Praise for *Development with the Force.com Platform, Second Edition*

"When the first edition of this book came out, it was welcomed by everyone working on the Force.com platform. The book did an excellent job of locating the Force.com platform in the overall code development sphere. And it was the first comprehensive guide to the platform. But that was 2009, before Chatter, before the REST API, before releases 16 through 21 of the Force.com platform.

"The second edition adds a whole new chapter on Chatter. In the new chapter, Mr. Ouellette continues his clear, logical explanation of the underlying data models and explains what you can, and cannot, do with Chatter and Apex code and Visualforce pages. I learned more about using and developing Chatter apps in 30 minutes with the new edition than in countless Salesforce.com keynotes, sessions, and webinars.

"REST (Representational State Transfer), another new topic, also is covered in detail. Many of the coding examples in the original edition have been reworked to use REST. This not only provides the reader with a good understanding of how to use REST but also explains when to use REST."

—**David Claiborne**, Principal, The Claiborne Company

"*Development with the Force.com Platform* continues to be the only book with beginning-to-end information on developing Force.com applications. This second edition keeps readers up-to-date with the latest additions to the platform."

—**John Rotenstein**, Author of *theEnforcer.net* blog on Force.com development

"Jason Ouellette's book is a must-have for all Salesforce developers. It can act as an introductory text on the Salesforce platform for a new developer and can also act as a reference book for an experienced Salesforce developer. The book provides depth as well as breadth on Apex, Visualforce, and other related technologies."

—**Naveen Gabrani**, CEO, Astrea IT Services

"There is no substitute for learning the unique aspects of the Force.com platform and Apex language directly from an expert such as Jason Ouellette, who shares his practical experience in this well-written and updated guide. This invaluable resource for learning to use the platform correctly and efficiently is truly a gift for anyone learning to build applications in the Salesforce.com cloud."

—**Mark Richer**, Internet Consultant, Able Minds

"Literally everything you need to know to develop a product on Force.com…who you need on the team, what tools to use, and how to use them in a clear, concise, and complete package. A must-have for Force.com development teams."

—**Jason Monberg**, VP of Product Management, MarkLogic Corporation

"*Development with the Force.com Platform* is a perfectly practical and consistently useful guide to developing on the leading cloud business platform. It is for beginners and pros alike, without any of the usual dogma or fluff that often serves as filler in technical publications."

—**Titash Bardhan**, Product Manager, PSA, FinancialForce.com

"Jason Ouellette is clearly a master of this domain. He distills its complexity into simplified, choice paths, creating the perfect companion for any Force.com aspirant. This second edition includes an exceptional chapter on social applications where Jason combines his experience with his intuitive and accessible writing style to demystify the Collaboration Cloud. Using this book as your guide with the latest Force.com technical documentation as your library, you will have all you need to succeed on the platform."

—**Adam Purkiss**, Force.com Architect and Twilio Developer Contest Winner

"Jason does a thorough job explaining how to develop a business application on the Force.com platform, leaving out the hype often surrounding Salesforce.com. Web developers and DBAs will find the book valuable in learning to apply their relational modeling skills to the Force.com data model, designed to reduce development time. Experienced Force.com developers are likely to find new features of the platform that they may have overlooked in the quarterly updates to the platform."

—**Christian G. Warden**, Director of Marketing Systems, CRC Health Group

"This is an indispensable reference for all Force.com developers. If there is something we need to know about building on Force.com, we turn to *Development with the Force.com Platform, Second Edition*. It is that good."

—**Howard A. Brown**, Founder and CEO, DemandResults

Development with the Force.com Platform

Second Edition

Development with the Force.com Platform

Second Edition

Building Business Applications in the Cloud

Jason Ouellette

✦✦ Addison-Wesley

Upper Saddle River, NJ • Boston • Indianapolis • San Francisco
New York • Toronto • Montreal • London • Munich • Paris • Madrid
Cape Town • Sydney • Tokyo • Singapore • Mexico City

The publisher offers excellent discounts on this book when ordered in quantity for bulk purchases or special sales, which may include electronic versions and/or custom covers and content particular to your business, training goals, marketing focus, and branding interests. For more information, please contact:

U.S. Corporate and Government Sales
(800) 382-3419
corpsales@pearsontechgroup.com

For sales outside the United States, please contact:

International Sales
international@pearson.com

Visit us on the Web: informit.com/aw

Copyright © 2012 Pearson Education, Inc.

Pearson Education, Inc.
Rights and Contracts Department
501 Boylston Street, Suite 900
Boston, MA 02116
Fax (617) 671 3447

Screenshots © 2012 Salesforce.com, Inc. All rights reserved.

ISBN-13: 978-0-321-76735-6
ISBN-10: 0-321-76735-7
First printing July 2011

Library of Congress Cataloging-in-Publication Data

Ouellette, Jason, 1973-
   Development with the Force.com platform : building business applications in the cloud / Jason Ouellette.
      p. cm.
   ISBN 978-0-321-76735-6 (pbk. : alk. paper)
 1. Web services. 2. Application software—Development. 3. Force.com (Electronic resource) 4. Cloud computing. 5. Business—Data processing. 6. Service-oriented architecture (Computer science) I. Salesforce.com (Firm) II. Title.
   TK5105.88813.O94 2012
   004.6'54—dc23
                              2011015142

Editor-in-Chief
Mark Taub

Acquisitions Editor
Trina MacDonald

Development Editor
Songlin Qiu

Managing Editor
Kristy Hart

Project Editor
Betsy Harris

Copy Editor
Paula Lowell

Indexer
Erika Millen

Proofreader
Water Crest Publishing

Technical Reviewers
David Cheng
Naveen Gabrani
Colin Loretz

Publishing Coordinator
Olivia Basegio

Book Designer
Gary Adair

Compositor
Nonie Ratcliff

To Tracey

"Life can only be understood backwards;
but it must be lived forwards."

—Søren Kierkegaard

Table of Contents

Preface

I wrote this book to help developers discover Force.com as a viable, even superior tool for building business applications.

I'm always surprised at how many developers I meet who aren't aware of Force.com as a platform. They know of Salesforce, but only that it's a CRM. Even those who have heard of Force.com are amazed when I describe what Appirio and other companies are building with it. "I didn't know you could do that with Force.com" is a common reaction, even to the simplest of things such as creating custom database tables.

Since this book was first published, Salesforce has continued to innovate, adding many new capabilities to the Force.com platform. Thanks to solid demand for the book, I got the chance to write this second edition. It contains updates throughout to reflect exciting developments like aggregate functions in SOQL, simplified governor limits, and the REST API. It also features two entirely new chapters: "Batch Processing" (Chapter 9) and "Social Applications" (Chapter 13).

I hope that the second edition of this book is effective in introducing business application developers to what Force.com offers. This is a combination of its features as a development platform and the benefits of it being "in the cloud," delivered over the Internet as a service rather than installed on your own servers. I believe you'll find, as I did, that Force.com can save you significant time and effort throughout the software development lifecycle of many types of applications.

Key Features of This Book

This book covers areas of Force.com relevant to developing applications in a corporate environment. It takes a hands-on approach, providing code examples and encouraging experimentation. It includes sections on the Force.com database, Apex programming language, Visualforce user interface technology, integration to other systems, and supporting features such as workflow and analytics. SFA, CRM, customer support, and other pre-built applications from Salesforce are not discussed, but general Force.com platform skills are helpful for working in these areas as well. The book does not cover cloud computing in general terms. It also avoids comparing Force.com with other technologies, platforms, or languages. Emphasis is placed on understanding Force.com on its own unique terms rather than as a database, application server, or cloud computing platform.

Although Force.com is a commercial service sold by Salesforce, all the material in this book was developed using a free Force.com Developer Edition account. Additionally, every feature described in this book is available in the free edition.

Throughout the text, you will see sidebar boxes labeled Note, Tip, or Caution. Notes explain interesting or important points that can help you understand key concepts and techniques. Tips are little pieces of information that will help you in real-world situations, and often offer shortcuts to make a task easier or faster. Cautions provide information about detrimental performance issues or dangerous errors. Pay careful attention to Cautions.

Target Audience for This Book

This book is intended for application developers who use Java, C#.NET, PHP, or other high-level languages to build Web and rich-client applications for end users. It assumes knowledge of relational database design and queries, Web application development using HTML and JavaScript, and exposure to Web services.

Code Examples for This Book

The code listings in this book are also available on the book's Web site: http://www.informit.com/title/9780321767356. They are also available as a Force.com package, freely available on Force.com AppExchange: https://sites.secure.force.com/appexchange/listingDetail?listingId=a0N30000003KG5cE AG. The package can be installed directly into your own Force.com organization.

Acknowledgments

There are many people to thank for this book.

- **Mark Taub:** Mark is the Editor-in-Chief at Pearson. At Dreamforce 2008, Mark attended my presentation on using Google Data APIs with Force.com. During the Q&A session, he approached me with an idea on a book for Force.com development.

- **Trina MacDonald:** Trina is the Acquisitions Editor at Pearson. She's not only a talented editor and wrangler of introverted authors, but a smooth salesperson as well. I don't know how else to explain the existence of this second edition.

- **David Cheng, Naveen Gabrani, Colin Loretz:** The technical reviewers for this book have consistently provided insightful feedback and fact-checking of the material.

- **Songlin Qiu:** Songlin is my development editor at Pearson. I continue to appreciate and benefit from her detailed feedback on my chapters.

- **Olivia Basegio:** Olivia is the Editorial Assistant at Pearson. She worked behind the scenes to make the publishing process run smoothly.

- **Heather Fox:** As my publicist at Pearson, Heather has repeatedly succeeded in getting me out of my headphoned comfort zone and into activities to promote the book.

- **Kavindra Patel, Nick Tran, Jon Mountjoy:** These three work for Salesforce.com and have been longtime supporters of the book, especially this second edition. I can't thank them enough.

- **Steve Fisher:** Steve is EVP of Technology at Salesforce.com. I'm honored to have him as the book's foreword author.

- **Craig Weissman:** Craig is CTO of Salesforce.com. I'm very grateful to him for writing the stellar foreword for the first edition book.

- **Kraig Swensrud:** Kraig is SVP of Marketing at Salesforce.com and the provider of much support over the years.

- **Jeff Douglas, Kyle Roche:** Jeff and Kyle are always on the social media circuit promoting the book. Never mind a beer: I owe them a keg at this point.

- **David Schach, Abhinav Gupta, Ajay Deewan, Tom Hedgecoth, Adam Toups:** Thanks to these super-fans who have gone the extra mile to contribute to the book.
- **Tracey:** This book would not be possible without my wife Tracey. She is my ultimate, unconditional supporter, cheerleader, caretaker, family, and source of sanity.

About the Author

Jason Ouellette led the development of popular AppExchange applications such as Appirio Cloud Sync, CloudWorks, and Professional Services Enterprise. He is an independent technology consultant with deep experience in cloud and enterprise integration. He has been inventing cutting-edge enterprise software for more than 15 years at Appirio, Composite Software, and webMethods. He was recognized by Salesforce as a Force.com MVP in 2011 and Force.com Developer Hero in 2009.

He lives with his wife and two geriatric cats in San Francisco, California.

Foreword

In the time since the first edition of *Development with the Force.com Platform*, technology's influence in our lives has grown and changed. The world we live in is now social and mobile: Facebook has more than 500 million users. 110 million tweets are posted to Twitter each day. Smartphone sales are expected to outpace PC sales by 2012 (Morgan Stanley).

This monumental shift toward technology becoming a pivotal position in our personal lives is also, naturally, happening in the workplace. Employees expect the same immediacy that epitomizes these consumer applications, coupled with proven trust, security, and scalability required by businesses. As such, the way we work is changing, as are the applications we use. Building the applications to drive this new era is not only a tremendous opportunity for today's developers but the path to long-term career success.

Development on traditional platforms such as J2EE, Microsoft .NET, or LAMP stacks is not designed for what we demand from technology today. The increasing consumption of apps via mobile devices results in massive backlogs of app requests because developers must master multiple programming languages to build and maintain apps across different mobile operating systems. Building social applications requires learning a new skill set, and integration is painstaking. As a result, app development using traditional platforms is complex, slow, and expensive.

The Force.com cloud platform-as-a-service is changing the way developers work in stride with how technology is changing. It makes it easier and faster to build social, mobile, and open cloud apps that meet the myriad of ways businesses use technology in this new era. Apps that run in the cloud are delivered as a service so companies don't have to buy and maintain hardware and software to run them—or manage and maintain complicated client/server deployments.

Force.com gives developers application development velocity to increase for multiple uses, devices, and operating systems. Because it is cloud-based, developers can build and deploy powerful applications much faster and for half the cost, allowing them to focus on innovation and not infrastructure.

Force.com is

- 100% cloud—requires no hardware or software
- Mobile—runs your apps on any platform or device
- Social—adds collaboration features to every app

- Open—supports open standards, APIs, and multiple languages, giving developers choice
- Proven—runs more than 185,000 apps for enterprises around the world

It's no wonder that Force.com has quickly become the leading cloud platform for business apps with a rapidly growing developer community responsible for building 185,000 apps and counting. The Force.com developer ecosystem encompasses companies of all sizes and across all industries building a wide variety of applications.

Kelly Services, a global provider of workforce solutions, has taken advantage of the time-to-market and productivity benefits of cloud development by building custom apps on Force.com that have enabled it to close new business, retain existing customers, and expand customers into new areas. For example, it used Force.com to provide a major insurance company client with a centralized database of prescreened insurance sales producer candidates for its franchised agents to search, interview, and hire more efficiently on demand. Kelly Services was able to design, develop, test, and deploy this solution in just 10 days.

As a result, the insurance company experienced a 78% cost reduction over previous methodologies.

Smaller companies like Critical Systems, a fire alarm inspection and testing company, have used Force.com to build a custom inspections app for the iPhone and deploy it to its field inspection team in less than four weeks. The company estimates building the app on Force.com was about 10 times faster than it would have taken using an on-premise development platform.

There are also independent software vendors (ISVs) who are using Force.com to deliver their cloud strategies to customers. For example, BMC's RemedyForce offering built on the Force.com platform provides businesses a simple and fast path to transform how they think about IT service management and provide tangible results such as streamlined IT support processes and reduced costs.

ServiceMax has built its business from the ground up on the Force.com platform to reinvent field service management, particularly enabling the mobility of its field service or "man in the van" agents using custom Force.com iPad apps. As a result, customers are up and running quickly in a low-cost subscription model, tightly integrated to their CRM, and can quickly take advantage of new cloud innovations, such as social collaboration with Salesforce Chatter, that are built right into the Force.com platform. ServiceMax has been able to focus all its resources on its business and not on maintaining IT infrastructure.

These examples only begin to illustrate the myriad of ways that apps built on Force.com can revolutionize businesses and enable them to harness the opportunities of the social and mobile world we now live in. As such, Jason Ouellette's second edition *Development with the Force.com Platform* is a timely and important guide to app development in this new era. Developers today, whether at an in-house IT department big or small or at an ISV, see the light at the end of tunnel and are looking for ways to get started developing in this new paradigm.

As one of the foremost Force.com developers and architects, Ouellette's expertise provides guidance to other developers on how to build today's social, mobile, and open enterprise cloud applications. With the addition of a new chapter on building social apps, he is one of the first to detail how to be successful in an enterprise environment. As with the first edition of *Development with the Force.com Platform*, Ouellette's talent is in striking the optimal balance of defining and illustrating technical concepts in an understandable and applicable way. With a sample application for every topic, he provides the tangible guidance enterprise developers need to succeed in this exciting era of innovation brought to us through the power of cloud computing.

—Steve Fisher
Executive Vice President, Technology, Salesforce.com

1

Introducing Force.com

This chapter introduces the concepts, terminology, and technology components of the Force.com platform and its context in the broader Platform as a Service (PaaS) landscape. The goal is to provide context for exploring Force.com within a corporate software development organization. If any of the following sentences describe you, this chapter is intended to help:

- You have read about cloud computing or PaaS and want to learn how Force.com compares to other technologies.
- You want to get started with Force.com but need to select a suitable first project.
- You have a project in mind to build on Force.com and want to learn how you can leverage existing development skills and process.

This chapter consists of three sections:

- **Force.com in the Cloud Computing Landscape:** Learn about PaaS and Force.com's unique features as a PaaS solution.
- **Inside a Force.com Project:** Examine how application development with Force.com differs from other technologies in terms of project selection, technical roles, and tools.
- **Sample Application:** A sample business application is referenced throughout this book to provide a concrete basis for discussing technical problems and their solutions. In this chapter, the sample application's requirements and use cases are outlined, as well as a development plan, mapped to chapters of the book.

Force.com in the Cloud Computing Landscape

Phrases like "cloud computing" and "Platform as a Service" have many meanings put forth by many vendors. This section provides definitions of the terms to serve as a basis for understanding Force.com and comparing it with other products in the market. With this background, you can make the best choice for your projects, whether that is Force.com, another PaaS product, or your own in-house infrastructure.

Platform as a Service (PaaS)

The platform is infrastructure for the development of software applications. The functionality of a platform's infrastructure differs widely across platform vendors, so this section focuses on a handful of the most established vendors. The suffix "as a Service" (aaS) means that the platform exists "in the cloud," accessible to customers via the Internet. Many variations exist on this acronym, including SaaS (Software as a Service), IaaS (Infrastructure as a Service), and so forth.

PaaS is a category within the umbrella of cloud computing. "Cloud computing" is a phrase to describe the movement of computing resources away from physical data centers or servers in a closet in your company and into the network, where they can be provisioned, accessed, and deprovisioned instantly. You plug a lamp into an electrical socket to use the electrons in your region's power grid. Running a diesel generator in your basement is usually not necessary. You trust that the power company is going to provide that service, and you pay the company as you use the service.

Cloud computing as a general concept spans every conceivable configuration of infrastructure, well outside the scope of this book. The potential benefits are reduced complexity and cost versus a traditional approach. The traditional approach is to invest in infrastructure by acquiring new infrastructure assets and staff or redeploying or optimizing existing investments. Cloud computing provides an alternative.

Many companies provide PaaS products. The following subsections introduce the mainstream PaaS products and include brief descriptions of their functionality. Consult the Web sites of each product for further information.

Amazon Web Services

Amazon Web Services refers to a family of cloud computing products. The most relevant to PaaS is Elastic Beanstalk, a platform for running Java applications that provides load balancing, auto-scaling, and health monitoring. The platform is actually built on several other Amazon Web Services products that can be independently configured by advanced users, with the most significant being Elastic Compute Cloud (EC2). EC2 is a general-purpose computing platform, not limited to running Java programs. You can provision virtual instances of Windows or Linux machines at will, loading them with your own custom operating-system image or one prebuilt by Amazon or the community. These instances run until you shut them down, and you are billed for usage of resources such as CPU, disk, and network.

A raw machine with an OS on it is a great start, but to build a business application requires you to install, manage access to, maintain, monitor, patch and upgrade, back up, plan to scale, and generally care and feed in perpetuity an application platform on the EC2 instance. Many of these tasks are still required of Amazon's higher-level Elastic Beanstalk offering. If your organization has the skills to build on .NET, J2EE, LAMP, or other application stacks, plus the OS, database administration, and IT operations experience, Amazon's virtual servers in the cloud could be a strong alternative to running your own servers in-house.

Amazon provides various other products that complement Elastic Beanstalk and EC2. These include Simple Queue Service for publish-and-subscribe-style integration between applications, Simple DB for managing schemaless data, and Simple Storage Service, a content repository.

Microsoft Azure

Azure consists of two products. The first is Windows Azure, an operating system that can utilize Microsoft's data centers for general computation and storage. It is a combination of infrastructure and platform designed to take existing and new .NET-based applications and run them in the cloud, providing similar features for scalability and elasticity as Amazon Web Services. Most Azure applications are developed in C# using Microsoft Visual Studio, although other languages and tools are supported. The second part is SQL Azure, a hosted version of Microsoft SQL Server. The cost of these products is based on resource consumption, defined as a combination of CPU, network bandwidth, storage, and number of transactions.

Google App Engine

App Engine is a platform designed for hosting Web applications. App Engine is like having an unlimited number of servers in the cloud working for you, preconfigured with a distributed data store and Python or Java-based application server. It's much like Amazon's Elastic Beanstalk but focused on providing a higher-level application platform. It lacks the configurable lower-level services like EC2 to provide an escape hatch for developers requiring more control over the infrastructure. App Engine includes tools for managing the data store, monitoring your site and its resource consumption, and debugging and logging.

App Engine is free for a set amount of storage and page views per month. Applications requiring more storage or bandwidth can purchase it by setting a maximum daily dollar amount they're willing to spend, divided into five buckets: CPU time, bandwidth in, bandwidth out, storage, and outbound email.

Force.com

Force.com is targeted toward corporate application developers and independent software vendors. Unlike the other PaaS offerings, it does not expose developers directly to its own infrastructure. Developers do not provision CPU time, disk, or instances of running operating systems. Instead, Force.com provides a custom application platform centered around the relational database, one resembling an application server stack you might be familiar with from working with .NET, J2EE, or LAMP.

Although it integrates with other technologies using open standards such as SOAP and REST, the programming languages and metadata representations used to build applications are proprietary to Force.com. This is unique among the PaaS products but not unreasonable when examined in depth. Force.com operates at a significantly higher level of abstraction than the other PaaS products, promising dramatically higher productivity to developers in return for their investment and trust in a single-vendor solution.

To extend the reach of Force.com to a larger developer community, Salesforce and VMware provide a product called VMforce. VMforce brings some of the features of the Force.com platform to Java developers. It consists of development tools from the Salesforce community and virtualized computing resources from VMware. With VMforce, you can create hybrid applications that use Force.com for data and services, but are built with Java standard technologies such as Spring. Along the same lines, Salesforce's acquisition of Heroku is expected to extend Force.com features to Ruby developers.

Force.com is free for developers. Production applications are priced primarily by storage used and number of unique users.

Facebook

Facebook is a Web site for connecting with your friends, but it also provides developers with ways to build their own socially aware applications. These applications leverage the Facebook service to create new ways for users to interact while online. The Facebook platform is also accessible to applications not built inside Facebook, exposing the "social graph" (the network of relationships between users) where permitted.

Much of the value of Facebook as a platform stems from its large user base and consistent yet extensible user experience. It is a set of services for adding social context to applications. Unlike Force.com and App Engine, for example, Facebook has no facility to host custom applications.

Force.com as a Platform

Force.com is different from other PaaS solutions in its focus on business applications. Force.com is a part of Salesforce.com, which started as a SaaS Customer Relationship Management (CRM) vendor. But Force.com is not CRM. It provides the infrastructure commonly needed for any business application, customizable for the unique requirements of each business through a combination of code and configuration. This infrastructure is delivered to you as a service on the Internet.

Because you are reading this book, you have probably developed a few business applications in your time. Consider the features you implemented and reimplemented in multiple applications, the unglamorous plumbing, wiring, and foundation work. Some examples are security, user identity, logging, profiling, integration, data storage, transactions, workflow, collaboration, and reporting. This infrastructure is essential to your applications but expensive to develop and maintain. Business application developers do not code their own relational database kernels, windowing systems, or operating systems. This is basic infrastructure, acquired from software vendors or the open-source community and then configured to meet user requirements. What if you could do the same for your application infrastructure? This is the premise of the Force.com.

The following subsections list differentiating architectural features of Force.com with brief descriptions.

Multitenancy

Multitenancy is an abstract concept, an implementation detail of Force.com, but one with tangible benefits for developers. Figure 1-1 shows a conceptual view of multitenancy. Customers access shared infrastructure, with metadata and data stored in the same logical database.

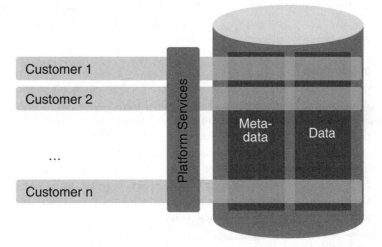

Figure 1-1   Multitenant architecture

The multitenant architecture of Force.com consists of the following features:

- **Shared infrastructure:** Every customer (or tenant) of Force.com shares the same infrastructure. They are assigned an independent logical environment within the Force.com platform.

  At first, some might be uncomfortable with the thought of handing their data to a third-party where it is co-mingled with that of competitors. Salesforce's whitepaper on its multitenant technology includes the technical details of how it works and why your data is safe from loss or spontaneous appearance to unauthorized parties.

Note

The whitepaper is available at http://wiki.developerforce.com/index.php/Multi_Tenant_ Architecture.

- **Single version:** Only one version of the Force.com platform is in production. The same platform is used to deliver applications of all sizes and shapes, used by 1 to 100,000 users, running everything from dog-grooming businesses to the Japanese national post office.

- **Continuous, zero-cost improvements:** When Force.com is upgraded to include new features or bug fixes, the upgrade is enabled in every customer's logical environment with zero to minimal effort required.

Salesforce can roll out new releases with confidence because it maintains a single version of its infrastructure and can achieve broad test coverage by leveraging tests, code, and configurations from their production environment. You, the customer, are helping maintain and improve Force.com in a systematic, measurable way as a side effect of simply using it. This deep feedback loop between the Force.com and its users is something impractical to achieve with on-premise software.

Relational Database

The heart of Force.com is the relational database provided as a service. The relational database is the most well-understood and widely used way to store and manage business data. Business applications typically require reporting, transactional integrity, summarization, and structured search, and implementing those on nonrelational data stores requires significant effort. Force.com provides a relational database to each tenant, one that is tightly integrated with every other feature of the platform. There are no Oracle licenses to purchase, no tablespaces to configure, no JDBC drivers to install, no ORM to wrangle, no DDL to write, no queries to optimize, and no replication and backup strategies to implement. Force.com takes care of all these tasks.

Application Services

Force.com provides many of the common services needed for modern business application development. These are the services you might have built or integrated repeatedly in your past development projects. They include logging, transaction processing, validation, workflow, email, integration, testing, reporting, and user interface.

These services are highly customizable with and without writing code. Although each service can be valued as an individual unit of functionality, their unification offers tremendous value. All the features of Force.com are designed, built, and maintained by a single responsible party, Salesforce. Salesforce provides documentation for these features as well as support staff on-call, training and certification classes, and accountability to its customers for keeping things running smoothly. This is in contrast to many software projects that end up as a patchwork of open-source, best-of-breed tools and libraries glued together by you, the developer, asked to do more with fewer people, shorter timelines, and cheaper, often unsupported tools.

Declarative Metadata

Almost every customization configured or coded within Force.com is readily available as simple XML with a documented schema. At any point in time, you can ask Force.com for this metadata via a set of Web services. The metadata can be used to configure an identical environment or managed with your corporate standard source control system. It is also helpful for troubleshooting, allowing you to visually compare the state of two environments. Although a few features of Force.com are not available in this declarative metadata form, Salesforce's stated product direction is to provide full coverage.

Programming Language

Force.com has its own programming language, called Apex. It allows developers to script interactions with other platform features, including the user interface. Its syntax is a blend of Java and database stored procedure languages like T/SQL and can be written using a Web browser or a plug-in to the Eclipse IDE.

Other platforms take a different approach. Google's App Engine simultaneously restricts and extends existing languages such as Python so that they play nicely in a PaaS sandbox. This offers obvious benefits, such as leveraging the development community, ease of migration, and skills preservation. One way to understand Apex is as a domain-specific language. Force.com is not a general-purpose computing platform to run any Java or C# program you want to run. Apex is kept intentionally minimalistic, designed with only the needs of Force.com developers in mind, built within the controlled environment of Salesforce R&D. Although it won't solve every programming problem, Apex's specialized nature leads to some advantages in learning curve, code conciseness, ease of refactoring, and ongoing maintenance costs.

Force.com Services

Force.com can be divided into four major services: database, business logic, user interface, and integration. Technically, many more services are provided by Force.com, but these are the high-level categories that are most relevant to new Force.com developers.

Database

Force.com is built around a relational database. It allows the definition of custom tables containing up to 800 fields each. Fields contain strongly typed data using any of the standard relational database data types, plus rich types such as currency values, picklists, formatted text, and phone numbers. Fields can contain validation rules to ensure data is clean before being committed, and formulas to derive values, like cells in a spreadsheet. Field history tracking provides an audit log of changes to chosen fields.

Custom tables can be related to each other, allowing the definition of complex data schemas. Tables, rows, and columns can be configured with security constraints. Data and metadata is protected against accidental deletion through a "recycling bin" metaphor. The database schema is often modifiable instantly, without manual migration. Data is imported from files or other sources with free tools, and APIs are provided for custom data-loading solutions.

Data is queried via a SQL-like language called SOQL (Salesforce Object Query Language). Full-text search is available through SOSL (Salesforce Object Search Language).

Business Logic

Apex is the language used to implement business logic on Force.com. It allows code to be structured into classes and interfaces, and it supports object-oriented behaviors. It has strongly typed collection objects and arrays modeled after Java.

Data binding is a first-class concept in Apex, with the database schema automatically imported as language constructs. Data manipulation statements, trigger semantics, batch processing, and transaction boundaries are also part of the language.

The philosophy of test-driven development is hard-wired into the Force.com platform. Methods are annotated as tests and run from a provided test harness or test API calls. Test methods are automatically instrumented by Force.com and output timing information for performance tuning. Force.com prevents code from being deployed into production that does not have adequate unit test coverage.

User Interface

Force.com provides two approaches for the development of user interfaces: Page Layouts and Visualforce. Page Layouts are inferred from the data model, including validation rules, and then customized using a WYSIWYG editor. Page Layouts feature the standard Salesforce look-and-feel. For many applications, Page Layouts can deliver some or all of the user interface with no development effort.

Visualforce allows developers to build custom user interfaces. It consists of a series of XML markup tags called components with their own namespace. As with JSP, ASP.NET, Velocity, and other template processing technologies, the components serve as containers to structure data returned by the Controller, a class written in Apex. To the user, the resulting Web pages might look nothing like Salesforce, or adopt its standard look-and-feel. Visualforce components can express the many types and styles of UIs, including basic entry forms, lists, multistep wizards, Ajax, Adobe Flex, mobile applications, and content management systems. Developers can create their own components to reuse across applications.

User interfaces in Visualforce are public, private, or some blend of the two. Private user interfaces require a user to log in before gaining access. Public user interfaces, called Sites, can be made available to anonymous users on the Internet.

Integration

In the world of integration, more options are usually better, and standards support is essential. Force.com supports a wide array of integration technologies, almost all of them based on industry-standard protocols and message formats. You can integrate other technologies with Force.com using an approach of configuration plus code. Here are some examples:

- Apex Web Services allows control of data, metadata, and process from any platform supporting SOAP over HTTP, including JavaScript. This makes writing composite applications that combine Force.com with technology from other vendors in many interesting and powerful ways possible. Force.com's Web services API has evolved over many years, spanning more than 20 versions with full backward compatibility.

- The Force.com database is accessible via Representational State Transfer (REST) calls. This integration method is much lighter weight than Web Services, allowing Web applications to query and modify data in Force.com with simple calls accessible to any development language.

- Business logic developed in Apex can be exposed as a Web service, accessible with or without a Force.com user identity. Force.com generates the WSDL from your Apex code. Additionally, Force.com converts WSDL to Apex bindings to allow access to external Web services from within the platform.

- You can create virtual email inboxes on Force.com and write code to process the incoming email. Sending email from Force.com is also supported.

- Force.com provides an API for making HTTP requests, including support for client-side certificates, SSL, proxies, and HTTP authentication. With this, you can integrate with Web-based resources, everything from static Web pages to REST services returning JSON.

- Salesforce-to-Salesforce (S2S) is a publish-and-subscribe model of data sharing between multiple Force.com environments. If the company you need to integrate with already uses Force.com and the data is supported by S2S, integration becomes a relatively simple configuration exercise. There is no code or message formats to maintain. Your data is transported within the Force.com environment from one tenant to another.

If your requirements dictate a higher-level approach to integration, software vendors like IBM's Cast Iron Systems and Informatica offer adapters to Force.com to read and write data and orchestrate complex transactions spanning disparate systems.

Inside a Force.com Project

This section discusses what makes a Force.com project different from a typical corporate in-house software development effort, starting with project selection. Learn some tips for selecting a project in Force.com's sweet spot. Then examine how traditional technical roles translate to development activities in a Force.com project and how technologies within Force.com impact your product development lifecycle. Lastly, get acquainted with the tools and resources available to make your project a success.

Project Selection

Some projects are better suited to implementation on Force.com than others. Running into natural limits of the PaaS approach or battling against the abstraction provided by the platform is possible. Always strive to pursue projects that play into Force.com strengths.

No absolute rules exist for determining this, but projects with the following characteristics tend to work well with Force.com:

- **The project is data-centered, requiring the storage and retrieval of structured data.**

  Structured data is the most important point. Implementing a YouTube-like application on Force.com is not the best idea, because it primarily works with unstructured data in the form of video streams. Force.com supports binary data, so a video-sharing Web site is certainly possible to build. But handling large amounts of binary data is not a focus or core competency of Force.com. A hotel reservation system is an example of a more natural fit.

- **The user interface is composed primarily of wizards, grids, forms, and reports.**

  Force.com does not restrict you to these user interface patterns. You can implement any type of user interface, including "rich" clients that run using Flash in the browser, and even full desktop applications that integrate with Force.com via its Apex Web Services API. But to capture the most benefit from the platform, stick with structured, data-driven user interfaces that use standard Web technologies such as HTML, CSS, and JavaScript.

- **The underlying business processes involve email, spreadsheets, threaded discussions, and hierarchies of people who participate in a distributed, asynchronous workflow.**

  Standard Force.com features such as Chatter, workflow, approvals, and email services add a lot of value to these applications. They can be configured by business analysts or controlled in-depth by developers.

- **The rules around data sharing and security are fine-grained and based on organizational roles and user identity.**

  User identity management and security are deep subjects and typically require high effort to implement in a custom system. With Force.com, they are standard, highly configurable components that you can leverage without coding. You can then spend more time thinking through the "who can see what" scenarios rather than coding the infrastructure to make them possible.

- **The project requires integration with other systems.**

  Force.com is built from the ground up to interoperate with other systems at all its layers: data, business logic, and user interface. The infrastructure is taken care of, so you can focus on the integration design. Exchange a million rows of data between your SQL Server database and Force.com. Call your Apex services from a legacy J2EE application or vice versa. Add an event to a Google calendar from within your Visualforce user interface. These scenarios and more are fully supported by the platform.

- **The project manipulates data incrementally, driven by user actions rather than a calendar.**

  Force.com is a shared resource. Simultaneously, other customers of varying sizes are using the same infrastructure. This requires Force.com to carefully monitor and fairly distribute the computing resources so that all customers can accomplish their goals with a high quality of service. If one customer's application on Force.com was allowed to consume a disproportionate share of resources, other customers' applications would suffer resource starvation. The limitations in place, called governors, prevent too much memory, CPU, disk, or network bandwidth from being concentrated in the hands of any one customer. The platform strongly enforces these governor limits, so the best Force.com applications involve computing tasks that can be split into small units of work.

- **The data volume is limited, below a few million records per table.**

  Data volume is important to think about with any system: How large is my data going to grow and at what rate? Force.com consists of a logical single transactional database. No analytical data store exists. Applications that require access to large volumes of data, such as data warehousing and analytics, cannot be built on Force.com. Other software vendors such as GoodData provide solutions in this area, but all involve copying data from Force.com to their own products.

Force.com is not an all-or-nothing proposition. If your project does not fit within these guidelines, you might still want to explore Force.com but in conjunction with other PaaS solutions such as Amazon's EC2. Thanks to Force.com's integration capabilities, EC2 and Force.com can be used together as a composite solution, EC2 augmenting Force.com where general-purpose computing is needed. VMforce takes a similar augmentation approach to give Java developers a streamlined way to extend the platform without the hassles of maintaining their own hardware, or even managing their own EC2-based environments.

Team Selection

The best people to staff on Force.com projects might already work at your company. Projects do not require brand-new teams staffed with Force.com experts. With the majority of the platform based in mature technology such as relational databases and Web development, adapting existing teams can be a straightforward task.

Here are some examples of traditional software development roles and how they can contribute to a Force.com project:

- **Business Analyst**

  Substantial Force.com applications can be built entirely by configuration, no computer science background or coding skills required. Salesforce refers to this as "clicks, not code." Business analysts who are proficient with Microsoft Excel and its macro language, or small-scale databases like Microsoft Access and FileMaker Pro, can get hands-on with the Force.com data model, validation rules, workflows, approval rules, and page layouts.

- **Data Modeler**

  A data model forms the core of a Force.com application. Data modelers can use their existing Entity-Relationship tools and techniques to design the data layer, with some deltas to account for Force.com-specific idiosyncrasies. Rather than scripts of DDL statements, their work output is Force.com's metadata XML or manual configuration of the data objects. Data modelers can also design reports and report types, which define data domains available to business users to build their own reports.

- **Database Administrator**

  Many traditional DBA tasks are obsolete in Force.com because there is no physical database to build, monitor, and tune. But a DBA still has plenty of work to do in planning and implementing the Force.com object model. There are objects to define or permissions to configure, and the challenges of data transformation and migration are still as relevant in Force.com as in any database-backed system.

- **Database Developer**

  The design of Force.com's programming language, Apex, has clearly been inspired by stored procedure languages like T-SQL and PL/SQL. Existing database developers can adapt their skills to writing Apex code, particularly when it requires detailed work on the data like triggers.

- **Object-Oriented Analysis and Design Specialist**

  Force.com includes an object-oriented language, and persistent data is represented as objects. With all of these objects floating around, people with skills in traditional techniques like Unified Modeling Language (UML) are valuable to have on your project team. Larger applications benefit from a well-designed object model, and as in any language, designing before writing Apex code can be a real timesaver.

- **User Interface Designer**

  Force.com supports modern Web standards for creating usable, flexible, and maintainable UIs. UI designers can help by building screen mock-ups, page layouts, and the static portions of Visualforce pages to serve as templates and assets for developers.

- **Web Developer**

  Developers who have built Web applications can quickly learn enough Apex and Visualforce and build similar applications on Force.com, typically with much less effort. Skills in HTML, CSS, JavaScript, or Adobe Flex are needed to build custom Force.com user interfaces.

- **4GL Developer**

  Developers proficient in fourth-generation languages such as Java, C#.NET, and PHP usually have no problem picking up Apex code. It has the same core syntax as Java, without the Java-specific libraries and frameworks.

- **Integration Specialist**

  Force.com is a producer and consumer of Web services and supports REST as well as any integration strategy based on HTTP. An integration expert can design the interaction between systems, define the remote operations, and implement them using Force.com or a specialized integration product.

- **Quality Assurance Engineer**

  Testing is a critical part of any software project, and on Force.com testing is mandatory before code is deployed to production. A QA engineer can write automated unit tests in Apex and test plans for security and integration testing. Standard tools like Selenium can be used to automate UI testing.

- **Operations Specialist**

  Although there are no servers or operating systems to manage, larger deployments of Force.com can involve integration with on-premise systems. Single Sign-On (SSO) integration and data migration are two common examples. Operations experts can help in this area, as well as with application deployment and Force.com administration tasks such as user maintenance.

Lifecycle

The software development lifecycle of a Force.com project is much like an on-premise Web application development project, but with less toil. Many moving parts exist in J2EE, .NET, or LAMP projects. Most require a jumble of frameworks to be integrated and configured properly before one line of code relevant to your project is written.

This section describes areas of Force.com functionality designed to streamline the development lifecycle and focus your time on the value-added activities related to your application. Each of these areas has implicit costs and benefits. On the cost side, there is usually a loss of control and flexibility versus technologies with less abstraction. Evaluating these features and judging whether they constitute costs or benefits for your project is up to you.

Integrated Logical Database

Relational databases are still the default choice for business applications, despite the availability of alternatives like NoSQL, XML, and object-oriented databases. The relational model maps well onto business entities, data integrity is easily enforceable, and implementations scale to hold large datasets while providing efficient retrieval, composition, and transactional modification.

For business applications coded in an object-oriented language, accessing relational databases introduces an impedance mismatch. Databases organize data in terms of schemas, tables, and columns. Programs organize data and logic into objects, methods, and fields. Many ways exist to juggle data between the two, none of them ideal. To make matters more complicated, many layers of protocol are needed to transport queries, resultsets, and transactions between the program and the database.

In Force.com, the database tables are called objects. They are somewhat confusingly named because they do not exhibit object-oriented behavior. The name comes from the fact that they are logical entities that act as tables when being defined, loaded with data, queried, updated, and reported on, but are surfaced to programs as typed data structures. No mismatch exists between the way data is represented in code and the way it's represented in the database. Your code remains consistent and concise whether you are working with in-memory instances of your custom-defined Apex classes or objects from the database. This enables compile-time validation of programs, including queries and data manipulation statements, to ensure that they adhere to the database schema. This one seemingly simple feature eliminates a whole category of defects that were previously discovered only through unit tests or in production by unfortunate users.

The logical aspect of the database is also significant. Developers have no direct access to the physical databases running in Salesforce's data centers. The physical data model is a meta-model designed for multitenant applications, with layers of caches and fault tolerance, spanning servers in multiple data centers. When you create an object in Force.com, no corresponding Oracle database table is created. The metadata describing your new table is stored and indexed by a series of physical tables, becoming a unified, tenant-specific vocabulary baked into the platform's higher-level features. The synergy of integrated, metadata-aware functionality makes Force.com more than the sum of its individual features.

Metadata-Derived User Interface

As described previously, the definition of your objects becomes the vocabulary for other features. Nowhere is this more evident than in the standard Force.com user interface, commonly referred to as the "native" UI. This is the style pioneered by the Salesforce Sales and Service Cloud products: lots of tabular displays of data, topped with fat bars of color with icons of dollar signs and telescopes, and a row of tabs for navigation.

It is worth getting to know the capabilities of native UI even if you have reservations about its appearance or usability. To some, it is an artifact of an earlier era of Web applications. To others, it is a clean-cut business application, consistent and safe. Either way, as a developer, you cannot afford to ignore it. The native UI is where many configuration tasks are performed, often for features not yet visible to Eclipse and other tools.

If your project's user interface design is amenable to the native UI, you can build screens almost as fast as users can describe their requirements. Rapid application prototyping is an excellent addition or alternative to static screen mock-ups. Page layouts are descriptions of which fields appear on a page in the native UI. They are automatically created when you define an object and configured with a simple drag-and-drop layout tool.

Simplified Configuration Management

Configuration management is very different from what you might be accustomed to from on-premise development. Setting up a development environment is trivial with Force.com. You can provision a new development environment in a few clicks and deploy your code to it using the familiar Eclipse IDE.

When added to your Eclipse IDE or file system, Force.com code and metadata are ready to be committed to an existing source control system. Custom Ant tasks are available to automate your deployments. Sandboxes can be provisioned for testing against real-world volumes of data and users. They are automatically refreshed from snapshots of production data per your request. Force.com's packaging feature allows you to partition your code into logical units of functionality, making it easier to manage and share with others at your company or in the larger community.

Integrated Unit Testing

The ability to write and execute unit tests is a native part of the Apex language and Force.com development environment. Typically, a test framework is an optional component that you need to integrate into your development and build process. With the facility to test aligned closely with code, writing and executing tests becomes a natural part of the development lifecycle rather than an afterthought.

In fact, unit tests are required by Force.com to deploy code into production. This applies to all Apex code in the system: user interface logic, triggers, and general business logic. To achieve the necessary 75% test coverage often requires as much if not more code than the actual Apex classes.

To make sure you don't code yourself into a corner without test coverage, a great time to write tests is while you code. Many development methodologies advocate test-driven development, and writing tests as you code has benefits well beyond simply meeting the minimum requirements for production deployment in Force.com. For example, a comprehensive library of tests adds guardrails to refactoring and maintenance tasks, steering you away from destabilizing changes.

Integrated Model-View-Controller (MVC) Pattern

The goal of the MVC pattern is maintainable user interface code. It dictates the separation of data, visual elements that represent data and actions to the user, and logic that mediates between the two. If these three areas are allowed to collide and the codebase grows large enough, the cost to fix bugs and add features becomes prohibitive.

Visualforce adopts MVC by design. For example, its view components do not allow the expression of business logic and vice versa. Like other best practices made mandatory by the platform, this can be inconvenient when you just want to do something quick and dirty. But it is there to help. After all, quick-and-dirty demos have an uncanny tendency to morph into production applications.

Integrated Interoperability

Force.com provides Web services support to your applications without code. You can designate an Apex method as a Web service. WSDL is automatically generated to reflect the method signature. Your logic is now accessible to any program that is capable of calling a Web service, given valid credentials for an authorized user in your organization. You can also restrict access by IP address or open up your service to guests.

As in other languages, Apex provides you with a WSDL-to-Apex tool. This tool generates Apex stubs from WSDL, enabling you to integrate with SOAP-enabled business processes existing outside of Force.com. Lower-level Apex libraries are also available for raw HTTP and XML processing.

End of Life

Retiring a production application requires a few clicks from the system administrator. Users can also be quickly removed or repurposed for other applications. Applications can be readily consolidated because they share the same infrastructure. For example, you might keep an old user interface online while a new one is being run in parallel, both writing to the same set of objects. Although these things are possible with other technologies, Force.com removes a sizable chunk of infrastructure complexity, preserving more intellectual bandwidth to devote to tackling the hard problems specific to your business.

Tools and Resources

Force.com has a rich developer ecosystem, including discussion groups for reaching out to the development community on specific subjects, a source-code repository for open-source projects, a Web site called AppExchange where you can browse for free and paid extensions to the platform, services companies to help you plan and implement your larger projects, and Ideas, a site for posting your ideas for enhancing the platform.

The following subsections list some tools and resources that exist to make your Force.com projects successful.

Developer Force (http://developer.force.com)

Developer Force is a rich source of information on Force.com. It contains documentation, tutorials, e-books written by Salesforce, a blog, and a wiki with links to many more resources inside and outside of Salesforce.

Developer Discussion Boards (http://community.salesforce.com)

The developer discussion boards are a public discussion forum for the Force.com development community, divided into a dozen separate boards by technology area. Users post their questions and problems, gripes, and kudos. Other users in the community contribute answers and solutions, including Salesforce employees. The boards are a great way to build a reputation as a Force.com expert and keep current on the latest activity around the platform.

Ideas (http://ideas.salesforce.com)

If you have a suggestion for improving Force.com or any Salesforce product, visit the Ideas site and post it. Other users in the community can vote for it. If your idea is popular enough, it might be added to the next release of Force.com. Incidentally, Ideas is a reusable component of Force.com, so you can build your own customized idea-sharing sites for your company.

Code Share (http://developer.force.com/codeshare)

Code Share is a directory of open-source code contributions from the Force.com community, with links to the source code hosted on Google Code. Salesforce employees have contributed many projects here. Code Share projects include the Facebook Toolkit, a library for integrating with Facebook, and the Toolkit for PayPal X Payments platform, to leverage PayPal's Adaptive Payments API in Force.com applications.

Platform Documentation

Salesforce provides documentation through online, context-sensitive help within the Web user interface, as well as HTML and PDF versions of its reference manuals. You can find all documentation at Developer Force.

AppExchange (http://www.appexchange.com)

AppExchange is a directory of ready-to-install applications developed on Force.com. The applications consist of metadata, such as Visualforce pages and Apex code, deployable into your Force.com environment. Users can rate applications from one to five stars and write reviews. Many free applications are written by Salesforce employees to illustrate new platform features. Commercial applications are also available for trial and purchase. AppExchange is how independent software vendors distribute their Force.com applications to Salesforce customers.

Dreamforce

Salesforce has a series of user conferences every year called Dreamforce. San Francisco hosts the largest Dreamforce venue, with thousands attending to participate in training sessions, booths, product demos, keynote speeches, breakout sessions, executive briefings, and, of course, the parties. Dreamforce is a fun way to stay up to date with the technology.

Systems Integrators

For deployments including significant numbers of users, integration with other enterprise systems, or complex data migrations, consider contracting the services of a systems integrator. You can find systems integrators who have competency with Force.com, Sales Cloud, Service Cloud, and other Salesforce products. They include pure-play cloud consultancies such as Appirio and Model Metrics, as well as traditional players like Accenture and Deloitte.

Technical Support

When you encounter undocumented or incorrect behavior in the system, submit a defect report. If the issue can be described simply, like a cryptic error message, search for it in the discussion groups. In many cases, someone else has already run into the same problem before you, posted about it, and attracted the attention of Salesforce employees. If not, the ability to log and track Force.com platform support cases is available in Force.com's Web user interface.

Sample Application: Services Manager

Every following chapter in this book contributes to the construction of a sample application called Services Manager. Services Manager is designed for businesses that bill for their employees' time. These businesses need accurate accounting of when and where employees are staffed, numbers of hours worked, skills of the employees, project expenses, amounts billed to customers, and so forth. This section describes these features in preparation for later discussions of their design and implementation.

The goal is not to build a fully functional application for operating a professional services business, but to provide a logically related set of working code samples to accompany the technical concepts covered in this book.

Background

Imagine you own a professional services business. The services your company provides could be architecture, graphic design, software, law, or anything with the following characteristics:

- High cost, highly skilled employees
- Complex projects lasting a week or more
- Resources billed out at an hourly rate
- High cost of acquiring new customers

Your profit comes from the difference between the billing rate and the internal cost of resources. This is typically small, so your process must be streamlined, repeatable, and scalable. To increase profit, you must hire more resources and win more customer projects.

User Roles

The users of the Services Manager application span many roles in the organization. The roles are covered in the following subsections, with a summary of their responsibilities and how they use Services Manager.

Services Sales Representative

Sales reps work with customers to identify project needs and manage the relationship with the customer. Reps use the Sales Cloud product from Salesforce to manage their sales process. In general, they do not use Services Manager directly, but start the process by winning the contract.

Staffing Coordinator

Staffing coordinators manage and schedule resources for projects. When the opportunity is closed, they are notified via email. They then create a project using Services Manager and staff it by matching the availability and skills of resources against the scheduling and skill requirements of the project.

Project Manager

Project managers are responsible for success of projects on a daily basis. They direct and prioritize project activities. They use Services Manager to manage the detailed weekly schedules of their consultants and monitor the health and progress of their projects.

Consultant

The consultant is engaged directly with the customer and is responsible for the project deliverables. In Service Manager, he or she logs time spent on the project, indicates the completion of project milestones, and submits expenses.

Accounts Receivable

Accounts receivable is responsible for invoicing and collecting customers based on work that has been delivered. At the end of each billing cycle, they use Services Manager to generate invoices for customers.

Services Vice President

The VP is responsible for the services P&L and success of the team. Services Manager provides the VP with reports on utilization and other metrics for assessing the team's overall performance.

Development Plan

The Services Manager sample application is developed incrementally throughout this book, each chapter building on the previous. Every chapter covers a set of technical concepts followed by the relevant Services Manager requirements, design, and implementation. The goal is to expose you to the abstract technology and then make it practical by getting your hands dirty on the sample application.

The following list names the remaining chapters in this book, with brief descriptions of the features of Services Manager to be covered:

- **Chapter 2, "Database Essentials":** Design and create the database and import data.
- **Chapter 3, "Database Security":** Define users, roles, and profiles. Configure sharing rules.
- **Chapter 4, "Additional Database Features":** Define fields for reporting and make a subset of data accessible offline.
- **Chapter 5, "Business Logic":** Build triggers to validate data and unit test them.
- **Chapter 6, "Advanced Business Logic":** Write services to generate email notifications based on user activity.
- **Chapter 7, "User Interfaces":** Construct a custom user interface for tracking the skills of consultants.
- **Chapter 8, "Advanced User Interfaces":** Enhance the skills-tracking user interface with Ajax.
- **Chapter 9, "Batch Processing":** Locate missing timecards using a batch process.
- **Chapter 10, "Integration":** Calculate and transmit corporate performance metrics to a fictional industry benchmarking organization.
- **Chapter 11, "Advanced Integration":** Develop a Java program to update Force.com with information from a human resources database.
- **Chapter 12, "Additional Platform Features":** Build a custom dashboard component to visualize the geographic distribution of consultants on projects.
- **Chapter 13, "Social Applications":** Automate built-in platform collaboration features to help project teams communicate.

Summary

This chapter has introduced you to Force.com, explained how it differs from other PaaS technologies and what infrastructure it's designed to replace, and given guidelines for its use on your projects. Here are a few thoughts to take away from this chapter:

- Force.com is a PaaS uniquely designed to make business applications easy to build, maintain, and deliver. It consists of database, business logic, user interface, and integration services, all of them interoperable and interdependent, accessible through configuration or code.
- The most suitable applications for implementation on Force.com operate primarily on structured data. Traditional software development roles are still relevant in the Force.com world, particularly Web and client/server developers. Data modeling

takes on a new importance with the platform, as data objects are tightly integrated with the rest of the technology stack, and unit testing is mandatory.

- Services Manager is the sample application built on throughout this book. It's designed to serve companies in the professional services space, those selling projects to customers and billing them for the time of its skilled employees.

2

Database Essentials

In Force.com, the database provides the framework for the rest of your application. Decisions you make on how to represent data have significant consequences for flexibility and maintainability. Understanding the unique behaviors of the Force.com database is critical for successful applications. Force.com operates at a higher level of abstraction than a relational database, so although existing relational database skills are helpful, the Force.com database is a completely different animal.

This chapter covers topics in Force.com database design and development:

- **Overview of Force.com's Database:** Get an overview of the Force.com database and how it's different from familiar relational databases.
- **Working with Custom Objects:** Custom objects are components within the Force.com database that store your data. Learn how they are created and then test them by entering and browsing their data.
- **Sample Application:** Design a logical data model for the Services Manager, map it to Force.com objects, implement the objects, and import sample data.

Overview of Force.com's Database

This section provides background on the database functionality within Force.com. It covers objects, fields, relationships, queries, and how data is integrated with your application logic. Each Force.com-specific database feature is described and contrasted with its equivalent in a standard relational database.

Objects

Strictly speaking, Force.com does not store objects in its database. Force.com's objects are more closely related to database tables than they are to anything in object-oriented programming. Objects contain fields, which are equivalent to the columns of a database table. Data is stored in objects in the form of records, like rows in a database table.

Objects belong to one of two categories: standard and custom. Standard objects provide data for Salesforce applications like CRM or core platform functionality such as user identity. They are built in to Force.com and cannot be removed, although you can extend them by adding your own fields. Custom objects are defined by you, the developer, and you'll be spending most of your time with them as you build your own applications.

Beyond the name, custom objects differ from their relational table counterparts in some significant ways.

Logical, Not Physical, Objects

Unlike relational database tables, custom objects have no physical representation accessible to the developer. There are no physical storage parameters to tune, no tablespace files to create and manage. Force.com does not even create physical database tables for your custom objects. This abstraction layer allows Force.com to make decisions about how best to represent, index, back up, migrate, relate, and tune your database.

Delegated Tuning and Operations

Force.com does not provide access to its database indexes. It is the job of Salesforce to tune their physical databases, and they use everything from standard database indexes to proprietary, tenant-optimized SQL generation that accounts for the characteristics of your data storage and access patterns. You as a developer reap the benefits of this tuning by virtue of the fact that you are building on the platform. Improving its product is in Salesforce's best interest. If you do encounter problems with database performance, file a support request with Salesforce.

When you run your own database software and hardware, you inevitably face operational tasks such as backup, recovery, and replication for scalability. Although nothing prevents you from exporting the data from your Force.com instance and backing it up to your own servers, normally no reason exists to do so.

Undelete Support

Normally when a row is deleted in a standard relational database and you need to recover it after a commit, you're out of luck unless you have backups of the database or are using a database that provides some proprietary technology, such as Oracle's Flashback. To avoid this situation, you could implement your own support for undeleting rows, such as triggers to copy data to an audit table or a "deleted" column to accomplish a "soft" delete. Or, you could use Force.com, which provides undelete functionality on every object. When records are deleted, they go into a "Recycle Bin," where they stay until they expire and are gone for good or an administrator undeletes them. Deleted records can be queried and programmatically undeleted as well.

Accidentally dropping a table or another database object can also lead to a lot of unpleasant work for a system administrator. If your database vendor doesn't offer specialized recovery features, you are stuck recovering data from backups. In Force.com, deleting objects sends them to the Recycle Bin. They stay there until they expire (30 days after deletion) or are explicitly erased or undeleted by an administrator. If an object is undeleted, its definition and all its data are restored.

Fields

Fields are like columns in a database. They belong to a parent table (custom object) and have a name and constraints such as data type and uniqueness.

Force.com has two classes of fields: standard and custom. Standard fields are fields that are created by Force.com for its own internal use, but that are also available to users. They can be hidden from view and unused, but not completely removed or redefined. They are a part of the Force.com data model that is static, relied on to exist by other layers of Force.com technology. Examples of standard fields are Id (unique identifier) and Created By (the user who created the record). Custom fields are created by you, the developer, to store data specific to your applications.

Logical, Not Physical, Fields

When you define a new field for your custom object, Force.com does not create a corresponding field in its physical database. Instead, it associates your new field with an existing "Flex" field, a VARCHAR column of its generic data table. This provides Force.com with the flexibility to redefine data types, add richer data types, and perform other processing on the data outside of the database's typically rigid rules. Although this implementation detail of Force.com is not relevant to learning how to use Force.com's database, it does help explain some of its underlying behavior.

Unique Identifiers

Typical database tables include one or more columns to contain the primary key, the unique identifier for each row. In Force.com, every object has a standard field called Id. This field is automatically populated with an 18-character, case-insensitive, alphanumeric string to uniquely identify your records. Unique identifiers can also be expressed as 15-character, case-sensitive strings, and this is how they appear in the Salesforce user interface. In most cases, the two styles of unique identifiers can be used interchangeably. So, when you are designing your Force.com database, you do not need to add a field to contain a unique identifier.

Validation Rules

Validation rules place restrictions on the values of a new or updated record. They prevent users and programs from inserting data that your application defines as invalid. Rules are defined in an expression language similar to the function language found in the cells of a Microsoft Excel worksheet. The validation rule in Listing 2-1 prevents a record from containing a Start Date greater than its End Date.

Listing 2-1   **Sample Validation Rule**

```
AND(
  NOT(
    ISNULL(Start_Date__c)
  ),
  NOT(
    ISNULL(End_Date__c)
  ),
  (Start_Date__c > End_Date__c)
)
```

When the expression evaluates to true, it is treated as a validation failure. For the rule to evaluate as `true`, the value in the fields `Start_Date__c` and `End_Date__c` must be non-null, and the value of `Start_Date__c` must be greater than `End_Date__c`.

Formula Fields

Formula fields contain values that are automatically calculated by Force.com, derived from other fields in the same object or in different objects. They use the same expression language as validation rules.

For example, Listing 2-2 shows a formula for a field called `Billable_Revenue__c`. It's defined on a Timecard object and calculates the billable revenue contained in the Timecard.

Listing 2-2   **Sample Formula Field**

```
Billable Revenue (Currency) = Week_Total_Hrs__c * Rate_Per_Hour__c
```

`Week_Total_Hrs__c` and `Rate_Per_Hour__c` are custom fields on the Timecard object. When a new record is inserted in the Timecard object, the two fields are multiplied, and the result is stored in the `Billable_Revenue__c` field.

Rich Data Types

Force.com supports a few flavors of the typical string, number, date/time, and Boolean data types. It also supports richer data types that lend themselves to direct usage in user interfaces with prebuilt validation, input masks, and output formatting. The rich types are phone, picklist, multi-select picklist, email, URL, and rich text area. Picklists are the most powerful types of the bunch because they address the clutter of "lookup tables" dangling off of most relational data models. Lookup tables usually contain only a key and description and can be readily replaced with picklist fields. Internally, picklists maintain their own identifiers for values, allowing their labels to be modified without updating the records that reference them.

History Tracking

Most databases do not provide developers a way to track every change made to records in a table. Typically this is something that you implement using another table and some code. In Force.com, any object can have History Tracking enabled on it, which allows up to 20 fields to be audited. Every field with History Tracking enabled that is changed gets a new record inserted in a corresponding History object containing the old and new values. Records in the History object cannot be deleted.

Relationships

The capability to define and manage relationships between data entities is the basis for much of the value of relational databases. Relationships allow data from one entity to be logically separated from others. With this separation, data can be modified without integrity loss, and combined with other entities for analysis.

Data relationships in Force.com resemble those found in standard relational databases. You can express one-to-one, one-to-many, and many-to-many relationships. But relationships in Force.com are closely controlled and managed by the platform and also integrated with many platform features. Some important points are listed in the subsections that follow.

Integrity Enforced

When you define a relationship in Force.com, a relationship field is created to contain the foreign key. Force.com prevents you from using a foreign key to a different object. It enforces that the foreign key points to an object of the correct type.

This is basic foreign key constraint checking, like in a relational database. The difference in Force.com is that you can never elect to turn it off. It is a mandatory, always-on feature, protecting your data from inconsistency.

This rule has one minor exception. Many standard objects contain special fields that can be related to multiple object types. For example, a support case can be assigned to an individual user or a group representing a collection of users. In the Case object, the OwnerId field can contain the ID of a record in the User object or the Group object. Both types of foreign keys are valid. Note that these polymorphic foreign key fields are not permitted in custom objects.

Explicitly Defined

In Force.com, all relationships are predefined, established when objects and fields are created. With the exception of semi- and anti-joins, you do not specify join conditions when you write queries. Instead you specify the fields you want, and Force.com takes care of traversing the necessary relationships to retrieve the data.

Query Language

Force.com has two query languages. One is called Salesforce Object Query Language (SOQL) and is used for structured queries. The other language, Salesforce Object Search Language (SOSL), is used for searching the full text of one or more objects.

SOQL

Don't let the name confuse you. Despite some similarities in syntax, SOQL is very different from SQL. It has more in common with a reporting or object query language than its more mathematically grounded ancestor.

Listing 2-3 shows a sample SOQL query on a custom object. It returns the names, statuses, and expected revenue amounts for the top-ten largest uninvoiced projects started in the last quarter, in descending order by pending revenue.

Listing 2-3   **Sample SOQL Query**

```
SELECT Name, Total_Billable_Revenue_Pending_Invoice__c, Project_Status__c
  FROM Proj__c
  WHERE Invoiced__c = FALSE and Start_Date__c = LAST_QUARTER
  ORDER BY Total_Billable_Revenue_Pending_Invoice__c DESC LIMIT 10
```

The query specifies a list of columns to be returned (SELECT), the object to query (FROM), filter conditions (WHERE), sorting results (ORDER BY) in descending (DESC) order, and a hard limit on the maximum number of rows to return (LIMIT).

Selecting a single object is the simplest type of SOQL query. More advanced queries select fields from multiple related objects, nested resultsets from child objects using subqueries, and perform semi-joins and anti-joins using IN and NOT IN.

The following subsections describe the four most significant differences between SQL and SOQL.

Implicit Join

In SQL, you can join any table with any other table, typically with one or more Boolean expressions involving pairs of columns. Assuming that the data types of the columns in the join expression are comparable, the join query returns the corresponding rows of both tables as specified in your join expression.

In Force.com, data from multiple standard and custom objects can be combined, but only in ways predetermined by you when you designed your database. SOQL itself does not support any concept of joins, other than semi-join and anti-join. Using SOQL, you tell the Force.com platform which fields of which objects to retrieve, and the platform does the work of traversing the data, maintaining the integrity between objects in accordance with the relationships you defined.

This behavior has its pros and cons. You cannot perform truly ad-hoc queries, in which data from multiple objects is combined in ways possibly unanticipated by the database designer. But it results in much simpler, more concise queries that can be optimized entirely by the platform.

Nested Resultsets

In SQL, querying two tables in a one-to-many relationship without aggregate functions and GROUP BY results in a cross product of the rows. For example, assume you have a table containing orders and another table with their line items, and issue the query in Listing 2-4.

Listing 2-4   **Relationship Query in SQL**

```
SELECT Orders.OrderId, OrderLineItems.LineItemId
  FROM Orders, OrderLineItems
  WHERE Orders.OrderId = OrderLineItems.OrderId
```

Assume that there are two orders (1 and 2), each with three line items (1–3 and 4–6). Table 2-1 shows the results of executing the query.

Table 2-1   **Results of SQL Join Query**

Orders.OrderId	OrderLineItems.LineItemId
1	1
1	2
1	3
2	4
2	5
2	6

To begin comparing this to Force.com, Listing 2-5 shows an equivalent query in SOQL.

Listing 2-5   **Relationship Query in SOQL**

```
SELECT OrderId, (SELECT LineItemId FROM OrderLineItems)
  FROM Orders
```

Note the lack of a WHERE clause to perform the join and the use of a subquery to nest the line items. Force.com is aware of the parent-child relationship between Orders and OrderLineItems, so it performs the join automatically. The result can be visualized as arrays of nested records, as shown in Figure 2-1. The outer record is the order, and each order contains an array of line items.

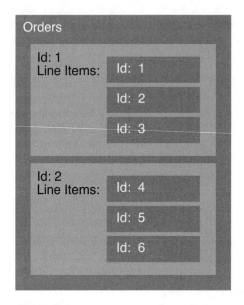

Figure 2-1   Nested results of SOQL query

No Functions in Column List

You might have included functions like LEFT, RIGHT, MID, LEN, and IFF along with your columns in a SQL SELECT statement. SOQL does not permit functions in the SELECT list. The only exceptions are built-in aggregate functions such as COUNT, which returns the number of records in the query. But aggregate functions can't be used in a query containing any other fields in the SELECT list.

Governor Limits

Force.com prevents a single user from consuming more than its fair share of system resources. This ensures a consistent level of system performance for all tenants. Limitations placed on resource consumption are called governor limits. A few examples of governor limits are the number of records that can be queried at one time, the amount of memory used by your code, and the size of messages sent between Force.com and external hosts. Some governor limits vary based on the type of licensing agreement you have in place with Salesforce.

SOSL

SOSL provides full-text search capabilities across many objects and fields simultaneously. This task is inefficient and often impossible in SOQL. SOSL statements can perform a search over all records, or incorporate SOQL to narrow the search scope and achieve the best of both worlds: structured and unstructured search. The SOSL expression in Listing 2-6 returns the IDs of records in four custom objects that begin with the word `java` in any of their fields.

Listing 2-6   **Query in SOSL**

```
FIND 'java*' IN ALL FIELDS
  RETURNING Project__c, Resource__c, Assignment__c, Skill__c
```

Data Integration

Integration refers to the incorporation of the database into the rest of your application, the business logic and user interface. If your application consists solely of stored procedures, there is no integration; your code runs inside the database process and hits database objects directly. More commonly application servers exist that need to communicate with the database.

With Force.com, either you are coding "on the platform," which is akin to writing stored procedures, or you are developing a "composite application," which executes somewhere else but integrates with Force.com data and logic. The following subsections describe how integrating data in Force.com differs from traditional Web application development.

Web Services API

Force.com provides a Web services API for accessing data from outside of its platform. This is the equivalent to a JDBC or ODBC driver, but uses SOAP and HTTP instead of lower-level protocols. You can run SOQL and SOSL queries, update the data using Data Manipulation Language (DML) operations, and query metadata.

To make using the raw SOAP services easier, language-specific bindings are available for Adobe Flex, Microsoft C#.NET and Visual Basic, Ruby, Perl, Java, JavaScript, PHP, and Python.

Object-Relational Mapping

In traditional Web application development, one of the most important integration technologies is Object Relational Mapping (ORM). This layer of infrastructure maps data objects from the database to and from the data structures in your program. Any ORM technology must be well integrated into your development process, efficient at runtime, and flexible to accommodate all data access patterns required by your application and allow for future schema changes. Java developers use Hibernate, Ruby has ActiveRecord, and so forth.

With Force.com, the ORM layer is built in to the platform. Data objects, metadata objects, and queries have direct representation in Apex code. When you create a new custom object, it's immediately accessible by name in Apex code. If you accidentally mistype the name of a field in your new object, your code will not compile.

For example, the snippet of Apex code in Listing 2-7 selects a single record from the Resource object, updates the value of its Hourly Cost Rate field, and commits the updated record to the database.

Listing 2-7   **Apex Code Snippet**

```
public void grantRaise(String resourceName, Decimal newRate) {
  Resource__c r = [ select Id, Hourly_Cost_Rate__c
      from Resource__c
      where Name = :resourceName limit 1 ];
  if (r != null) {
    r.Hourly_Cost_Rate__c = newRate;
    update r;
  }
}
```

Note the use of an inline SOQL query (in square brackets), the custom object as a first-class object in code (Resource__c), and inline DML (update statement).

Metadata in XML

Metadata in Force.com is created using a Web user interface, the Eclipse IDE, or the Metadata API. Force.com does not use Data Definition Language (DDL), but has its own XML schema for metadata. Listing 2-8 shows a simple example of Force.com's XML metadata.

Listing 2-8   **Metadata XML for a Custom Object**

```
<?xml version="1.0" encoding="UTF-8"?>
<CustomObject xmlns="http://soap.sforce.com/2006/04/metadata">
    <deploymentStatus>Deployed</deploymentStatus>
    <fields>
        <fullName>Start_Date__c</fullName>
        <label>Start Date</label>
        <type>Date</type>
    </fields>
    <label>Project</label>
    <nameField>
        <label>Project Name</label>
        <type>Text</type>
    </nameField>
    <pluralLabel>Projects</pluralLabel>
    <searchLayouts/>
    <sharingModel>ReadWrite</sharingModel>
</CustomObject>
```

This XML describes an object with a human-readable name of Project. It contains a single custom field called Start Date, of type Date. The Sharing Model of ReadWrite means that all users in the organization can edit the records in the Project object. Force.com provides a Metadata API for importing metadata XML into the platform. This is how development tools such as the Force.com IDE operate.

Generated User Interfaces

In the process of defining a custom object, described in the next section, you will see a number of settings related to the visual appearance of your object. These settings help Force.com generate a user interface for manipulating the data in your object. From here on, this is referred to as the "native" user interface, native meaning that it is built in to Force.com.

Force.com's native user interface is tightly integrated with your data model. The definitions of your objects, fields, and relationships are combined with additional configuration settings to create full-featured user interfaces that can perform CRUD (create, replace, update, delete) operations on your data.

Working with Custom Objects

This section describes how to create and manage custom objects in Force.com. This is an introduction to the process, so you can experiment with your own objects and data. It starts with instructions for getting your own Force.com Developer Edition account and gives a brief introduction to the tools available for working with custom objects. The rest of the section covers object creation and customization, field creation, and entering and viewing data using the native user interface.

Force.com Developer Edition

To get hands-on with Force.com development, you need a development environment. Environments are known as organizations, or "orgs" for short. Orgs come in different shapes and sizes based on the licensing agreement with Salesforce. Salesforce gives its Developer Edition (DE) away free. DE orgs are full-featured but have hard limits on the amount of storage (20MB of files, 20MB of data) and number of users (two full users and three platform-only users). When you are ready to test your application with production data and user volumes, license a Force.com Sandbox or Force.com Enterprise Edition (EE).

Salesforce offers one other licensing option geared toward developers called Free Edition (FE). As its name suggests, FE is free for a single application with up to 100 users, 10 custom objects, 1GB of storage, and an additional linked DE org called a Developer Sandbox. The Sandbox can be refreshed with the full contents of your FE account (metadata and data) with a single click. Although its increased user and storage limits are helpful, FE is not a drop-in replacement for DE due to its license restrictions. It is most useful for testing your app with a larger org before upgrading to EE.

> **Tip**
>
> Contact a Salesforce sales representative for more information about the different licensing options for Force.com.

Registration

Visit http://developer.force.com with your Web browser. On this page is a link or button to create a free DE account. Complete the sign-up form. Within a few minutes, two emails are sent to the address you provide. The first email is a login confirmation containing a temporary password and a link to log in. The second email is a welcome message to Force.com, with links to resources for developers.

Logging In

Click the login link in the first email. Your browser is directed to a page that forces you to change your password. Passwords must be at least eight characters long and alphanumeric. Here you also choose a security question and answer, as shown in Figure 2-2. The security challenge is used in the event that you forget your password.

At this point, you are logged in to your own Force.com organization.

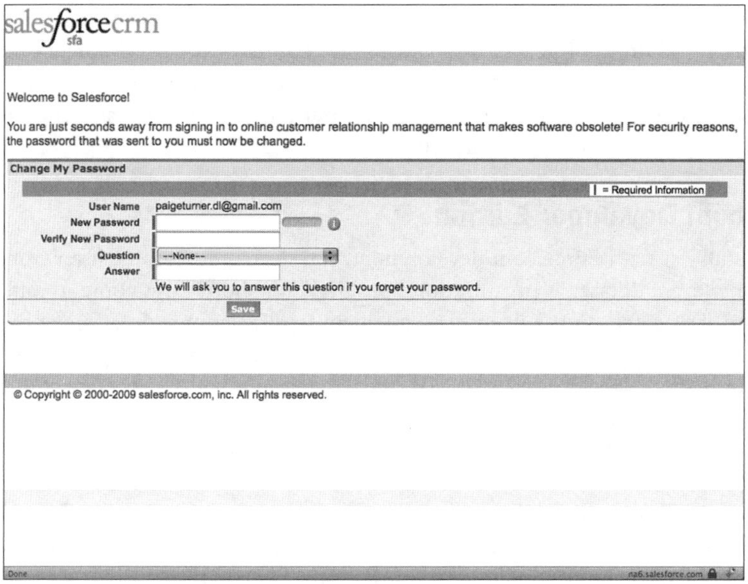

Figure 2-2   Force.com password change page

Tools for Custom Objects

Many tools are available that work with Force.com, created by Salesforce and independent software vendors. But if you're new to Force.com, starting with the free tools supported by Salesforce is best. Unless noted otherwise, all tools are available from the Developer Force Web site (http://developer.force.com). After you're comfortable with the standard tools, explore the range of solutions offered by the Force.com community.

Tools for Metadata

Metadata is the description of a Force.com application, from the data model to the user interface and everything in between. In this chapter, the focus is on the data model, and two tools are available from Salesforce for building it.

Force.com App Builder Tools

App Builder Tools are built in to the native Web user interface of Force.com. They are the easiest and most full-featured tools for working with objects and many other features. When new features are added to Force.com, you'll find them supported in the App Builder Tools first. For an example of using the App Builder Tools, log in to Force.com and click Setup. In the App Setup area, click Create → Objects.

Force.com IDE

The Force.com IDE is an Eclipse-based development environment. Its strength is developing Apex code and Visualforce pages and managing the metadata for larger deployments involving multiple Force.com organizations. It provides some functionality for working with custom objects, but the objects are presented in Metadata XML, not in a friendly user interface. This makes the Force.com IDE a better tool for maintaining objects than for creating new ones from scratch.

Tools for Data

Data tools enable you to import and export data in bulk. You usually use them in a migration, in which data you load from an existing system into Force.com.

Force.com Data Loader

Data Loader has the richest data import features of any Salesforce-provided data tool. It is available for Windows only, although a Mac port is available in the community. Find it by logging in to Force.com, going to the Administration Setup area, and clicking Data Management → Data Loader.

Import Wizard

The Import Wizard is a tool built in to the native user interface. It allows bulk data to be imported as new or updated records of custom objects. To use it, log in to Force.com and click Setup. In the Administration Setup area, click Data Management → Import Custom Objects. The Import Wizard walks you through a seven-step process for getting the data from a Comma Separated Values (CSV) file into Force.com.

Force.com Excel Connector

Excel Connector is an add-in to Microsoft Excel that allows bidirectional data movement between a worksheet and a Force.com object. You can fill an Excel worksheet with records from a Force.com object. In the worksheet, you can change values by simply editing the corresponding cells. The modified values can then be written back to the Force.com object. If you're an Excel power user, you will appreciate this tool. You can download it at http://wiki.developerforce.com/index.php/Force.com_Excel_Connector.

Object Creation

The easiest way to understand the object creation process is to try it. Log in to Force.com using your DE account and click Setup. In the App Setup area, click Create → Objects. Figure 2-3 shows the screen as it appears in a new Force.com organization, with no objects yet defined.

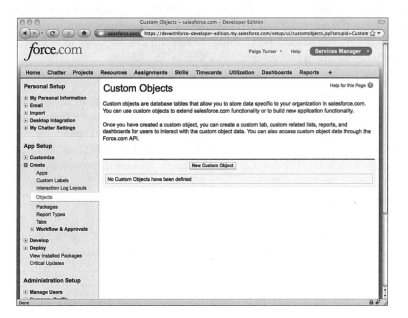

Figure 2-3   Custom objects in Force.com App Builder Tools

To begin, click the New Custom Object button.

Object Definition

The first step of building the custom object is its definition screen. This looks like a complex screen, but only two values are required: the label and its plural form. From that, Force.com does the rest. The label is the human-readable name of your custom object.

Setting a description for your object if you're working with other developers is a good practice.

Before leaving this screen, glance at the other options:

- **Object Name:** This is a very important name. It is how you refer to your custom object when you write Apex code, formula fields, and validation rules. It is automatically populated from the label, but it can be set manually. Although it is not shown on this screen, internally Force.com appends the Object Name with "__c" to differentiate it from standard objects.

- **Record Name Label and Format:** Every object has a standard field called Name. It is used in the native user interface as a label for your record. Name can have an Auto Number data type, which causes names to be automatically generated from a pattern, or a Text data type with a maximum length of 80 characters. Name values are not required to be unique.

- **Allow Reports:** If checked, this custom object can participate in the reporting feature of Force.com.

- **Allow Activities:** If this is checked, users can associate calendar events and tasks to records of your custom object. You can find the calendar and tasks features on the Home tab.

- **Track Field History:** If this option is checked, Force.com creates an additional object to work alongside yours, recording changes to selected fields.

- **Deployment Status (in development, deployed):** If an object is in development status, it is hidden from the users in your org, except those with the Customize Application permission. Deployed objects become visible to any user, as dictated by the security configuration of the object and org.

- **Object Creation Options:** Unlike the other options, which can be changed later, these options are available only when a custom object is first created. Add Notes and Attachments Related List to Default Page Layout allows external documents to be attached to records of your custom object, like attachments on an email. Launch New Custom Tab Wizard is a shortcut for building a custom tab at the same time as you define your object.

- **Help Settings:** This setting dictates how the Help for This Page link in the corner of every page behaves on your custom object. By default, it shows the standard Force.com help. You can configure it to display a custom Visualforce page instead. Visualforce pages are discussed in Chapter 7, "User Interfaces."

After you've clicked the Save button on the definition page, the detail page of your new custom object is shown. It contains a series of bordered boxes with titles. Each box contains configuration options for a different aspect of the object. Most aspects are described in the following subsections.

Standard Fields

Standard fields are automatically part of every object. They are used for platform-wide functions. The Created By, Last Modified By, and Owner fields help provide record-level access control of your data. Data security is discussed further in Chapter 3, "Database Security."

Custom fields are created by you, the developer, to store data specific to your applications. Custom relationships express associations between the records in a pair of objects, such as a purchase order and its line items. Initially your object does not contain any custom fields or relationships. After you've added some, they are listed here and can be edited and deleted.

Validation Rules

Validation rules define what constitutes a valid record, preventing records that do not conform from being stored in the database. When a validation rule is added, it applies to data coming from anywhere: a bulk import process, a user interface, or a Web service call from another application. When validation rules are defined, they are shown in this list and can be edited and deleted.

Triggers

Triggers are much like triggers in relational databases, except written in Apex code. They fire before or after a data manipulation action, such as insert, update, delete, and undelete. They can inhibit the action or extend it by acting on other database objects, modifying data, or even calling out to external Web services.

Standard Buttons and Links

When a custom object is created, a native user interface is also created for that object to enable CRUD operations without coding. The native user interface contains a collection of standard buttons, and this list allows you override their behavior. With overrides, you can use Visualforce to develop a custom user interface to be shown for actions that require special treatment, such as the creation of a new record in your object.

Custom Buttons and Links

This section allows the definition of one or more custom buttons to appear in the native user interface for your object. For example, you might want to add a Verify button, which would pop up a new window and allow the user to view the results of some analysis performed on the record.

Page Layouts

A Page Layout brings together all the native user interface elements for a custom object. This includes the buttons along the top and bottom of the screen, the fields displayed, and related lists, which are records of child objects.

Page Layouts are assigned to profiles. This allows different user interfaces to be shown to different types of users. For example, you need one user interface for entering a contact for a support case, but a different one for entering job applicant information. Both end up as records in the Contact object, but the user interfaces can appear very different.

Search Layouts

In this section, you can customize the display of your object in the native search user interfaces. Make a point of editing the Tab layout. It is the most frequently used and worth customizing to save yourself time. The Tab layout displays recently viewed, created, or modified objects on your custom tab. By default, it contains only the Name field.

Field Creation

As in object creation, the easiest way to understand field creation is to try it. Return to your custom object detail page and click the New button in the Custom Fields & Relationships section. The first page of the New Custom Field Wizard prompts for field type. The data types can be thought of in terms of seven categories:

1. **Text, Text Area, Text Area (Long), Text Area (Rich):** Text fields are varying lengths of Unicode text. Force.com does not allow fields with other encodings. Text stores 1 to 255 characters, Text Area stores the same number of characters but allows line breaks, and Text Area (Long) and Text Area (Rich) store up to 32,000 characters. The Rich Text Area field allows images, links, and basic formatting information to be stored inline with the text. One limitation of both the Long and Rich Text Areas is that Force.com's full-text search feature looks at only the first 2,048 characters.

2. **Picklist, Picklist (Multi-Select):** A Picklist is a list of suggested values that is presented to the user. Multi-Select enables a user to select multiple values. Record Types can be used to create multiple lists of suggested values for the same field, to be shown to different types of users. Picklist values are not enforced at the database level without the addition of a trigger or validation rule.

3. **Number, Percent, Currency:** Number can store signed values from 1 to 18 digits long, decimal places included. Currency and Percent are also Numbers but add type-specific formatting, such as a dollar sign.

4. **Checkbox:** Checkbox is a Boolean field. It stores a `true` or `false` value, and is represented in the native user interface as a check box.

5. **Date, Date/Time:** In the native user interface, dates are rendered with a calendar picker component and times with a separate, time-masked field with AM/PM selector.

6. **Email, Phone, URL:** These types are provided to enhance the experience in the native user interface. For example, URLs are clickable and open in a new Web browser window.

7. **Relationship (Lookup, Master–Detail):** These define relationships between two objects. They are covered in more detail in the section, "Relationship Fields."

After you've established the field type, the detail page is shown. The only required fields are Label and Name. The label is the human-readable name of your field. Setting a description for your field to document its purpose if not readily apparent from the label is good practice.

Before leaving this screen, examine the other detail settings:

- **Field Name:** Like Object Name, this is an important name. It is the name used to refer to your field in Apex Code, formula fields, and validation rules. It is automatically populated from the label, but it can be set manually. Field names cannot contain spaces. Although it is not shown on this screen, internally Force.com appends the Field Name with "__c" to differentiate it from Standard Fields.

- **Help Text:** If you provide help text for your field, a small blue circle icon containing the letter "i" is shown beside it in the native user interface. If a user hovers the mouse over this icon, your help text is displayed.

- **Required:** If this is checked, a record cannot be saved unless this field contains a value. This applies to records created anywhere, in the native user interface, imported from other systems, and programmatically.

- **Unique:** Text and Number fields allow a uniqueness constraint to be applied. If this is checked, new records must contain a unique value for this field, one that does not occur in other records, or it cannot be saved. Like the Required attribute, this is enforced at the database level.

- **External ID:** Text and Number fields can be designated as External IDs. By default, the only unique identifier on an object is the standard Id field. But if External ID is checked, your custom field can be used to uniquely identify records. External IDs are also searchable from the Search sidebar. Note that each object can have at most three External ID fields.

- **Default Value:** In a new record, this optional expression is evaluated and shown as a default value, but can be overwritten by the user. The expression is written in the same language as formula fields and validation rules. It can be as simple as a static value or a series of calculations performed on other fields.

Relationship Fields

Relationship fields can express one-to-one, one-to-many, and many-to-many relationships between objects. Creating relationships keeps data normalized, but also adds to the complexity of the data model, causing greater complexity in code and user interfaces that rely on it. When moving to Force.com from a relational database, do not blindly create an object for every table and expect to join them all together with relationships. Force.com has hard limits on the distance between objects that can be joined together for purposes of user interface, reporting, formulas, and triggers. When you are querying a child object and referencing data from parent objects, the maximum number of objects that can be referenced is five. In the reverse scenario in which the query is against a parent and references the child, the maximum is one. You can use workarounds, such as using formula fields to consolidate fields from distant objects, but keeping your object and relationship count low pays dividends later in the development process.

The two types of relationship fields are Lookup and Master-Detail. Lookup relationships are the default choice. They are the most flexible and transparent in their operation. You can create up to 25 of them on a single object, they maintain their own record of ownership, child records can be reassigned to a new parent, and they do not have any automatic behaviors such as cascade delete.

Master-Detail relationships are useful for enforcing mandatory relationships, in which a child record cannot exist without its parent record. All child records in a Master-Detail relationship must have a parent record specified. When the master record in a Master-Detail relationship is deleted, all associated detail records are also deleted. Up to four nested levels of Master-Detail relationships can be created, counting from the master object to the most deeply nested child object. Master-Detail relationships have some other special behaviors, such as allowing aggregation of child records through roll-up summary fields, discussed in Chapter 4, "Additional Database Features."

Table 2-2 summarizes the differences between Lookup and Master-Detail relationships.

Table 2-2   **Comparing Lookup and Master-Detail Relationships**

Lookup Relationship	Master-Detail Relationship
Child records exist independent of parent	Child records cannot exist without parent
Independent ownership	Always owned by parent record
No cascading behavior	Deletion of parent cascades to delete children
No roll-up fields	Roll-up summary fields supported
Unlimited nesting, although limited by SOQL	Up to four nested levels

Additional Field Types

Some field types have special behavior, different than simply storing a value. These are listed here:

- **Auto Number:** Most databases have an identity or sequence field, a field that automatically increments itself when a new record is added. In Force.com, Auto Number fields are read-only text fields with a maximum length of 30 characters. You define the length, a display format used to generate values, and the starting number. For example, if you define an Auto Number field with a display format of `Project-{0000}` and a starting number of 100, the Auto Number field in your first record will contain a value of `Project-0100`.

- **Formula:** Formula fields are read-only fields that are calculated by Force.com based on an expression you provide when defining the field. The output of a formula can be a currency, date, date/time, number, percent, or text value.
- **Roll-Up Summary:** Roll-up summary fields allow child records in a Master-Detail relationship to be summarized and the result stored in the parent record.

Entering and Browsing Data

Force.com's native user interface might or might not be suitable for presenting directly to users of your application. But few people can argue its value as a database front end for developers and administrators.

Use it to test your data model by creating records with dummy values. This helps identify missing fields, non-intuitive Page Layouts, and additional validation rules needed. After your object contains some records, browse them using Views and Search. Customize Views to show the optimal set of columns. Usable Views are helpful later in the development process for troubleshooting data problems.

Getting Started

Salesforce often adds new features that users must opt-in to use. For example, users must opt-in to features that involve significant changes to the user interface. Salesforce recently released a faster, more powerful user interface for working with lists of records and for editing records with fewer clicks. Before starting this section, check to make sure your org has these features enabled. Go to the Setup, App Setup area, click Customize → User Interface, and then check the Enable Enhanced Lists and Enable Inline Editing options; click the Save button.

Entering Data

Custom tabs are containers for developer-defined user interfaces. These tabs, such as the Home tab, are displayed at the top of the page. Tabs are the gateway to the native list view and CRUD user interfaces for an object and can also present entirely custom user interfaces built in Visualforce.

If you have not created a custom tab for your object, do so now by going to Setup and, in the App Setup area, clicking Create → Tabs. Click the New button in the Custom Object Tabs section. In the details page, select your custom object from the drop-down list, pick a tab style, and optionally enter a description. Skip through the remaining pages, accepting the default values.

To create a new record in your custom object, click the Create New drop-down on the left side of the screen and select your object from the list. An edit screen is shown, as in Figure 2-4, which shows editing a new record in a custom object named Resource. This screen is defined by the Page Layout. Make note of things you don't like as you enter test data and return to the Page Layout to fix them.

When your new record is saved, the page changes to a view mode. This is also controlled by the Page Layout. If you've enabled Inline Editing, you can double-click the editable fields to change their values.

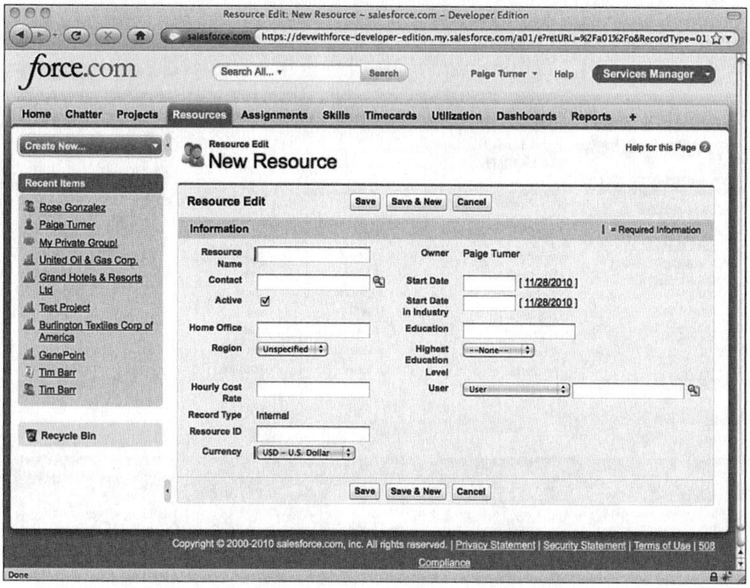

Figure 2-4   Creating a new record

Browsing Data

Your first encounter with a list of records is usually on the home page of your custom object. Click your custom object's tab, and you'll see a section listing recently viewed records. It shows only the Name of your records. To customize this list of recently viewed records to show more fields, go to the custom object definition, Search Layouts section, and edit the Tab layout to add more fields. Figure 2-5 shows an example of a tab layout with several fields visible.

Another way to browse data is a View. A View is a native user interface that displays the records of a single object as a list. It includes such features as sorting, pagination, columns that can be dragged to reorder, and the capability to delete and edit data inline without switching to another user interface. To define a View, you specify the list of fields to be displayed and, optionally, filter criteria to restrict the list to a manageable size.

To show a View on your own object's data, click its tab and then click the Go button. This displays the selected View, which is All by default. Unless you've already customized your All View, it contains only the Name field. Customizing Views is another task, like building tabs and Page Layouts, that can increase developer productivity, even if you don't plan to use the native user interface outside of administration. Figure 2-6 shows a View customized with additional fields.

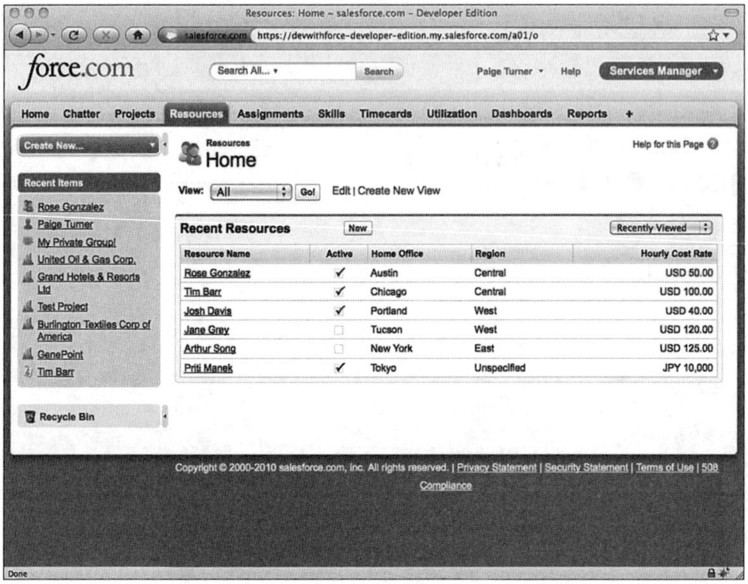

Figure 2-5 Custom tab home

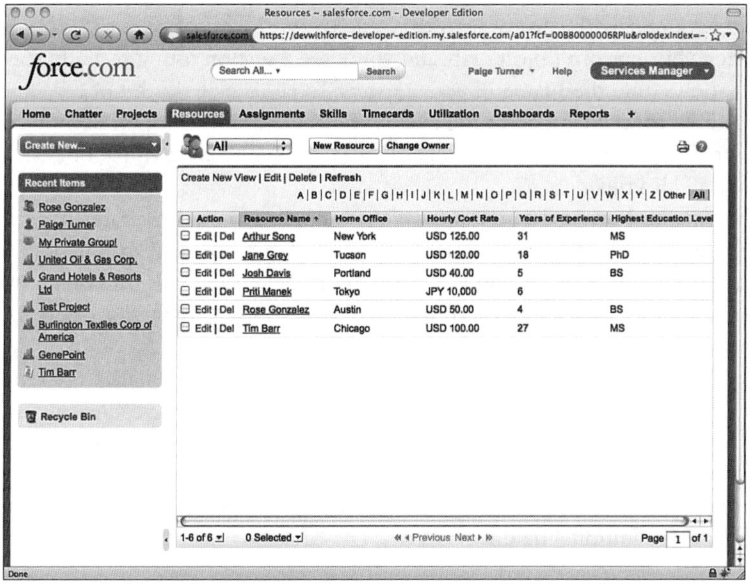

Figure 2-6 View of custom object

Sample Application: Data Model

In this section, you'll build a first iteration of the Force.com database for the Services Manager sample application and populate it with data. It starts with a discussion of the design of the Services Manager data model. The remainder of the section describes how to implement the data model on Force.com and load it with sample data.

Logical Data Model

To build a database in Force.com, begin with a logical model. Identify the data entities, the logical groupings for information. Draw these as boxes and add lines connecting related entities. Annotate these lines with the cardinality of the relationship.

The logical data model of the Services Manager sample application is illustrated in Figure 2-7.

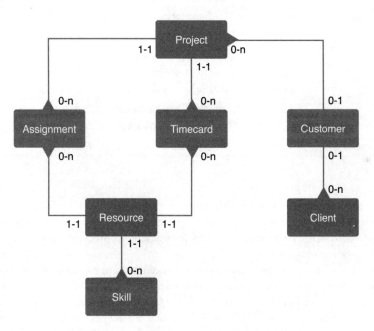

Figure 2-7   Logical data model for Services Manager

The seven data entities are described here.

Customer

The customer is the organization to which professional services are delivered. Customers have a mailing address, a phone number, and zero or more clients associated with them. Table 2-3 lists the columns in the Customer entity.

Table 2-3 **Customer Columns**

Column Name	Type	Description
Name	Text	Customer name
Address	Text	Customer billing address
Phone	Phone	Customer phone number

Client

The client is a person who is employed by a customer. Each client has a first and last name, an email address, a phone number, and a mailing address. Clients also have a named position within an organizational unit of their company. Clients are associated with a single customer at a time. Table 2-4 contains the columns in the Client entity.

Table 2-4 **Client Columns**

Column Name	Type	Description
First Name	Text	Client first name
Last Name	Text	Client last name
Address	Text	Client address
Phone	Phone	Client phone number
Email	Email	Client email address
Title	Text	Title (e.g., VP of Sales)
Department	Text	Organizational unit (e.g., Sales)

Project

A project is a unit of work that the customer has contracted. It has financial attributes such as the number of hours allocated for its completion, the expected revenue, and how billing is to be handled. It also has attributes for tracking its lifecycle, such as start and end date, status, stage, and notes.

Projects have zero or more resources associated with them to deliver the scope of work. Projects also have zero or more timecards logged to them. Performing aggregate calculations on the timecards and resources provides important project financial metrics, such as total billable hours, total assigned hours, total billable revenue, total projected revenue, and total cost. Table 2-5 contains the full list of columns in the Project entity.

Table 2-5 **Project Columns**

Column Name	Type	Description
Name	Text	Project name
Type	Text	Type of project (e.g., Billable, Non-Billable)
Start Date	Date	Date project begins
End Date	Date	Date project ends

Table 2-5   **Project Columns**

Column Name	Type	Description
Billable Hours	Number	Number of billable hours allocated for this project, usually specified in the SOW
Consulting Budget	Currency	Amount budgeted for consulting portion of this project
Expense Budget	Currency	Amount budgeted for expenses
Invoiced	Boolean	Has the customer been invoiced?
Location	Text	Geographic location of this project
Project ID	Text	Human-readable unique ID for this project
Notes	Long Text	General notes on the project
Stage	Picklist	Stage of the project (Planned, In Progress, Completed, Canceled)
Status	Picklist	Status of the project (Green, Yellow, Red)
Status Notes	Text	Explanation of the project status

Resource

A resource is a consultant, a person who works for the services organization to deliver the project. Resources contain basic contact information, such as first and last name, email address, phone number, and mailing address. They also have information specific to services delivery, such as primary skill, number of years of experience, education, and the hourly cost rate. The full list of columns is shown in Table 2-6.

Table 2-6   **Resource Columns**

Column Name	Type	Description
First Name	Text	Resource first name
Last Name	Text	Resource last name
Address	Text	Resource address
Phone	Phone	Resource phone number
Email	Email	Resource email address
Active	Boolean	If `false`, this consultant has left the company or is otherwise unavailable
Education	Text	College(s) attended, degrees attained
Highest Education Level	Picklist	High School, AA, BS, MS, MA, PhD
Hourly Cost Rate	Currency	Internal cost of resource, per hour
Home Office	Text	Office that this consultant typically works out of and/or lives nearest to
Region	Picklist	Area in the country this consultant works in (Unspecified, East, West, Central)

Table 2-6   **Resource Columns**

Column Name	Type	Description
Start Date	Date	Date started with consulting company
Start Date in Industry	Date	Date started in the field
Years of Experience	Number, Calculated	Calculated from Start Date in Industry

Assignment

Projects are staffed with resources by the creation of assignments. Assignments associate a resource with a project for a specified period. Projects can have many resources assigned to them, and a single resource can be assigned to multiple projects. Assignments contain a status, the role the resource is performing on the project, information about the hours billed and remaining, and expected and actual revenue. All Assignment columns are listed in Table 2-7. Assignments are not valid unless they are associated with a Project and a Resource.

Table 2-7   **Assignment Columns**

Column Name	Type	Description
Start Date	Date	Date that the assigned resource begins work on the project
End Date	Date	Date that the assigned resource finishes work on the project
Description	Text	Description of this assignment (e.g., Design, Development)
Role	Text	Role of the resource on this project (e.g., Developer, Instructor)
Currently Assigned?	Boolean, Calculated	If true, today is between Start Date and End Date
Status	Text	Tentative, Scheduled, Closed
Total Hours	Number	Number of hours to be worked during this assignment
Hourly Cost	Currency	Internal cost of the assigned resource
Hourly Rate	Currency	Rate at which the assigned resource is billed out
Planned Cost	Currency, Calculated	Expected cost of this assignment, equal to Total Hours multiplied by Hourly Cost
Planned Revenue	Currency, Calculated	Expected revenue from this assignment, equal to Total Hours multiplied by Hourly Rate
Planned Margin	Currency, Calculated	Expected margin from this assignment, equal to Planned Cost minus Planned Revenue

Skill

To ensure that projects are staffed with qualified resources, the application must store information about the skills of each resource. Each resource has zero or more associated skills, but a skill must be associated with a resource. A skill contains a name, description, and numeric rating of the competency level of the associated resource. Table 2-8 provides the list of columns in the Skill entity.

Table 2-8 **Skill Columns**

Column Name	Type	Description
Type	Text	Type of skill (e.g., Java)
Rating	Picklist	On a scale of 0 (none) to 5 (expert), proficiency of associated resource in this skill
Notes	Text	Additional detail to back up the rating

Timecard

As resources work on projects, they keep track of their time. The hours spent each day are logged to a Timecard. Each Timecard represents a week of work on the project. Multiplying the number of hours worked by the internal cost of the consultant produces a cost. Timecards are not valid unless they are associated with both a Resource and a Project. You can find the full list of columns in the Timecard entity in Table 2-9.

Table 2-9 **Timecard Columns**

Column Name	Type	Description
Billable	Boolean	If `true`, hours in this timecard are billable
Sunday Hours	Number	Hours worked on Sunday
Monday Hours	Number	Hours worked on Monday
Tuesday Hours	Number	Hours worked on Tuesday
Wednesday Hours	Number	Hours worked on Wednesday
Thursday Hours	Number	Hours worked on Thursday
Friday Hours	Number	Hours worked on Friday
Saturday Hours	Number	Hours worked on Saturday
Invoiced	Boolean	If `true`, this timecard has been invoiced
Invoice Number	String	Invoice number associated with this timecard
Invoice Date	Date	Date timecard was invoiced
Status	Picklist	Saved, Submitted, or Approved
Notes	Text	Any comments on the timecard, entered by the consultant

Table 2-9 **Timecard Columns**

Column Name	Type	Description
Week Ending	Date	Last day in the week recorded by this Timecard (a Saturday)
Total Hours	Number, Calculated	Total number of hours worked this week, equal to the sum of the individual hours columns (Sunday to Saturday)

Force.com Data Model

In this section, the logical design is translated to a design that can be implemented on Force.com. To do this requires knowledge of how Force.com represents relationships and fields and how standard objects can be leveraged to save development time and create a consistent, maintainable, interoperable application.

Figure 2-8 diagrams the Force.com standard and custom objects for the Services Manager sample application.

As you can see, the Force.com data model closely resembles the logical model. The main changes are the addition of object type (standard versus custom) and the translation of cardinality to Force.com's relationship types of Lookup and Master-Detail. The incorporation of standard objects and the use of relationships are critical to making a successful Force.com data model. They are examined in more detail in the subsections that follow.

Standard Objects

The logical diagram contained the Client and Customer entities. These are replaced by the standard objects Contact and Account. Force.com comes built in with these objects. They contain many standard fields for such things as name, addresses, phone numbers, and email address, which can be customized to meet the needs of your application. If the standard fields are not sufficient, you can also add custom fields, the same type of fields you add to custom objects.

Many advantages exist to using standard objects wherever possible. They are the foundation of Force.com's CRM heritage, so special tools, functionality, and support for them is built in to the platform. Also, if you plan to build or install other applications in your Force.com environment, they probably also use CRM concepts. Interoperating and coexisting is usually much easier when applications share the same core data objects.

Relationship Types

Table 2-10 lists the relationships in the logical model and the Force.com relationship types corresponding to them.

The Lookup relationships in the Services Manager are between Contact and Account, and Account and Project. A relationship between Contact and Account already exists, so you do not need to create one. Between Account and Project is a Lookup relationship because it is optional. An Account does not require a Project, and a Project does not require an Account.

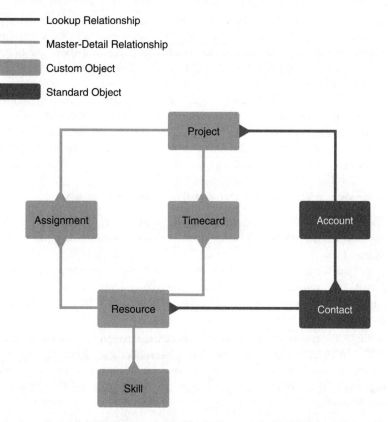

Figure 2-8   Force.com data model for Services Manager

Table 2-10   **Relationships in Service Manager**

Parent	Child	Child Requires Parent?	Force.com Relationship Type
Account	Project	No	Lookup
Project	Timecard	Yes	Master-Detail
Resource	Timecard	Yes	Master-Detail
Project	Assignment	Yes	Master-Detail
Resource	Assignment	Yes	Master-Detail
Resource	Skill	Yes	Master-Detail
Contact	Resource	No	Lookup
Account	Contact	No	Lookup

The remainder of the relationships are Master-Detail. In all of them, the child record requires a parent record. For example, Skill records cannot exist without a corresponding Resource. For mandatory relationships like this, Master-Detail is a good starting point because referential integrity is enforced. If a Resource record is deleted, all child Skill records are also deleted.

You might wonder why Skill and Resource are not a many-to-many relationship. It would be the more normalized way to go. But with the simpler, single Master-Detail relationship, the only repeated field is Skill Type. You can use a Picklist field to keep users working from the same list of valid skills and a validation rule to increase data integrity. If Skill had a larger set of its own attributes and they could not be expressed as Picklists, it would be a good candidate for a many-to-many relationship.

Here are some limitations of Master-Detail relationships to be aware of:

- Force.com supports a maximum of four levels of cascading Master-Detail relationships. So, a child object in a Master-Detail relationship can be the parent of another Master-Detail relationship, and so on. The four-level limit in genealogical terms means that a child can have a great-grandparent object but not a great-great-grandparent. The canonical example of cascading Master-Detail is the purchase order: A purchase order contains one or more line items, and each line item contains one or more line item details.

- A single object cannot be the child in more than two Master-Detail relationships. When an object is the child of two Master-Detail relationships, that object is referred to as a Junction Object. It joins two parent objects in a many-to-many relationship. In the Services Manager data model, Assignment and Timecard are Junction Objects.

- After a child record has referenced its parent record, it cannot be reassigned to a new parent record. This is a significant restriction. In Services Manager, that means if some Timecard records were mistakenly entered to the wrong Project, they must be deleted and re-created as children of the correct Project. They cannot simply be reassigned to the Project.

In Force.com, as in any technology, many ways exist to do the same things, some better than others. Given this first cut of the Services Manager data model, these restrictions on Master-Detail do not seem to be a problem. Incidentally, all the reasons that Master-Detail relationships were chosen can be also satisfied using Lookup fields in conjunction with other Force.com features, to be discussed in later chapters.

Implementing the Data Model

This section walks through the creation of the Services Manager data model in Force.com using Force.com App Builder Tools. This includes a Custom Application to contain the user interface components, the five custom objects, and the relationship fields required between them.

The Force.com App Builder Tools are used in all the instructions in this section. To begin, log in to your DE account and click Setup to navigate to the Builder.

Creating a Custom Application

Defining your application first so that you can add tabs to it as you build them is a good practice:

1. In the App Setup section, click Create → Apps. A list of applications appears. Ignore the built-in applications. Most come with the DE account and cannot be removed. Click the New button.

2. Enter a label for the application, a name, and a description, and then click the Next button. The label is the human-readable label for the application, displayed to users. Name is an internal name, used by Force.com at the API level.

3. Optionally, select an image to be displayed as the logo for your application. This image is shown in the upper-left corner when your application is active. When you're done, click the Next button.

Tip

To prepare an image for use as an application logo, first go to the Documents tab and click the New button. Check the Externally Available Image check box, enter a name to identify the image, and click the Browse button to locate a file on your computer. Click the Save button to upload the image.

4. This screen is for selecting the tabs to be included in the custom application. Home tab is a system-provided tab included in every application and cannot be removed. No tabs are defined for the application yet, so do nothing here. Click the Next button.

5. You can restrict access to your application by Profile, a grouping of users discussed in the following chapter. For now, grant access to System Administrator by clicking the last check box in the Visible column. Then click the Save button.

You are returned to the list of applications, but it now contains your new application. If you activate your application by selecting it from the list in the upper-right corner dropdown, you'll see that it contains a single tab, the Home tab.

Project Custom Object

The following steps define the custom object for Project, including its custom tab and fields:

1. In the App Setup section, click Create → Objects. Click the New Custom Object button.

2. Enter `Project` for the label, `Projects` for plural. Object name defaults to Project, but change it to `Proj` to avoid collision with a Force.com reserved word. Enter a

one-line description of the object in the description field. Select the Launch New Custom Tab Wizard option. This is a shortcut to launch the Custom Tab Wizard. Although not every custom object in Services Manager needs its own tab, tabs tend to come in handy and can always be deleted. Enter `Project Name` for the Record Name Label, and leave the data type Text. Click the Save button to continue.

3. The object has been created, and the New Custom Object Tab wizard is now displayed. Note that the Object field is already prepopulated with Project. Click the Lookup icon (magnifying glass) to select a style for the tab and then click the Next button.

4. Visibility of this tab by Profile is easy to change later, so leave this screen unchanged and click the Next button. This means the new tab is visible for all profiles.

5. Click the Include Tab check box at the top to uncheck it for all applications, and then check it for Services Manager only. Click the Save button to complete the creation of the custom tab.

6. You are now viewing the details of the Project object. To begin adding its fields, click the New button in the Custom Fields & Relationships section.

7. Project Name is already a standard field, so start with the Type field. It can contain one of three predetermined values, making it a Picklist. Select Picklist and then click the Next button.

8. Enter `Type` for the label. When your cursor exits the label, the Field Name is automatically populated. For the list of values, enter `Billable`. Press Enter to start a new line, and then enter `Non-Billable`. Select to use the first value as the default. Click the Next button.

9. Skip the field-level security settings by clicking the Next button.

10. The last screen adds the new field to the default Page Layout. Leave this option checked. Click the Save and New button to save this field and start the wizard over again for a new field.

Repeat steps 7 through 10 until all the fields of Project are created. A few notes on the fields:

- Billable Hours is Number with a length of 7 and 0 decimal places.
- Currency fields (Consulting Budget, Expense Budget) have a length of 16, with 2 decimal places.
- Make the Location field a length of 255, the maximum for a Text type.
- Project ID is an Auto Number Field; format `Project-{00000}`, starting with number 1, and make sure that External ID is checked.

- Stage and Status are Picklists.
- Status Notes is a Text Area, to allow for multiple lines of text.

At this point, you have finished defining the first custom object of the Services Manager sample application. To create the remainder of the objects, follow the same steps, starting with the corresponding table from the logical model. The following sections highlight Force.com-specific details on the fields in each object.

Resource Custom Object

The first five fields on the Resource object contain basic information about the person, such as name and address. This is CRM stuff, so it is more effectively incorporated into the Resource object through a relationship to the Contact object rather than as a series of custom fields. Do not add these fields to the Resource object. The following list provides detail on the remaining fields:

- The first field is Active, a Checkbox, with a default value of Checked.
- Education and Home Office are Text fields, length 255.
- Highest Education Level is a Picklist field with no default value.
- Hourly Cost Rate is a Currency field with length 16, decimal places 2.
- Region is a Picklist with the first value the default.

Years of Experience is a Formula field. Set it to Number type with 0 decimal places. The formula subtracts the current date from the date the Resource started in the industry, rounded down to the nearest whole number of years. If the Resource does not yet have a value for its industry start date, the formula should evaluate to a blank value, designating it as unknown rather than a misleading zero.

The formula in Listing 2-9 is one way to approximate the number of years of experience.

Listing 2-9   **Formula for Years of Experience Field**

```
FLOOR((TODAY() - Start_Date_in_Industry__c) / 365)
```

Assignment Custom Object

In Project and Resource, the standard field Name has been left to its default behavior—that is, a Text of length 80. Projects and Resources have well-defined, meaningful names for storage in the Name field. But an Assignment does not. It is a housekeeping object, maintaining the link between a Resource and Project. Users, both end users and Force.com developers on your team working with this object, should not be required to provide a name for an Assignment record. So, in step 2, in the Record Name Label and Format section, set the Record Name to Assignment #, Type Auto Number, Format {MMDDYYYY}-{000}. This defaults the name to the current date plus a counter value.

The following list describes the rest of the fields in the Assignment object:

- Description and Role are Text, length 255.
- Currently Assigned is a Formula field, type Text.

  Listing 2-10 shows the formula, which returns Yes if today's date is greater than or equal to the start date and less than or equal to the end date, and No otherwise.

Listing 2-10   **Formula for Currently Assigned Field**

```
IF (AND (Start_Date__c <= TODAY(), End_Date__c >= TODAY()), "Yes", "No")
```

- Status is a Picklist, with the first value as the default.
- Total Hours is a Number field, length 5, decimal places 2.
- Hourly Cost and Hourly Rate are Currency fields, length 4, decimal places 2.
- Planned Cost, Planned Revenue, and Planned Margin are all Formula fields of Currency type with 2 decimal places, and treat blank fields as blanks. The formulas are `Total_Hours__c * Hourly_Cost__c`, `Total_Hours__c * Hourly Rate__c`, and `Planned_Revenue__c - Planned_Cost__c`, respectively.

Skill Custom Object

Use the following list to help you create the fields of the Skill object:

- Skill is a Detail object in a Master-Detail relationship with Resource. The standard field Name is not valuable for this object, because individual Skill records do not have names. So, define Name as an Auto Number, type Text, format `Skill-{00000}`.
- Type is a Picklist of valid Skills; for example, Java, C#, Ruby, Perl, PHP, and Apex Code.
- Rating is a Picklist with values 0 to 5 (with text descriptions), using the first value as the default value.
- Notes is a Text of length 255.

After creating the fields, define a new validation rule to enforce that Type contains a value. Having a Skill record without a Skill Type doesn't make sense. The error condition formula in Listing 2-11 checks for an empty Picklist value.

Listing 2-11   **Validation Rule for Skill Type**

```
ISPICKVAL(Type__c, '')
```

Timecard Custom Object

The following list provides details on the fields of the Timecard object:

- Timecard is another housekeeping object, maintaining a link between a Resource and Project for financial purposes. It does not need an editable standard Name field. Set the Record Name to type Auto Number, Format {MMDDYYYY}-{00000}. This defaults the name to the current date plus a counter value.

- All the fields named after days of the week are Number, length 2, decimal places 2, defaulting to 0.

- Invoice Number is a Text, length 255.

- Week Ending is a Date field, and a value is required.

- Notes is a Long Text Area.

- Total Hours is a Formula field, Number type with 2 decimal places. The formula is the sum of the hours fields, as shown in Listing 2-12.

Listing 2-12   **Formula for Total Hours**

```
Sunday_Hours__c + Monday_Hours__c +
  Tuesday_Hours__c + Wednesday_Hours__c +
  Thursday_Hours__c + Friday_Hours__c +
  Saturday_Hours__c
```

Relationships

For each relationship listed earlier in Table 2-10 except the last one, which is already provided in the platform, create a relationship field by following this procedure:

1. Navigate to the child object in Force.com App Builder Tools. To do this, click Setup → Create → Objects. Then click the label of the child object.

2. In the Custom Fields & Relationships section, click the New button.

3. Select the relationship type; this is either Lookup or Master-Detail. Then click the Next button.

4. In the Related To drop-down list, select the parent object and then click the Next button.

5. Click the Next button to navigate past the remaining screens, accepting the default values. These screens control who is allowed to see the new relationship field and how it appears in the native UI on the Page Layouts of both the parent and the child.

One of the most important parts of creating relationships is making sure that they are created on the correct object. In the one-to-many relationship, the "one" side is the parent, and "many" is the child. Always create the relationship field on the child, relating it to the parent. You can always delete the field and start over if you make a mistake.

When you're done, return to the list of custom objects (Setup → Create → Objects). Figure 2-9 shows the list. Compare it with yours, paying particular attention to the values in the Master Object column.

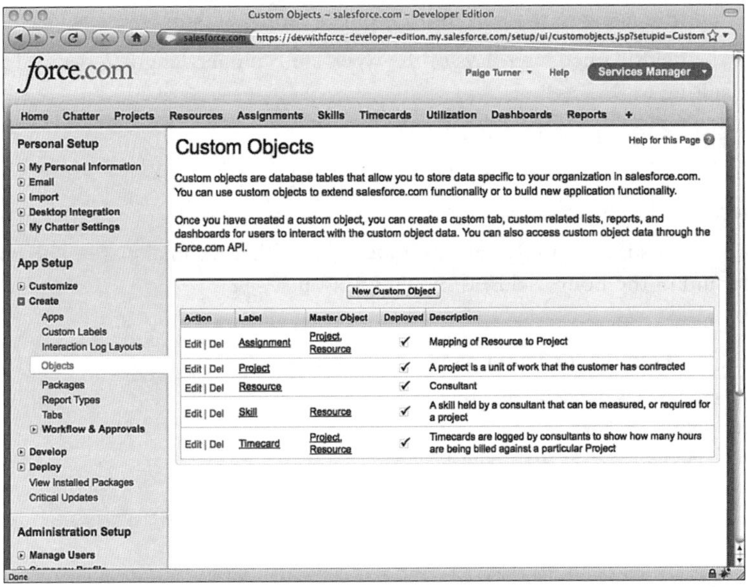

Figure 2-9   Service Manager custom objects list

Importing Data

In this section, you will import sample project and resource data into the Force.com database using the Data Loader tool. This process is divided into three stages: preparing the data, importing it, and then verifying it visually using the native user interface. This is certainly not the only way to import data into Force.com, and probably not the easiest. But it employs a free, widely used, fully supported tool from Salesforce that can scale up to support large numbers of records and complex objects.

Data Preparation

Data Loader operates on CSV files. The first line of the file contains a header listing the columns present in the data. The following lines are the body of the data, with each line a record, values separated by commas. You should have access to Microsoft Excel or an equivalent tool for working with CSV files.

To begin, export CSV files for the Project and Resource objects. Because no data exists yet in the database, these files will be empty except for the header line. This serves as a template for the import file, conforming the data to the layout expected by the Data Loader.

To export, perform the following steps:

1. Launch Data Loader. Click the Export button.

2. Enter your username and password and click the Log In button. Make sure your password includes a Security Token appended to it. If you have not yet obtained a Security Token, log in to Force.com using your Web browser, navigate to Setup → My Personal Information → Reset My Security Token, click the Reset Security Token button, and get the Security Token from the email sent to you by Force.com. Click the Next button when your login is completed.

3. Select the object to export, and click the Browse button to name the export file and specify its directory. Name the file the same as the object name, and save it where you'll readily find it, such as the desktop. Then click the Next button.

4. Click the Select All Fields button. Then remove the system fields, which are ID, OwnerId, IsDeleted, CreatedDate, CreatedById, LastModifiedDate, LastModified-ById, and SystemModstamp. Click the Finish button.

5. Answer Yes to the confirmation dialog. The export is performed, and a summary dialog is shown. Click the OK button to dismiss it. You now have a CSV file on your desktop containing a single line with the names of the exported fields.

Repeat this process for both the Project and the Resource objects. Repeat the process for Account and Contact as well, but this time select only the ID and Name fields for export. Force.com is preconfigured with a handful of Account and Contact records, used in this section as related records for the Projects and Resources.

You should have four files on your desktop. Open account.csv using Excel. Create a new worksheet and import contact.csv into it. Repeat this for project.csv and resource.csv. Reverse the order of the ID and Name columns in the contact and account worksheets so that Name is before ID.

Importing relationships can be a messy process, depending on the tool you're using for the import. Projects are related to Accounts, and Resources are related to Contacts. In the absence of external ID fields, Force.com requires the ID of the related record in order to perform a successful import. Account and Contact do not have External ID fields defined by default, so the ID field must be used.

Because you're working with a small number of records, you could manually enter the ID of each Account and Contact. But for a more realistic scenario, imagine you have a much larger data set. To automate the resolution of ID from Name, use the VLOOKUP function in Excel. In the Resource worksheet, CONTACT_C column, enter the formula given in Listing 2-13 and fill it downward to populate five rows.

Listing 2-13 **Excel Formula for Populating Contact ID**

```
=VLOOKUP(A2, contact!$A$1:$B$32, 2, FALSE)
```

The formula tells Excel to look up the Resource name (in Column A) in the contact worksheet and, if a match is found, set the cell's value to the second column of the contact worksheet corresponding to the match, which is the ID of the Contact.

Enter the formula given in Listing 2-14 in the Project worksheet's ACCOUNT_C column and copy it down five rows.

Listing 2-14   Excel Formula for Populating Account ID

```
=VLOOKUP(A2, account!$A$1:$B$32, 2, FALSE)
```

Listing 2-15 is a sample import file containing five Resource records. Listing 2-16 contains five sample Project records. You can use these samples, replacing the last column with the IDs valid for your Force.com environment, or create your own sample data. Make sure you save the Project and Resource Excel worksheets as two separate CSV files when you're done. (Note: Only a certain number of code characters will fit on one line on the page. The arrow symbol indicates where code that should be entered as one line wrapped to the next line.)

Listing 2-15   CSV Import File for Resource

```
NAME,ACTIVE__C,EDUCATION__C,HIGHEST_EDUCATION_LEVEL__C,
➥HOURLY_COST_RATE__C,HOME_OFFICE__C,REGION__C,START_DATE__C,
➥START_DATE_IN_INDUSTRY__C,YEARS_OF_EXPERIENCE__C,CONTACT__C
Tim Barr,TRUE,University of Chicago,MS,
➥100,Chicago,Central,2/3/2003,
➥6/1/1983,,0038000000YzufcAAB
Rose Gonzalez,TRUE,St. Edwards University,BS,
➥50,Austin,Central,5/15/2006,
➥5/15/2006,,0038000000YzufXAAR
Josh Davis,TRUE,Cascade College,BS,
➥40,Portland,West,7/1/2008,
➥1/1/2005,,0038000000YzufhAAB
Jane Grey,TRUE,University of Arizona,PhD,
➥120,Tucson,West,10/15/2004,
➥3/1/1992,,0038000000YzufiAAB
Arthur Song,TRUE,Fordham University,MS,
➥125,New York,East,6/28/2007,
➥5/1/1979,,0038000000YzufjAAB
```

Listing 2-16   CSV Import File for Project

```
NAME,TYPE__C,START_DATE__C,END_DATE__C,BILLABLE_HOURS__C,
➥CONSULTING_BUDGET__C,EXPENSE_BUDGET__C,INVOICED__C,LOCATION__C,
➥PROJECT_ID__C,NOTES__C,STAGE__C,STATUS__C,STATUS_NOTES__C,ACCOUNT__C
GenePoint,Billable,1/12/2009,,800,
➥200000,20000,FALSE,"Mountain View, CA",
➥,Phase 2,In Progress,Green,,0018000000PAmpWAAT
```

```
Grand Hotels & Resorts Ltd,Billable,2/16/2009,,100,
➥30000,0,FALSE,"Chicago, IL",
➥,,In Progress,Green,,0018000000PAmpdAAD
United Oil & Gas Corp.,Billable,2/9/2009,,500,
➥75000,10000,FALSE,"New York, NY",
➥,,In Progress,Green,,0018000000PAmpgAAD
Burlington Textiles Corp of America,Billable,2/2/2009,,200,
➥40000,5000,FALSE,"Burlington, NC",
➥,,In Progress,Green,,0018000000PAmpaAAD
Express Logistics and Transport,Non-Billable,3/1/2009,,0,
➥0,0,FALSE,"Portland, OR",
➥,Presales,In Progress,Green,,0018000000PAmpeAAD
```

Data Import

Now that the data is prepared, you're ready to import it. Launch Data Loader again, log in, and then follow these steps:

1. From the File menu, select Insert.

2. Select Resource from the list of Salesforce objects.

3. Click the Browse button and locate your `Resource.csv` file, and then click the Next button.

4. The file structure is verified, and a small dialog is displayed showing the number of records contained in the file. Check to make sure that this matches the number of records you expected. Click the OK button to continue.

5. The mapping dialog takes columns from your file and matches them with fields in the Force.com object. Click the Create or Edit a Map button.

6. The easiest way to create the mapping is to click the Auto-Match Fields to Columns button. Because the import files were actually once export files, the columns should match perfectly. Figure 2-10 shows the result of this mapping. All the available Force.com fields except for OwnerId were mapped to columns of the CSV file. The YEARS_OF_EXPERIENCE__C column has no mapping because it is an Auto Number field and cannot be modified. Click the OK button to continue.

7. The new mapping is copied to the current mapping screen. Click the Next button.

8. Click the Browse button to locate a directory to save the results of the import. Data Loader creates two files, one containing errors and another containing success messages. Click the Finish button to begin the import and click Yes to confirm.

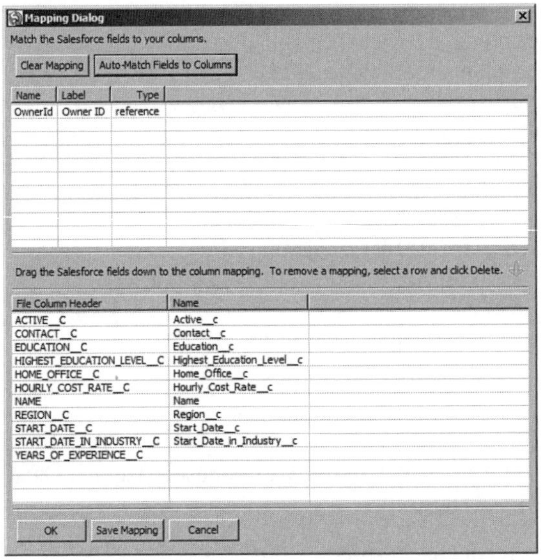

Figure 2-10　Column to field mapping
for `Resource.csv`

9. A dialog is shown with the results of the import. If you received errors, click the View Errors button to examine them, fix your import file accordingly, and try the import again.

Repeat this process for the Project CSV file.

Verify the Data

Data Loader outputs a CSV file containing the records successfully imported. But a friendlier way to look at the successfully imported data is to log in to Force.com and browse the records using the native user interface.

After you log in, select the Services Manager application from the application drop-down list in the upper-right corner of the screen. It contains five tabs, one for each of the custom objects defined in this chapter. Click the Resources tab and then click the Go button to display the view named All, which contains all the records of the Resource object.

You should see a list of the resources you just imported. By default, only the names are shown. You can modify this view to show more fields by clicking the Edit link to the right of the Create New View link and then adding fields in the Select Fields to Display section. Figure 2-11 shows a modified All view of Resources.

Figure 2-12 shows the detail of an individual Resource record. Verify that the currency and dates imported correctly. Notice that the number of years of experience was calculated from the Start Date in Industry field. Examine the Contact field. It should contain a link to the Contact record corresponding to this Resource.

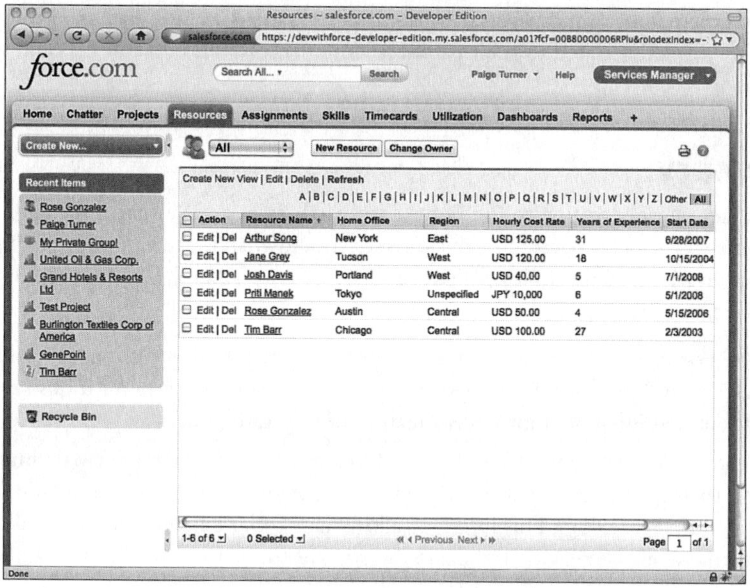

Figure 2-11   Modified All Resources view

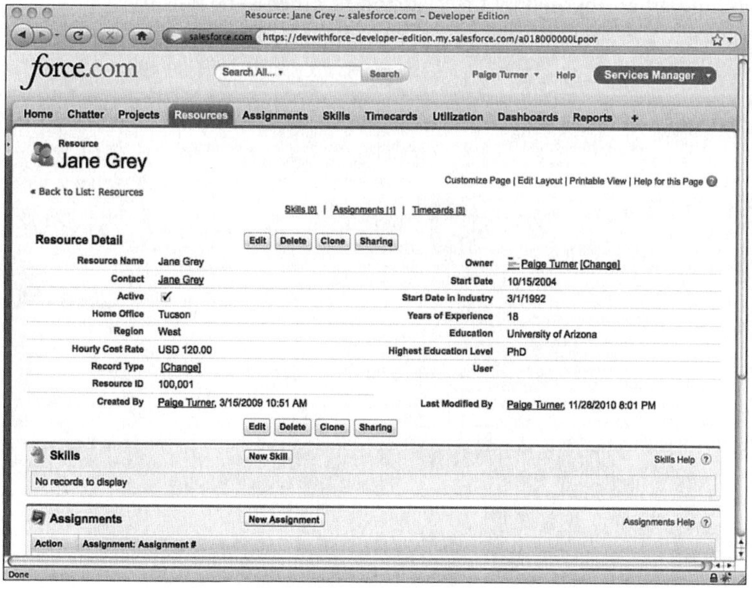

Figure 2-12   Resource record detail

To complete your rounds, browse to the Projects tab. Make sure that the Project records are properly related to their parent Account records and that all the field types were imported correctly.

Summary

This chapter engaged you with the Force.com database in areas essential for application development. The skills covered in this chapter should enable you to build various data-driven applications, all through configuration rather than coding. Here are some key points to take forward.

- The Force.com database is not a standard relational database. It is a logical database based on Objects and Fields, like Tables and Columns but tuned for business applications and integrated into every feature of the platform.
- Custom objects are the backbone of development in Force.com. By defining them and their fields, you are also defining a user interface that is programmatically generated by Force.com. This interface allows data to be entered and browsed without coding, while preserving the data integrity called for in your object definition.
- Services Manager consists of five custom objects and leverages two standard objects (Account and Contact). The process of translating a logical data model to a Force.com database must account for the unique field data types, relationship types, and limitations imposed by the platform in order to be effective.

3

Database Security

For many developers, securing an application is the drudge work left after the fun and challenging development work is done. The good news is that Force.com makes security relatively painless, whether you think about it before, during, or after an application is built. The concepts of user identity, data ownership, and fine-grained access control are baked into the platform, requiring configuration rather than coding in most cases.

You might wonder why this chapter is about only database security rather than being a general discussion of security. After all, Force.com is more than a database. The reason is that the database is the center of Force.com development. Just as object definitions are leveraged throughout the platform to construct native user interfaces and strongly typed procedural code expressions, data security measures are equally pervasive.

This chapter contains the following sections:

- **Overview of Database Security:** Take a high-level view of the database security features available in Force.com and how they interact to protect your data.
- **Object-Level Security:** Get into depth on the methods for protecting individual data objects and their fields.
- **Record-Level Security:** Learn how to control access to individual records within your Force.com database.
- **Sample Application:** Walk through the design and implementation of the security model for the Services Manager.

Overview of Database Security

Force.com provides a multilayered approach to data security. Each layer secures data using a different approach, and the layers build on each other to provide a deep, configurable defense. Figure 3-1 identifies the layers of security and their relationship to data and other layers.

The box enclosing the Object represents object-level security, which is provided by profiles. A profile is a unit of Force.com metadata used to group users with common data access requirements. It contains a set of permissions for every object defined in the

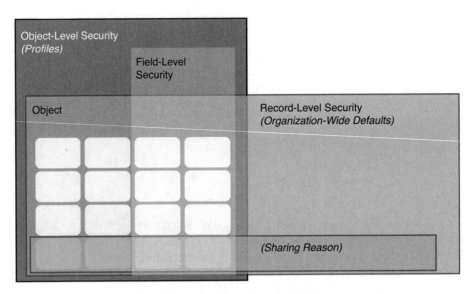

Figure 3-1   Security architecture

Force.com organization. These permissions determine whether users belonging to the profile are authorized to read, create, edit, and delete records of each object. Also within the profile are rules determining access to individual fields of an object. Fields can be hidden entirely or defined as read-only directly in the profile or in page layouts.

Record-level security is layered on top of object-level security. It further restricts access to data based on the concept of record ownership. But it can never override object-level security. Organization-wide defaults define the default, most restrictive sharing behavior of each object, and sharing reasons create exceptions to this default behavior, granting access to specific groups of users.

Another way to think about Force.com security features is to imagine them as a funnel, as in Figure 3-2. Requests for data enter the top of the funnel and descend, filtered through successive layers of security technology. If the requests survive until the bottom of the funnel, they have passed security clearance and are granted.

The four filters in the funnel are described here:

1. **Object Permissions:** At the top of the funnel, the data request is evaluated against the object permissions. They ensure that the requesting user is authorized by its profile to take the desired action on this object. The solid line under this level indicates that requests denied at this point stop moving through the funnel.

2. **Field Accessibility:** The requesting user's profile is consulted again to determine whether fields are included in the request that are read-only or hidden.

3. **Sharing Model:** If the user is not the owner of this record or otherwise privileged with an administrative profile, organization-wide defaults are applied. These defaults

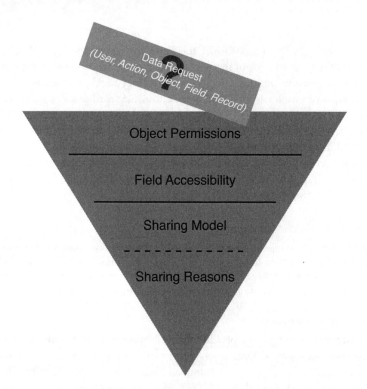

Figure 3-2   Security architecture as a funnel

designate records of each object as private, public with read and write access, or public with read-only access. In a slight break of the funnel concept indicated by the dashed line, if the sharing model prohibits access, the request has one more chance to be granted through exceptions called sharing reasons.

4. **Sharing Reasons:** Sharing reasons override the organization–wide defaults. The owner of the requested record is matched against a list of sharing reasons relevant to its group affiliation. If a sharing reason is found, access is granted. Groups are defined as simple lists of users and other groups or as a hierarchy, allowing permissions of subordinates to be inherited by their superiors.

Object-Level Security

Object-level security is governed by the profile. Profiles control data access for a group of users on the level of objects and fields. This section describes profiles and how they are configured.

Profiles

Profiles are the primary way to customize the Force.com user experience. They contain a large number of settings to control the user interface and data security of your organization. Users are assigned to profiles based on the tasks they need to perform in your system.

The two types of profiles are standard and custom. Standard profiles are provided with Force.com and cannot be renamed or deleted, although they can be reconfigured. Custom profiles have the same functionality as standard profiles but can be named. They can also be deleted if no users are assigned to them.

To manage profiles, click Setup, and in the Administration Setup area, click Manage Users → Profiles. In the realm of data security, the two primary sections to focus on are Administrative Permissions and Object Permissions.

> **Tip**
>
> Make sure Enhanced Profile List Views are enabled for your organization. This feature allows up to 200 profiles at a time to be compared and modified easily, with far fewer clicks than the default user interface. To enable it, click Setup, and in the App Setup area, click Customize → User Interface and select Enable Enhanced Profile List Views.

Administrative Permissions

Two administrative privileges in a profile trump all other security features in Force.com: Modify All Data and View All Data. Users of a profile with these permissions can modify and view all records of all objects, overriding all Force.com security measures. These permissions are powerful, so grant them with extreme care in a production environment. Developers need these permissions to work with tools such as the Force.com IDE, but this applies only in a sandbox or development environment.

Object Permissions

Object permissions are divided into two sections, one for standard objects and another for custom objects. They have identical functionality. Note that object permissions cannot be edited on standard profiles. Figure 3-3 shows the section of a custom profile that defines object permissions.

Each object name is followed by a row of check boxes. Each check box corresponds to a permission for that object. The permissions are described in the following list:

- **Read:** The Read permission allows users to view records of this object. Unless overridden with field-level permissions, this access applies to all fields of the object.
- **Create:** The Create permission permits Read access and the addition of new records to the object.
- **Edit:** The Edit permission allows records in this object to be read and modified.
- **Delete:** This permission enables users to read, edit, and remove records from this object. Deleted records are moved to the Recycle Bin, where they can be undeleted or permanently erased.

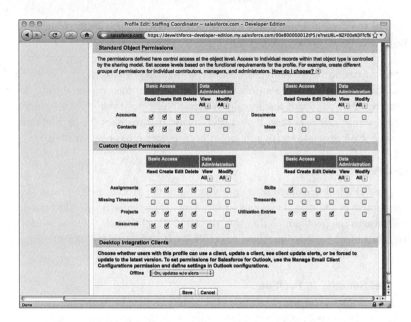

Figure 3-3   Configuring object permissions on a custom profile

- **View All:** The View All permission is like the system-wide View All administrative permission but scoped to a single object. It's designed for use in exporting data because it circumvents other security features of the platform, ensuring that all records are accessible.

- **Modify All:** Like View All, this permission is intended for bulk data operations such as migration and cleansing. It allows users to modify all fields of all records in this object, overriding every other security measure.

New custom objects initially have all permissions disabled for all profiles, except those with View All Data or Modify All Data permission. This platform behavior of defaulting to the most secure configuration ensures that your data is not unintentionally exposed.

Licensing

Profiles are associated with a user license. Licenses are how Salesforce charges for the Force.com platform when you're ready to go into production with an application. Salesforce has many license types to provide flexibility in pricing, but the most basic licenses are Salesforce and Salesforce Platform. The Salesforce Platform license allows full use of Force.com but disables the business domain-specific functionality such as CRM or SFA. For example, a Salesforce license grants you the use of the Opportunity and Case objects, but a Salesforce Platform license does not. Sometimes even infrastructure features are downgraded. For example, profiles for a full Salesforce license can delegate administration on standard and custom objects. The Salesforce Platform license limits this feature to custom objects only.

Planning ahead pays in regard to licensing Force.com. If you are sure you do not need the extra features of the Salesforce license, select the Salesforce Platform license for your profiles. This cuts down on the number of objects and features you see during development and prevents you from accidentally referencing one of them. Also, in order to assign a user to a profile, that user must have a user license that matches the profile. Your custom profile cannot be associated with a different license after it has been created.

Field-Level Security

Security of fields is determined by a combination of the profile and the page layout. The more restrictive of the two always takes precedence. The two ways to edit field-level security are through the profile directly using the Field-Level Security section or through a feature called Field Accessibility. Field Accessibility is a bit more sophisticated because it provides a consolidated view of fields across page layouts and profiles.

Field-Level Security in Profiles

To reach the field-level security section, click Setup, and in the Administration Setup area, click Manage Users → Profiles. Select a profile by clicking its name and scroll down to the Field-Level Security section. Click the View link next to the object name, such as Project, shown in Figure 3-4.

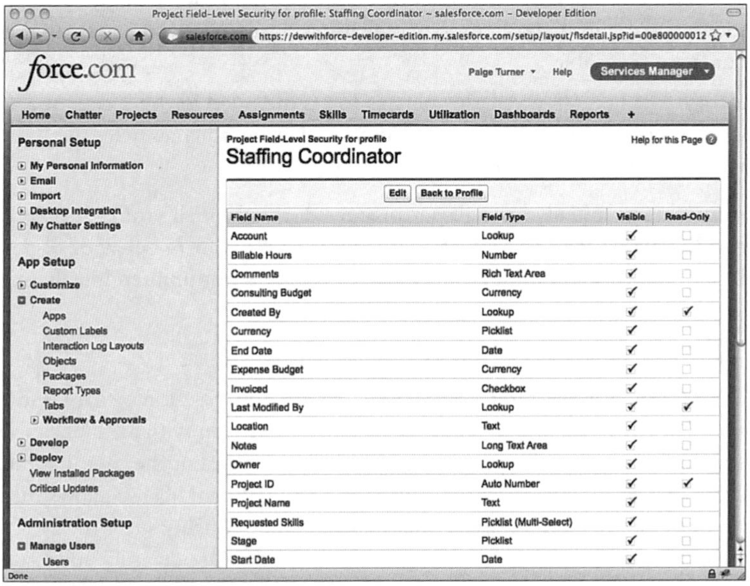

Figure 3-4   Configuring field-level security for the Project object

The two possible states for a field are visible and read–only. Fields marked as visible are available for display on page layouts belonging to this profile. Read-only fields might also be visible on a page layout, but values in these fields cannot be modified.

Field Accessibility

Field Accessibility addresses the finer control of fields provided through the combination of page layout and profile. The more restrictive of two settings always wins. So, if a page layout defines a field as read-only that is defined in the profile as being invisible, the profile takes precedence, and the field is hidden. Field Accessibility provides an easy way to see this behavior in action.

To use Field Accessibility, click Setup, and in the Administration Setup area, click Security Controls → Field Accessibility. Select an object and then drill in by Field or Profile to see the corresponding field accessibility table. Each field has one of four accessibility values:

- **Required:** If a field is defined as required in its page layout and visible in its profile, it is a required field. This means for a record to be saved, it must contain a value for this field.

- **Editable:** A field defined as visible in both the page layout and the profile is designated as editable. This field appears to the user and can be modified.

- **Read-Only:** If a field is declared read-only on its profile or visible in its profile and read-only in its page layout, then it is a read-only field. It appears in the page layout, but its value cannot be modified.

- **Hidden:** Fields that are set to invisible on their profile or page layout are hidden. Hidden fields are never shown to the users of this profile.

Try marking a field as read-only in its page layout but invisible in its profile. Then hover the cursor over the word *Hidden* in the Field accessibility table. You'll see the message that the field is hidden because of Field Security. If you edit the field again and make it visible via the profile, the field becomes read-only per the page layout.

Record-Level Security

In Force.com, individual data records within an object are secured through a combination of three concepts:

1. **Record Ownership:** All records except those on the child side of a Master–Detail relationship have a single named owner. Record owners are individual users or groups of users. Ownership of a record can be transferred manually to another user or group.

2. **User Groups:** Users can be organized into flat lists and placed in a hierarchy. Groups can contain individual users as well as other groups.

3. **Sharing Model:** The sharing model consists of two parts, organization-wide defaults and sharing reasons. The organization-wide defaults can be configured to lock down all records by object, regardless of their owner. Sharing reasons selectively override the defaults to allow access based on record ownership or arbitrary criteria.

This section discusses each concept in more depth.

Record Ownership

When a new record is created, it's owned by the user who created it. The owner has full control over the record. The owner can read, edit, and delete the record; share with other users; and transfer ownership to a different user.

You can experiment with record ownership by creating a record in the native user interface and examining its detail. Notice that its owner field is set to your user, the user creating the record. To share the record with others, click the Sharing button. To transfer ownership, click the Change link beside the owner name.

Owners are typically individual users, but a queue can be also an owner. A queue is a holding area for records to which users are assigned. When a user takes ownership of a record in queue, it leaves the queue and is assigned directly to that user. To configure queues, go to the Administration Setup area and click Manage Users → Queues.

Most objects support record ownership. The notable exception is child objects in a Master-Detail relationship. Records in these child objects have no owners. They inherit ownership from their parent records.

User Groups

Record-level sharing operates on groups of users, not individual users. Force.com provides two mechanisms for grouping users relevant to sharing: Public Groups and Roles.

Public Groups

At its simplest level, a public group is a named list of users included in the group. This list can also contain other public groups. To define a public group, click Setup. In the Administration Setup area, click Manage Users → Public Groups.

A best practice for public groups is to keep the membership list as short as possible. This improves performance and simplifies maintenance. Build larger groups up from smaller subgroups rather than working with individual users.

Roles

Roles are also groups of users but are organized in a hierarchy. Users in roles can inherit the privileges of the roles below them in the hierarchy. This includes record ownership.

A user belongs to one role at a time, and all applications in your Force.com organization use a single role hierarchy.

To define roles, click Setup. In the Administration Setup area, click Manage Users →
Roles. The first time you use this feature, Force.com asks you to select a sample set of
roles to get started. Figure 3-5 shows the territory-based sample configuration of roles.

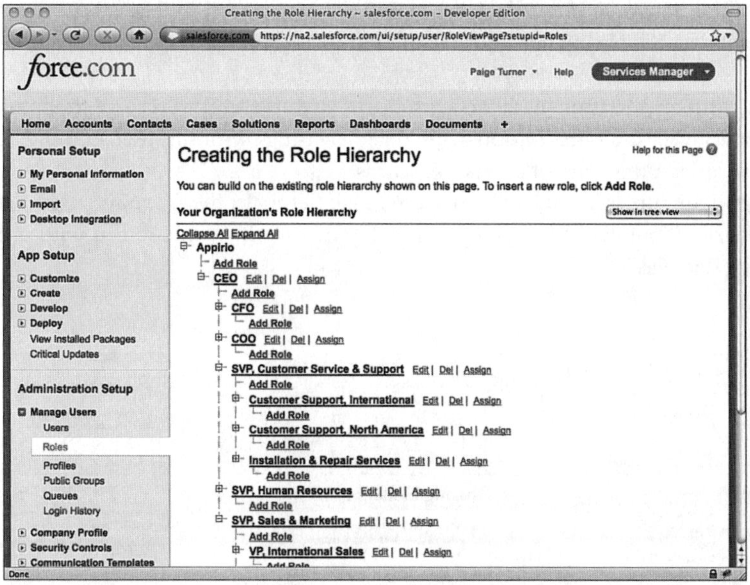

Figure 3-5   Sample roles configuration

Sharing Model

The sharing model defines how record-level privileges are granted to users who do not
own the record. Configuring the sharing model is a two-part process. Organization-wide
defaults are used to establish the most restrictive level of access for each object. Sharing
reasons override the defaults to grant access to individual records.

Organization-Wide Defaults

Every object that allows record ownership has an organization-wide default setting dictat-
ing how records are shared between the owner and other users. Custom objects have
several default settings:

- **Private:** Records belong to the owner and only the owner. With the exception of
  the data administration-level privileges View All and Modify All, records are accessible only to their owners.

- **Public Read-Only:** Any user can view records in this object but cannot edit or
  delete them. Only the owner and users with administrative privileges have rights to
  edit and delete.

- **Public Read/Write:** Any user can view, edit, and delete records in this object. All newly created custom objects default to this setting.
- **Controlled by Parent:** This option is available only to child objects in Lookup relationships. It delegates record-sharing decisions to the parent record. The child records behave as if they lack an owner. Objects with this default setting have the same record-sharing behavior as children in a Master-Detail relationship.

When setting organization-wide defaults, begin with the user to receive the minimum access to data. Set the organization-wide default settings with this user in mind. All users then have at least this level of access to records.

To configure organization-wide defaults, click Setup. In the Administration Setup area, click Security Controls → Sharing Settings. Figure 3-6 shows the screen with organization-wide defaults.

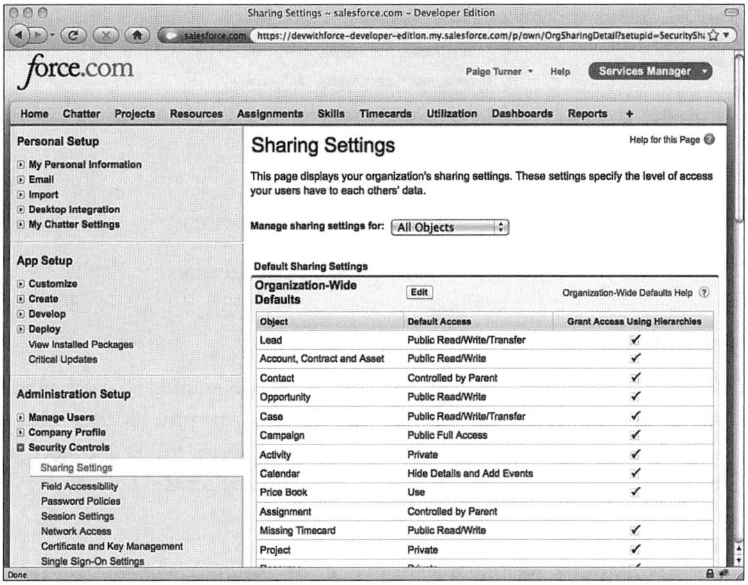

Figure 3-6   Configuring organization-wide defaults

The rightmost column of check boxes called Grant Access Using Hierarchies determines whether the role hierarchy is used on this object to propagate permissions upward to superior roles. By default, this behavior is enabled. Disabling it causes roles to function like public groups. Record permissions are shared only between a pair of roles, never aggregated up the role hierarchy.

Sharing Reasons

Sharing reasons override the organization-wide defaults to allow individual records to be shared between groups of users. The groups can be roles or public groups. The behavior of the sharing reason depends on the groups involved and the type of sharing reason.

Sharing between roles results in asymmetric privileges. Users in subordinate roles do not receive any privileges of their superiors, but superiors receive all the privileges of their subordinates. Sharing with public groups is symmetric, granting equal rights to both parties. In other words, a user has access to all records that are accessible to its descendants in role hierarchy. For example, in Figure 3-5, the SVP of Customer Service & Support has access to records that are accessible to Customer Support, International and Customer Support, North America.

The four types of sharing reasons are as follows:

1. **Manual:** The owner of a record can elect to manually share it with another user or group of users. The owner specifies the level of access (Read Only or Read/Write) to be granted. To configure manual sharing, click the Sharing button on a detail record in the Force.com native user interface. Figure 3-7 shows the user interface for sharing a record named GenePoint in the Project object.

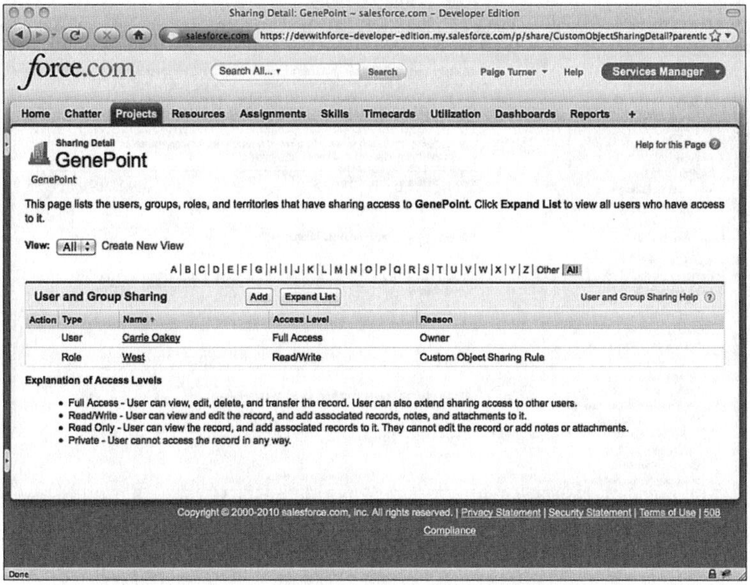

Figure 3-7   Manually sharing a Project record

2. **Sharing Rules:** Sharing rules allow records to be shared automatically by Force.com based on group membership or arbitrary criteria. In Figure 3-8, a sharing rule is being created for the Project object. It specifies that members of the Central business unit can automatically read and write all Project records owned by their colleagues in the same business unit. In Figure 3-9, a criteria-based sharing rule is being defined to provide users in the Executive role with read and write access to billable projects.

3. **Procedural:** Records can be shared programmatically using Apex code. This allows a developer to define the conditions that govern the sharing of a record. This is discussed in Chapter 6, "Advanced Business Logic."

4. **Delegated Administration:** Profiles contain a special object permission category called Data Administration. It contains View All and Modify All permissions. If these are granted, they exempt users in that profile from all sharing rules, giving them access to all records regardless of owner. This privilege is intended for data import, export, and cleansing programs that need to run unencumbered by sharing rules.

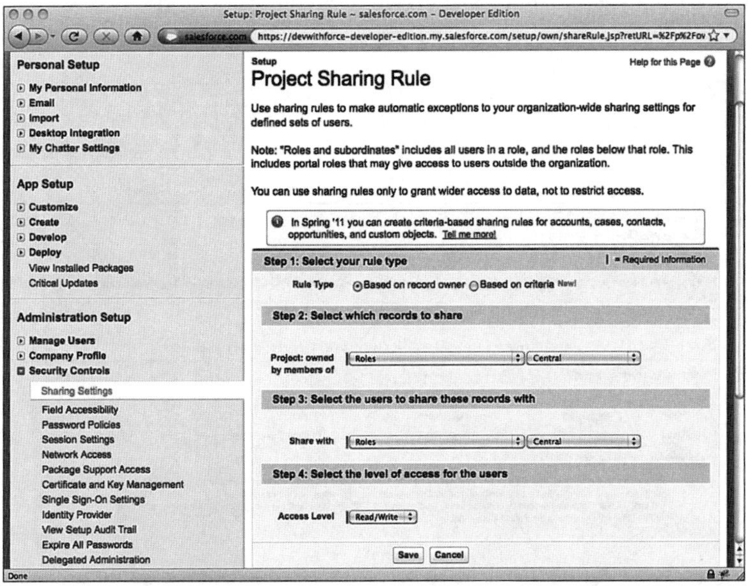

Figure 3-8   Creating a sharing rule for projects

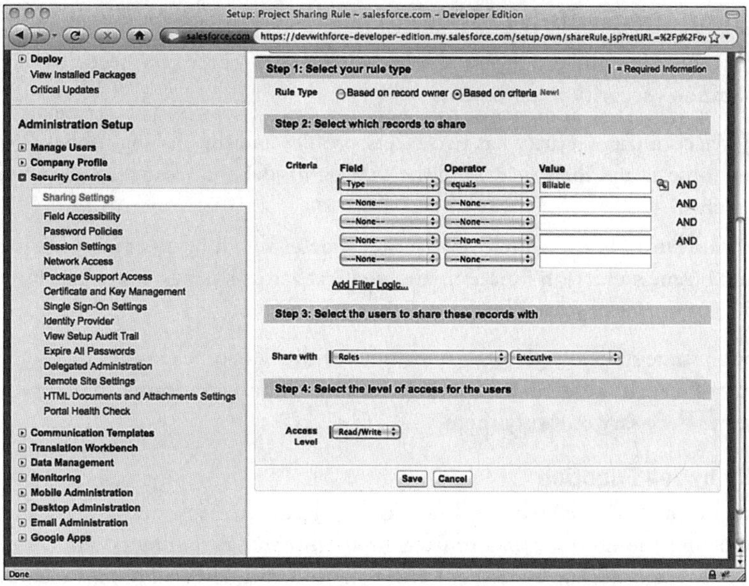

Figure 3-9   Creating a criteria-based sharing rule for projects

Sample Application: Securing Data

The fictional organization driving the development of your Services Manager sample application is organized into independent business units by geography. Business units generally do not share resources or projects, but might do so in special circumstances. All business units roll up to an executive team, which has access to all data. The employees of each business unit perform essentially the same tasks: booking deals, staffing projects, billing time on projects, and invoicing their clients.

From this description of the organization's structure, consider how to make the best use of the data security features of Force.com. The goal is to allow users access to precisely the right data they need in order to perform their jobs, no more and no less. The configuration of Force.com security features necessary to achieve the goal will be referred to as the security model.

In this section, you will walk through the design, implementation, and testing of the security model for the Services Manager application.

Designing the Security Model

To begin the design process, review the fundamentals of Force.com security and the sample application's security requirements:

- Force.com data security has two facets: profiles and the sharing model. Profiles protect objects and their fields, and the sharing model controls access to individual records.

- Data security in the sample application is determined by an employee's job function and business unit. Job functions are identical across business units, and business units do not normally share data.

The design strategy followed in the remainder of this section examines each of the sample application's security requirements and discusses the configuration of the Force.com security features necessary to satisfy them.

Security by Job Function

Job functions dictate what type of data a user is allowed to view and modify. For example, consultants should not create projects or assignments. A staffing coordinator creates projects and assigns resources to them. But a consultant is allowed to create and edit timecards.

As you're thinking about job functions, you're naturally discussing the objects that make up the application. In Force.com, profiles control access to objects and fields. To design profiles for the Services Manager application, start by listing all job functions and objects in a grid. At the intersection of each job function and object, determine the level of access needed. The level of access is expressed as a series of permissions. The permissions are read, create, edit, and delete. Table 3-1 shows the output of this exercise.

Table 3-1   **Services Manager Profiles**

Profile	Project	Resource	Timecard	Assignment	Skill	Account	Contact
Sales Rep	Read	Read			Read	Read	Read
						Create	Create
						Edit	Edit
						Delete	Delete
Staffing Coordinator	Read	Read		Read	Read	Read	Read
	Create	Create		Create		Create	Create
	Edit	Edit		Edit		Edit	Edit
	Delete	Delete		Delete			
Project Manager	Read	Read	Read	Read	Read	Read	Read
	Edit		Create		Create		
			Edit		Edit		
			Delete		Delete		

Table 3-1   **Services Manager Profiles**

Profile	Project	Resource	Timecard	Assignment	Skill	Account	Contact
Consultant	Read	Read	Read Create Edit	Read	Read Create Edit Delete	Read	Read
Accounts Receivable	Read Create Edit Delete	Read	Read Edit	Read	Read	Read Create Edit	Read Create Edit
Vice President	Read Create Edit Delete	Read Create Edit Delete	Read Create Edit Delete	Read Create Edit Delete	Read Create Edit Delete	Read Create Edit Delete	Read Create Edit Delete

Security by Business Unit

Business units are autonomous minicompanies that have a somewhat competitive relationship with each other. All business units report to an executive team. The sample organization is shown in Figure 3-10.

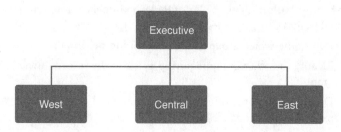

Figure 3-10   Services Manager business units

The Force.com security model must account for the following facts about the organization:

- In normal day-to-day operations, business units do not share data. This includes projects, resources, customers, and contacts. All data is private, belonging to the business unit that created it.

- In some cases, business units might need to share records. For example, a consultant with specialized skills is needed on projects in all three business units.

- Members of the executive team are able to read and write all data.

In the preceding section, you designed profiles to provide each job function in the organization with access to objects and fields. Now you must look at the requirements to protect each record of data. This is where Force.com's record-level security features come into play. To design for record-level security, use the following three steps:

1. **Establish the Sharing Model:** For each object, determine the most restrictive mode of sharing that is called for on its records. For the custom objects found in Services Manager, the options are Private, Public Read Only, and Public Read/Write. Private means that records remain under the control of their owners. Do not consider objects on the Detail side of Master-Detail relationships because records in these objects inherit ownership from their parent record. The output of this step is a list of objects, each with a default access setting (Private, Public Read Only, or Public Read/Write).

2. **Build Groups of Users:** Identify scenarios in which users need to share data outside of the restrictive defaults defined in the sharing model. Look for groups of users involved in these exceptions to the sharing model. Examine the flow of information between the two groups. It can be symmetric, with both groups getting equal access to the data. Or it can be one-sided, with one group receiving elevated rights to another group's data without reciprocation. The output of this step is a list of Roles and Public Groups. Use Roles where the sharing relationship is one-sided, and Public Groups where the relationship is equal.

3. **Set Sharing Rules:** Using the list of Roles and Public Groups from the preceding step, build a list of sharing rules. To build each rule, follow three steps, as shown here:

   1. Determine which group owns the record to be shared.
   2. Identify the other group requiring access to the records owned by the first group.
   3. Decide whether the other group requires Read Only or Read/Write access to the shared record.

Following the first step creates the results given in Table 3-2, which shows the sharing model chosen for each object. Note that Contact is a child in a Lookup relationship, so it has the option of deferring sharing decisions to its parent (Controlled by Parent). This causes it to function like the child in a Master-Detail relationship.

In the second step, the groups of users are defined. In Services Manager, the only groups relevant to sharing are the business units. Each business unit will become a role, including the executive team.

Table 3-2   **Sharing Model for Services Manager**

Object	Sharing Model
Project	Private
Resource	Private
Account	Private
Contact	Controlled by Parent

For the final step of defining sharing rules between the groups, the requirement is to allow users in the same business unit to collaborate on records. To accomplish this task, grant each business unit Read/Write access to records owned by users in their business unit.

Implementing the Security Model

In the preceding section, you designed the sharing model for the Services Manager sample application. In this section, you will implement it in your Force.com DE organization. The implementation involves five separate tasks:

1. **Create Profiles:** Profiles control access to objects and fields. The profiles in Services Manager are modeled after job functions such as Consultant and Project Manager.

2. **Configure Field Accessibility:** Profiles also provide fine-grained control over the fields within an object. In Services Manager, several cases exist in which a particular type of user needs Read access to an object, but not the whole object. Some fields are sensitive and should be hidden. Supporting these cases using field-level accessibility settings is easy.

3. **Set Organization-Wide Defaults:** This is the first step in defining record-level control over data. All records have an owner, initially the user who created the record. Organization-wide defaults are defined on each object and dictate which users besides the owner, if any, also receive access to the records.

4. **Establish Role Hierarchy:** Roles provide a way to group users into a hierarchy. Users at higher levels in the hierarchy receive access to all records owned by their subordinates. In the Services Manager example, roles are used to model geographically distinct business units. By default, business units do not share data with each other. An executive team at the top of the hierarchy receives access to all data.

5. **Add Sharing Rules:** Sharing Rules are one way to override the organization-wide defaults. They automatically share records between two groups of users based on record ownership and group membership. In Services Manager, sharing rules are used to allow record owners in the same business unit to collaborate on the same data. For example, if two Project Managers are in the West, they should be able to see each other's Project records because they work on the same team.

Create Profiles

On the Setup screen in the Administration Setup area, click Manage Users → Profiles. For each profile identified in Table 3-1, follow these steps:

1. Click the New Profile button.

2. Select an existing profile to use as the starting point for the new custom profile. Use Standard Platform User.

3. Enter the profile name and click the Save button.

4. The new profile is created—a copy of the existing one. Click the Edit button to customize it.

5. In Custom App Settings, select Services Manager as the default.

6. Scroll down to the Standard Object Permissions section. Check off the boxes as appropriate to grant access to Accounts and Contacts. Repeat the same process in the Custom Object Permissions section for the five custom objects in the Services Manager application.

7. Click the Save button. As a shortcut to create more profiles, click the Clone button and start building the next profile from step 3.

When you're done, your Profiles screen should look as shown in Figure 3-11.

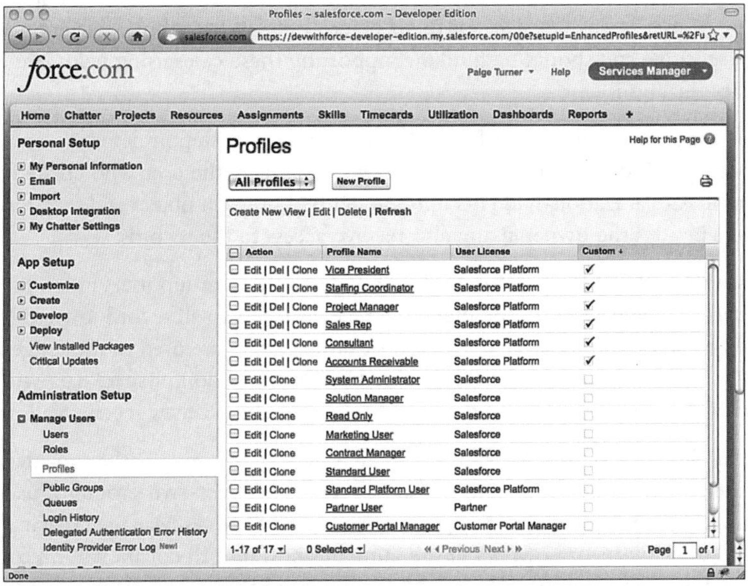

Figure 3-11   Services Manager profiles

Configure Field Accessibility

In addition to object-level security, you also need to protect sensitive fields. By default, all fields of an object are visible. For example, you have granted all profiles at least Read access to the Project object. But a Consultant should not see the finance-related fields Consulting Budget, Expense Budget, and Invoiced.

Follow this procedure to change the visibility of fields in an object:

1. Click Setup, and in the Administration Setup area, click Security Controls → Field Accessibility.

2. Click the object to configure—for example, Project.

3. Click View by Profiles.

4. Select the profile—for example, Consultant. At a glance, you can see the access level of every field in the profile.

5. For each field to change, click its corresponding field access value.

6. Click the first Visible check box to make the field invisible to this profile.

7. Click the Save button.

8. Repeat from step 4 until every profile is assigned the correct access levels for this object.

When you're done with these steps for the Project object, your Field Accessibility screen for the Consultant profile should resemble that shown in Figure 3-12.

Repeat this process on the following objects:

- **Timecard:** Hide the invoice-related fields (Invoiced, Invoice Number, Invoice Date) from the Consultant profile.

- **Assignment:** Hide the finance-related fields (Hourly Cost, Hourly Rate, Planned Cost, Planned Margin, Planned Revenue) from the Consultant profile.

- **Resource:** Hide the Hourly Cost Rate from the Consultant profile.

Set Organization-Wide Defaults

Follow these steps to configure the organization-wide defaults:

1. Click Setup. In the Administration Setup area, click Security Controls → Sharing Settings.

2. Click the Edit button.

3. In the Project row, select Private. Also select Private in the Resource row.

4. Click the Save button.

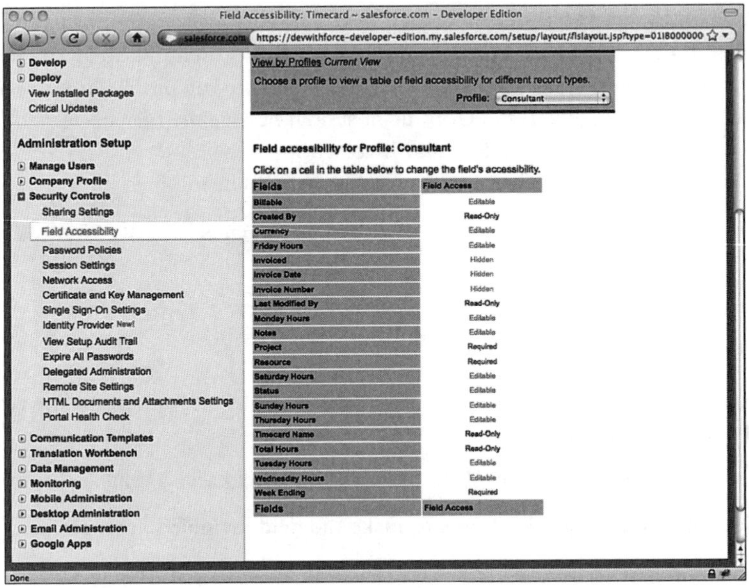

Figure 3-12   Accessibility of invoiced field in Project object

All Projects and Resources are now private. This means that only the owner of a Project and Resource is able to see it. Although this is not the desired behavior, it is the most restrictive setting. From there, you will use Sharing Rules to open access to members of the same business unit.

Establish Role Hierarchy

In the Services Manager sample application, business units are represented using Roles. Roles are chosen over Public Groups because they provide the one-way sharing needed between business units and the executive team.

To configure the Roles, follow these steps:

1. Click Setup. In the Administration Setup area, click Manage Users → Roles. If you've never used this feature before, click the Set Up Roles button to continue past the display of sample role hierarchies.

2. Rename CEO to Executive.

3. Rename three of the roles reporting to Executive to West, Central, and East.

4. Delete the unneeded roles, starting with those at the lowest level of the hierarchy.

When you're done, your role hierarchy should appear as shown in Figure 3-13.

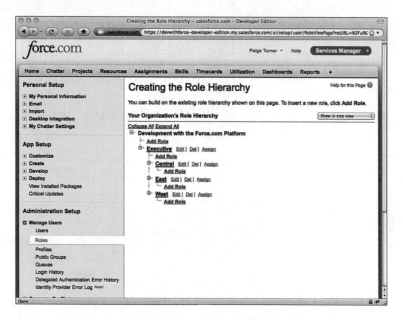

Figure 3-13   Services Manager roles

Add Sharing Rules

The goal in using Sharing Rules is to allow users in the same business unit to collaborate and share data. A record created by one user should be available to all users in the same business unit and their superiors, the executive team.

To configure Sharing Rules, follow these steps:

1. Click Setup. In the Administration Setup area, click Security Controls → Sharing Settings.

2. Scroll to the bottom of the screen. Click the New button in the Project Sharing Rules section.

3. The first pair of drop-down lists identifies the record owners who will be sharing. Select Roles from the first drop-down list and a Role from the second—for example, West.

4. Select the group of users to share with. To share records within the same business unit, set this pair of drop-downs to the same values as those in the preceding step—for example, Roles and West.

5. The final drop-down list, Access Level, specifies the level of access that the second group of users receives to the shared records. Select Read/Write.

Repeat this process to share Project records within the other two business units, Central and East, and Resource records in all three business units. Records are automatically shared with executives because they lie above the business units on the role hierarchy. Figure 3-14 shows the completed list of Sharing Rules.

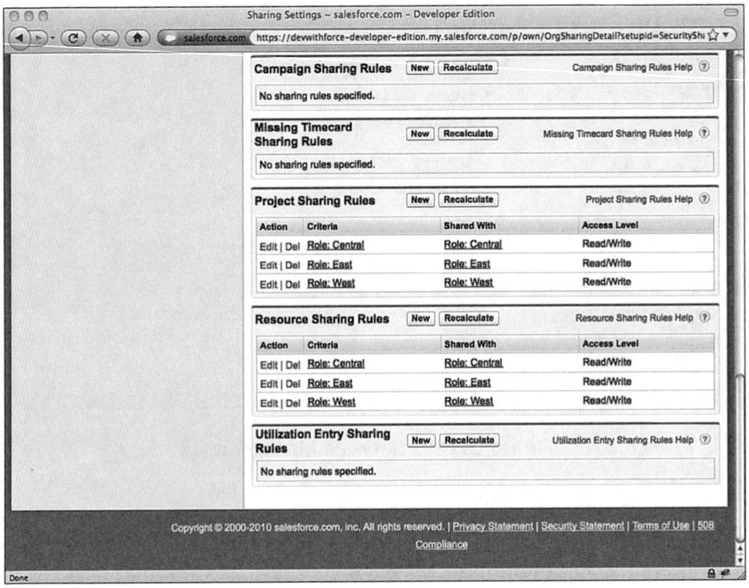

Figure 3-14   Services Manager Sharing Rules

Testing the Security Model

Although Services Manager is a sample application, it's a good idea to get into the habit of testing the security of all Force.com applications before you go into production with them. If you do not take the time to test methodically, a user or group of users could be unable to perform their jobs or become exposed to confidential data intended for other users.

Security testing requires the same level of patience and attention to detail as the actual configuration. If you've kept a spreadsheet or another document with the details of your configuration, you can use it to construct a test plan. Where feasible, make sure you test from the perspective of every group of uniquely privileged users. The native user interface is a great tool for security testing, since it exposes the underlying security model accurately, without the distortion of potentially buggy custom code found in custom user interfaces.

Test object and field visibility by visiting tabs. Test access levels by looking for buttons that modify the state of the record on the pages in these tabs. Test sharing rules by creating records with different owners and checking their visibility to other users.

In the following subsections, you will create three additional users for testing, prepare some test data, verify object and field visibility for three profiles, and test manual sharing between two Roles.

Creating Additional Users

Force.com Developer Edition provides you with up to five free users for your testing. Two of the users are licensed to use the full Salesforce functionality, which includes all the standard objects. Three of the users are Salesforce Platform Users, meaning they have access to a subset of the standard objects. Service Manager can be tested using Salesforce Platform Users.

Although you could use one user and cycle him through the various roles and profiles, creating as many users as you can makes testing more efficient and intuitive. Start with a Staffing Coordinator in the West, a Consultant in the West, and a Vice President in the Executive team.

Follow these steps to create each new Salesforce Platform user:

1. Click Setup. In the Administration Setup area, click Manage Users → Users.

2. Click the New User button.

3. Enter First and Last name, and Email. Set Profile to one of the custom Services Manager profiles and select a Role. Make sure that the check box Generate New Password and Notify User Immediately is selected. Then click the Save button.

4. You will receive an email with a link to log in as your new user. Visit this login link.

5. Set your new password.

6. Click Setup. In the Personal Setup area, click My Personal Information → Grant Login Access.

7. Grant login access to your administrator by entering a date in the second input field and clicking the Save button. This is a time-saving step that allows you, the administrator, to log in temporarily as the user without going through the full login process of entering a username and password.

Repeat this process for each new user. When you're done, you should have a list of users resembling the one shown in Figure 3-15.

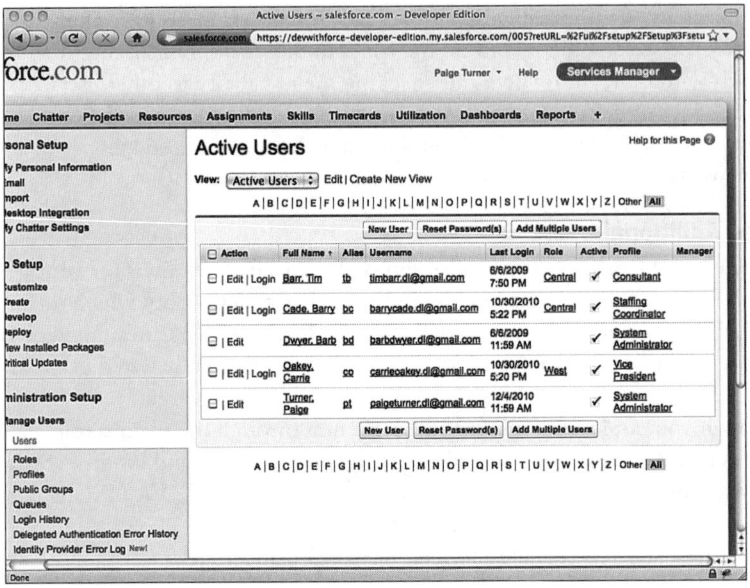

Figure 3-15   Services Manager users

Data Preparation

If you log in as a non-administrator, you'll notice that no Project or Resource records are visible. But you imported some in the preceding chapter, so where are they? Because your sharing model is set to Private for these objects, they are accessible only to the owner, which is the administrator user you used to import them.

To get started with testing profiles, you need to transfer ownership of some records. Log in as the administrator. Grant your Consultant user ownership of a Resource record by visiting the record and clicking the Change link beside the owner name. Figure 3-16 shows the record with a new owner. Note that the owner is different from the user who created the record.

Repeat the same process to transfer ownership of a Project to your user in the Staffing Coordinator profile.

Testing the Consultant Profile

Now log in as a user in the Consultant profile. Click the Resources tab and click the Go button. You should see the Resource record. There are New Timecard and New Skill buttons, but not a New Assignment button. That's because the Consultant profile prohibits this user from creating an Assignment record. Also notice that the Hourly Cost field is hidden.

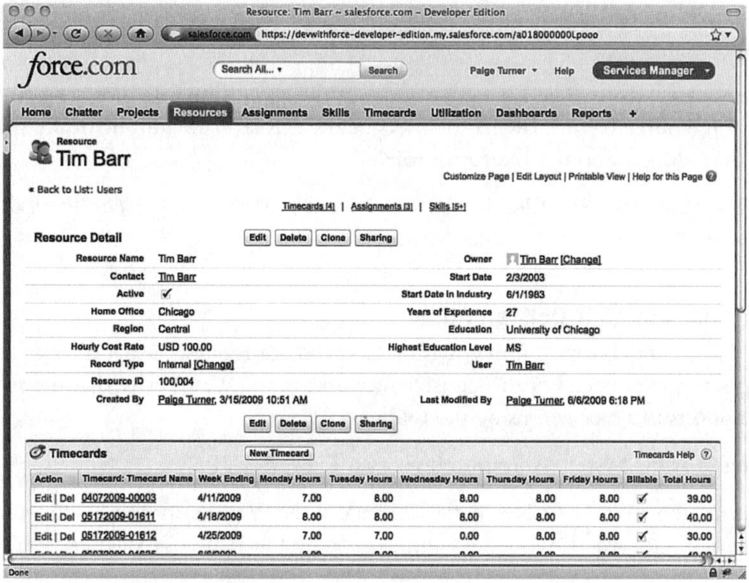

Figure 3-16   Resource record with new owner

Before you leave this record, click the New Skill button and add a few skills to the consultant. Then click around in the other tabs to verify that the consultant cannot create a Project or Resource and cannot see the hidden fields in these objects.

Testing the Staffing Coordinator Profile

When you're satisfied with the Consultant, log out and log in as a Staffing Coordinator. Verify the following behaviors of this profile:

- Can create, edit, and delete Projects and view all their fields
- Can create, edit, and delete Assignments
- Can create, edit, and delete Resources
- Cannot create, edit, or delete Skills
- Cannot create, read, edit, or delete Timecards

Testing the Executive Role, Vice President Profile

Log in as your Executive VP user and verify that this user has full access to any of the records owned by the other users. This includes the ability to edit, delete, and change ownership and share the records.

Recall that the privileged access of this user stems from a combination of two Force.com security features:

1. **Executive Role:** The Executive role is at the top of the role hierarchy. All Project and Resource records owned by users below this level are automatically shared with users belonging to the Executive role.

2. **Vice President Profile:** The Vice President profile has full access to all the objects and fields used in the Services Manager.

Testing Business Unit Collaboration

Say that the Central business unit's Staffing Coordinator requests a specialized consultant for a high-profile project, but this consultant works in the West. Verify that the security model supports this scenario using the following steps:

1. Log in as the System Administrator or an Executive VP user.

2. Locate the record of a Resource working in the West. Verify this by clicking the Resource record's Owner field and examining the value of that user's Role.

3. Click the Sharing button.

4. Click the Add button.

5. In the Search drop-down list, select Roles.

6. Select Role: Central and click the Add button. The Share With list now contains Role: Central. Keep the Access Level at Read Only because you do not want the Central users to be modifying this West-owned resource.

7. Click the Save button.

The sharing detail screen for this Resource should look as shown in Figure 3-17. Note the presence of both the sharing rule and the newly added manual share.

Now that the record is shared with Central, it's time to test it. Make sure you're logged in as the System Administrator. Modify the Staffing Coordinator user so that it belongs to the Central role, and log in as that user. Staff the West consultant to a project by creating an Assignment, setting this consultant as the Resource. If you are able to do this, the manual share is working as intended.

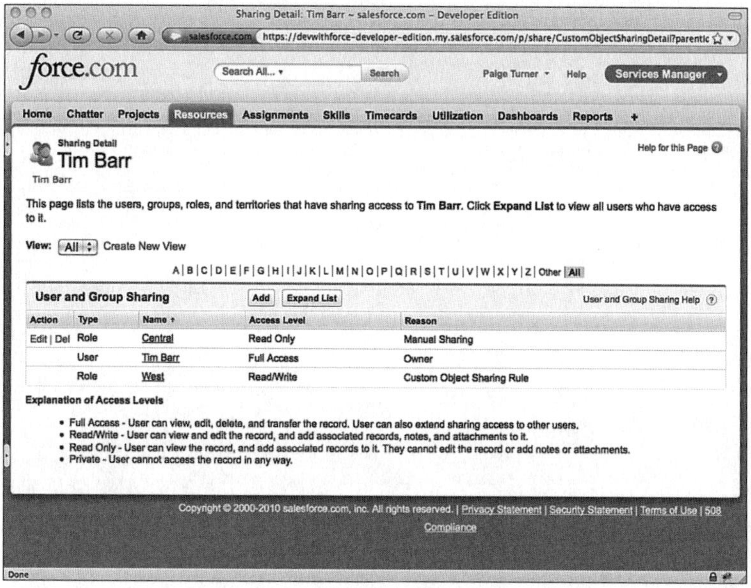

Figure 3-17   Sharing detail for Resource record

Summary

This chapter introduced the data security features provided by the Force.com platform. These features can eliminate much of the effort required in traditional application development to build basic security infrastructure. Here are a few points to consider before moving on:

- Data can be protected at the object, field, and record level.
- Profiles control access to objects and fields. A combination of object and field permissions plus page layouts determines the degree to which a field is accessible to users.
- Most records have a built-in concept of ownership. The record's owner, plus organization-wide defaults and sharing reasons that override these defaults, determines non-owners' rights to view and modify records.

4

Additional Database Features

This chapter introduces a set of features that go hand-in-hand with the Force.com database. Their configuration and behavior build on the definition of objects and fields, extending them to support more complex native user interfaces, calculations performed on groups of records, and offline access to your data.

The following features are discussed in this chapter:

- **Dependent Fields:** Dependent fields enable the standard "cascading picklist" user interface pattern, in which user selection in one picklist filters the available values in a second.

- **Record Types:** Record types allow records in a single object to take on multiple personalities in the native user interface. For example, the standard object Account is designed to store information on businesses, but with minor adjustments can support data on individuals as well. This can be accomplished with record types.

- **Roll-Up Summary Fields:** Roll-up summary fields are like formula fields that operate on a group of records, calculating their sum, minimum, maximum, or a record count.

- **Field History Tracking:** Field History Tracking is an audit trail for your objects. As records are updated, details of the changes are stored in a separate history object. Details include the user modifying the record, the fields modified, and the old and new values.

- **Tags:** Tags are an alternative way to search for records. They are user-created, informal annotations of records that can be easily searched and shared to drive collaboration.

- **Force.com Connect Offline:** This feature brings portions of your Force.com database directly to your desktop. You can work disconnected from the Internet, and your data is synchronized with Force.com when you reconnect.

- **Custom Settings:** Custom settings store and manage user preferences, aspects of an application that can be configured by users rather than hard-coded by developers.
- **Sample Application:** Three of the preceding features are applied to enhance the Services Manager sample application.

Dependent Fields

Dependent fields are primarily used to define cascading picklists. Cascading picklists are a user interface pattern in which the values in one picklist depend on the selection in another picklist. For example, a picklist for state/province might depend on another picklist for country. When a user selects a country, the state/province picklist is populated with a set of values that make sense given the selected country. In Force.com, the first picklist is called the dependent field, and the second is the controlling field. The controlling field can be a standard or custom picklist (with at least 1 and fewer than 300 values) or a check box field, but cannot be a multi-select picklist. The dependent field can be a custom picklist or multi-select picklist.

A dependent field is an ordinary picklist field with an additional attribute to relate it to a controlling field. To visualize the relationship between the fields, modify your object's page layout so that the controlling field appears above the dependent field. Then perform the following steps to define the relationship between their values:

1. Navigate to the Custom Field Definition Detail page for the dependent field.

2. In the Picklist Options subsection, click the New link next to the label for Controlling Field.

3. Select the controlling field and click the Continue button.

4. Use the grid to specify which values of the controlling field should be included in the dependent field. Picklist values of the controlling field are shown as columns. Values of the dependent field appear as rows. Double-click individual values to include or exclude them or hold down the Shift key while clicking multiple values and click the Include Values and Exclude Values buttons to make changes in bulk.

Dependent fields can be challenging to incorporate in dynamic user interfaces and are not supported in Force.com Connect Offline. The main alternative to dependent fields is a Lookup relationship between two objects that contain your valid values. If you already have an investment in picklists and want to migrate, create two objects. One object contains the values of the controlling field; the other contains the dependent field's values. Add a lookup relationship field on the second object, relating it to the first. Load the first object with records, one for each of the controlling field's picklist values. Then add records to the second object, assigning them the correct parent controlling record.

Record Types

Record types overload the native user interface behavior of a single object. This allows you to get more mileage out of your existing objects or limit the complexity of a new data model.

For example, Salesforce uses this feature in its CRM product. Person Accounts are a record type of the Account object. Accounts ordinarily store information about businesses, but the Person Account record type adapts Account to store information about individuals. Salesforce opted to overload Account with a record type rather than creating an entirely new object.

Before creating a separate object to represent every business entity, ask yourself whether the entity is truly new or merely a slight variation of another entity. Where you find slight variations, consider using a single object to do the work of many. The single object contains a superset of the objects' fields. The record type of each record determines which variation of the business entity is stored. Force.com consults the record type and the user's profile to display the correct native user interface.

Even if you don't plan to use the native user interface, record types can expand the flexibility of your data model. By using record types, you gain an additional standard field called RecordTypeId. In custom user interfaces, you can use this to drive different functionality. Of course, you can always add your own custom field to accomplish the same thing, but record types force you to make your design explicit at the native Force.com level and provide tight integration with native Force.com security.

Record types can be tricky to configure because they interact with many other features of Force.com. This section examines record types across three areas:

1. **Defining Record Types:** Record types enable picklist fields to be customized to show different values for different record types of an object. They also add another dimension of flexibility when designing page layouts.

2. **Securing Record Types:** Users gain access to record types through their profiles.

3. **Using Record Types:** The native user interface changes in some significant ways when a user has rights to multiple record types.

Defining Record Types

Record types are defined at the object level after an object is created. In the object definition is a section called Record Types for creating, editing, and deleting record types. Click the New button there to start.

Every object has a default record type called Master. It contains the master list of values for all picklist fields in the object. New record types are cloned from the Master record type if no other record types exist, and given a name, label, and description. Normally record types are in an active state, which makes them available to users who are creating and editing records. Deactivating a record type is required before it can be deleted.

The list at the bottom of the page is a shortcut for adding this record type to many profiles at once. You can skip it. If you do use it, do so with caution. If you add your record type to many profiles and later decide you want to delete it, you must manually visit each profile to remove the record type first. Record types cannot be deleted if they are referenced by profiles.

The next page allows you to associate your new record type with one or more page layouts. This determines which native user interface is shown when a user creates or edits a record of this type. The default is to show one page layout to all users, regardless of their profiles. This page can also be skipped. There is another user interface to do the same thing, but across multiple record types and profiles simultaneously.

After the record type is saved, it enters an edit mode. Edit mode permits the maintenance of picklist values for the record type. The list of picklist type fields in the object is shown, with Edit links beside each. These Edit links take you to Figure 4-1, a screen that allows picklist values to be customized. Here you can select all, or a subset of the picklist values, and provide a custom default value.

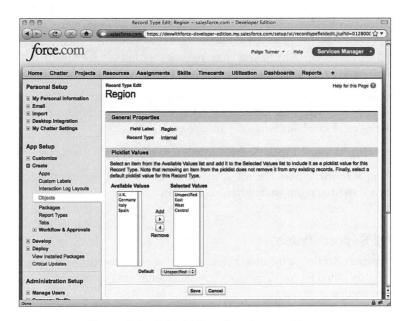

Figure 4-1   Edit picklist values for record type

This is just one way to manipulate the picklist values of a record type. When adding new picklist values in an object with more than one record type defined, you are asked which record types they apply to. Figure 4-2 depicts this scenario. By default, new picklist values are added only to the Master record type, leaving other record types unchanged.

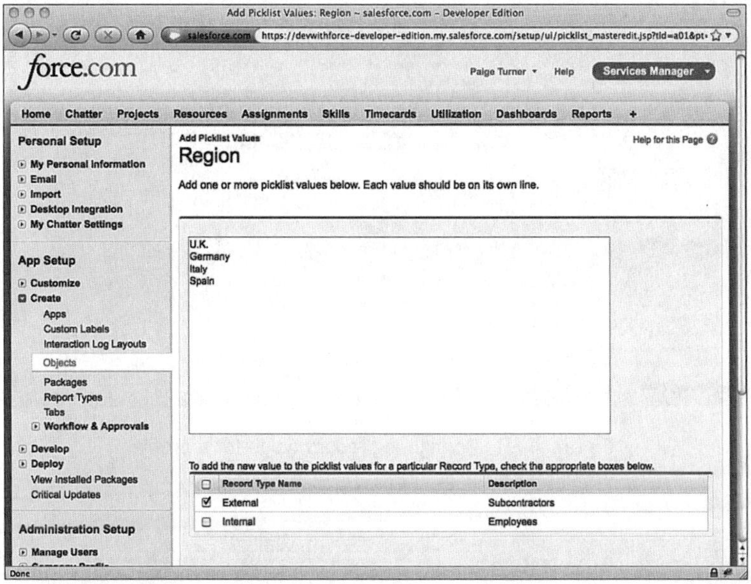

Figure 4-2   Adding picklist values with multiple record types

Securing Record Types

Users are granted access to record types according to their profiles. Profiles contain a section called Record Type Settings. Every one of your custom objects is displayed there, along with a list of the record types the profile is allowed to access and an Edit link. Figure 4-3 is the result of clicking the Edit link on a custom object called Resource in the System Administrator profile. It shows that the System Administrator profile is allowed to access two record types. The default record type is Internal, and the impact of this is discussed in the subsequent section.

Another part of security is field visibility, which is partially determined by the page layout. Record types add another dimension of configurability for assigning page layouts to users. Without record types, the page layout is determined by a user's profile. But with record types, you have the additional option of splitting the decision by record type. This configuration matrix of profiles and record types is shown in Figure 4-4. You reach the screen by clicking the Page Layout Assignment button in the Page Layouts section of the object definition.

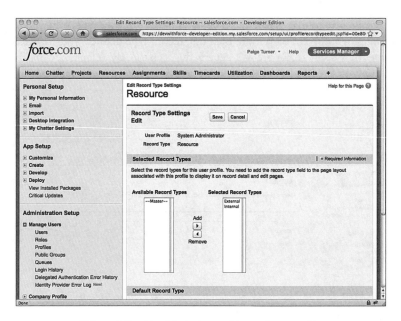

Figure 4-3   Configuring record types for a profile

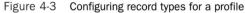

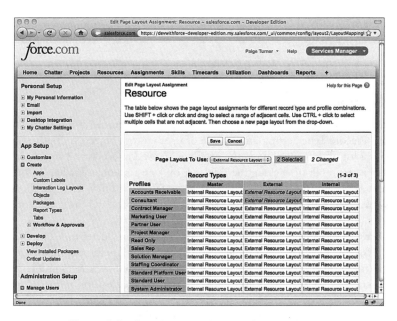

Figure 4-4   Page layout assignment for record types

In this screen, an administrator can quickly review and modify the page layouts assigned to all combinations of record type and profile.

Using Record Types

You've learned how to define record types and how they help determine which page layout is shown to a user and the picklist values within it. But how does a record get assigned a record type in the first place?

If a user has access to only one record type, that record type is automatically assigned to the record. Things become more interesting for users with access to more than one record type. The first step of creating a new record becomes selecting its record type, as shown in Figure 4-5.

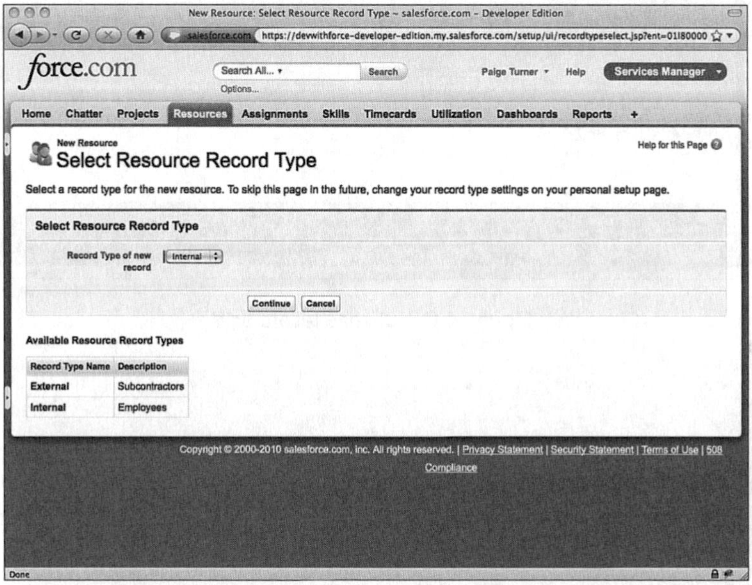

Figure 4-5   New record creation with multiple record types

Users who find this extra step in record creation unnecessary can disable it by visiting their Personal Setup area and clicking My Personal Information → Record Type Selection. Here they can opt to always use the default record type. The default record type is chosen by the administrator and stored in the user's profile.

A record begins life as a particular record type, but its type can be changed later by the record owner. If the Record Type field is added to your page layout, you'll see a Change link beside it. Clicking it reveals the screen shown in Figure 4-6. After the record type is changed, the Force.com user interface automatically enters edit mode on the record to allow you to fix any picklist values that are no longer valid.

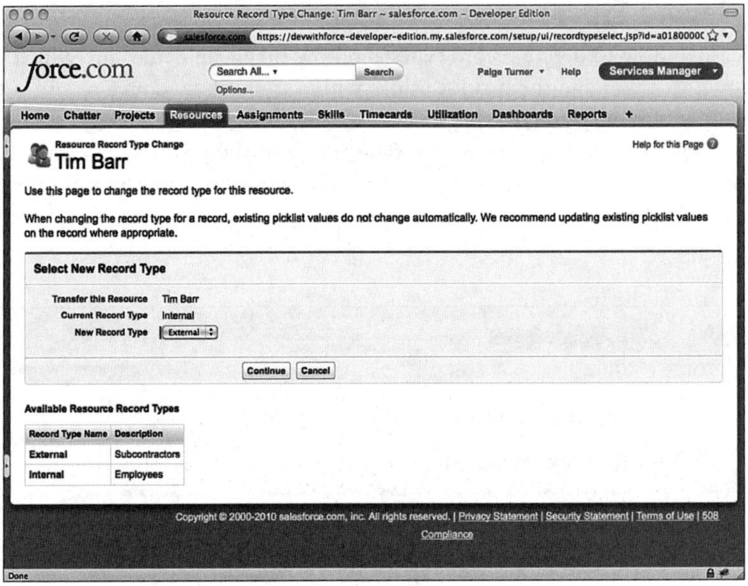

Figure 4-6   Change record type

> **Note**
> Every object has a special field named `RecordTypeId` to indicate the record type of individual records. This allows record types to be queried and assigned to records programmatically.

Roll-Up Summary Fields

Summarizing data in SQL databases is a routine matter of invoking GROUP BY and an aggregate function like SUM. Force.com's SOQL query language supports summarization as well but comes with limitations. Built-in reporting in Force.com provides some summarization functionality, but it's an independent feature with its own user interface, not integrated with your custom application's user interface. For the flexibility to use summary data anywhere, Force.com requires that it be calculated incrementally, either by the database itself or in Apex code. As a result, planning for summary-level data as the database is designed is best.

Roll-up summary fields are the mechanism for instructing the database that you would like summary data to be calculated without custom code or ad-hoc queries. You specify the child object to summarize, the function to apply to the child records, and filter criteria on the child records. The database then takes care of keeping the roll-up summary values up to date as child records are created, modified, and deleted. For example, given an Invoice Header object and Invoice Line Item child object, you could use a roll-up summary field on the Invoice Header to maintain a running count of invoice line items.

Roll-up summary fields are added to objects using the same process as adding other types of fields. After you have provided a label and selected the Roll-Up Summary Field type, the summary calculation is defined as shown in Figure 4-7.

The summary calculation consists of three parts:

- **Summarized Object:** A drop-down list contains the objects you are permitted to summarize. This is restricted to child objects in a Master-Detail relationship with the object on which you're creating the roll-up summary field. Lookup relationships are not supported.

- **Roll-Up Type:** Select the calculation to be performed on the child records and the field of the child object to perform it on. The fields available in this list depend on the calculation. If your calculation is Sum, the list contains fields of type Number, Currency, and Percent. With Min or Max, you can also summarize Date and Date/Time fields. Note that you cannot roll up other roll-up summary fields or formula fields that contain references to other objects, merge fields, or functions returning dynamic values, such as TODAY and NOW.

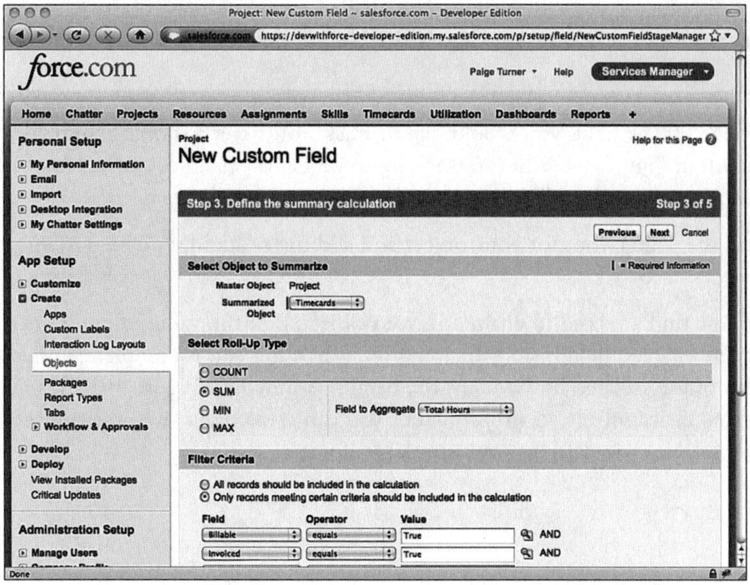

Figure 4-7   Defining a roll-up summary field

- **Filter Criteria:** By default, all records are included in the summary calculation. Alternatively, you can also specify one or more filter criteria to restrict the records involved in the calculation. Build filter criteria by selecting a field to filter, the operator to apply, and the value. If you add more than one criteria, the effect is additive. All filter criteria must be satisfied for the record to be included in the summary calculation.

After you have specified the summary calculation and saved the new field, Force.com begins calculating the summary values on existing records. This can take up to 30 minutes. An icon is displayed beside the field to indicate that the calculation is running.

You can define at most ten roll-up summary fields per object. Make a point of creating them toward the end of your database design process, because they make changing your objects more difficult. For example, you can't convert a Master-Detail relationship to a Lookup relationship without first removing the roll-up summary fields.

Field History Tracking

Field history tracking provides an audit trail of changes to one or more fields of your objects. This audit trail is accessible in the native user interface by adding a special related list to your page layout and also in your own custom code. No user can remove or edit entries in the audit trail, not even a system administrator.

To get started with field history tracking, follow these steps:

1. Go to your custom object's definition page and click the Edit button.

2. In the Optional Features section, select Track Field History and click the Save button.

3. Click the Set History Tracking button in the Custom Fields & Relationships section.

4. Check off the fields you would like to track. Your screen should resemble what's shown in Figure 4-8. You can track up to 25 fields per object. You cannot track the history of formula, roll-up summary, or auto-number fields.

5. Edit the page layout for your object and add the related list corresponding to your object's history.

6. To test, find a record to change in your object. Edit the value of one of the fields you've enabled field history tracking on. When the edit is complete, notice that the field history related list contains the details, as shown in Figure 4-9. This field history related list cannot be customized, but you can create your own custom user interface for viewing field history using Visualforce.

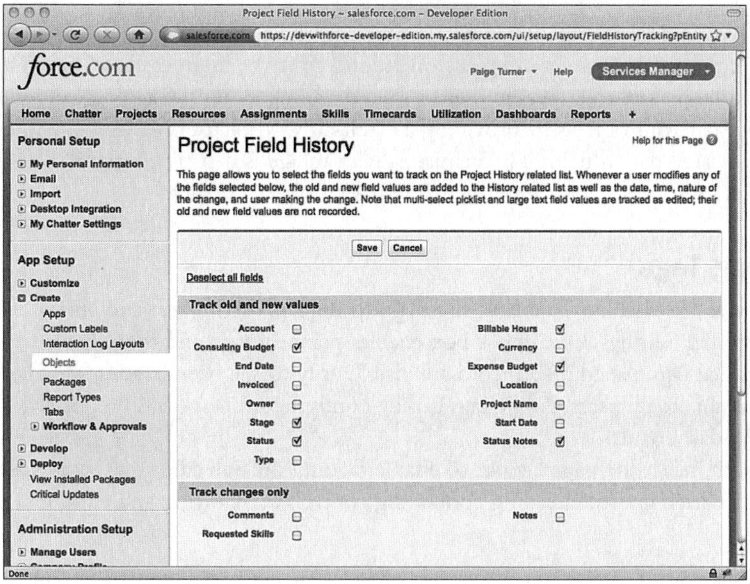

Figure 4-8   Configuring field history tracking

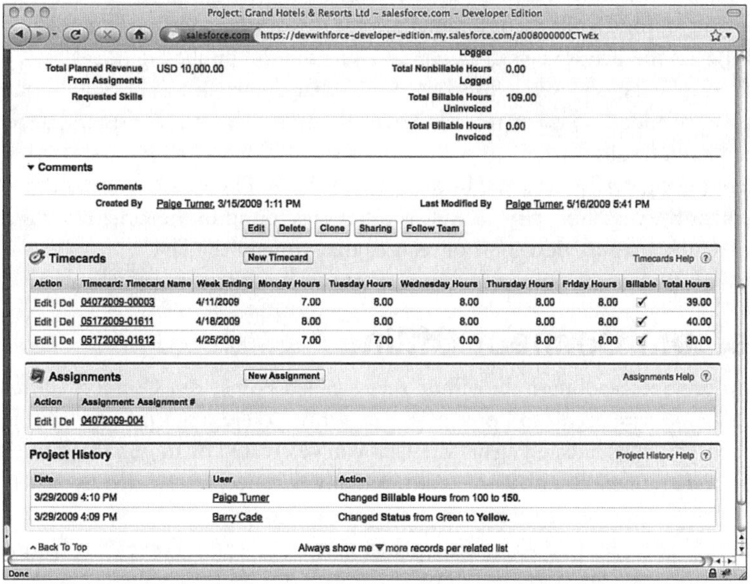

Figure 4-9   Field history related list

Tags

Tags are keywords that users can place on records to make them easier to find. These key-words can be private to a specific user or shared among all users. Tagging can reduce the complexity of your objects by providing a catch-all way for users to search, without addi-tional dedicated search fields. The primary disadvantage is that the search is unstructured. Tags are always strings and cannot be treated as numbers or dates.

Enabling Tags

Initially, tags are disabled. To enable them, go to the App Setup area and click Customize → Tags → Tag Settings. One check box enables personal tags, and the other enables public tags. Personal tags placed on a record are visible only to the user creating the tags. Public tags are visible to all users. Public tags can be configured to appear on reports, documents, notes, and dashboards.

To finish, select the page layouts to enable tagging on. Selected page layouts are enhanced with a gray subheading containing controls for viewing and editing tags.

Using Tags

Visit a record whose page layout has tagging enabled on it. Click the Add Tags link. Depending on how you've configured tags, you could see an input field for public tags, private tags, or both. Enter tags separated by commas.

When you're done, your record contains a list of your tags across the top. The record in Figure 4-10 has the private tags `delayed` and `hot` and the public tag `hotel`.

If you create a tag on a second record, notice that Force.com assists you by suggesting tags that you've added on other records. This helps make the tags consistent, improving the quality of search results.

To search using tags, enter a tag in the search sidebar. The tags section of the search results returns the matching tags, as well as other tags found in the same records as your search tag. Click a tag to view a list of records that contain the tag.

Force.com Connect Offline

Force.com provides a solution for offline access called Force.com Connect Offline. It allows read and write access to Force.com data while you're disconnected from the net-work. When you're connected again, the data you've created or modified offline is syn-chronized and reconciled with Force.com, and any new records created by other users while you were disconnected are cached on your computer.

You should consider two viewpoints when getting to know Force.com Connect Offline. First, an administrator configures the feature for users, specifying the data available for offline access. Then there are the users themselves, who must be running a Windows operating system. They use a dedicated client application to access Force.com when dis-connected, in place of their normal Web browsing application.

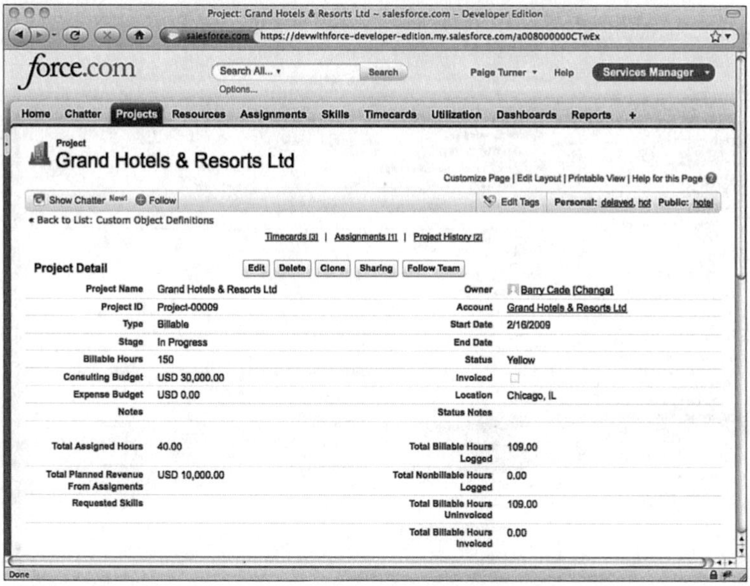

Figure 4-10   Record with personal and public tags

Administration of Force.com Connect Offline

Two independent tracks exist within offline configuration. One is called the Briefcase, and it allows users to directly control the data they need to access offline. The Briefcase is limited to sales objects: accounts, contacts, opportunities, and leads. This option is not discussed further because it is a CRM-specific feature and does not work with custom objects.

The full version of offline configuration is performed by administrators at the profile level. It allows any custom object to be available for offline access and provides filters to limit the amount of data.

To define your own offline configuration, in the Administration Setup area, click Desktop Administration → Offline Briefcase Configurations. Figure 4-11 shows an offline configuration. Two profiles are granted access to a data set made up of records from seven objects.

The majority of the work in creating an offline configuration is in defining the data sets. A data set is simply a group of records cached on users' machines that they can interact with while disconnected from the network. Data sets consist of the following components:

- **Objects:** Select one or more objects to enable for offline access. Objects can be nested in a hierarchy, leveraging relationships between objects to filter records.

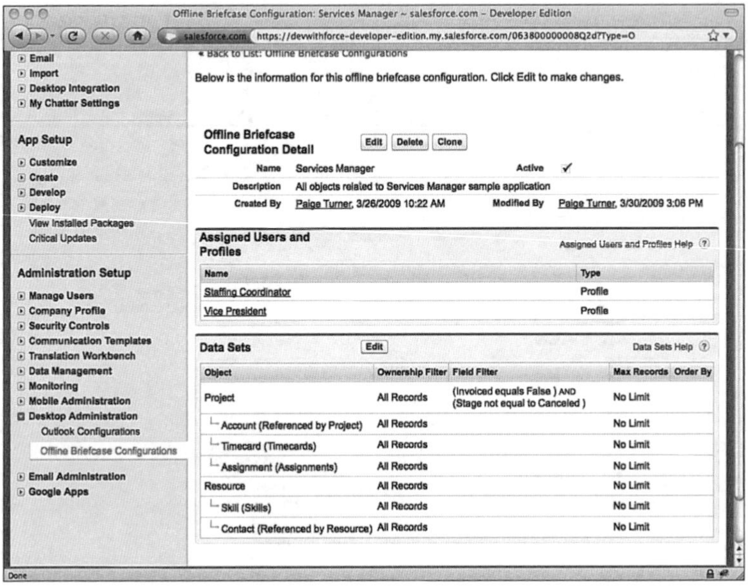

Figure 4-11   Offline configuration

- **Record Ownership Filters:** Four options are available for restricting data by owner. The default is to include all records the user has access to read. Two other options filter on owner, limiting records to those owned by the user directly or by the user and its subordinates in the role hierarchy. The final option provides search access to all records but doesn't actually synchronize the data.

- **Field Filters:** Field filters restrict data based on their values. Filters consist of a field, an operator to compare the values, and a static value. Multiple filters are additive by default but can be chained together in more complex ways using the Advanced Filter Conditions.

- **Record Limits:** You can set a maximum number of records to retrieve for a given data set. If you do not set a limit, Force.com internally limits the data set to 5,000 records per object.

Using Force.com Connect Offline

In the Personal Setup area, click Desktop Integration → Force.com Connect Offline. Click the Install Now button to download the desktop client. It is available only for Windows operating systems. After proceeding through the installation program, you should have an icon on your desktop and in your Start menu called Offline Edition. Launch it and enter your username and password in the login dialog. Be sure to include your security token after your password.

After you're logged in and the initial synchronization is performed, you should see the tabs associated with objects included in your offline configuration. You are now working offline. Figure 4-12 shows a detail record in the offline client application. The user interface is similar to the standard Force.com native user interface, with some elements removed. The list of applications in the upper-right corner is gone, so the tabs from all applications are shown together in a single line.

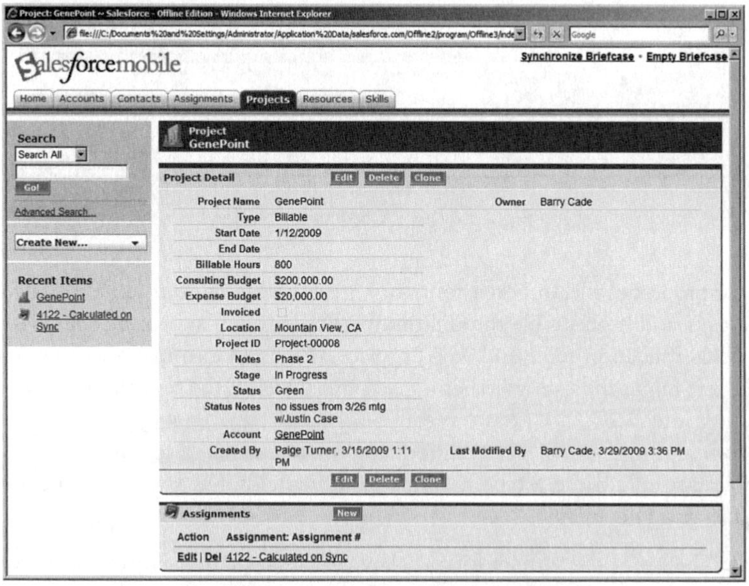

Figure 4-12   Offline client application

At this point, you can browse your offline data sets, search, create new records, edit existing records, and delete records. Click the Synchronize Briefcase link in the upper-right corner to send your changes back to Force.com when you're connected to the network.

If conflicts occur between the data entered offline and data in Force.com, you get the opportunity to manually reconcile the changes. Figure 4-13 illustrates the data reconciliation user interface. Each pair of conflicting changes is displayed side-by-side, and you decide which version of the data is correct.

Custom Settings

Custom settings are a special data storage feature designed for relatively simple, frequently accessed data. The type of data stored in custom settings is ancillary, used to configure or control your application rather than the operational data itself, which belongs in standard and custom objects. For example, user preferences in a Java application might be stored in

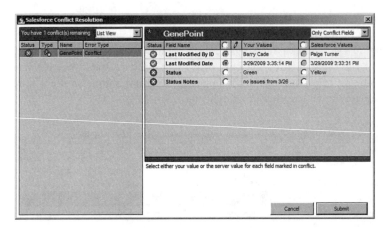

Figure 4-13   Conflict resolution

an XML or properties file. In Force.com, they are stored in custom settings. Data in custom settings is readily accessible throughout the Force.com platform in Apex, Visualforce, formula fields, validation rules, and Web Services API. As an example, a custom setting named Expert might indicate whether a given user receives the default or advanced version of a user interface.

A custom setting is an object definition, much like a standard or custom database object. It consists of a name, a type, and one or more fields. The two types of custom settings are List and Hierarchy:

- **List:** The List is the simpler form, behaving like a database object except for the fact that records are accessed one at a time, by unique name. For example, you might define a custom setting with fields representing configurable options in your application, and each named record representing a collection of those options, such as Test and Production.

- **Hierarchy:** The Hierarchy type expands upon the List type, adding the ability to relate data to organization, profile, and user. If a value is not provided for a given level, it defaults to the levels above it. With Hierarchy types, you can create applications that manage settings for individual users, but defer to a profile or organization-wide default when necessary without storing and maintaining redundant, overlapping information.

Using List Custom Settings

The following steps describe how to build a simple custom settings object and manage the values stored in it:

1. Go to the App Setup area and click Develop → Custom Settings. This is where you define custom settings and maintain their values.

2. Click the New button to define a new custom settings object. Label is the display name for your object; Object Name is the name you'll refer to it by in programs. Enter Config Setting as the Label, and ConfigSetting as the Object Name. For Setting Type, select List. Visibility controls how this setting behaves when packaged. Leave it as Protected. Use the Description field to explain the purpose of your custom setting to other developers in your organization.

Tip

Following a naming convention for your custom settings so that they can be easily differentiated from custom objects is a good practice. For example, append the word "Setting" to the end of any custom setting name. The value of naming conventions will become more apparent when you write Apex code that interacts with the database.

3. Click the Save button. Your custom setting is now created and needs some fields and data. Each custom setting can have up to 300 fields.

4. In the Custom Fields section, click the New button to create a new field. Custom settings fields use a subset of the data types available to custom object fields. They are Checkbox, Currency, Date, Date/Time, Email, Number, Percent, Text, Text Area, and URL. Select Checkbox for your field and click the Next button. For the field label, enter Debug. The Field Name, used to refer to the field in code, is automatically populated. Click the Next button.

5. Click the Save button to finish your field definition. You should see a page resembling Figure 4-14.

You're ready to store values in your custom settings object. Force.com provides a standard user interface for this purpose. Click the Manage button and then the New button. There is a field for the Name of the setting record, which serves as a human-readable identifier for the record. Following the name are the custom fields you've defined on the custom setting. In this case, you have a single checkbox field named Debug. Enter Default for the name, select the Debug box, and click the Save button.

Using Hierarchy Custom Settings

Hierarchy type custom settings provide additional options when storing values. To see them in action, create a new custom setting object called Hierarchy Setting with an object name of HierarchySetting. Again, add a checkbox field named Debug. The default value of Debug selected here is the organization-level setting, which applies if no values are defined for a user or profile.

When you've finished creating the custom setting, add a new value to it. You are prompted to set the value of the Debug field as with the List custom setting example. But there is an additional system field called Location. Location determines at which level in the hierarchy the setting applies. The two options are Profile and User. Try to create two custom setting records, one with Debug selected for the System Administrator profile, and

Figure 4-14   Custom settings object definition

the other a user in that profile with Debug deselected. Figure 4–15 shows the result of this, with a custom view (named Custom View) that pulls in the value of the Debug field to show it varying across the two custom settings records.

Caution

Storage limits exist on custom settings data. For example, in a Developer Edition organization, you cannot store more than 2MB total in all of your custom setting objects. Current usage and the limit for your organization is shown on the Custom Settings main page. To view it, go to the App Setup area and select Develop → Custom Settings.

Sample Application: Applying the Features

This section walks through three scenarios to enhance the Services Manager sample application with features discussed in this chapter. The following list describes the three features to be covered and their contribution to Services Manager:

1. **Dependent Fields for Skill Types:** Services Manager users have outgrown the skill type picklist you built in Chapter 2, "Database Essentials." It contains too many values to effectively navigate. Add a skill category picklist field to filter the values of skill type down to a more manageable size.

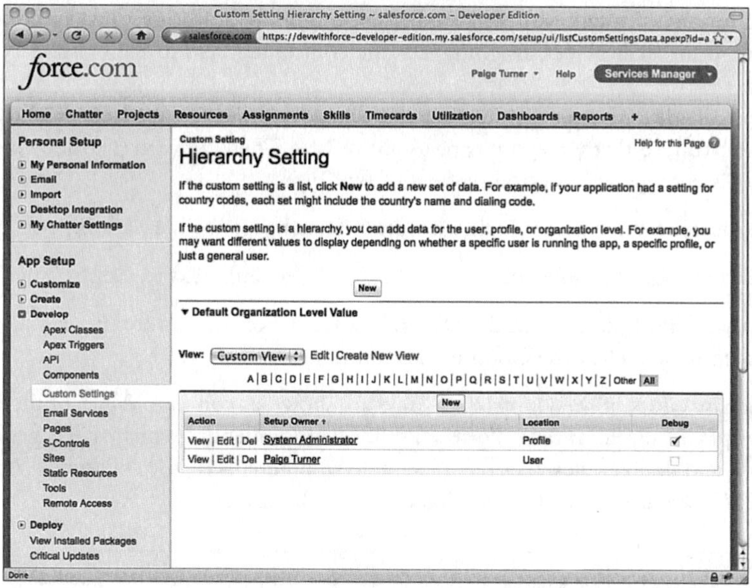

Figure 4-15   Hierarchy custom setting data

2. **Roll-Up Summary Fields for Project Reporting:** Management has requested summary information about projects on the project records themselves. Add roll-up summary fields to the Project object that calculate sums on Timecard and Assignment fields.

3. **Force.com Connect Offline for Staffing:** Make portions of the Services Manager database available offline so that staffing coordinators and project managers can browse, search, and assign resources to projects while disconnected.

Dependent Fields for Skill Types

The Services Manager data model includes a Skill object, which is a child of the Resource object. This pair of objects allows each consultant to have zero or more skills. The Skill object contains a picklist to capture the type of skill and another picklist to store a rating value, measuring the strength of the resource in the selected skill type.

Imagine that consultants and staffing coordinators using the system have complained that a single list of skill types is too limited. The list of skill types has grown and become difficult to scroll through. They agree that grouping skills into categories would address the issue. The users would like to select a skill category and see a shorter list of types belonging to that category.

To accomplish this task, you will use the dependent fields feature to add a skill category field to the Skill object, assigning it as the controlling field to the existing Type picklist.

To start, create a new picklist field named Category on the Skill object. Modify the Skill page layout so that Category appears above Type. Then perform the following steps to assign Category as the controlling field of skill Type:

1. Navigate to the Custom Field Definition Detail page for the Skill Type field.

2. In the Picklist Options subsection, click the New link next to Controlling Field.

3. Type is already selected as the Dependent Field. For the Controlling Field, select Category and click the Continue button.

4. Picklist values of the Controlling Field are shown as columns. Values of the Dependent Field appear as rows. For each skill category, identify which skill types belong to it and double-click them. For example, in Figure 4-16, the skill types "Apex" and "C#" have been added to the skill category, "Languages."

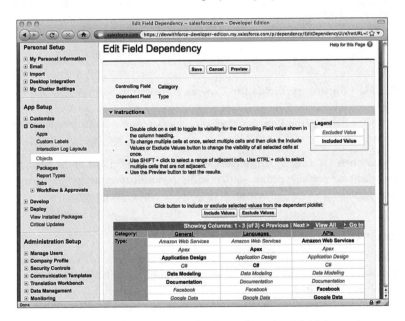

Figure 4-16   Editing values in a dependent picklist

5. Optionally, click the Preview button to test your new dependent picklist. If it doesn't behave as expected, make modifications and preview again. When you're satisfied, click the Save button.

6. To test, create or edit a Skill record. It should look as shown in Figure 4-17. Now your users can select the skill category to get a relevant list of skill types.

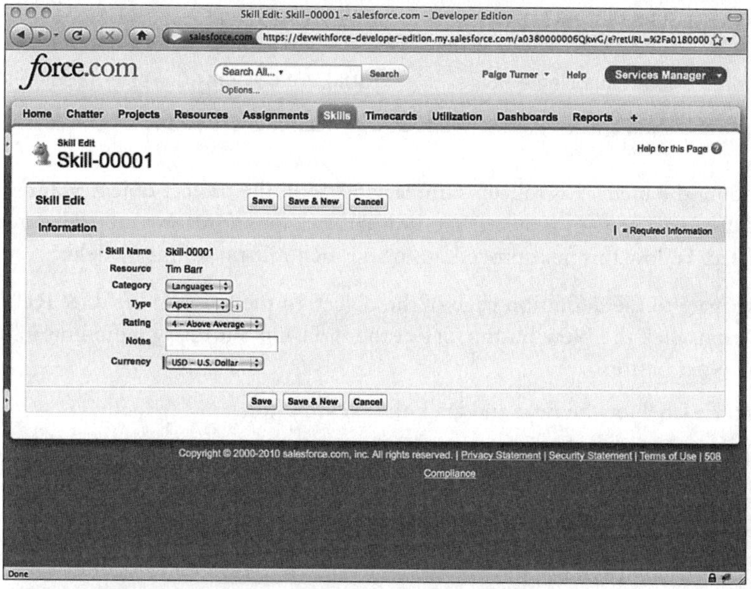

Figure 4-17   Skill record with dependent picklist

Roll-Up Summary Fields for Project Reporting

Executive management spends a lot of time in the native user interface, searching and browsing projects. But the project detail page lacks the metrics to help them run the business. These metrics are simple calculations performed on the assignments and timecards in the project. Table 4-1 lists the metrics that management would like to see, expressed as roll-up summary fields.

Table 4-1   Roll-Up Summary Fields on Project Object

Object	Roll-Up Summary Field Name	Roll-Up Type, Field	Filter Criteria
Assignment	Total Assigned Hours	SUM, Total Hours	
Assignment	Total Planned Revenue from Assignments	SUM, Planned Revenue	
Timecard	Total Billable Hours Invoiced	SUM, Total Hours	`Billable = True and Invoiced = True`
Timecard	Total Billable Hours Logged	SUM, Total Hours	`Billable = True`

Table 4-1   **Roll-Up Summary Fields on Project Object**

Object	Roll-Up Summary Field Name	Roll-Up Type, Field	Filter Criteria
Timecard	Total Billable Hours Uninvoiced	SUM, Total Hours	`Billable = True and Invoiced = False`
Timecard	Total Nonbillable Hours Logged	SUM, Total Hours	`Billable = False`

By adding the metrics as roll-up summary fields on the project object, you ensure that they are always accurate as project, timecard, and assignment records are added, removed, and updated. Follow this next procedure to add each roll-up summary field:

1. Navigate to the definition page of the object. In the Custom Fields & Relationships section, click the New button. Select the Roll-Up Summary radio button and click the Next button.

2. Enter a label for the field and click the Next button.

3. Select an object to summarize. The drop-down list contains Detail objects related to the Master object.

4. Select a roll-up type and a field to aggregate.

5. Specify filter criteria, if any. For each filter criteria, select its field, operator, and value.

6. Click the Next button twice to make the new field available to all profiles and add it to the page layout, and then click the Save button.

Repeat this process for each of the roll-up summary fields listed in Table 4-1. When you're done, your Project object should resemble what's shown in Figure 4-18. To finish, add some assignment and timecard records to watch the roll-up summary fields in action.

Management would also like revenue information at the project level. However, Timecards lack the billable rate of the consultant. This data is available on the Resource object and could be copied into the Timecard using a Formula field.

Before you go down this road, recall that roll-up summary fields cannot be created on fields containing cross-object formulas. That reference to the Resource object from Timecard to get its hourly rate qualifies it as a cross-object formula. Workarounds exist, but they involve custom user interfaces or Apex code to copy the resource's hourly rate into an ordinary Number field.

Force.com Connect Offline for Staffing

Staffing coordinators and project managers have requested offline access to the data in Services Manager. They are Windows users and have already installed the Force.com Connect Offline application. They have asked to see all noninvoiced, noncanceled projects and their associated data, including Account, Timecard, Assignment, Resource, Skill, and Contact.

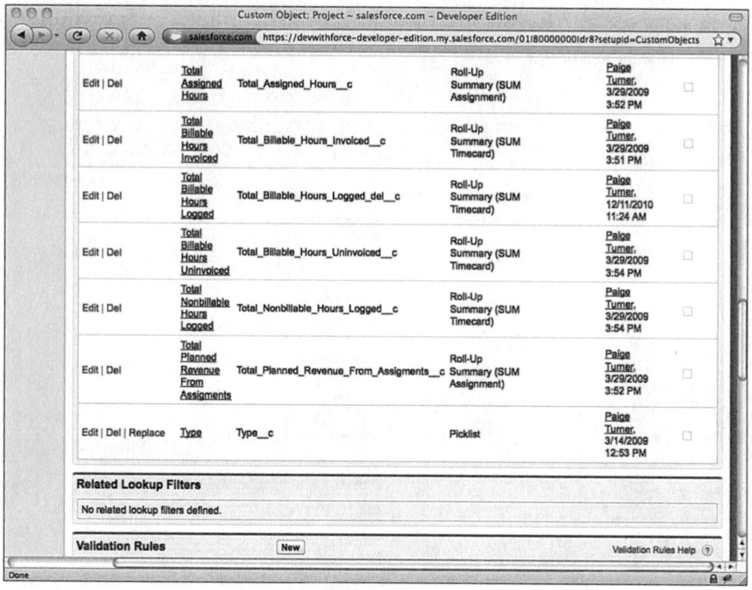

Figure 4-18   Roll-up summary fields on Project object

Use the following steps to build the new offline configuration:

1. In the Administration Setup area, click Desktop Administration → Offline Briefcase Configurations.

2. Click the New Offline Briefcase Configuration button.

3. Enter a name, select the Active check box, and provide a description.

4. Select the Staffing Coordinator and Project Manager profiles from the Available Members list and click the Add button to move them to the Assigned Members list. Click the Save button.

5. Your offline configuration is now created. Click the Edit button in the Data Sets section to add data sets to it.

6. Click the Add button to add a data set. In the dialog that appears, select the object to make available offline.

7. Set the record ownership, field filters, and record limit. For example, add two filters to the Project object, one on the Invoiced field and another on the Stage field.

8. Repeat steps 6 and 7 for each of the data sets. Your offline configuration should resemble that shown in Figure 4-19.

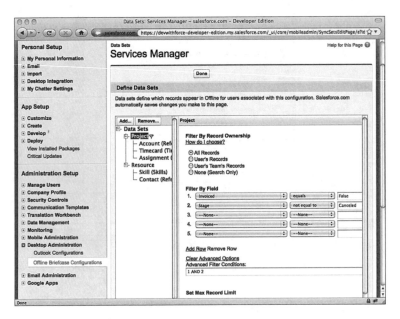

Figure 4-19   Defining an offline data set

9. Click the Done button to complete the process. Your offline configuration is now ready for use.

Test your offline configuration by logging in to the Offline Client application. It should contain the records you defined in the data set and adhere to the same security rules governing the online version of the application. Click the Synchronize Briefcase link when you're done editing data. Log in to Force.com using the Web browser and verify that the data created, modified, and deleted offline has been reflected in the online environment.

Summary

This chapter introduced seven features that extend the functionality already provided by the Force.com database. Here are a few points to consider before moving on:

- Record types offer the ability to create variations of a single object. Records are assigned a record type, used by Force.com to deliver the correct picklist values and page layout for the variation.

- Roll-up summary fields provide a simple way to summarize the data contained in a group of records but require the use of Master-Detail relationships to work.
- Offline access to Force.com data is an exercise in configuration rather than coding. Assuming your users can run Windows, they can easily work with data offline and synchronize it upon reconnection without learning a new user interface.

5

Business Logic

Business logic in Force.com is developed in Apex, a programming language designed for the Force.com platform. Through Apex code, many platform features, such as the database and user interface, can be customized to meet the needs of individual users and companies.

This chapter introduces Apex as a language for writing business logic, specifically where it interacts with the Force.com database. It uses a combination of explanatory text and code snippets to introduce concepts and encourage experimentation. This approach assumes you're already experienced in some other high-level, object-oriented programming language and would like to see for yourself how Apex is different.

The chapter consists of the following sections:

- **Introduction to Apex:** Learn basic facts about Apex and how it differs from other programming languages.
- **Introducing the Force.com IDE:** Take a brief tour of the Force.com IDE, a user interface for developing, debugging, and testing Apex code.
- **Apex Language Basics:** Learn the building blocks of the Apex language, such as data types and loops.
- **Database Integration in Apex:** Incorporate the Force.com database into your Apex programs through queries, statements that modify data, and code executed automatically when data is changed.
- **Object-Oriented Apex:** Learn how to use object-oriented principles in your Apex code.
- **Debugging and Testing:** Get familiar with the tools and techniques for debugging Apex code and how unit tests are written.
- **Sample Application:** Walk through the implementation of a data validation rule for the Services Manager sample application.

Introduction to Apex

Apex is a stored procedure-like language that runs entirely on the Force.com platform. It provides object-oriented features and tight integration with the Force.com database. It's mainly used in custom user interfaces and in triggers, code that is executed when data is changed in the database.

Apex is not a general-purpose programming language like Java or C. Its scope is limited to business and consumer applications that operate on relational data and can benefit from the feature set of the surrounding Force.com platform.

Apex programs exist in a multitenant environment. The computing infrastructure used to execute Apex is operated by Salesforce and shared among many developers or tenants of the system. As a result, unlike general-purpose programming languages you are familiar with, the execution of Apex programs is closely controlled to maintain a consistently high quality of service for all tenants.

This control is accomplished through governor limits, rules that Force.com places on programs to keep them operating within their allotted share of system resources. Governor limits are placed on database operations, memory and bandwidth usage, and lines of code executed. Some governor limits vary based on the type of licensing agreement you have in place with Salesforce or the context that the code is running in, and others are fixed for all users and use cases.

> **Note**
>
> The most prevalent governor limits are discussed throughout this book, but it is not a complete treatment of the subject. The authoritative guide to governor limits is the Force.com Apex Code Developer's Guide, available at http://developer.force.com. Educate yourself on governor limits early in the development process. This education will alter the way you architect your Apex code and prevent costly surprises. Additionally, test all of your Apex code with production-like data volumes. This helps to expose governor-related issues prior to a production deployment.

Here are a few important facts about Apex:

- **It includes integrated testing features.** Code coverage is monitored and must reach 75% or greater to be deployed into a production environment.
- **It is automatically upgraded.** Salesforce executes all of its customers' unit tests to verify that they pass before deploying a major release of the Force.com platform. Your code is always running on the latest version of Force.com and can take advantage of any and all new functionality without the hassle and risks of a traditional software upgrade process.
- **There is no offline runtime environment for Force.com.** You can edit your code on your desktop computer, but it must be sent to Force.com for execution.
- **Apex is the only language that runs on the Force.com platform.** You can integrate Apex with programs running outside of Force.com using HTTP-based techniques such as Web services.

- **The Force.com database is the only database integrated into the Apex language.** Other databases can be integrated through Web services or other technology using HTTP.

The two primary choices for developing Apex code are the Web-based App Builder Tools and the Force.com IDE, provided as a standalone application as well as a plugin to the standard Eclipse IDE. The Force.com IDE is the more powerful and developer-friendly of the two, so it is used throughout this book.

Introducing the Force.com IDE

The Force.com IDE is an extension to the standard Eclipse development tool for building, managing, and deploying projects on the Force.com platform. This section covers installation and gives a brief walkthrough of the Force.com IDE components used throughout this book.

Installation

Force.com IDE is distributed in two forms: a standalone application, and a plugin to the Eclipse IDE. If Force.com is your primary development language or you are not an existing Eclipse IDE user, the standalone version is a good choice. The plugin version of the Force.com IDE requires Eclipse, which you can find at www.eclipse.org. Only specific versions of Eclipse are supported by the Force.com IDE. If you are already using Eclipse but it's an unsupported version, keep your existing Eclipse version and install the supported version just for use with the Force.com IDE. Multiple versions of Eclipse can coexist peacefully on a single computer.

Visit http://wiki.developerforce.com/index.php/Apex_Toolkit_for_Eclipse to learn how to install the standalone and plugin versions of the Force.com IDE.

Force.com Perspective

A perspective is a concept used by Eclipse to describe a collection of user interface components. For example, Eclipse has built-in perspectives called Java and Java Debug. By installing the Force.com IDE, you've added a perspective called Force.com. Figure 5-1 shows the Force.com perspective, indicated in the upper-right corner.

If you do not see the Force.com perspective, click the menu option Window → Open Perspective → Other, select Force.com from the Open Perspective dialog, and click the OK button. The Open Perspective dialog is shown in Figure 5-2.

The Force.com perspective includes several user interface panels, called views. You can see two of them at the bottom of Figure 5-1: Execute Anonymous and Apex Test Runner. It also adds a new type of project called the Force.com Project, which is shown in the left-side Navigator tab. The first step to using the Force.com IDE is to create a Force.com Project.

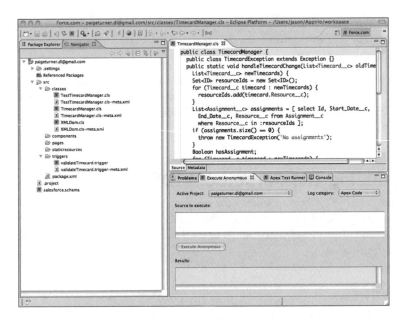

Figure 5-1   Force.com perspective

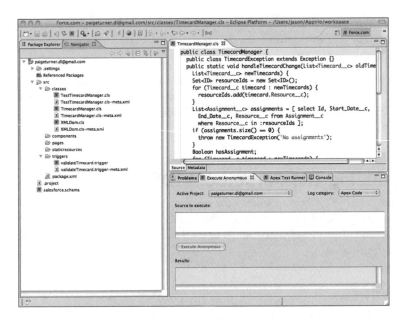

Figure 5-2   Open Perspective dialog

Force.com Projects

A Force.com Project allows you to read and write code, user interfaces, and other meta-data objects within a Force.com organization from your local computer. Although this metadata is edited locally, it must be deployed to the Force.com service to run. Deployment to Force.com occurs automatically every time you make a modification to an object in a Force.com Project and save the changes.

> **Note**
>
> Force.com does not provide its own integrated source control system, but Force.com Projects can be integrated into your company's source control system through the built-in Team features of Eclipse. Refer to the Eclipse documentation for more information.

Problems View

The Force.com IDE leverages the standard Eclipse view called Problems to display compilation errors. When you save changes to an object in a Force.com Project, it is sent over the network to the Force.com service for compilation. If compilation fails, Force.com-specific errors are added to the Problems view. In most cases, you can double-click a problem row to navigate to the offending line of code.

Schema Explorer

The Schema Explorer allows direct interaction with the Force.com database. Use it to inspect objects and fields and to execute database queries and preview their results. To open the Schema Explorer, double-click the object named salesforce.schema in any Force.com Project. In Figure 5-3, the Schema Explorer is open and displaying the fields in the Resource object in its right panel. In its left panel, a query has been executed and has returned five records.

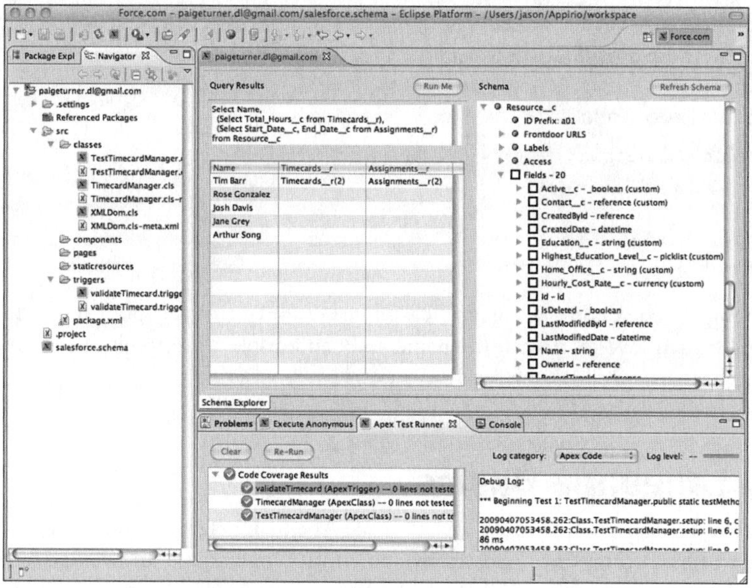

Figure 5-3   Force.com IDE Schema Explorer

Apex Test Runner View

All business logic written in Force.com must be accompanied by unit tests to deploy it to a production environment. Apex Test Runner view is a user interface to run unit tests and view test results, including statistics on code performance and test coverage. If the Apex Test Runner is not already visible on the bottom of your screen, go to the Window menu and select Show View → Apex Test Runner.

Execute Anonymous View

The Execute Anonymous view provides an interactive, immediate way to execute arbitrary blocks of Apex code. Unless noted otherwise, you can execute all the code snippets in this chapter directly from the Force.com IDE using the Execute Anonymous view.

To try the Execute Anonymous view, first create a new Force.com Project. Go to the File menu and select File → New Force.com Project. Enter a project name; enter your Force.com username, password, and security token; and click the Next button. If you receive an error on this step, double-check your username, password, and security token. Also make sure you're providing the credentials for a Developer Edition organization, given that other types of organizations might not have access to the Force.com API. Click the Finish button to create the project.

After you've created a project for your Development Edition organization, the Execute Anonymous view should be visible in the lower-right half of the screen. If not, go to the Window menu and select Show View → Execute Anonymous. In the Source to Execute text box, enter the code given in Listing 5-1. If the text box is not visible, resize your Execute Anonymous view until it's tall enough to see it. After you've entered the code, click the Execute Anonymous button to run it.

Listing 5-1   **Hello World**

```
String helloWorld(String name) {
  return 'Hello, ' + name;
}
System.debug(helloWorld('Apex'));
```

This sample code defines a function called `helloWorld` that accepts a single `String` parameter. It then invokes it with the name `Apex` and displays the results, `Hello Apex`, to the debug log.

Apex Language Basics

This section describes the building blocks of the Apex language. The building blocks are variables, operators, arrays and collections, and control logic. Basic knowledge of the syntax and operation of Apex is valuable for almost any custom development task in Force.com, including triggers, custom user interfaces, and integration with external systems. The section concludes with an introduction to Apex governor limits. Knowledge of governor limits is a critical part of writing business logic that scales from Developer Edition organizations to production organizations with real-world data volumes.

Variables

This subsection covers variable declaration, data types, constants and enums, and type conversions. It also provides detail on rounding numbers and converting dates to and from strings, common tasks in business applications.

Variable Declaration

Apex is a strongly typed language. All variables must be declared before they're referenced. At minimum, a variable declaration consists of the data type followed by the variable name. For example, Listing 5-2 is a valid statement.

Listing 5-2   **Variable Declaration**

```
Integer i;
```

The variable i is declared to be an Integer. Apex does not require variables to be initialized before use, but doing so is good practice. The variable i initially contains a null value.

Variable names cannot start with numbers or symbols and must not conflict with Apex reserved words. These are special keywords used by the Apex language itself. The list of reserved words is available in the *Force.com Apex Code Developer's Guide*.

Variable names are not case-sensitive. Try defining two variables with the same name, one in uppercase and one in lowercase to prove this, as in Listing 5-3. If you try to execute this code, you will receive a compilation error citing a duplicate variable.

Listing 5-3   **Case Insensitivity of Variable Names**

```
Integer i;
String I;
```

Data Types

In Apex, all data types are objects. There is no concept of a primitive type such as an int in Java. Table 5-1 lists Apex's standard atomic data types. These types contain a single value at a time or a null value.

Table 5-1   **Standard Atomic Data Types**

Data Type	Valid Values
String	Zero or more Unicode characters.
Boolean	True or false.
Date	Date only; no time information is included.
Datetime	Date and time value.
Time	Time only; no date information is included.
Integer	32-bit signed whole number (–2,147,483,648 to 2,147,483,647).
Long	64-bit signed whole number (–2^{63} to 2^{63}–1).
Decimal	Signed number with whole (m, Integer) and fractional components (n), expressed as m.n. Total length of number, including sign and decimal point, cannot exceed 19 characters.
Double	64-bit signed number with a decimal point (–2^{63} to 2^{63}–1).
Blob	Binary data.
ID	ID is a variation of the String type to store the unique identifiers for Force.com database records. ID values are restricted to 18 characters. Values are checked at compile and runtime, and a `StringException` is thrown if they do not conform.
Object	Object is the generic type. Variables defined as Object are essentially typeless and can receive any value. Typeless code is vulnerable to run-time errors because it is invisible to the compiler's type checking functionality.

Constants and Enums

A constant is a variable that cannot be modified after it has been initialized. It is declared using the `final` keyword and can be initialized only in constructors, in initializers, or in the declaration itself.

An enum is a set of identifiers. Listing 5-4 provides an example of a constant as well as an enum. The constant is an Integer type; the enum is named `MyConstants` and contains three members. The variable x is initialized to the first member, and its data type is the enum itself, which can be thought of as a user-defined data type.

Listing 5-4   **Defining an Integer Constant and an Enum**

```
final Integer MAGIC_NUMBER = 42;
Enum MyConstants { One, Two, Three }
MyConstants x = MyConstants.One;
```

After it has been declared, an enum can be referenced in Apex code like any built-in data type. It can also be converted into an Integer from its zero-indexed position using its `ordinal` method or into a String using its `name` method.

Converting Data Types

The two ways to convert one data type to another are implicit, and through conversion methods. Implicit conversion means that no method calls or special notation is required to convert one type into another. Conversion methods are functions that explicitly convert a value from one type to another type.

Implicit conversion is supported for numeric types and String types. For numbers, the rule is this: Integer → Long → Double → Decimal. Conversions can move from left to right without casting, as Listing 5-5 demonstrates.

Listing 5-5   **Implicit Conversion of Numeric Types**

```
Integer i = 123;
Long l = i;
Double d = l;
Decimal dec = d;
```

For Strings, ID and String are interchangeable, as shown in Listing 5-6. If conversion is attempted from String to ID but the String is not a valid ID, a System.StringException is thrown.

Listing 5-6   **Converting Between ID and String**

```
String s = 'a0I80000003hazV';
ID id = s;
String s2 = id;
```

When implicit conversion is not available for a pair of types, you must use a conversion method. Data type objects contain a static conversion method called valueOf. Most conversions can be handled through this method. Listing 5-7 is a series of statements that convert a string into the various numeric types.

Listing 5-7   **Type Conversion Methods**

```
String s = '1234';
Integer i = Integer.valueOf(s);
Double d = Double.valueOf(s);
Long l = Long.valueOf(s);
Decimal dec = Decimal.valueOf(s);
```

When a type conversion method fails, it throws a TypeException. For example, when the code in Listing 5-8 executes, it results in an error: System.TypeException: Invalid integer: 1234.56.

Listing 5-8   **Type Conversion Error**

```
String s = '1234.56';
Integer i = Integer.valueOf(s);
```

Rounding Numbers

Rounding occurs when the fractional component of a Decimal or Double is dropped
(round), or when a Decimal is divided (divide) or its scale (number of decimal places)
reduced (setScale). Apex has a set of rounding behaviors called rounding modes that apply
in all three of these situations. By default, the rounding mode is HALF_EVEN, which rounds
to the nearest neighbor, or to the even neighbor if equidistant. For example, .5 rounds to 0,
and .6 to 1. For the complete list of rounding modes, refer to the *Force.com Apex Code
Developer's Guide* at www.salesforce.com/us/developer/docs/apexcode/index.htm.

Listing 5-9 demonstrates the three operations that can cause rounding.

Listing 5-9   **Three Rounding Operations**

```
Decimal d = 123.456;
Long rounded = d.round(RoundingMode.HALF_EVEN);
Decimal divided = d.divide(3, 3, RoundingMode.HALF_EVEN);
Decimal reducedScale = d.setScale(2, RoundingMode.HALF_EVEN);
```

Converting Strings to Dates

Strings can be converted to Date and Datetime types using the valueOf conversion methods, but the string values you're converting from must be in a specific format. For Date,
the format is YYYY-MM-DD; for Datetime, YYYY-MM-DD HH:MM:SS, regardless of the locale
setting of the user. Time does not have a valueOf method, but you can create one with its
newInstance method, providing hours, minutes, seconds, and milliseconds. Listing 5-10
shows the creation of all three types.

Listing 5-10   **Creating Date, Datetime, and Time**

```
Date d = Date.valueOf('2009-12-31');
Datetime dt = Datetime.valueOf('2009-12-31 02:30:00');
Time t = Time.newInstance(2,30,0,0);
```

Converting Dates to Strings

Dates can be converted to strings through the String.valueOf method. This applies a
default format to the date values. If you want control over the format, Datetime has a
format method that accepts a Date pattern. This pattern follows the SimpleDateFormat

pattern found in the Java API, which is documented at the following URL: http://down-load.oracle.com/javase/1.4.2/docs/api/java/text/SimpleDateFormat.html. For example, the code in Listing 5-11 outputs `Thu Dec 31, 2009`.

Listing 5-11   **Formatting a Datetime**

```
Datetime dt = Datetime.valueOf('2009-12-31 00:00:00');
System.debug(dt.format('E MMM dd, yyyy'));
```

Operators

Apex supports the standard set of operators found in most languages. Each operator is listed in Table 5-2 along with its valid data types, precedence if mathematical, and a brief description. In an expression with two operators, the operator with lower precedence is evaluated first.

Table 5-2   **Operators, Their Data Types, and Precedence**

Operators	Operands	Precedence	Description
=	Any compatible types	9	Assignment
+, -	Date, Datetime, Time	4	Add or subtract days on Date, Datetime, milliseconds on Time, argument must be Integer or Long
+	String	N/A	String concatenation
+, -, *, /	Integer, Long, Double, Decimal	4	Numeric add, subtract, multiply, divide
!	Boolean	2	Logical negation
-	Integer, Long, Double, Decimal	2	Arithmetic negation
++, —	Integer, Long, Double, Decimal	1	Unary increment, decrement
&, |, ^	Integer, Long, Boolean	10	Bitwise AND, OR, XOR
<<, >>, >>>	Integer, Long	10	Signed shift left, signed shift right, unsigned shift right
==, <, >, <=, >=, !=	Any compatible types	5 (<, >, <=, >=), 6 (==, !=)	Not case-sensitive, locale-sensitive comparisons: equality, less than, greater than, less than or equal to, greater than or equal to, not equal to

Table 5-2   **Operators, Their Data Types, and Precedence**

Operators	Operands	Precedence	Description
`&&`, `||`	Boolean	7 (&&), 8 (||)	AND, OR, with short-circuiting behavior (second argument is not evaluated if first argument is sufficient to determine result)
`===`, `!==`	Map, List, Set, Enum, SObject	N/A	Exact equality, exact inequality
`()`	Any	1	Group an expression and increase its precedence
`? :`	Boolean	N/A	Shortcut for `if/then/else` expression

Operators not included in Table 5-2 are the assignment variations of date, string, and numeric (`+=`, `-=`, `*=`, `/=`) and bitwise (`|=`, `&=`, `^=`, `<<=`, `>>=`, `>>>=`) arithmetic. For example, x = x + 3 assigns x to itself plus 3, but so does x += 3.

Arrays and Collections

Arrays and collections are a family of data types that contain a sequence of values. It includes Lists and Arrays, Sets, and Maps. This subsection covers each of the three types and describes how to create them and perform some basic operations. Each collection type is different, but there are four methods you can invoke on all of them:

1. **clear:** Removes all elements from the collection.
2. **clone:** Returns a copy of the collection.
3. **isEmpty:** Returns `false` if the collection has elements, `true` if empty.
4. **size:** Returns the number of elements in the collection as an Integer.

Lists and Arrays

Lists and Arrays contain an ordered sequence of values, all the same type. Duplicate values are allowed. Unlike Lists, the length of an Array is fixed when you initialize it. Lists have a dynamic length that is adjusted as you add and remove elements.

To declare a List variable, use the `List` keyword followed by the data type of its values in angle brackets. Because Lists and Arrays are containers for other values, they must be initialized before values can be added to them. The `new` keyword creates an instance of the List. Listing 5-12 declares a variable called `stringList` that contains Strings, initializes it, and adds a value.

Listing 5-12   **Creating a List**

```
List<String> stringList = new List<String>();
stringList.add('Hello');
```

To create an Array, specify a variable name, data type, and length. Listing 5-13 creates an Array of Strings named `stringArray`, initializes it to accommodate five elements, and then assigns a value to its first element.

Listing 5-13   **Creating an Array**

```
String[] stringArray = new String[5];
stringArray[0] = 'Hello';
```

Multidimensional Arrays are not supported. But you can create a two-dimensional List object by nesting a List within another List. In Listing 5-14, `list2` is defined as a List containing Lists of Strings. A String List called `childList` is initialized, populated with a value, and added to `list2`.

Listing 5-14   **Nested List Usage**

```
List<List<String>> list2 = new List<List<String>>();
List<String> childList = new List<String>();
childList.add('value');
list2.add(childList);
```

Arrays and Lists have interchangeable behavior and syntax in Apex, as demonstrated in Listing 5-15. Lists can be initialized using an Array initializer, and its elements accessed using the square-bracket notation. Arrays can be initialized using the List constructor, and accessed using the List getters and setters. But for the sake of code clarity, picking one usage style and sticking with it is a good idea. In this book, List is the standard because it better reflects the object-oriented nature of these collection types.

Listing 5-15   **Mixed Array and List Syntax**

```
List<Integer> intList = new Integer[3];
intList[0] = 123;
intList.add(456);
Integer[] intArray = new List<Integer>();
intArray.add(456);
intArray.set(0, 123);
```

Arrays and Lists preserve the order in which elements are inserted. They can also be sorted in ascending order using the sort method of the List object. It takes no arguments, sorts in ascending order, and is valid only on Lists of primitive data types.

Sets

The Set is another collection type. Like a List, a Set can store only one type of element at a time. But Sets do not allow duplicate values and do not preserve insertion order. Sets are initialized like Lists. In Listing 5-16, a set named `stringSet` is created, and two values are added.

Listing 5-16   **Basic Set Usage**

```
Set<String> stringSet = new Set<String>();
stringSet.add('abc');
stringSet.add('def');
System.debug(stringSet.contains('abc'));
```

The final statement in Listing 5-16 outputs `true`, illustrating one of the most valuable features of the Set collection type: its `contains` method. To test whether a particular String exists in an Array or a List, every element of the List must be retrieved and checked. With a Set, this test can be done more efficiently thanks to the `contains` method.

Maps

The Map type stores pairs of keys and values and does not preserve their insertion order. It maintains the relationship between key and value, functioning as a lookup table. Given a key stored in a Map, you can retrieve its corresponding value.

Maps are initialized with a key data type and value data type. Keys are limited to primitive data types, but values can be any data type. Listing 5-17 initializes a new Map called `myMap` to store Integer keys and String values. It inserts a single value using the `put` method and then retrieves it using the `get` method. The last line of code prints `abc` because that is the value associated with the key `123`.

Listing 5-17   **Basic Map Usage**

```
Map<Integer, String> myMap = new Map<Integer, String>();
myMap.put(123, 'abc');
System.debug(myMap.get(123));
```

Other useful methods of Maps include `containsKey` (returns `true` if the given key exists in the Map), `remove` (returns and removes an element by key), `keySet` (returns a Set of all keys), and `values` (returns an Array of all values).

Control Logic

This subsection describes how to control the flow of Apex code execution. It covers conditional statements, loops, exception handlers, recursion, and asynchronous execution.

Conditional Statements

Conditional statements evaluate a Boolean condition and execute one code block if true, another if false. Listing 5-18 provides an example, defining a function that prints `true` if an Integer argument is greater than 100, `false` otherwise.

Listing 5-18   **Conditional Statement Usage**

```
void testValue(Integer value) {
   if (value > 100) {
     System.debug('true');
   } else {
     System.debug('false');
   }
}
testValue(99);
testValue(101);
```

In addition to this simple `if`, `else` structure, you can chain multiple conditional statements together using `else if`.

> **Note**
>
> In conditional code blocks that contain a single statement, the curly braces around them can be omitted. This is true of all the control logic types in Apex. For example, `if (a > 0)` `return 1 / a; else return a;` is a valid statement.

Loops

Loops in Apex behave consistently with other high-level languages. Table 5-3 lists the loop statements available in Apex.

Table 5-3   **Types of Loops**

Name	Syntax	Description
Do-While Loop	`do { code_block }` `while (condition);`	Executes code block as long as Boolean condition is `true`. Evaluates `condition` after running code block, executing the code block at least once.
While Loop	`while (condition)` `{ code_block; }`	Executes code block as long as Boolean condition is `true`. Evaluates `condition` before running code block, so code block might not be executed at all.
Traditional For Loop	`for (init; exit` `condition; increment)` `{ code_block; }`	Executes `init` statement once. Loops on the following steps: exit loop if Boolean `exit` `condition` evaluates to `false`, executes code block, executes `increment` statement.
List/Set Iteration For Loop	`for (var : list/set)` `{ code_block }`	For every element of the list or set, assigns `var` to the current element and executes the code block. Cannot modify the collection while iterating.

The keywords break and continue can be used to further control the loops. To immediately exit a loop at any point in its execution, use break in the code block. To abort a
cycle of loop execution in the middle of a code block and move to the next cycle, use
continue.

Exception Statements

Exceptions are classes used to signal a problem at runtime. They abort the normal flow of
code execution, bubbling upward until explicitly handled by some other code, carrying
with them information about the cause of the problem.

Apex allows custom exception classes to be defined that are meaningful to your programs. It also provides system exception classes corresponding to areas of the Force.com
platform. Some common system exceptions are DmlException (issues with changes to the
database), NullPointerException (attempt to dereference a null value), QueryException
(issues with database queries), and TypeException (issues converting data types).

The two ways to use exceptions in your code are to raise an exception with the throw
keyword, and handle an exception with the try, catch, and finally keywords:

1. **Raise an Exception:** When your code cannot proceed due to a problem with its
   input or other issue, you can raise an exception. An exception stops execution of the
   code and provides information about the problem to its callers. Only custom exceptions, classes that are subclasses of Force.com's Exception class, can be raised. The
   names of all custom exception classes must end with the word *Exception*. Construct
   an instance of your exception class using an optional message or another exception
   as the preceding cause and provide it as an argument to the throw keyword.

2. **Handle an Exception:** An exception handler in Apex is a code block defined to
   expect and take action on one or more named exception classes. It consists of a try
   code block, zero or more catch code blocks, and optionally a finally code block.
   The try code block is executed first. If an exception is raised, Apex looks for a
   catch code block that matches the exception class. If it's found, execution skips to
   the relevant catch. If not, the exception is bubbled upward to the caller. After the
   code in the try completes, successfully or not, the finally code block is executed.

Listing 5-19 demonstrates both forms of exception statements. It inserts a Timecard record
within a try block, using a catch block to handle a database exception (DmlException).
The code to handle the database exception itself raises an exception, a custom exception
class called MyException. It ends by printing a final message in the finally block.

Listing 5-19   **Sample Exception Statements**

```
class MyException extends Exception {}
Timecard__c timecard = new Timecard__c();
try {
  insert timecard;
} catch (DMLException e) {
```

```
    throw new MyException('Could not create Timecard record: ' + e);
} finally {
    System.debug('Exiting timecard creation code');
}
```

Recursion

Apex supports the use of recursion in code. The maximum stack depth is not documented, so experiment with your own code before committing to a recursive algorithm. For example, the code in Listing 5-20 fails with System.Exception: Maximum stack depth reached: 90.

Listing 5-20   **Recursion with Unsupported Depth**

```
Integer counter = 0;
void recursive() {
    if (counter < 100) {
        counter++;
        recursive();
    }
}
recursive();
```

Asynchronous Execution

Code in Apex normally is executed synchronously. From the user's point of view, there is a single thread of execution that must complete before another can begin. But Apex also supports an asynchronous mode of execution called future methods. Code entering a future method completes immediately, but the body of the method isn't executed until later, at a time determined by the Force.com platform.

The code in Listing 5-21 declares a future method called asyncMethod with a single parameter: a list of strings. It might use these strings to query records via SOQL and perform DML operations on them.

Listing 5-21   **Future Method Declaration**

```
@future
public static void asyncMethod(List<String> idsToProcess) {
    // code block
}
```

Future methods typically are used to perform expensive tasks that are not time-critical. A regular synchronous method can begin some work and invoke a future method to finish it. The future method starts fresh with respect to governor limits, described in Table 5-4.

Table 5-4   **Subset of Governor Limits**

Resource Type	Governor Limit
Heap	3MB
Apex code	200,000 lines of code executed
Database	50,000 records retrieved via SOQL

Future methods have many limitations, as follows:

- You cannot invoke more than ten future methods in a single scope of execution. There is no guarantee of when these methods will be executed by Force.com or in what order.

- Future methods cannot call other future methods.

- Future method signatures are always static and return void. They cannot use custom classes or database objects as parameters—only primitive types such as String and Integer and collections of primitive types.

- You cannot test future methods like ordinary methods. To write testable code that includes future methods, keep your future methods limited to a single line of code that invokes a normal method to perform the actual work. Then in your test case, call the normal method so that you can verify its behavior.

- Force.com limits your usage of future methods to 200 per licensed user within a 24-hour period.

> **Note**
>
> Batch Apex is an additional feature for asynchronous execution. It provides much greater control than future methods and supports processing of millions of records. Batch Apex is covered in Chapter 9, "Batch Processing."

Understanding Governor Limits

Governor limits are imposed on your running Apex code based on the type of resource consumed. When a governor limit is encountered, your code is immediately terminated with an exception indicating the type of limit reached. Examples of resource types are heap (memory used during execution) and SOQL (Salesforce Object Query Language) queries.

Table 5-4 lists a few of the most important governor limits. Additional governor limits are introduced later in the book.

> **Note**
>
> Namespaces are used to separate and isolate Apex code and database objects developed by different vendors so that they can coexist and interoperate in a single Force.com organization. Governor limits are applied independently to each namespace. For example, if you install a package from Force.com AppExchange, the resources consumed by code running inside that package do not count against the limits applied to your code.

Database Integration in Apex

In Apex, the Force.com database is already integrated into the language and runtime environment. There are no object-relational mapping tools or database connection pools to configure. Your Apex code is automatically aware of your database, including all of its objects and fields and the security rules protecting them.

This section examines the five ways the database is exposed in Apex code, which are summarized here:

1. **Database Records as Objects:** Database objects are directly represented in Apex as classes. These classes are implicitly imported into your code, so you're always developing from the latest database schema.

2. **Database Queries:** SOQL is a concise expression of the records to be queried and returned to your programs.

3. **Persisting Database Records:** Apex has a built-in Data Manipulation Language (DML), providing verbs that create, update, or delete one or more records in the database.

4. **Database Triggers:** Triggers are code that register interest in a specific action or actions on a database object, such as an insert or delete on the Account object. When this action occurs, the trigger code is executed and can inhibit or enhance the behavior of the database action.

5. **Database Security in Apex:** Normally, Apex code runs in a privileged mode, granting it full access to all the data in the system. Alternatively, you can configure it to run under the same restrictions imposed on the current user, including object and record-level sharing rules.

Database Records as Objects

All database objects, standard and custom, are available as first-class members of the Apex language, automatically and transparently. This eliminates the mind-numbing, error-prone work of importing, mapping, and translating between relational and program data structures, chores commonly required in general-purpose programming languages. In Apex, references to database objects are verified at compile time. This reduces the possibility of runtime surprises caused by field or object mismatches. Listing 5-22 shows an example of creating a record in the Resource custom database object and setting its name field.

Listing 5-22   **Creating a Record**

```
Resource__c resource = new Resource__c();
resource.Name = 'Larry';
```

Database relationships are also exposed in Apex. The __r syntax refers to a relationship field, a field that contains a reference to another object or list of objects. Listing 5-23 builds on the previous listing, creating a standard Contact record and associating it with the Resource record.

Listing 5-23 **Creating a Record with Relationship**

```
Contact c = new Contact();
c.FirstName = 'Larry';
resource.Contact__r = c;
```

The Force.com IDE's Schema Explorer can take the mystery out of relationship fields like `Contact__r`. It displays the correct syntax for referring to fields and relationships, based on the actual schema of the database object. Its Schema list on the right side displays all objects, custom and standard. Drilling into an object, the `Fields` folder lists all fields in the object and their types. A reference type indicates that a field is the child object in a Lookup relationship. Expand these fields to reveal their parent object's type and name. For example, `Contact__r` is the foreign key to the Contact object. This is demonstrated in Figure 5-4.

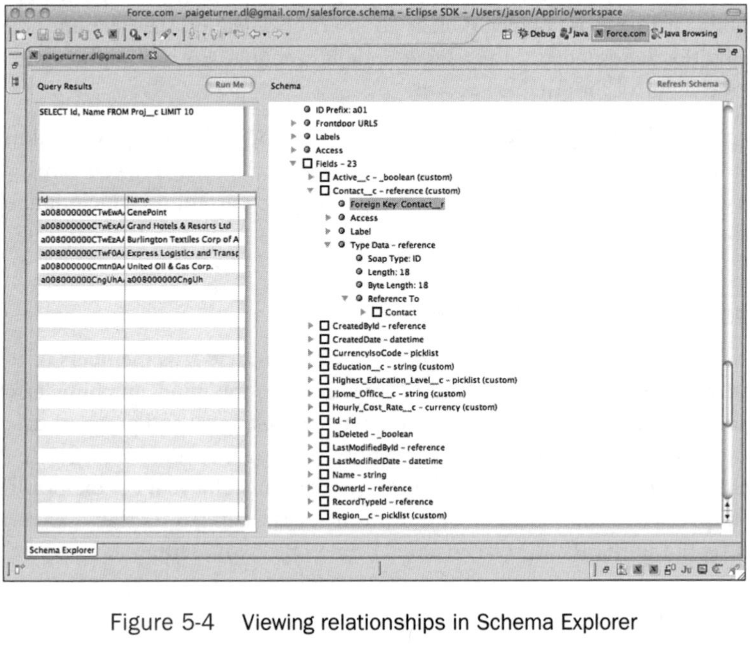

Figure 5-4   Viewing relationships in Schema Explorer

Data integrity is protected in Apex at compile and runtime using object metadata. For example, `Name` is defined as a read-only field in Contact, so the code in Listing 5-24 cannot be compiled.

Listing 5-24   **Attempted Assignment to Read-Only Field**

```
Contact c = new Contact();
c.Name = 'Larry';
```

After a database object is referenced in Apex code, that object cannot be deleted or edited in a way that invalidates the code. This protects your code from changes to the database schema. Impacted code must be commented out before the database objects are modified.

Database Queries

You've seen how data structures in Apex are implicitly defined by the objects in your database. Force.com provides two query languages to populate these objects with data: Salesforce Object Query Language (SOQL) and Salesforce Object Search Language (SOSL). SOSL, addressed in Chapter 6, "Advanced Business Logic," provides unstructured, full-text search across many objects from a single query.

The focus of this section is SOQL because it is the workhorse of typical business applications. This section includes subsections on the basics of SOQL, filtering and sorting, how to query related objects, and how to use SOQL from Apex code.

As you read this section, you can experiment with the sample SOQL queries using the Force.com IDE's Schema Explorer. Enter a query in the text box in the upper-left corner and click the Run Me button. The results appear in the table below the query. In Figure 5-5, a query has been executed against the Project object, returning five records. Note that many of the queries rely on objects from the Services Manager sample application rather than standard Force.com objects.

> **Note**
>
> This book does not cover every feature and nuance of SOQL. For the complete specification, visit http://developer.force.com and download the latest Force.com Web Services API documentation.

SOQL Basics

Despite being one letter away from SQL and borrowing some of its syntax, SOQL is completely different and much easier to understand on its own terms. Just as Apex is not a general-purpose programming language like Java, SOQL is not a general-purpose database query language like SQL. SOQL is specifically designed and optimized for the Force.com database.

A SOQL statement is centered on a single database object, specifying one or more fields to retrieve from it. The fields to select are separated by commas. Listing 5-25 is a simple SOQL statement that returns a list of Account records with Id and Name fields populated. SOQL is not case-sensitive. SOQL keywords are shown throughout the book in uppercase and metadata objects in title case for readability only.

Listing 5-25   **Simple SOQL Statement**

```
SELECT Id, Name
   FROM Account
```

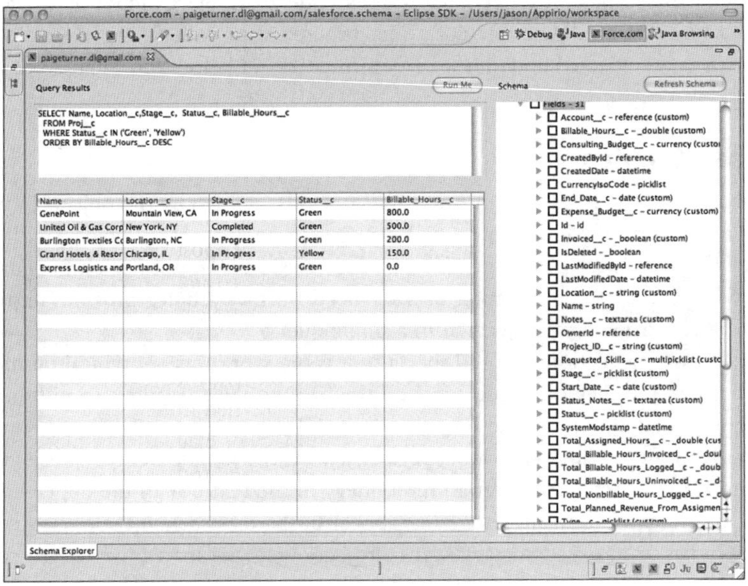

Figure 5-5   Running SOQL queries in Schema Explorer

Filtering Records

SOQL supports filter conditions to reduce the number of records returned. A filter condition consists of a field name to filter, an operator, and a literal value.

Valid operators are > (greater than), < (less than), >= (greater than or equal to), <= (less than or equal to), = (equal to), != (not equal to), IN and NOT IN (matches a list of literal values, and supports semi-joins and anti-joins), and INCLUDES and EXCLUDES (match against multi-select picklist values). On String fields the LIKE operator is also available, which applies a pattern to filter records. The pattern uses the % wildcard to match zero or more characters, _ to match one character, and the \ character to escape the % and _ wildcards, treating them as regular characters.

Multiple filters are combined in a single SOQL statement using the Boolean operators AND and OR and grouped with parentheses. Listing 5-26 returns the names of accounts with a type of direct customer, a modification date sometime during the current year, and more than $100 million in annual revenue.

Listing 5-26 **SOQL Statement with Filter Conditions**

```
SELECT Name
  FROM Account
  WHERE AnnualRevenue > 100000000
  AND Type = 'Customer - Direct'
  AND LastModifiedDate = THIS_YEAR
```

Notice the way literal values are specified. Apostrophes must be used around String literals but never with other data types. THIS_YEAR is a built-in relative time function. The values of relative time functions vary based on when the query is executed. Other relative time functions are YESTERDAY, TODAY, TOMORROW, LAST_WEEK, THIS_WEEK, NEXT_WEEK, and so forth.

Absolute dates and times can also be specified without apostrophes. Dates must use the YYYY-MM-DD format. Datetimes can be YYYY-MM-DDThh:mm:ssZ, YYYY-MM-DDThh:mm:ss+hh:mm, or YYYY-MM-DDThh:mm:ss-hh:mm, indicating the positive or negative offset from Coordinated Universal Time (UTC).

In addition to filter conditions, SOQL supports the LIMIT keyword. It sets an absolute upper bound on the number of records that can be returned from the query. It can be used in conjunction with all the other SOQL features. For example, the SOQL statement in Listing 5-27 returns up to ten Account records modified today.

Listing 5-27 **SOQL Statement with Record Limit**

```
SELECT Name, Type
  FROM Account
  WHERE LastModifiedDate = TODAY
  LIMIT 10
```

Sorting Query Results

Results of a query can be sorted by up to 32 fields in ascending (ASC, the default) or descending (DESC) order. Sorting is not case-sensitive, and nulls appear first unless otherwise specified (NULLS LAST). Multi-select picklists, long text areas, and reference type fields cannot be used as sort fields. The SOQL query in Listing 5-28 returns records first in ascending order by Type, and then in descending order by LastModifiedDate.

Listing 5-28 **SOQL Statement with Sort Fields**

```
SELECT Name, Type, AnnualRevenue
  FROM Account
  ORDER BY Type, LastModifiedDate DESC
```

Querying Multiple Objects

The result of a SOQL query can be a simple list of records containing rows and columns or hierarchies of records containing data from multiple, related objects. Relationships between objects are navigated implicitly from the database structure. This eliminates the work of writing accurate, efficient join conditions common to development on traditional SQL databases.

The two ways to navigate object relationships in SOQL are child-to-parent and parent-to-child. Listing 5-29 is an example of a child-to-parent query, returning the name, city, and Force.com username creating its contact of all resources with a mailing address in the state of Illinois. It selects and filters fields of the Contact object, the parent object of Resource. It also selects the Name field from the User object, a parent two levels removed from Resource via the Contact's CreatedBy field.

Listing 5-29   **SOQL with Child-to-Parent Relationship**

```
SELECT Name, Contact__r.MailingCity, Contact__r.CreatedBy.Name
  FROM Resource__c
  WHERE Contact__r.MailingState = 'IL'
```

> **Note**
>
> The results of child-to-parent relationship queries are not completely rendered in the Force.com IDE. You can double-click a row and column to view fields from a parent record, but this is limited to direct parents only. Fields from parent-of-parent objects, such as the Contact__r.CreatedBy relationship in Listing 5-29, are omitted from the results. This is a limitation not of SOQL, but of the Force.com IDE.

At most, five levels of parent objects can be referenced in a single child-to-parent query, and the query cannot reference more than 25 relationships in total.

The second form of relationship query is the parent-to-child query. Listing 5-30 provides an example. The parent object is Resource, and the child is Timecard. The query selects from every Resource its Id, Name, and a list of hours from its Timecards in the current month.

Listing 5-30   **SOQL with Parent-to-Child Relationship**

```
SELECT Id, Name,
  (SELECT Total_Hours__c
    FROM Timecards__r
    WHERE Week_Ending__c = THIS_MONTH)
  FROM Resource__c
```

A parent-to-child query cannot reference more than twenty child objects. Double-clicking the parent record in the results table brings up the child records for viewing in the Force.com IDE.

Using SOQL in Apex

Like database objects, SOQL queries are an integrated part of the Apex language. They are developed in-line with your code and verified at compile time against your database schema.

Listing 5-31 is an example of a SOQL query used in Apex. It retrieves a list of Project records for this year and loops over them, summing their billable hours invoiced in the variable `totalHours`. Note the usage of the variable named `statuses` directly in the SOQL query, preceded by a colon. This is known as a *bind variable*. Bind variables can appear on the right side of a WHERE clause, as the value of an IN or NOT IN clause, and in the LIMIT clause.

Listing 5-31   **SOQL Query in Apex**

```
Decimal totalHours = 0;
List<String> statuses = new String[] { 'Green', 'Yellow' };
List<Proj__c> projects = [ SELECT Total_Billable_Hours_Invoiced__c
  FROM Proj__c
  WHERE Start_Date__c = THIS_YEAR and Status__c IN :statuses ];
for (Proj__c project : projects) {
  totalHours += project.Total_Billable_Hours_Invoiced__c;
}
```

This code relies on a List to store the results of the SOQL query. This means the entire SOQL query result must fit within the heap size available to the program. A better syntax for looping over SOQL records is a variation of the List/Set Iteration For Loop called a SOQL For Loop. The code in Listing 5-32 is a rewrite of Listing 5-31 using the SOQL For Loop. This allows it to run when the Project object contains up to 50,000 records for this year without consuming 50,000 records worth of heap space at one time.

Listing 5-32   **SOQL Query in Apex Using SOQL For Loop**

```
Decimal totalHours = 0;
for (Proj__c project : [ SELECT Total_Billable_Hours_Invoiced__c
  FROM Proj__c
  WHERE Start_Date__c = THIS_YEAR ]) {
  totalHours += project.Total_Billable_Hours_Invoiced__c;
}
```

An additional form of the SOQL For Loop is designed for use with Data Manipulation Language (DML). Consider how the code in Listing 5-32 could be adapted to modify Project records returned from the SOQL query rather than simply summing them. With the existing code, one Project record would be modified for each loop iteration, an inefficient approach and a quick way to run afoul of the governor limits. But if you change the type of variable in the For loop to a list of Project records, Force.com provides up to 200 records per loop iteration. This allows you to modify a whole list of records in a single operation.

> **Note**
>
> Looping through a list of records to calculate the sum of a field is provided as an example of using SOQL with Apex. It is not an optimal way to perform calculations on groups of records in the database. Chapter 6 introduces aggregate queries, which enable calculations to be returned directly from a SOQL query, without Apex.

Any valid SOQL statement can be executed in Apex code, including relationship queries. The result of a child-to-parent query is returned in a List of objects whose types match the child object. Where fields from a parent object are included in the query, they are available as nested variables in Apex code. For example, running the query in Listing 5-29 within a block of Apex code returns a `List<Resource__c>`. If this List is assigned to a variable named `resources`, the first Resource record's mailing city is accessible by `resources[0].Contact__r.MailingCity`.

Parent-to-child queries are returned in a List of objects, their type matching the parent object. Each record of the parent object includes a nested List of child objects. Using Listing 5-30 as an example, if `results` contains the `List<Resource__c>` returned by the query, `results[0].Timecards__r[0].Total_Hours__c` accesses a field in the first Resource's first Timecard child record.

> **Note**
>
> Usage of SOQL in Apex is subject to governor limits. For example, you are limited to a total of 100 SOQL queries, or 300 including parent-to-child queries. The cumulative maximum number of records returned by all SOQL queries, including parent-to-child, is 50,000.

Persisting Database Records

Changes to database records in Force.com are saved using Data Manipulation Language (DML) operations. DML operations allow you to modify records one at a time, or more efficiently in batches of multiple records. The five major DML operation types are listed next. Each is discussed in more detail later in this subsection.

- **Insert:** Creates new records.
- **Update:** Updates the values in existing records, identified by Force.com unique identifier (Id) field or a custom field designated as an external identifier.
- **Upsert:** If records with the same unique identifier or external identifier exist, this updates their values. Otherwise, it inserts them.
- **Delete:** Moves records into the Recycle Bin.
- **Undelete:** Restores records from the Recycle Bin.

DML operations can be included in Apex code in one of two ways: DML statements and database methods. Beyond the syntax, they differ in how errors are handled. If any one record in a DML statement fails, all records fail and are rolled back. Database methods allow for partial success. This chapter uses DML statements exclusively. Chapter 6 provides information on database methods.

> **Note**
>
> Usage of DML in Apex is subject to governor limits. For example, you are limited to a total of 150 DML operations. The cumulative maximum number of records modified by all DML operations is 10,000.

Insert

The `Insert` statement adds up to 200 records of a single object type to the database. When all records succeed, they contain their new unique identifiers. If any record fails, a `DmlException` is raised and the database is returned to its state prior to the `Insert` statement. For example, the code in Listing 5-33 inserts a Contact record and uses it as the parent of a new Resource record.

Listing 5-33   **Inserting a Record**

```
try {
  Contact c = new Contact(FirstName = 'Justin', LastName = 'Case');
  insert c;
  Resource__c r = new Resource__c(
    Contact__c = c.Id, Hourly_Cost_Rate__c = 75, Region__c = 'West');
  insert r;
} catch (DmlException e) {
  System.debug(LoggingLevel.ERROR, e.getMessage());
}
```

Update

`Update` saves up to 200 existing records of a single object type. Existing records are identified by unique identifier (Id). Listing 5-34 illustrates the usage of the `Update` statement by creating a Resource record for Doug and updating it. Refresh the Resources tab in the native user interface to see the new record.

Listing 5-34   **Updating Records**

```
Resource__c doug = new Resource__c(Name = 'Doug Hole');
insert doug;
doug.Hourly_Cost_Rate__c = 100;
doug.Home_Office__c = 'London';
update doug;
```

Upsert

`Upsert` combines the behavior of the `Insert` and `Update` operations on up to 200 records of the same object type. First, it attempts to locate a matching record using its unique identifier or external identifier. If one is found, the statement acts as an `Update`. If not, it behaves as an `Insert`.

The syntax of the Upsert statement is identical to Update and Insert, but adds a second, optional argument for specifying an external identifier. If an external identifier is not provided, the record's unique identifier is used. The code in Listing 5-35 upserts a record in the Resource object using the field Resource_ID__c as an external identifier. If a Resource record with a Resource_ID__c value of 1001 exists, it is updated. If not, it is created.

Listing 5-35   **Upserting a Record**

```
Resource__c r = new Resource__c(Resource_ID__c = 1001, Name = 'Terry Bull');
upsert r Resource_ID__c;
```

Delete and Undelete

Delete and Undelete statements move up to 200 records of the same object type to and from the Recycle Bin, respectively. Listing 5-36 shows an example of the Delete statement. A new Resource record named Terry is added and then deleted.

Listing 5-36   **Deleting Records**

```
Resource__c terry = new Resource__c(Name = 'Terry Bull');
insert terry;
delete terry;
```

Listing 5-37 builds on Listing 5-36 to undelete the Terry record. Concatenate the listings in the Execute Anonymous view to test. The database is queried to prove the existence of the undeleted record. Try running the code a second time with the undelete statement commented out to see that it is working as intended.

Listing 5-37   **Undeleting Records**

```
undelete terry;
Resource__c terry2 = [ SELECT Id, Name
  FROM Resource__c WHERE Name LIKE 'Terry%' LIMIT 1 ];
System.debug(terry2.Name + ' exists');
delete terry;
```

Database Triggers

Triggers are Apex code working in concert with the Force.com database engine, automatically invoked by Force.com when database records are modified. Trigger code can perform any necessary processing on the modified data before or after Force.com completes its own work. The following list describes scenarios commonly implemented with triggers:

- A validation rule is required that is too complex to define on the database object using formula expressions.
- Two objects must be kept synchronized. When a record in one object is updated, a trigger updates the corresponding record in the other.
- Records of an object must be augmented with values from another object, a complex calculation, or external data via a Web service call.

This subsection covers the essentials of trigger development, including definition, batch processing, and error handling.

Definition

A trigger definition consists of four parts:

1. A unique trigger name to differentiate it from other triggers. Multiple triggers can be defined on the same database object.

2. The name of the database object on which to create the trigger. You can create triggers on standard and custom objects.

3. A comma-separated list of one or more trigger events that cause the trigger code to be executed. An event is specified using two keywords. The first keyword is either `before` or `after`, indicating that the trigger is to be executed before or after the database operation is saved. The second keyword is the DML operation: `insert`, `update`, `delete`, or `undelete`. For example, the trigger event `before update` means that the trigger is fired before a record is updated. Note that `before undelete` is an invalid trigger event.

4. The block of Apex code to execute when the trigger event occurs. The code typically loops over the list of records in the transaction and performs some action based on their contents. For `insert` and `update` triggers, the list of records in the transaction is provided in the variable `Trigger.new`. In a `before` trigger, these records can be modified. In `update`, `delete`, and `undelete` triggers, `Trigger.old` contains a read-only list of the original versions of the records. Also available to your trigger code is a set of Boolean variables indicating the event type that fired the trigger. They are useful when your trigger is defined on multiple events yet requires separate behavior for each. These variables are `Trigger.isBefore`, `Trigger.isAfter`, `Trigger.isInsert`, `Trigger.isUpdate`, `Trigger.isDelete`, and `Trigger.isUndelete`.

Listing 5-38 is an example of a trigger named `validateTimecard`. It is triggered before inserts and updates to the Timecard custom object. It doesn't do anything yet because its code block is empty.

Listing 5-38   **Trigger Definition**

```
trigger validateTimecard on Timecard__c(before insert, before update) {
  // code block
}
```

Triggers cannot be created in the Execute Anonymous view. Create them in the Force.com IDE by selecting File → New → Apex Trigger. To test triggers, use the native user interface to manually modify a relevant record, or write a unit test and invoke it from the Apex Test Runner or Execute Anonymous view.

Batch Processing in Triggers

Manual testing in the native user interface and simplistic unit tests can lull you into the false belief that triggers operate on a single record at a time. Not to be confused with Batch Apex, triggers can always be invoked with a list of records and should be optimized accordingly. Many ways exist to get a batch of records into the Force.com database, including the Data Loader and custom user interfaces. The surest way to a production issue with governor limits is to write a trigger that operates inefficiently when given a batch of records. The process of hardening a trigger to accept a batch of records is commonly called *bulkifying* the trigger.

Batches can be up to 200 records. When writing your trigger code, look at the resources consumed as you loop over `Trigger.new` or `Trigger.old`. Study the governor limits and make sure your code splits its work into batches, doing as little work as possible in the loop. For example, if you have some additional data to query, build a set of IDs from the trigger's records and query them once. Do not execute a SOQL statement for each loop iteration. If you need to run a DML statement, don't put that in the loop either. Create a List of objects and execute a single DML statement on the entire List. Listing 5-39 shows an example of looping over a batch of Contact records (in the variable `contacts`) to produce a list of Resource records to insert.

Listing 5-39   **Batching DML Operations**

```
List<Resource__c> toInsert = new List<Resource__c>();
for (Contact contact : contacts) {
  toInsert.add(new Resource__c(
    Name = contact.FirstName + ' ' + contact.LastName));
}
insert toInsert;
```

Error Handling

Errors are handled in triggers with `try`, `catch` blocks, consistent with other Apex code. But uncaught errors within a trigger differ from other Apex code in how they can impact execution of the larger database transaction the trigger participates in.

A common use of errors in triggers is for validation. Strings describing validation errors can be added to individual records or fields using the addError method. Force.com continues to process the batch, collecting any additional errors, and then rolls back the transaction and returns the errors to the initiator of the transaction.

> **Note**
>
> Additional error-handling behavior is available for transactions initiated outside of Force.com; for example, through the Web services API. Records can fail individually without rolling back the entire transaction. This is discussed in Chapter 11, "Advanced Integration."

If an uncaught exception is encountered in a trigger, whether thrown by the system or the trigger code itself, the batch of records is immediately aborted, and all changes are rolled back.

Database Security in Apex

Outside of Anonymous blocks, Apex always runs in a privileged, system context. This gives it access to read and write all data. It does not honor object, field, and record-level privileges of the user invoking the code. This works well for triggers, which operate at a low level and need full access to data.

Where full access is not appropriate, Apex provides the with sharing keyword. For example, custom user interfaces often require that access to data is limited by the privileges of the current user. Using with sharing, the sharing rules applying to the current user are evaluated against the data requested by queries and updated in DML operations. This option is discussed in detail in Chapter 7, "User Interfaces."

Object-Oriented Apex

Apex is an object-oriented language. This section describes Apex in terms of five standard characteristics of object-oriented languages, summarized here:

- **Encapsulation:** Encapsulation combines the behavior and internal state of a program into a single logical unit.
- **Information Hiding:** To minimize tight coupling between units of a program, information hiding limits external visibility into the behavior and state of a unit.
- **Modularity:** The goal of modularity is to establish clear boundaries between components of a program.
- **Inheritance:** Inheritance allows one unit of code to define its behavior in terms of another.
- **Polymorphism:** Polymorphism is the capability to interact with multiple units of code interchangeably without special cases for each.

These principles of object-oriented programming can help you understand Apex syntax and behaviors from a language-neutral point of reference.

> **Note**
>
> Some of the code examples in this chapter cannot be tested in the Execute Anonymous view of the Force.com IDE. Examples using inner classes or static methods or variables can be run by creating a standalone test class and then invoking it from the Execute Anonymous view. To create a standalone class in the Force.com IDE, select your Force.com Project and then select File → New → Apex Class.

Encapsulation

Encapsulation describes the bundling of a program's behavior and state into a single definition, usually aligned with a real-world concept. In Apex, that definition is a class.

When a class is defined, it becomes a new data type in Apex. It can be used everywhere primitive data type classes are used, except in Sets and as the keys of a Map. In Listing 5-40, a class named MyClass is defined. The variable c is initialized with an instance of MyClass and then placed into the List myList.

Listing 5-40   **List of User-Defined Classes**

```
public class MyClass {}
MyClass c = new MyClass();
List<MyClass> myList = new List<MyClass>();
myList.add(c);
```

Classes can contain variables, methods, properties, constructors, initializers, and inner classes. These components are described in the following subsections.

Variables and Their Scope

Variables hold the state of an object instance or class. By default, variables declared inside a class are scoped to individual object instances and are called member variables. Every instance of an object gets its own member variables and can read and write their values independently without interfering with the values stored in other object instances.

Class variables are declared using the static keyword and are also known as static variables. Static variables are shared across all instances of the object. If one object instance updates the value of a static variable, this updated value is visible to all other object instances. The contents of static variables live for the duration of an Apex execution context, which is a user action such as a button click or a trigger action on a batch of records. When working with the Force.com database, static variables are useful for sharing state among multiple triggers.

Variables can also be declared with the final keyword. This means they must be assigned a value once, in initialization code, a declaration, or a constructor. The value cannot be updated after it is set or a runtime exception is thrown.

Typically, final is used in conjunction with static to produce a constant. A constant is a variable whose value is set once, for all object instances, and never changes.

Listing 5-41 shows examples of member, static, and constant variable declarations. Constant names are typically in uppercase for code clarity, but this is not required.

Listing 5-41   **Variable Declarations**

```
Integer memberVar;
static Integer classVar;
static final Integer CONSTANT = 1;
```

Methods

Methods define the verbs in a class, the actions to be taken. By default, they operate within the context of individual object instances, able to access all member variables. Methods can also be static, operating on the class itself. Static methods have access to static variables but never member variables.

At a minimum, a method declaration consists of a return type and a method name. Typically it also has an implementation, a block of code to execute, and one or more named, typed arguments. There are several other ways to define methods, covered later in this chapter.

Listing 5-42 shows four basic method declarations.

Listing 5-42   **Method Declarations**

```
void doNothing() {}
void doNothingWithArgs(String a, Integer b, Date c) {}
void returnsNothing() { Integer i = 1; }
Integer returnsInteger() { return 2009; }
```

Properties

A property is a shortened form of a method that provides access to a static or instance variable. Without the use of a property, exposing a variable for read and write access requires code like that in Listing 5-43.

Listing 5-43   **Variable with Accessor Methods**

```
private Integer cost;
public Integer getCost() { return cost; }
public void setCost(Integer cost) { this.cost = cost; }
```

This code defines a private variable named cost, with a getCost method to return the current value of the variable and a setCost method to update its value. Listing 5-44 is a version of this code that uses properties to accomplish the same thing.

Listing 5-44   **Variable as Property**

```
public Integer cost { get { return cost; } set { this.cost = value; } }
```

The cost variable can now be accessed directly, as if it were a public member variable. But access to the variable is mediated by the getter and setter code blocks within the property declaration.

A more concise form of properties is called *automatic properties*. They are properties with no code body. When no code body is present, the getter and setter logic is implied. Getters return their value; setters set their value. Listing 5-45 rewrites the property in Listing 5-44 as an automatic property.

Listing 5-45   **Variable as Automatic Property**

```
public Integer cost { get; set; }
```

Access modifiers of accessors can be more restrictive than their containing property. Listing 5-46 contains an example of read-only and write-only properties.

Listing 5-46   **Read-Only and Write-Only Properties**

```
public Integer readOnly { get; private set; }
public Integer writeOnly { private get; set; }
```

Constructors

A constructor is a special method executed when a class is instantiated. Constructors are declared much like methods, but share their name with the class name, and have no return type declaration. Listing 5-47 shows a sample constructor that accepts two arguments and initializes instance variables from them. The this keyword specifies that x and y refer to member variables. Although unnecessary in this case because these variables are not ambiguous, using this is a good practice. The final line of code creates an instance of the object using its two-argument constructor.

Listing 5-47   **Constructor Declaration and Usage**

```
public class MyClass {
  String x;
  Integer y;
  MyClass(String a, Integer b) {
    this.x = a;
    this.y = b;
  }
}
MyClass c = new MyClass('string', 123);
```

Constructors can be chained together using the this method. This provides consumers of the object with multiple options for instantiation, without duplication of constructor code. Listing 5-48 provides an example of this usage. The last line validates that the constructor chain is working as expected by outputting the values (value, a, and b) of the three member variables.

Listing 5-48   **Constructor Chaining**

```
public class MyClass {
  String x, y, z;
  MyClass() { x = 'value'; }
  MyClass(String y) { this(); this.y = y; }
  MyClass(String y, String z) { this(y); this.z = z; }
}
MyClass c = new MyClass('a', 'b');
System.debug(c.x + ', ' + c.y + ', ' + c.z);
```

Constructors are optional. If no constructor is defined, an implicit public constructor with no arguments exists.

Initializers

An initializer contains code that runs before any other code in the class. The two types of initializers are static and instance. Static initializers are run only once, when a class is referenced for the first time. Instance initializers are run every time a new instance of the class is created, before the constructor.

Listing 5-49 demonstrates the usage of an instance initializer. If you run it, you'll see in the debug log that the initializer runs before the constructor.

Listing 5-49   **Instance Initializer**

```
public class MyClass {
  {
    System.debug('Instance initializer');
  }
  MyClass() {
    System.debug('Constructor');
  }
}
new MyClass();
```

Static initializers have the same syntax but add the static keyword before the opening curly brace. A class can contain any number of initializers. They are executed in the order in which they appear in the code. In general, you should avoid the use of initializers. Variables should be initialized in constructors or in variable declarations instead.

Inner Classes

An inner class is a class defined within another class. Other than a few restrictions, mentioned in the text that follows, they are declared like regular classes. Listing 5-50 shows an example of an inner class declaration.

Listing 5-50   **Inner Class Declaration**

```
public class MyClass {
  String x;
  class MyInnerClass {
    String y;
    void doSomething() {
      // cannot access x from here!
    }
  }
}
```

Inner classes are always static, so the `static` keyword is not permitted. They can't reference variables in their containing class. Additionally, inner classes cannot contain other inner classes and cannot contain static variables.

Information Hiding

Class definitions include notation to limit the visibility of their constituent parts to other code. This notation protects a class from being used in unanticipated and invalid ways and simplifies maintenance by making dependencies explicit. In Apex, information hiding is accomplished with access modifiers. The two places to use access modifiers are on classes, and on methods and variables.

Access Modifiers on Classes

Classes have two access modifiers:

1. `public:` The class is visible to the entire application namespace, but not outside it.

2. `global:` The class is visible to Apex code running in every application namespace. If an inner class is global, its outer class is required to be global. Several Force.com features described later in this book, such as Web services and Batch Apex, require your code to live within global methods.

Access modifiers on outer classes are required. Inner classes are private by default, accessible only by their containing classes.

Access Modifiers on Methods and Variables

Methods and variables have four access modifiers:

1. `private:` The method or variable is visible only within its defining class.

2. `protected:` It is visible to the defining class and subclasses.

3. **public:** It is visible to any Apex code in the same application namespace but not accessible to other namespaces.

4. **global:** It can be used by any Apex code running anywhere in the organization, in any namespace. If a method is global, its class must be global as well.

If no access modifier is provided, the method or variable is private.

Modularity

Apex supports interfaces, which are skeletal class definitions containing a list of methods with no implementation. A class built from an interface is said to implement that interface, which requires that its method names and the data types of its argument lists be identical to those specified in the interface.

The proper use of interfaces can result in modular programs with clear logical boundaries between components, making them easier to understand and maintain. Listing 5-51 shows an interface declaration and a class that implements it.

Listing 5-51   **Interface Declaration and Usage**

```
public interface MyInterface {
  void doSomething(String thing);
}
public class MyClass implements MyInterface {
  public void doSomething(String x) {}
}
```

If you change the access modifier, return data type, name of the method in `MyClass`, the data type of its argument, or add or remove an argument, compilation fails. Apex is enforcing the contract, specified in `MyInterface` and agreed to by `MyClass`.

The access modifiers of interfaces are identical to those of classes. Interfaces can be declared `public` or `global` and default to `public`. Access modifiers are not allowed on methods of an interface. They are governed by the access modifier specified on the interface declaration.

Inheritance

Apex supports single inheritance. It allows a class to extend one other class and implement many interfaces. Interfaces can also extend one other interface. A class extending another class is referred to as its subclass.

For a class to be extended, it must explicitly allow it by using the `virtual` or `abstract` keyword in its declaration. Without one of these keywords, a class is final and cannot be subclassed. This is not true of interfaces because they are implicitly virtual.

By default, a subclass inherits all the functionality of its parent class. All the methods defined in the parent class are also valid on the subclass without any additional code. This behavior can be selectively overridden if the parent class permits. Overriding a method is a two-step process:

1. The parent class must specify the `virtual` or `abstract` keywords on the methods to be overridden.

2. In the subclass, the `override` keyword is used on the virtual or abstract methods to declare that they're replacing implementations in the parent class.

After it's overridden, a subclass can do more than replace the parent implementation. Using the `super` keyword, the subclass can invoke a method in its parent class, incorporating its functionality and potentially contributing its own. Listing 5-52 is an example of subclassing and overriding a method. `MyClass` is a subclass of `MyParentClass` and overrides its method `doSomething`. The result is that both debug lines are printed.

Listing 5-52   **Subclass with Method Override**

```
public virtual class MyParentClass {
  public virtual void doSomething() {
    System.debug('something');
  }
}
public class MyClass extends MyParentClass {
  public override void doSomething() {
    super.doSomething();
    System.debug('something else');
  }
}
new MyClass().doSomething();
```

You've seen how classes declared as virtual can be inherited from by a subclass. The other way to accomplish inheritance is to declare a class abstract using the `abstract` keyword. An abstract class is allowed to contain abstract methods. Unlike virtual methods, abstract methods cannot have an implementation and are required to be overridden in subclasses. Overridden abstract methods can specify an identical or more restrictive access modifier than a parent, but never more permissive. Listing 5-53 shows an example of the subclass `MyClass` overriding an abstract method of its parent class.

Listing 5-53   **Abstract Method Declaration and Override**

```
public abstract class MyBaseClass {
  public abstract void doSomething();
}
public class MyClass extends MyBaseClass {
```

```
  public override void doSomething() {
    System.debug('something');
  }
}
new MyClass().doSomething();
```

Polymorphism

An object that inherits a class or implements an interface can always be referred to in Apex by its parent class or interface. References in variable, property, and method declarations treat the derived objects identically to objects they are derived from, even though they are different types.

This polymorphic characteristic of object types can help you write concise code. It works with the hierarchy of object types to enable broad, general statements of program behavior, behavior applying to many object types at once, while preserving the option to specify behavior per object type.

One example of using polymorphic behavior is method overloading, in which a single method name is declared with multiple argument lists. Consumers of the method simply invoke it by name, and Apex finds the correct implementation at runtime based on the object types. Listing 5-54 provides an example of method overloading.

Listing 5-54   **Method Overloading**

```
public class ClassA {}
public class ClassB extends ClassA {}
public class ClassC extends ClassB {}
public class Overloaded {
  public void doSomething(ClassA a) {
    System.debug('something with A');
  }
  public void doSomething(ClassB b) {
    System.debug('something with B');
  }
}
new Overloaded().doSomething(new ClassA());
new Overloaded().doSomething(new ClassB());
// new Overloaded().doSomething(new ClassC());
```

The last line of code is commented because it will not compile. Because ClassC inherits from both ClassB and ClassA, two forms of the doSomething method could apply to it, and Apex cannot determine which is correct.

You don't need to rely on Apex to find the right behavior for your object at a method level. You can also determine an object's type at runtime using the instanceof keyword.

This is useful for working with collections of a base type. Listing 5-55 provides an example, building on the classes defined in Listing 5-54.

Listing 5-55   **Using the `instanceof` Keyword**

```
List<ClassA> newList = new List<ClassA>();
newList.add(new ClassA());
newList.add(new ClassB());
newList.add(new ClassC());
System.debug(newList.get(2) instanceof ClassB);
```

The list `newList` is declared to contain instances of `ClassA`, but this implicitly allows its subclasses as well. The last line outputs `true` because the last list element, an instance of `ClassC`, inherits from `ClassB`.

Debugging and Testing

Because Apex code cannot be executed on your local machine, debugging and testing Apex requires some different tools and techniques than traditional software development. This section describes how to debug your code and monitor its performance using Force.com's built-in profiling information. It also describes how to develop and execute unit tests to keep your code free of defects.

Debugging

Force.com does not yet allow you to set breakpoints and step through the code executing on its remote infrastructure. But the Force.com IDE and the native user interface expose extensive diagnostic information about your running Apex code in the debug log.

Each entry written to the log is assigned a debug log category and level. Debug log categories correspond to the type of code executed. The full list of debug log categories is provided in Force.com's online help. Categories relevant to this chapter are Database, Apex Code, and Apex Profiling. Debug log levels are Error, Warn, Info, Debug, Fine, Finer, and Finest.

This subsection discusses how to view the debug log from the native user interface and the Force.com IDE. It also describes how to write custom entries to the debug log from within your Apex code.

Viewing Logs

In the Force.com IDE, a user interface is provided for the debug log on the right side of the Execute Anonymous and Test Runner views. It displays debug log entries resulting from code executed by these views. Each has a text area for the log entries, a drop-down list of debug log categories, and a slider for adjusting the log level. Each category receives its own independent log level, although only one can be shown at a time in the user interface. In Figure 5-6, the log level for Apex code has been set to Finest.

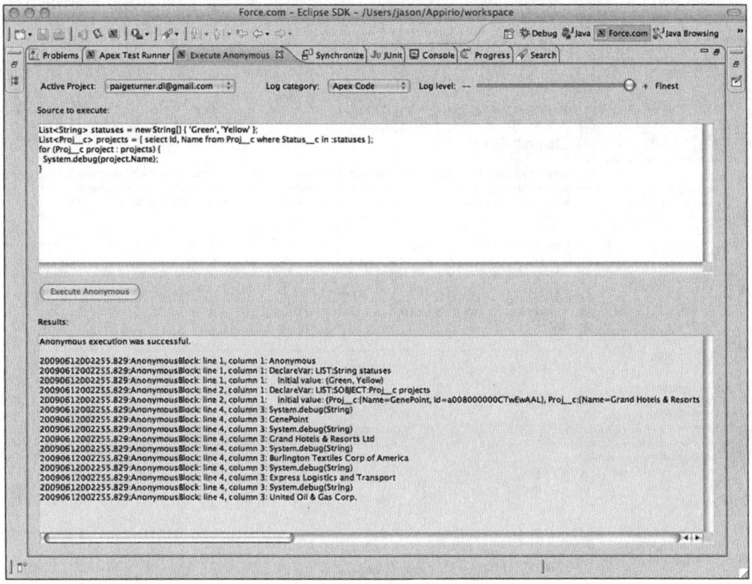

Figure 5-6   Debug log in the Execute Anonymous view

Testing or debugging code from a user's point of view, directly from the native user interface, is often necessary. To reach the debug log in the native user interface, click the System Log link at the top of the screen. This allows you to examine debug log entries caused by the current user.

To capture debug logs for any user, go to the Administration Setup and click Monitoring → Debug Logs. Click the New button, select one or more users to monitor, and then click the Save button. Figure 5-7 shows debug logging active for one user.

Debug logs can be verbose and hard to read. Filters are a way to control the verbosity of the logs. After debug logging is enabled for a user, click the Filters link for that user. Figure 5-8 shows the default state of the filters page. Each category of Force.com logging can be controlled independently by selecting a level for it. Level NONE disables the category entirely.

As a user with debug logging enabled interacts with Force.com, that user's log entries are recorded and become visible at the bottom of the Debug Logs page. This is the same page you used to configure the logs, as illustrated in Figure 5-9. Click the View link beside a log to view it.

Logging

If you have a relatively modest amount of code and you're not sure where it's failing, try setting the Apex code category to the Finest log level. It outputs an entry to the debug log for every Apex code statement executed.

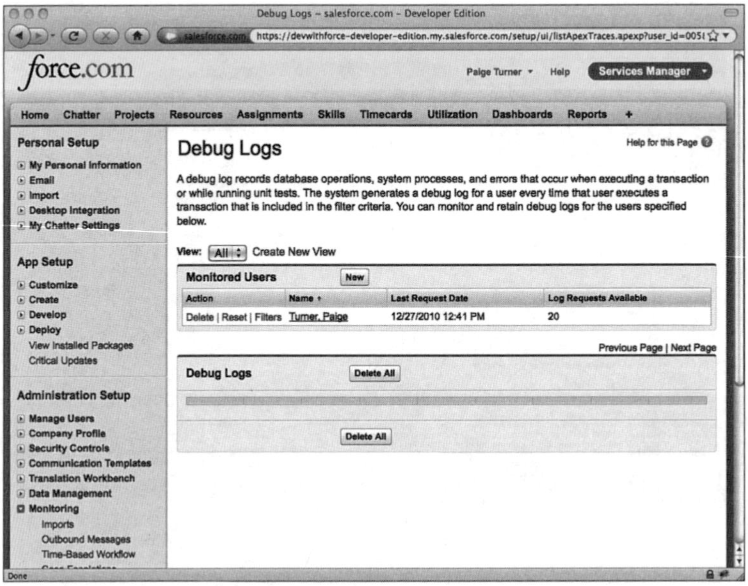

Figure 5-7   Monitoring the debug log for a user

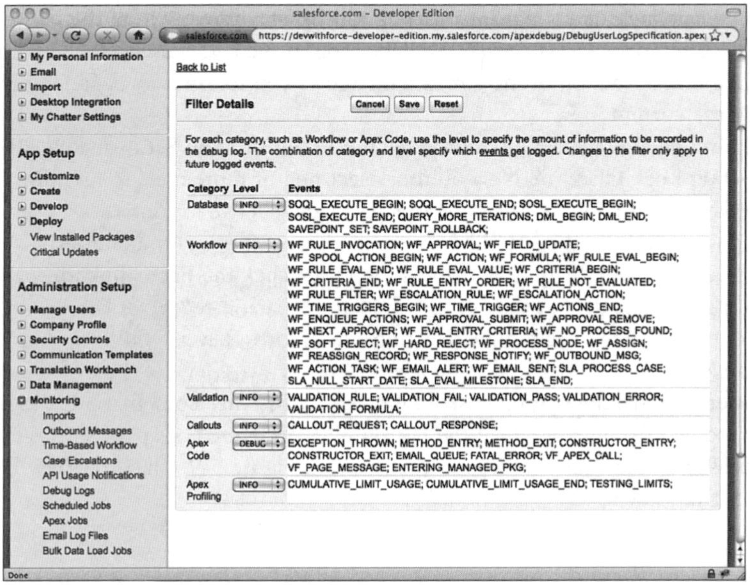

Figure 5-8   Filtering the debug log for a user

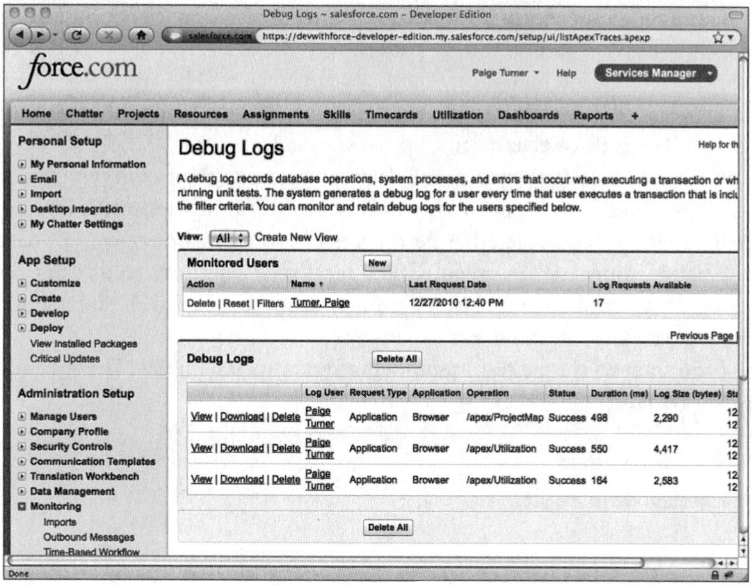

Figure 5-9   Viewing the debug logs in the native user interface

If you need to inspect the value of a variable and the Finest log level is too verbose to be useful, use the `System.debug` method. This method adds a log entry with a category of Apex Code and a level of Debug. To control the log level, specify it before the value. For example, `System.debug(LoggingLevel.INFO, 'Hello');` adds a log entry at the Info log level.

Testing

Testing Apex code consists of writing and executing unit tests. Unit tests are special methods written to exercise the functionality of your code. The goal of testing is to write unit tests that execute as many lines as possible of the target code. The number of lines of code executed during a test is called *test coverage* and is expressed as a percentage of the total lines of code. Unit tests also typically perform some pre-test preparation, such as creating sample data, and post-test verification of results.

Writing Test Methods

Test methods are static Apex code methods in an outer class with the `testMethod` keyword added. Alternatively, you can designate an entire class with the `@isTest` annotation to treat all methods as tests. Tests are subject to the same governor limits as all Apex code, but every test method is completely independent for the purposes of limit tracking, not cumulative.

A test is considered successful if its method is executed without encountering an uncaught exception. A common testing pattern is to make a series of assertions about the target code's state using the built-in method `System.assert`. The argument of `assert` is a Boolean expression. If it evaluates to `true`, the program continues; otherwise, a `System.Exception` is thrown and causes the test to fail.

Tests can rely on records already in the database or create their own temporary test data. All database modifications occurring during execution of a test method are rolled back after the method is completed. A best practice is to create your own test data in a setup phase before your tests are executed, and limit your assertions to that test data. If test data is not tightly controlled, spurious test failures can result due to the interaction of tests with unrelated data present at test execution time.

Listing 5-56 shows a simple test method. It asserts two statements. The second is false, so the test always fails.

Listing 5-56   **Test Method**

```
static testMethod void negativeTest() {
  Integer i = 2 + 2;
  System.assert(i == 4);
  System.assert(i / 2 == 1);
}
```

Running Tests

All tests are automatically executed when migrating code to a production environment, even unchanged and existing tests not included in the migration. Tests can and should be executed manually throughout the development process. The Force.com native user interface includes a test runner. In the App Setup area, click Develop → Apex Classes, and then click the Run All Tests button. The same functionality is available in the Force.com IDE; to access it, right-click an Apex class containing test methods and select Force.com → Run Tests.

Sample Application: Validating Timecards

This section applies Apex, SOQL, DML, and triggers to ensure that timecards entered into the Services Manager sample application have a valid assignment. An *assignment* is a record indicating that a resource is staffed on a project for a certain time period. A consultant can enter a timecard only for a project and time period he or she is authorized to work. Triggers are one way to enforce this rule.

The following subsections cover the process of configuring the Force.com IDE for Apex development, creating the trigger code to implement the timecard validation rule, and writing and running unit tests.

Force.com IDE Setup

Begin by creating the Force.com IDE Project for the Services Manager sample application, if you have not already done so. Select the menu option File → New → Force.com Project. Enter a project name, username, password, and security token of your Development Edition organization and click the Next button and then the Finish button. The Force.com IDE connects to Force.com, downloads the metadata in your organization to your local machine, and displays a new project node in your Navigator view.

Creating the Trigger

Listing 5-57 defines the trigger to validate timecards. It illustrates a best practice for trigger development: Keep the trigger's code block as small as possible. Place code in a separate class for easier maintenance and to encourage code reuse. Use naming conventions to indicate that the code is invoked from a trigger, such as the `Manager` suffix on the class name and the `handle` prefix on the method name.

Listing 5-57   **Trigger validateTimecard**

```
trigger validateTimecard on Timecard__c(before insert, before update) {
  TimecardManager.handleTimecardChange(Trigger.old, Trigger.new);
}
```

To create this trigger, select File → New → Apex Trigger. Enter the trigger name, select the object (`Timecard__c`), enable the two trigger operations (`before insert`, `before update`), and click the Finish button. This creates the trigger declaration and adds it to your project. It is now ready to be filled with the Apex code in Listing 5-57. If you save the trigger now, it will fail with a compilation error. This is because the dependent class, `TimecardManager`, has not yet been defined.

Continue on to creating the class. Select File → New → Apex Class to reveal the New Apex Class Wizard. Enter the class name (`TimecardManager`), leave the other fields (Version and Template) set to their defaults, and click the Finish button.

Listing 5-58 is the `TimecardManager` class. It performs the work of validating the timecard on behalf of the trigger. First it builds a Set of resource Ids referenced in the incoming set of timecards. It uses this Set to query the Assignment object. For each timecard, the assignment List is looped over to look for a match on the time period specified in the timecard. If none is found, an error is added to the offending timecard. This error is ultimately reported to the user or program initiating the timecard transaction.

Listing 5-58   **TimecardManager Class**

```
public class TimecardManager {
  public class TimecardException extends Exception {}
  public static void handleTimecardChange(List<Timecard__c> oldTimecards,
    List<Timecard__c> newTimecards) {
    Set<ID> resourceIds = new Set<ID>();
```

```
  for (Timecard__c timecard : newTimecards) {
    resourceIds.add(timecard.Resource__c);
  }
  List<Assignment__c> assignments = [ SELECT Id, Start_Date__c,
    End_Date__c, Resource__c FROM Assignment__c
    WHERE Resource__c IN :resourceIds ];
  if (assignments.size() == 0) {
    throw new TimecardException('No assignments');
  }
  Boolean hasAssignment;
  for (Timecard__c timecard : newTimecards) {
    hasAssignment = false;
    for (Assignment__c assignment : assignments) {
      if (assignment.Resource__c == timecard.Resource__c &&
        timecard.Week_Ending__c - 6 >= assignment.Start_Date__c &&
        timecard.Week_Ending__c <= assignment.End_Date__c) {
          hasAssignment = true;
          break;
      }
    }
    if (!hasAssignment) {
      timecard.addError('No assignment for resource ' +
        timecard.Resource__c + ', week ending ' +
        timecard.Week_Ending__c);
    }
  }
 }
}
```

Unit Testing

Now that the trigger is developed, you must test it. During development, taking note of the code paths and thinking about how they are best covered by unit tests is a good idea. An even better idea is to write the unit tests as you develop.

To create unit tests for the timecard validation code using the Force.com IDE, follow the same procedure as that for creating an ordinary Apex class. An optional variation on this process is to select the Test Class template from the Create New Apex Class Wizard. This generates skeleton code for a class containing only test methods.

Listing 5-59 contains unit tests for the TimecardManager class. Before each unit test, test data is inserted in a static initializer. The tests cover a simple positive case, a negative case in which no assignments exist for the timecard, a second negative case in which no valid assignments exist for the time period in a timecard, and a batch insert of timecards. The code demonstrates a best practice of placing all unit tests for a class in a separate test class with an intuitive, consistent naming convention.

Listing 5-59   **Unit Tests for `TimecardManager` Class**

```
@isTest
private class TestTimecardManager {
  private static ID resourceId, projectId;

  static {
    Resource__c resource = new Resource__c(Name = 'Bob');
    insert resource;
    resourceId = resource.Id;
    Proj__c project = new Proj__c(Name = 'Proj1');
    insert project;
    projectId = project.Id;
  }

  static testMethod void positiveTest() {
    Date weekEnding = Date.valueOf('2009-04-11');
    insert new Assignment__c(Project__c = projectId,
      Start_Date__c = weekEnding - 6, End_Date__c = weekEnding,
      Resource__c = resourceId);
    insert new Timecard__c(Project__c = projectId,
      Week_Ending__c = weekEnding, Resource__c = resourceId);
  }

  static testMethod void testNoAssignments() {
    Timecard__c timecard = new Timecard__c(Project__c = projectId,
      Week_Ending__c = Date.valueOf('2009-04-11'),
      Resource__c = resourceId);
    try {
      insert timecard;
    } catch (DmlException e) {
      System.assert(e.getMessage().indexOf('No assignments') > 0);
      return;
    }
    System.assert(false);
  }

  static testMethod void testNoValidAssignments() {
    Date weekEnding = Date.valueOf('2009-04-04');
    insert new Assignment__c(Project__c = projectId,
      Start_Date__c = weekEnding - 6, End_Date__c = weekEnding,
      Resource__c = resourceId);
    try {
      insert new Timecard__c(Project__c = projectId,
        Week_Ending__c = Date.today(), Resource__c = resourceId);
    } catch (DmlException e) {
      System.assert(e.getMessage().indexOf('No assignment for resource') > 0);
```

```
      return;
    }
    System.assert(false);
  }

  static testMethod void testBatch() {
    Date weekEnding = Date.valueOf('2009-04-11');
    insert new Assignment__c(Project__c = projectId,
      Start_Date__c = weekEnding - 6, End_Date__c = weekEnding,
      Resource__c = resourceId);
    List<Timecard__c> timecards = new List<Timecard__c>();
    for (Integer i=0; i<200; i++) {
      timecards.add(new Timecard__c(Project__c = projectId,
        Week_Ending__c = weekEnding, Resource__c = resourceId));
    }
    insert timecards;
  }
}
```

After saving the code in the unit test class, run it by right-clicking in the editor and selecting Force.com → Run Tests. After a few seconds, you should see the Apex Test Runner view with a green check box indicating that all tests passed, as shown in Figure 5-10. Expand the results node to see 100% test coverage of the `TimecardManager`, and scroll through the debug log to examine performance information and resource consumption for each of the tests.

Summary

This chapter is arguably the most important chapter in the book. It describes core Apex concepts and syntax that form the basis of all subsequent chapters. Absorb this chapter, augmenting it with the information available through the developer.force.com Web site and community, and you will be well prepared to write your own Force.com applications.

Before moving on, take a few minutes to review these major areas:

- Apex is the only language that runs inside the Force.com platform and is tightly integrated with the Force.com database. Apex is strongly typed and includes object-oriented features.

- The Force.com database is queried using SOQL and SOSL, and its records are modified using DML. All three languages can be embedded directly inside Apex code.

- Resources consumed by Apex programs are tightly controlled by the Force.com platform through governor limits. Limits vary based on the type of resource consumed. Learn the relevant governor limits as early as possible in your development process. This ensures that you write efficient code that scales up to production data volumes.

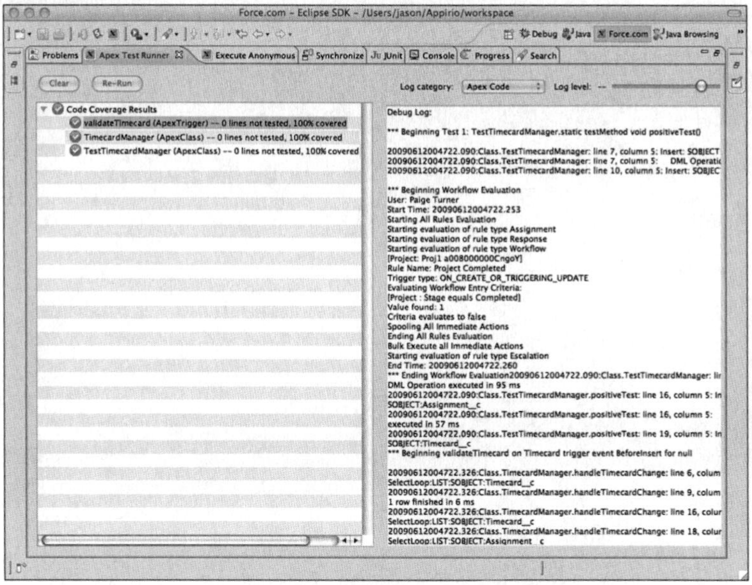

Figure 5-10   Viewing code coverage results

6

Advanced Business Logic

In the preceding chapter, you learned the basics of the Apex language for developing business logic. This chapter extends your knowledge of Apex to reach more features of the Force.com platform. The following topics are covered:

- **Aggregate SOQL Queries:** Aggregate queries operate on groups of records, summarizing data declaratively at the database level rather than in Apex.

- **Additional SOQL Features:** SOQL includes features for querying related objects and multi-select picklists.

- **Salesforce Object Search Language (SOSL):** SOSL is a full-text search language, a complement to SOQL, that allows a single query to search the textual content of many database objects and fields.

- **Transaction Processing:** Apex includes database methods to enable the partial success of transactions, saving and restoring of database state, and locking of records returned from a query.

- **Apex Managed Sharing:** Managed sharing allows programmatic control over record-level sharing.

- **Sending and Receiving Email:** Apex programs can send and receive email with support for text and binary attachments and templates for standardizing outbound messages.

- **Dynamic Apex:** Execute database queries that aren't hard-coded into your programs, query Force.com for your database's metadata, and write generic code to manipulate database records regardless of their type.

- **Custom Settings in Apex:** Data from custom settings can be retrieved, created, updated, and deleted from Apex.

- **Sample Application:** The Services Manager sample application is enhanced to send email notifications to users when a business event occurs.

Aggregate SOQL Queries

SOQL statements that summarize or group records are called *aggregate queries*. Rather than selecting a set of records and performing calculations on them in Apex, SOQL allows you to do this within the database. This results in much better performance and simpler code. This section covers three aspects of aggregate SOQL queries:

- **Aggregate Functions:** Rather than simply returning the discrete values of a database field in a SELECT statement, aggregate functions such as SUM apply a simple calculation on each record and return the accumulated result.
- **Grouping Records:** The GROUP BY syntax works with aggregate functions to return a set of summarized results based on common values.
- **Grouping Records with Subtotals:** SOQL provides two special forms of the GROUP BY syntax to calculate subtotals and return them in the query results.

Aggregate Functions

Aggregate functions in SOQL work much like their SQL counterparts. They are applied to fields in the SELECT list. After you include an aggregate function in a query, non-aggregate fields in the same query are not allowed. The six aggregate functions available in SOQL are:

- **AVG:** Calculates an average of the values in a numeric field.
- **COUNT:** Counts the values in a numeric, date, or string field, including duplicate values but not nulls. Unlike all other aggregate functions, the argument to COUNT is optional.
- **COUNT_DISTINCT:** Counts the unique values in a numeric, date, or string field, excluding nulls.
- **MIN:** Returns the minimum value in a numeric, date, or string field. The minimum of a string field is the first value when values are sorted alphabetically. If the string is a picklist type, the minimum is the first value in the picklist.
- **MAX:** Returns the maximum value in a numeric, date, or string field. The maximum of a string field is the last value when values are sorted alphabetically. If the string is a picklist type, the maximum is the last value in the picklist.
- **SUM:** Computes the sum of values in a numeric field.

All queries containing aggregate functions return a special Apex object called AggregateResult, except the no-argument form of COUNT, which returns an integer. The AggregateResult object contains the aggregate values calculated by running the query. They have default field names expr0 for the first field, expr1, and so forth. Alternatively, you can provide an alias immediately following the aggregate function column to provide a friendlier label for the value in your code. Aggregate result fields are accessed using the get method.

To get started with aggregate functions in Apex, open Force.com IDE's Execute Anonymous view and type in and run the code given in Listing 6-1.

Listing 6-1   **Returning the Record Count**

```
Integer i = [ SELECT COUNT() FROM Timecard__c ];
System.debug(i);
```

This code prints the number of records contained in the `Timecard__c` object to the debug log. The SOQL query returns an integer because it uses the no-argument form of the `COUNT` aggregate function. In contrast, the example in Listing 6-2 uses the `SUM` aggregate function and returns an `AggregateResult` object, with an alias `Total` specified on the aggregate column. Note that if an alias were not specified, the aggregate column would be named `expr0`.

Listing 6-2   **Calculating a Sum**

```
AggregateResult r = [ SELECT SUM(Total_Hours__c) Total
  FROM Timecard__c ];
System.debug(r.get('Total'));
```

> **Note**
>
> Normal SOQL governor limits apply to aggregate functions. The number of records used to compute an aggregate result are applied toward the limit on records returned. So although your COUNT query returns a single result record, if it counted more than 50,000 records, your query will fail with an exception. If such a failure is disruptive to your application, make sure you use a WHERE clause to reduce the number of records that are processed in the query. The LIMIT keyword is not allowed in queries with aggregate functions, except for the special form of the COUNT function that has no field argument.

Grouping Records

SOQL provides the `GROUP BY` syntax for grouping records by one or more fields. When a query contains a grouping, its results are collapsed into a single record for each unique value in the grouped field. Because you can no longer return individual field values, all fields not specified as grouped must be placed within aggregate functions.

Listing 6-3 shows a simple example of grouping records without aggregate functions. It examines all the records in the Resource custom object and returns only the unique values of the field `Region__c`.

Listing 6-3   **Returning Unique Records by Grouping Them**

```
for (AggregateResult r : [ SELECT Region__c FROM Resource__c
  GROUP BY Region__c ]) {
  System.debug(r.get('Region__c'));
}
```

Although aggregate functions can be used alone in a simple query, they are much more powerful when used in conjunction with record groupings. Listing 6-4 demonstrates aggregate functions with record groupings. It groups all Timecard records by the geographic region of the consultant (Resource) who performed the work, and sums their reported hours. This results in one record per geographic region with the region's name and a sum of their timecard hours.

Listing 6-4   **Using Aggregate Functions with Record Groupings**

```
for (AggregateResult r : [ SELECT Resource__r.Region__c,
  SUM(Total_Hours__c) FROM Timecard__c
  GROUP BY Resource__r.Region__c ]) {
  System.debug(r.get('Region__c') + ' ' + r.get('expr0'));
}
```

You're already familiar with the WHERE keyword in SOQL for filtering query results using Boolean expressions. Filtering on the results of aggregate functions requires the HAVING keyword. It works just like WHERE but the field being filtered must be wrapped with an aggregate function and included in the GROUP BY list.

The code in Listing 6-5 outputs the average hourly cost rates for resources by education level, but excludes records at or below an average cost rate of $100. The filtering of the average cost rates is specified by the HAVING keyword.

Listing 6-5   **Filtering Grouped Records by Aggregate Function Values**

```
for (AggregateResult r : [ SELECT Highest_Education_Level__c ed,
  AVG(Hourly_Cost_Rate__c) FROM Resource__c
  GROUP BY Highest_Education_Level__c
  HAVING AVG(Hourly_Cost_Rate__c) > 100 ]) {
  System.debug(r.get('ed') + ' ' + r.get('expr0'));
}
```

Grouping Records with Subtotals

Two special forms of grouping in SOQL produce subtotals and grand totals for the record groupings specified in the query. They are GROUP BY ROLLUP and GROUP BY CUBE, and they replace GROUP BY syntax and support up to three grouped fields. These functions make it easier for developers to produce cross-tabular, or pivot-style outputs common to reporting tools, where groups become the axes and aggregate values are the cells. The Force.com database calculates the totals and provides them in-line, in the results, eliminating the need to write Apex to post-process the data.

Listing 6-6 demonstrates GROUP BY ROLLUP to add subtotals to combinations of two fields: Status__c and Region__c. Because Status__c appears first in the GROUP BY ROLLUP function, the subtotals are calculated for each of its unique values. The function

GROUPING is used to identify subtotal records, and also to order the results so that the subtotals appear last.

Listing 6-6   **Subtotals on Two Field Groupings**

```
for (AggregateResult r : [ SELECT Project__r.Status__c, Resource__r.Region__c,
  SUM(Total_Hours__c) hours, COUNT(Id) recs,
  GROUPING(Project__r.Status__c) status, GROUPING(Resource__r.Region__c) region
  FROM Timecard__c
  GROUP BY ROLLUP(Project__r.Status__c, Resource__r.Region__c)
  ORDER BY GROUPING(Project__r.Status__c), GROUPING(Resource__r.Region__c) ]) {
  System.debug(LoggingLevel.INFO,
    r.get('Status__c') + ' ' + r.get('Region__c') + ' ' +
    r.get('region') + ' ' + r.get('status') + ' ' +
    r.get('hours') + ' ' + r.get('recs'));
}
```

Listing 6-7 shows the result of running the code in Listing 6-6 on a database containing 13 Timecard records spread across West and Central regions in Yellow and Green status. Note the third and fourth columns contain the value of the GROUPING function. Here a 1 indicates that the record is a subtotal, and 0 indicates a normal record. For example, the fifth record from the top is a subtotal on status because the 1 appears in the status column. The other values in that record indicate the sum of all Timecard hours for projects in Yellow status is 109, and that this constitutes three records' worth of data. The final record contains the grand totals, which you can verify by adding the record count of the Green subtotal (10) to the Yellow subtotal (3).

Listing 6-7   **Excerpt of Debug Log After Running Code in Listing 6-6**

```
16:04:43.207|USER_DEBUG|[7]|INFO|Green West 0 0 230.0 6
16:04:43.207|USER_DEBUG|[7]|INFO|Green Central 0 0 152.0 4
16:04:43.207|USER_DEBUG|[7]|INFO|Yellow Central 0 0 109.0 3
16:04:43.207|USER_DEBUG|[7]|INFO|Green null 1 0 382.0 10
16:04:43.207|USER_DEBUG|[7]|INFO|Yellow null 1 0 109.0 3
16:04:43.207|USER_DEBUG|[7]|INFO|null null 1 1 491.0 13
```

To experiment with GROUP BY CUBE, replace the word ROLLUP with CUBE in Listing 6-6 and run the code. The GROUP BY CUBE syntax causes all possible combinations of grouped fields to receive subtotals. The results are shown in Listing 6-8. Note the addition of two records, subtotals on the Region__c field indicated by a 1 in the region column.

Listing 6-8   **Excerpt of Debug Log After Changing Listing 6-6 to Group By Cube**

```
16:06:56.003|USER_DEBUG|[7]|INFO|Green Central 0 0 152.0 4
16:06:56.003|USER_DEBUG|[7]|INFO|Green West 0 0 230.0 6
16:06:56.004|USER_DEBUG|[7]|INFO|Yellow Central 0 0 109.0 3
```

```
16:06:56.004|USER_DEBUG|[7]|INFO|Green null 1 0 382.0 10
16:06:56.004|USER_DEBUG|[7]|INFO|Yellow null 1 0 109.0 3
16:06:56.004|USER_DEBUG|[7]|INFO|null West 0 1 230.0 6
16:06:56.004|USER_DEBUG|[7]|INFO|null Central 0 1 261.0 7
16:06:56.005|USER_DEBUG|[7]|INFO|null null 1 1 491.0 13
```

Additional SOQL Features

Although SOQL doesn't allow arbitrary joins, it provides some control over how related objects are navigated. This section discusses inner and outer joins, as well as semi-joins and anti-joins:

- **Inner Join and Outer Join:** SOQL statements that include related objects normally do so by outer join, but can perform an inner join instead using a WHERE clause.

- **Semi-Join and Anti-Join:** Semi-join and anti-join are types of relationship queries that use the results of a subquery to filter the records returned from the parent object.

- **Multi-Select Picklists:** A multi-select picklist is a form of picklist field that allows multiple values to be stored for a single record. The standard conditional filters of the SOQL WHERE clause do not suffice for handling multiple values within a single record and column, so SOQL provides special syntax to handle this case.

Inner Join and Outer Join

A SOQL statement consists of a single base object, specified using the FROM keyword. All fields in the base object can be retrieved in the query, as well as fields from parent and child objects depending on their distance away from the base object. Force.com takes care of joining related objects together to retrieve the requested fields.

These implicit joins are always outer joins. An outer join returns all records from the base object, including records that do not refer to a related object. To get a feel for this behavior, create a new Project record in the native user interface and leave all of its fields blank, but enter **Test Project** for the Name. Open Force.com IDE's Schema Explorer and enter and run the query given in Listing 6-9.

Listing 6-9   **SOQL Outer Join**

```
SELECT Name, Account__r.Name
  FROM Proj__c
```

This query returns the name and account name of the Projects. Account is the parent object of Project through a Lookup relationship. Because it is a Lookup relationship and not Master-Detail, it can contain a null value in Account__c, the Account foreign key field. With no foreign key to Account, Account__r, the foreign object reference, is also null.

You should see the five records imported from Listing 2-16 in Chapter 2, "Database Essentials," plus the newly added record, named Test Project. Figure 6-1 shows the result of running the query. The Test Project record contains no value for `Account__r` yet was included in the results anyway. This is due to the outer join behavior.

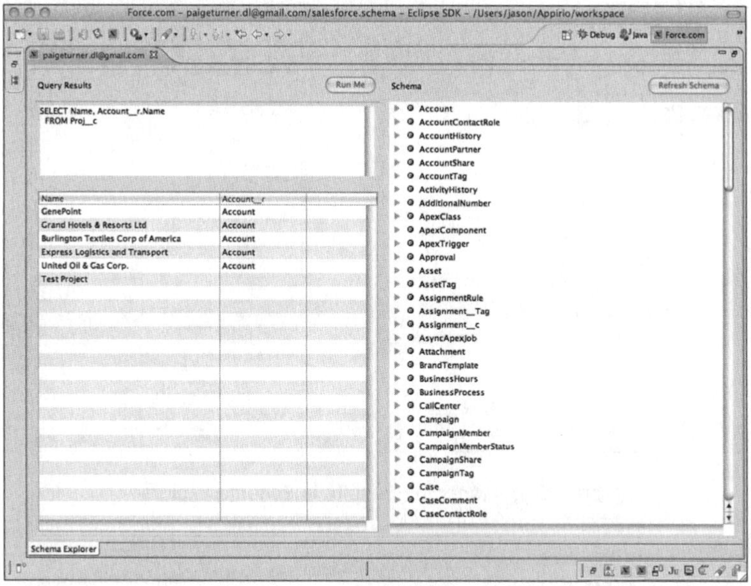

Figure 6-1   Outer join results in Schema Explorer

In a relational database, this same query translated to SQL would result in five rows. The Test Project row would not be returned because it does not match a row in the Account table. Joins in SQL are inner by default, returning only rows that match both tables of the join.

To duplicate this inner join behavior in SOQL, simply add a filter condition to eliminate records without a matching record in the related object. For example, Listing 6-10 adds a filter condition to Listing 6-9 to exclude Project records without a corresponding Account.

Listing 6-10   **SOQL Inner Join**

```
SELECT Name, Account__r.Name
  FROM Proj__c
  WHERE Account__c != null
```

The results of this query are shown in Figure 6-2. It has returned five records, each one with a corresponding parent Account record. The newly added Project record without the Account is correctly omitted.

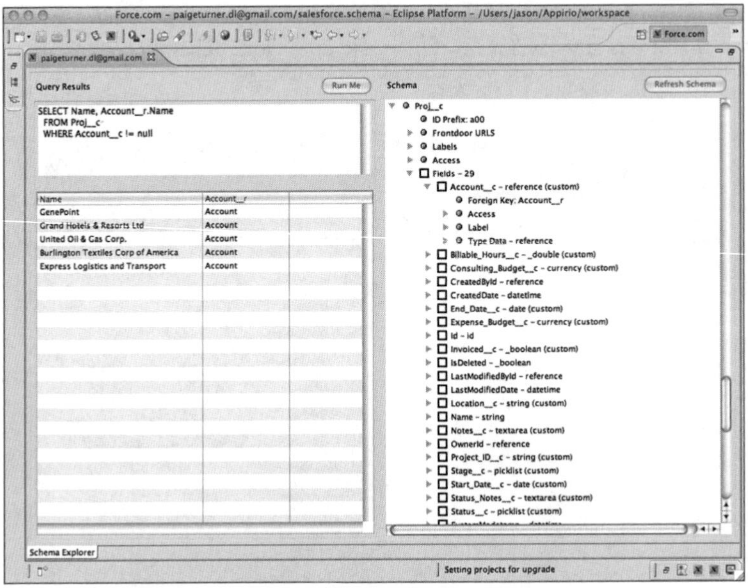

Figure 6-2   Inner join results in Schema Explorer

Semi-Join and Anti-Join

In Chapter 5, "Business Logic," you learned the two ways related objects can be included in SOQL: parent-to-child and child-to-parent queries. Semi-join and anti-join queries enhance the functionality of both queries, and add the ability to make child-to-child queries. In general, they allow records from one object to be filtered by a subquery against another object.

For example, suppose you need a list of all Account records that have at least one Project record in a yellow status. To make sure you have a valid test case, edit one of the Project records in the native user interface to set it to a yellow status. Try to write a query to return its Account, with Account as the base object.

You can't do this without using a semi-join. Listing 6-11 shows one attempt. But it returns the unique identifiers and names of all Accounts and the unique identifiers of any Projects in yellow status. You would still have to write Apex code to filter through the Account records to ignore those without Project child records.

Listing 6-11   **Parent-to-Child Query, Filter on Child**

```
SELECT Id, Name,
 (SELECT Id FROM Projects__r WHERE Status__c = 'Yellow')
  FROM Account
```

Figure 6-3 shows the result of executing this query. Grand Hotels & Resorts Ltd is the Project in yellow status, and you can see that its Project record has been returned in the relationship field `Projects__r`.

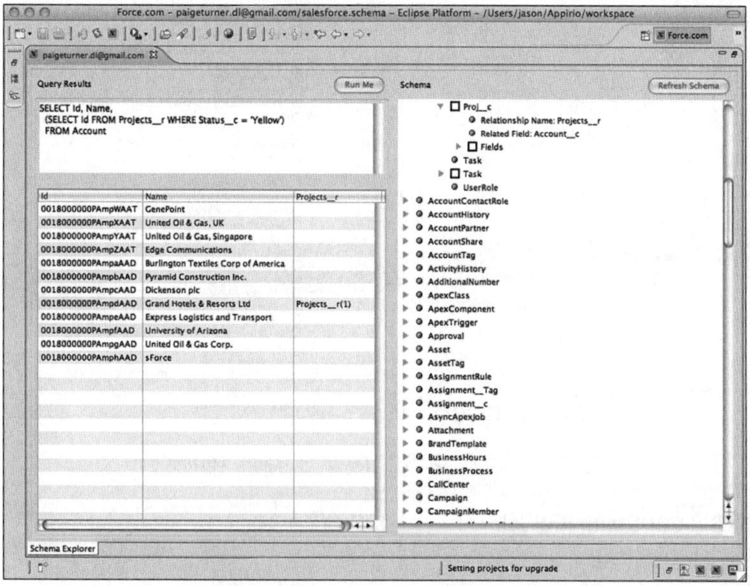

Figure 6-3   Parent-to-child query, filter on child

Listing 6-12 rewrites this query using a semi-join. Read it from the bottom up. A subquery identifies Projects in yellow status, returning their Account unique identifiers. This set of Account unique identifiers is used to filter the Account records returned by the query. The result is a single Account, as shown in Figure 6-4.

Listing 6-12   **SOQL with Semi-Join**

```
SELECT Id, Name
  FROM Account
  WHERE Id IN
    (SELECT Account__c FROM Proj__c WHERE Status__c = 'Yellow')
```

An anti-join is the negative version of a semi-join. It uses the NOT IN keyword to allow the subquery to exclude records from the parent object. For example, Listing 6-13 returns all Accounts except those containing Projects in a green status. Note that the results include the Project in yellow status, as well as all Account records not associated with a Project.

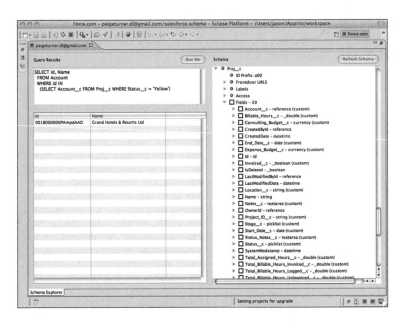

Figure 6-4   SOQL with parent-to-child semi-join

Listing 6-13   SOQL with Anti-Join

```
SELECT Id, Name
  FROM Account
  WHERE Id NOT IN
    (SELECT Account__c FROM Proj__c WHERE Status__c = 'Green')
```

Returning to semi-joins, Listing 6-14 provides an example of another type, called child-to-child. It joins two child objects that aren't directly related by relationship fields. The records in the Timecard object are filtered by resources that have at least one assignment as a consultant. This means Timecards logged by resources who are not assigned to a project as a consultant are excluded from the results. Child-to-child refers to the Timecard and Assignment objects, which are related to each other only in so much as they are children to other objects.

Listing 6-14   SOQL with Child-to-Child Semi-Join

```
SELECT Project__r.Name, Week_Ending__c, Total_Hours__c
  FROM Timecard__c
  WHERE Resource__c IN
    (SELECT Resource__c FROM Assignment__c WHERE Role__c = 'Consultant')
```

Listing 6-15 demonstrates a third type of semi-join, the child-to-parent. Timecards are filtered again, this time to include resources with an hourly cost rate of more than $100.

Child-to-parent refers to the relationship between the Timecard and Resource objects. Resource is the parent object, and it is being used to restrict the output of the query on Timecard, the child object.

Listing 6-15   **SOQL with Child-to-Parent Semi-Join**

```
SELECT Project__r.Name, Week_Ending__c, Total_Hours__c
  FROM Timecard__c
  WHERE Resource__c IN
    (SELECT Id FROM Resource__c WHERE Hourly_Cost_Rate__c > 100)
```

Several restrictions are placed on semi-join and anti-join queries:

- The selected column in the subquery must be a primary or foreign key and cannot traverse relationships. It must be a direct field on the child object. For example, it would be invalid to rewrite the subquery in Listing 6-12 to return `Account__r.Id` in place of `Account__c`.

- A single query can include at most two semi-joins or anti-joins.

- Semi-joins and anti-joins cannot be nested within other semi-join and anti-join statements, and are not allowed in subqueries.

- The parent object cannot be the same type as the child. This type of query can always be rewritten as a single query without a semi-join or an anti-join. For example, the invalid query `SELECT Name FROM Proj__c WHERE Id IN (SELECT Id FROM Proj__c WHERE Status__c = 'Green')` can be expressed without a subquery: `SELECT Name FROM Proj__c WHERE Status__c = 'Green'`.

- Subqueries cannot be nested and cannot contain the `OR`, `count()`, `ORDER BY`, or `LIMIT` keywords.

Multi-Select Picklists

Multi-select picklists are interchangeable with ordinary picklists in queries, except for being prohibited in the `ORDER BY` clause. SOQL includes two additional features for filtering multi-select picklists, described in the following list:

- **Semicolon AND Operator:** The semicolon is used to express multiple string literals. For example, `'Java;Apex'` means that the multi-select picklist has both Java and Apex items selected in any order. The semicolon notation can be used with the `=` and `!=` SOQL operators to make assertions about the selected items of multi-select picklists.

- **INCLUDES and EXCLUDES Keywords:** The `INCLUDES` and `EXCLUDES` keywords are followed by comma-separated lists of literal values. The `INCLUDES` keyword returns records in which the selected values of a multi-select picklist are included in the list of values. The `EXCLUDES` keyword returns records that match none of the values.

The semicolon notation can be combined with the INCLUDES and EXCLUDES keywords to express any combination of multi-select picklist values.

To try this out, create a multi-select picklist named Requested Skills on the Project object. Run the SOQL statement given in Listing 6-16 using the Force.com IDE's Schema Explorer. It returns Project records with the multiple selection of Apex, Java, and C# in the Requested Skills field and also records with only Python selected. Populate Project records with matching values to see them returned by the query.

Listing 6-16   **SOQL with Multi-Select Picklist**

```
SELECT Id, Name
  FROM Proj__c
  WHERE Requested_Skills__c INCLUDES ('Apex;Java;C#', 'Python')
```

Salesforce Object Search Language (SOSL)

Data stored in the Force.com database is automatically indexed to support both structured and unstructured queries. SOQL is the language for structured queries, allowing records from a single object and its related objects to be retrieved with precise, per-field filter conditions. SOSL is a full-text search language for unstructured queries. It begins by looking across multiple fields and multiple objects for one or more search keywords, and then applies an optional SOQL-like filter on each object to refine the results.

To decide which query language to use, consider the scope of the query. If the query spans multiple unrelated objects, SOSL is the only practical choice. If the query searches for words within many string fields, it can probably be expressed more concisely in SOSL than SOQL. Use SOQL for queries on a single object with filters on various data types.

SOSL Basics

At the highest level, a SOSL query specifies search terms and scope. The search terms are a list of string literals and can include wildcards. The search scope is fields containing string data from one or more objects. This excludes Number, Date, and Checkbox fields from being searched with SOSL.

SOSL query syntax consists of four parts, described in the list that follows:

- **Query:** The query is one or more words or phrases to search on. The query can include the wildcards * (matches any number of characters) and ? (matches any single character) at the middle or end of search terms. Enclose a search term in quotation marks to perform an exact match on multiple words. Use the logical operators AND, OR, and AND NOT to combine search terms and parentheses to control the order in which they're evaluated. Note that searches are not case-sensitive.

- **Search Group:** The search group is an optional part of the SOSL query indicating the types of fields to search in each object. Valid values are ALL FIELDS (all string fields), NAME FIELDS (the standard Name field only), EMAIL FIELDS (all fields of type Email), and PHONE FIELDS (all fields of type Phone). The default value is ALL FIELDS.

- **Field Specification:** The field specification is a comma-separated list of objects to include in the result. By default, the Id field of each object is included. Optionally, you can specify additional fields to return by enclosing them in parentheses. You can also specify conditional filters using the same syntax as the SOQL WHERE clause, set the sort order with the ORDER BY keyword, and use the LIMIT keyword to limit the number of records returned per object.

- **Record Limit:** This optional value specifies the maximum number of records returned by the entire query, from all the objects queried. If a record limit is not provided, it defaults to the maximum of 200.

These four parts are combined in the following syntax: FIND *'query'* IN *search group* RETURNING *field specification* LIMIT *record limit*. The apostrophes around query are required.

SOSL in Apex

SOSL in Apex works much like SOQL in Apex. Queries are enclosed in square brackets and compiled directly into the code, ensuring that the query syntax is correct and references valid fields and objects in the database.

As with SOQL, bind variables can be used to inject variable values from the running program into select parts of the query. This injection of values is performed in a secure manner because Apex automatically escapes special characters. Bind variables are allowed in the search string (following FIND), filter literals (in the WHERE block), and the LIMIT keyword.

SOSL is not allowed in triggers. It will compile, but will fail at runtime. It is allowed in unit tests and custom user interfaces, as covered in Chapter 7, "User Interfaces." In this chapter, you can experiment with SOSL using the Execute Anonymous view.

> **Note**
>
> You are limited to 20 SOSL queries returning a maximum of 200 rows per query.

Listing 6-17 is a sample SOSL query in Apex. It returns the names of records in the Project and Resource objects that contain the word *Chicago* in any of their fields.

Listing 6-17   **SOSL in Apex**

```
List<List<SObject>> result = [
  FIND 'Chicago'
  RETURNING Proj__c(Name), Resource__c(Name)
];
List<Proj__c> projects = (List<Proj__c>)result[0];
for (Proj__c project : projects) {
  System.debug('Project: ' + project.Name);
}
```

```
List<Resource__c> resources = (List<Resource__c>)result[1];
for (Resource__c resource : resources) {
  System.debug('Resource: ' + resource.Name);
}
```

Figure 6-5 shows the results of running this code in the Execute Anonymous view. If your debug log is cluttered with too many other entries to see the output of the query, set Apex code to the Debug level and all other Log categories to None.

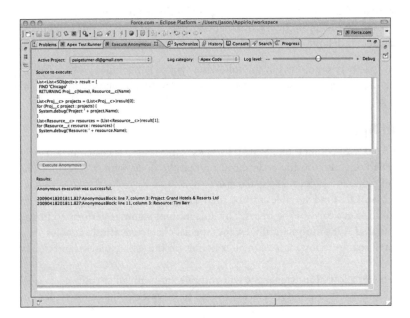

Figure 6-5   Results of SOSL in Apex

Transaction Processing

This section covers three features of Apex that control how transactions are processed by the database:

- **Data Manipulation Language (DML) Database Methods:** DML database methods are much like DML statements from Chapter 5, but add support for partial success. This allows some records from a batch to succeed while others fail.

- **Savepoints:** Savepoints designate a point in time that your code can return to. Returning to a savepoint rolls back all DML statements executed since the establishment of the savepoint.

- **Record Locking:** Apex provides a SOQL keyword to protect records from interference by other users or programs for the duration of a transaction.

Data Manipulation Language (DML) Database Methods

All database operations in Apex are transactional. For example, an implicit transaction is created when a trigger fires. If the code in a trigger completes without error, DML operations performed within it are automatically committed. If the trigger terminates prematurely with an uncaught exception, all DML operations are automatically rolled back. If multiple triggers fire for a single database operation, all trigger code succeeds or fails as a group.

In Chapter 5, you were exposed to DML statements. These statements accept a single record or batch of records. When operating on a batch, they succeed or fail on the entire group of records. For example, if 200 records are inserted and the last record fails with a validation error, none of the 200 records are inserted.

Apex offers a second way of making DML statements called DML database methods. DML database methods allow batch DML operations to fail on individual records without impacting the entire batch. To do this, they do not throw exceptions to indicate error. Instead they return an array of result objects, one per input record. These result objects contain a flag indicating success or failure, and error details in the event of failure.

A DML database method exists for each of the DML statements. Each method takes an optional Boolean parameter called opt_allOrNone to specify batch behavior. The default value is true, indicating that the behavior is "all or none." This makes the method identical to a DML statement, with one failed record causing the failure of all records and a DmlException. But if the opt_allOrNone parameter is false, partial success is allowed.

> **Note**
>
> DML database methods are subject to the same governor limits and general restrictions as DML statements. Refer to Chapter 5 for more information.

Listing 6-18 inserts a batch of two Skill records using the insert database method. It passes false as an argument to allow partial success of the DML operation. The insert method returns an array of SaveResult objects. They correspond one-to-one with the array passed as an argument to the insert method. Each SaveResult object is examined to check for failure, and the results are displayed in the debug log.

Listing 6-18   **DML Database Method Usage**

```
Resource__c tim = [ SELECT Id
  FROM Resource__c
  WHERE Name = 'Tim Barr' LIMIT 1 ];
Skill__c skill1 = new Skill__c(Resource__c = tim.Id,
  Type__c = 'Java', Rating__c = '3 - Average');
Skill__c skill2 = new Skill__c(Resource__c = tim.Id,
  Rating__c = '4 - Above Average');
Skill__c[] skills = new  Skill__c[] { skill1, skill2 };
Database.SaveResult[] saveResults =
  Database.insert(skills, false);
for (Integer i=0; i<saveResults.size(); i++) {
  Database.SaveResult saveResult = saveResults[i];
```

```
if (!saveResult.isSuccess()) {
  Database.Error err = saveResult.getErrors()[0];
  System.debug('Skill ' + i + ' insert failed: '
    + err.getMessage());
} else {
  System.debug('Skill ' + i + ' insert succeeded: new Id = '
    + saveResult.getId());
}
}
```

The result of executing this code is shown in Figure 6-6. Examining the debug log, the first record is inserted, but the second failed because it doesn't contain a value for the `Type__c` field. This is enforced by a validation rule created in Chapter 2. If you edit this code and remove the second argument to `Database.insert`, which enables partial success, the failure of the second record raises an exception and rolls back the successful insertion of the first record.

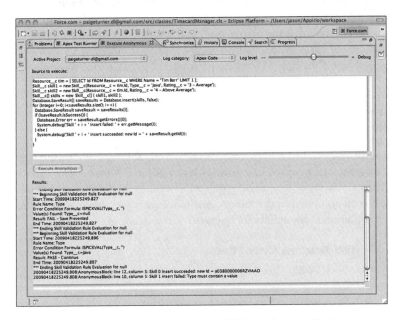

Figure 6-6   Results of `insert` DML database method

Savepoints

Savepoints are markers indicating the state of the database at a specific point in the execution of your Apex program. They allow the database to be restored to a known state in case of error or any scenario requiring a reversal of all DML operations performed since the savepoint.

Set a new savepoint using the `Database.setSavepoint` method, which returns a Savepoint object. To restore the database to a savepoint, call the `Database.rollback` method, which takes a Savepoint object as its only argument.

Several limitations exist on the use of savepoints. The number of savepoints and rollbacks contributes toward the overall limit on DML statements, which is 150. If you create multiple savepoints and roll back, all savepoints created after the savepoint you roll back to are invalidated. Finally, you cannot share a savepoint across triggers using a static variable.

Listing 6-19 is an example of using the `setSavepoint` and `rollback` methods. First, a savepoint is set. Then, all the Resource records in your database are deleted, assuming your database doesn't contain more than the governor limit of 10,000 records for DML. Finally, the database is rolled back to the savepoint. The number of records in the Resource object is counted before each operation in the program to illustrate its behavior.

Listing 6-19   **Savepoint and Rollback Usage**

```
void printRecordCount() {
  System.debug([ SELECT COUNT() FROM Resource__c ] + ' records');
}
printRecordCount();
Savepoint sp = Database.setSavepoint();

delete [ SELECT Id FROM Resource__c ];
printRecordCount();

Database.rollback(sp);
printRecordCount();
```

The results of running the code snippet in the Execute Anonymous view are shown in Figure 6-7. The debug log indicates that the Resource object initially contains five records. They are all deleted, leaving zero records. Then the database is rolled back to the savepoint established before the deletion, resulting in a count of five records again.

Record Locking

Apex code has many entry points. Code can be invoked from outside of Force.com via a Web service call, by modifying a record with a trigger on it in the native user interface, inside Force.com IDE in an Execute Anonymous view, or in a unit test. Additionally, multiple users or programs can be running the same code simultaneously or code that uses the same database resources.

DML operations using values returned by SOQL or SOSL queries are at risk for dirty writes. This means values updated by one program have been modified by a second program running at the same time. The changes of the second program are lost because the first program is operating with stale data.

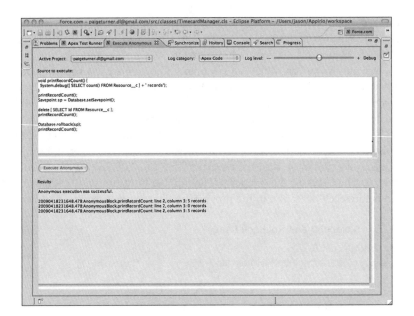

Figure 6-7   Results of savepoint and rollback sample code

For example, if your code retrieves a record and then modifies its value later in the program, it requires a write lock on the record. A write lock prevents the record from being concurrently updated by another program. Write locks are provided in Apex via the SOQL FOR UPDATE keyword. This keyword indicates to Apex that you intend to modify the records returned by the SOQL query. This locks the records, preventing them from being updated by another program until your transaction is complete. No explicit commit is necessary. The records are unlocked, and changes are automatically committed when the program exits successfully or is rolled back otherwise.

> **Note**
>
> You cannot use the ORDER BY keyword with FOR UPDATE. Query results are automatically ordered by Id field.

Listing 6-20 is an example of record locking in Apex. Tim Barr is given a raise of $20. His Resource record is retrieved and locked, the hourly cost is incremented, and the database is updated. The use of FOR UPDATE ensures that this code running simultaneously in two contexts still results in the correct outcome: a $40 increase in hourly cost rate, $20 from each of the two independent execution contexts, serialized with FOR UPDATE. Without the locking, a dirty write could cause one of the updates to be lost.

Listing 6-20   **Record Locking Example**

```
Resource__c tim = [ SELECT Id, Hourly_Cost_Rate__c
  FROM Resource__c
  WHERE Name = 'Tim Barr' LIMIT 1
  FOR UPDATE ];
tim.Hourly_Cost_Rate__c += 20;
update tim;
```

Apex Managed Sharing

Apex managed sharing allows Apex code to add, edit, and delete record sharing rules. This is the third and most advanced type of record sharing provided by Force.com. It provides the Apex developer with full control of record sharing. Apex managed sharing uses the same infrastructure as the other two types of record sharing, discussed in Chapter 3, "Database Security," and briefly reviewed here:

- **Force.com Managed Sharing:** These are record sharing rules maintained by Force.com. A native user interface enables administrators to add, edit, and delete these rules. Rules are based on user, group, or role membership and defined individually on each object. They are configured in the Administration Setup area, Security Controls → Sharing Settings.

- **User Managed Sharing:** Users who own records can grant permission to additional users from the native user interface. This is a manual process. The owner visits a record to share and clicks the Sharing button to add, edit, or remove its sharing rules.

This section is divided into two parts, described next:

- **Sharing objects:** Sharing objects are where Force.com stores record sharing rules. The fields of sharing objects are described, as well as restrictions on their use.

- **Creating sharing rules in Apex:** This walks you through the infrastructure behind sharing rules, finishing with a code sample to add a sharing rule in the Services Manager sample application schema.

Sharing Objects

Every custom object, except Detail objects in a Master-Detail relationship, has a corresponding sharing object to store its record-level sharing rules. The sharing object is created automatically by Force.com and is invisible to the native user interface. It can be seen in the Force.com IDE's Schema Explorer. Its name is the name of your object with __Share appended. For example, the sharing object for the Proj__c object is Proj__Share.

The sharing object contains explicit sharing rules. These are created by Force.com managed sharing, user managed sharing, and Apex managed sharing. It does not contain implicit shares such as organization-wide defaults.

Four fields of the sharing object control how records are shared between users and groups, as follows:

- **ParentID:** `ParentId` is the unique identifier of the record being shared.
- **UserOrGroupId:** This is the unique identifier of the user or group that the sharing rule is granting access to. Groups are public groups or roles.
- **AccessLevel:** This field stores the level of access granted to the user or group for this record. The three valid values are `Read` (Read Only), `Edit` (Read and Edit), and `All` (Full Control). Apex managed sharing cannot set a record to `All`. The value of `AccessLevel` must be more permissive than the organization-wide default or a run-time exception is thrown.
- **RowCause:** The purpose of the `RowCause` field is to track the origin of the sharing rule. Valid values are Manual (the default) or a custom sharing reason, defined on the object in the Apex Sharing Reasons related list. Manual sharing rules can be edited and removed by the record owner and are reset when record ownership changes. Sharing records with a custom reason are not reset when ownership changes and cannot be edited or removed without the administrative permission Modify All Data.

Restrictions

Two important restrictions exist on Apex managed sharing:

- Objects with an organization-wide default sharing level of Public Read/Write, the most permissive setting, cannot use Apex managed sharing. Set the level to Private or Public Read Only instead.
- After a sharing record is created, the only field that can be updated is the access level. If you need to change other fields, delete the sharing record entirely and re-create it.

Caution

When the organization-wide sharing default is changed for an object, all sharing rules are recalculated. This causes your Apex managed sharing rules to be deleted. To re-create them, you must implement an Apex class to participate in the recalculation event. This code uses the Apex batch processing feature to allow processing of millions of records in smaller groups of records, to stay within governor limits. The Apex batch processing functionality is covered in Chapter 9, "Batch Processing."

Creating Sharing Rules in Apex

Figure 6-8 shows the Force.com managed sharing settings for the Project object, configured in Chapter 3. The sharing rules specify that projects owned by members of one role are shared by all users in that role. This is defined three times because three separate roles exist, one for each region in the sample company.

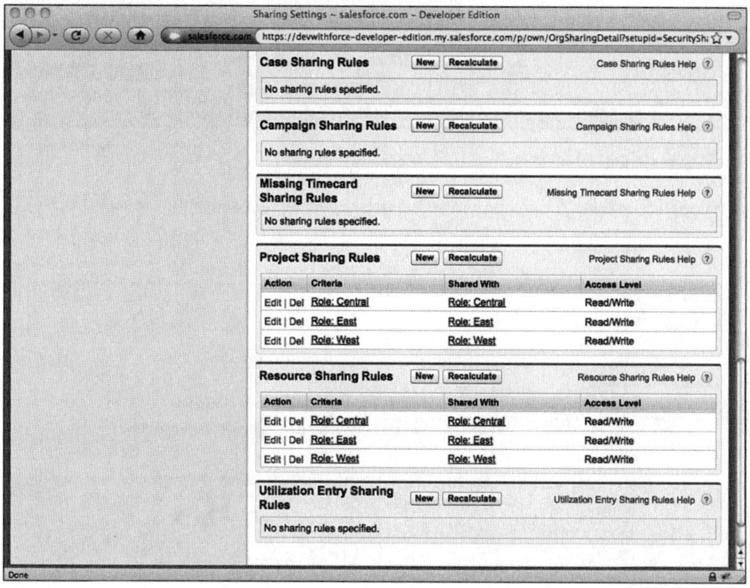

Figure 6-8   Sharing rules for Project object

Navigate to an individual Project record and click the Sharing button. Figure 6-9 is an example of the resulting screen. It lists the sharing rules in effect for this record. The first sharing rule is the default one, specifying that the owner has full control over the record. The second is the sharing rule maintained by Force.com managed sharing, configured using the screen shown in Figure 6-8, which allows users in the same role (Central) to edit the record.

You've visited screens in the native user interface where record sharing is taking place. Next, look a level deeper at the data driving the sharing behavior. Open the Force.com IDE's Schema Explorer and run the query shown in Listing 6-21. It illustrates how Force.com stores the information for the sharing rules in Figure 6-9 and what you will be manipulating with Apex managed sharing.

Listing 6-21   **SOQL Query on Project Share Object**

```
SELECT ParentId, UserOrGroupId, AccessLevel
  FROM Proj__Share
  WHERE Parent.Name = 'GenePoint'
```

Figure 6-10 is the result of running the query. Note that the identifiers in your Force.com organization will be different from those in the figure.

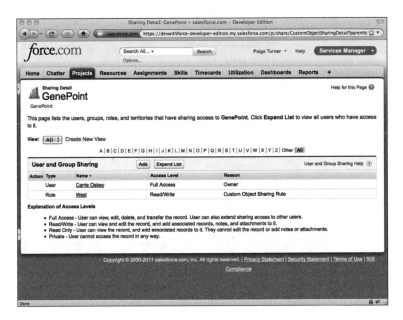

Figure 6-9   Sharing detail for Project record

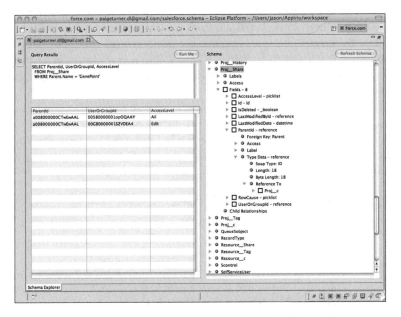

Figure 6-10   Results of SOQL query on Project Share object

Try to decode the meaning of each record. The `ParentId` field contains the unique identifier of the record being shared. The query has filtered by the name GenePoint, which is a Project record. The `UserOrGroupId` field contains the unique identifier of a User or Group record. The `AccessLevel` field is one of the four access levels (All, None, Edit, View), although only Edit and View can be set using Apex managed sharing.

The first record has All access, so it's the default sharing rule granting the owner of the record full access. The second record might be a mystery at first. The `UserOrGroupId` does not match up with the unique identifier of the Central region's role record. Run the query shown in Listing 6-22 to track down the meaning of this value.

Listing 6-22   **SOQL Query on Group Object**

```
SELECT Id, Type, RelatedId
  FROM Group
```

The Group object stores information about Roles and other groups in Force.com. Figure 6-11 displays the results of the query. The `RelatedId` field contains the same value as the `UserOrGroupId` value of the second sharing record. This is where Force.com

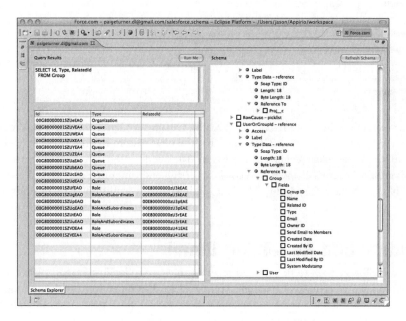

Figure 6-11   Results of SOQL query on Group object

managed sharing has stored the fact that the Project record named GenePoint is shared with other members of the Central role.

Apex managed sharing allows you to insert new rows into the `Proj__Share` object, and other sharing objects, and specify custom sharing reasons that are meaningful to your application. Custom sharing reasons are maintained for each object individually. To try adding one, go to the App Setup area and click Create → Objects and select the Project object. Scroll to the bottom of the page. In the Apex Sharing Reasons list, add a new reason with a label of My Sharing Reason. Force.com automatically suggests a Name, converting spaces to underscores. Refer to the custom sharing reason in your Apex code by adding __c to the end of the name.

Listing 6-23 contains sample code you can run in the Execute Anonymous view. It shares the GenePoint record with an additional user, specifying the custom sharing reason, with read-only access.

Listing 6-23   **Inserting Sharing Rule on Project Object**

```
User tim = [ SELECT Id FROM User
  WHERE Name = 'Tim Barr' LIMIT 1 ];
Proj__c genePoint = [ SELECT Id FROM Proj__c
  WHERE Name = 'GenePoint' LIMIT 1 ];
Proj__Share share = new Proj__Share(
  ParentId = genePoint.Id,
  UserOrGroupId = tim.Id,
  rowCause = Proj__Share.rowCause.My_Sharing_Reason__c,
  AccessLevel = 'Read');
insert share;
```

After executing this code, refresh the Sharing Details for GenePoint and you should see the screen shown in Figure 6-12. It shows that the new custom sharing rule has been added. Because the sharing rule was created by Apex code and uses a custom sharing reason, it's preserved across changes of record ownership and cannot be edited or deleted by users unless they have the Modify All Data administrative permission in their profile.

Sending and Receiving Email

Force.com allows emails to be sent and received in Apex code. This functionality can be helpful in many scenarios. For example, you could send an email from within a trigger to notify users of events occurring in the application, such as work that requires their attention. You could write code to automate the classification of incoming emails to customer support, searching for keywords and routing them to the proper support employees. This section describes how to use the objects and methods built in to Apex to process inbound and outbound email and introduces the administration screens of the native user interface that support them.

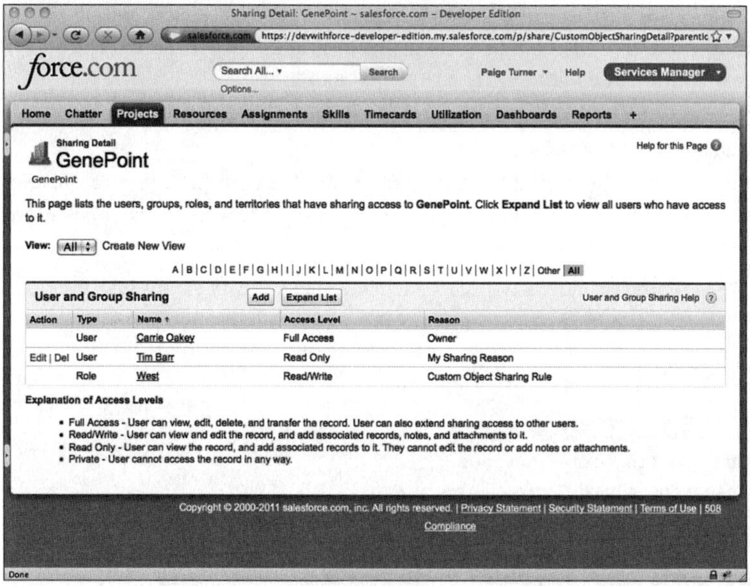

Figure 6-12   Sharing detail for Project record with Apex managed sharing
rule

Sending Email

The three ways to send email in Apex are the following:

- **SingleEmailMessage:** Sends an email to up to ten receivers. The email addresses of receivers are provided as strings. A string containing HTML or plain text is used as the message body.

- **SingleEmailMessage with Template:** Sends to up to ten receivers, but the unique identifiers of Contact, Lead, or User objects must be used instead of strings to provide the receivers' email addresses. The message body is constructed from a template. Templates are globally available to an organization as defined by an administrator or private to an individual user. Templates can include merge fields to dynamically substitute field values from the receiver's record and, optionally, field values from an additional, related object.

- **MassEmailMessage:** Behaves like a SingleEmailMessage with template but can send email to up to 250 receivers in a single call.

Each of these three ways of sending email contributes toward the maximum of 10 email calls within a single context, an instance of running Apex code. To translate that to the number of email messages, if you use the SingleEmailMessage object with 10 recipients, you can reach a maximum of 100 recipients (10 recipients times the 10 invocation maximum) within a single execution of your program. You can reach 2,500 recipients using the

`MassEmailMessage`. Force.com imposes a daily limit on mass emails, which varies based on the edition of Force.com being used. If this limit is exceeded, an exception is thrown with the exception code `MASS_MAIL_LIMIT_EXCEEDED`.

Using `SingleEmailMessage`

You can run the code in Listing 6-24 directly in the Execute Anonymous view. It looks up the User record for the current user and sends a test message to its email address.

Listing 6-24   **Sending Email**

```
User you = [ SELECT Email
  FROM User
  WHERE Id = :UserInfo.getUserId()
  LIMIT 1 ];
Messaging.SingleEmailMessage mail =
  new Messaging.SingleEmailMessage();
mail.setToAddresses(new String[] { you.Email });
mail.setSubject('Test message');
mail.setPlainTextBody('This is a test');
Messaging.sendEmail(new Messaging.SingleEmailMessage[] { mail });
```

Check the email account associated with your Force.com user for the new message. If you do not see the message, it might be in your junk mail folder. If it's not in your inbox or junk mail folder, your email server might have refused its delivery. In this case, Force.com will send you the returned message with any delivery error information, given that you are both the sender and the receiver.

> **Note**
>
> Force.com provides online tools to help you authorize its mail servers to ensure that its messages are delivered. Go to the Administration Setup area and click Email Administration → Deliverability and Test Deliverability for more information.

Notice that the sender and receiver of the email are identical. You have sent a message to yourself via Force.com. By default, Apex email methods run using the identity of the current user. The current user's email address becomes the "from" address in outbound emails. Alternatively, you can define an organization-wide email address and use it to set the "from" address. This enables all of your outbound emails to be sent from a single set of authorized, public email addresses. To define an organization-wide email address, go to the Administration Setup area and click Email Administration → Organization-Wide Addresses.

Using `SingleEmailMessage` **with Template**

Templates standardize the appearance and content of emails. They also make including dynamic content in messages without cumbersome, hard-to-maintain code full of string concatenations simple. To add a new email template, go to the Personal Setup area and click Email → My Templates.

When a template is used to send a message, you must provide a `targetObjectId` value. This is the unique identifier of a Lead, Contact, or User record. The email address associated with this record becomes the recipient of the email.

Optionally, a `whatId` can be provided. This is the unique record identifier of an Account, Asset, Campaign, Case, Contract, Opportunity, Order, Product, Solution, or any custom object. The fields from this record can be referenced in your template using merge fields. When the message is sent, the record is retrieved and its data substituted into the message body in the locations specified by the merge fields.

Listing 6-25 sends an email using a template. Before trying it, create a template with the unique name of `Test_Template`. Set its text or HTML content to `Hello {!User.FirstName}!` or the equivalent to demonstrate the use of merge fields. Mark the template as available for use. In Listing 6-25, a SOQL query is used to retrieve the template's unique identifier so that it isn't hard-coded into the program.

Listing 6-25   **Sending Email Using Template**

```
User you = [ SELECT Email
  FROM User
  WHERE Id = :UserInfo.getUserId()
  LIMIT 1 ];
EmailTemplate template = [ SELECT Id
  FROM EmailTemplate
  WHERE DeveloperName = 'Test_Template'
  LIMIT 1 ];
Messaging.SingleEmailMessage mail =
  new Messaging.SingleEmailMessage();
mail.templateId = template.Id;
mail.targetObjectId = you.Id;
mail.setSaveAsActivity(false);
Messaging.sendEmail(new Messaging.SingleEmailMessage[] { mail });
```

> **Note**
>
> The `setSaveAsActivity` method was called in Listing 6-25 to disable the HTML email tracking feature, which is not compatible with the User object (`targetObjectId`). The `setSaveAsActivity` method is described in the subsection titled, "Additional Email Methods."

Using `MassEmailMessage`

Mass emails can be sent to 250 recipients in a single method call. The code for sending a mass email is similar to that for sending a single email with a template. The difference is that a `MassEmailMessage` object is created instead of a `SingleEmailMessage`. At minimum, you must provide a value for `targetObjectIds` (an array of Lead, Contact, or User record unique identifiers) and a `templateId`.

Optionally, you can provide `whatIds`, an array of record unique identifiers corresponding to the array of `targetObjectIds`. Field values from these records add dynamic content to the message body. The records are limited to Contract, Case, Opportunity, and Product types. Note that none of these object types are available in a Force.com platform-only license.

Listing 6-26 demonstrates the use of the `MassEmailMessage`. It selects one Contact in the system and sends an email using the same template created for Listing 6-25.

Listing 6-26   **Sending a Mass Email**

```
User you = [ SELECT Email
  FROM User
  WHERE Id = :UserInfo.getUserId()
  LIMIT 1 ];
EmailTemplate template = [ SELECT Id
  FROM EmailTemplate
  WHERE DeveloperName = 'Test_Template'
  LIMIT 1 ];
Messaging.MassEmailMessage mail = new Messaging.MassEmailMessage();
mail.templateId = template.Id;
mail.targetObjectIds = new Id[] { you.Id };
mail.setSaveAsActivity(false);
Messaging.sendEmail(new Messaging.MassEmailMessage[] { mail });
```

Transactional Email

The transactional behavior of the `sendEmail` method is consistent with that of Force.com database DML methods. When an invocation of Apex code is completed without error, email is sent. If an uncaught error causes the program to be terminated prematurely, email is not sent. If multiple emails are sent, by default they all fail if one fails. Setting the optional `opt_allOrNone` parameter of the `sendEmail` method to `false` enables partial success of a group of outbound messages. In this case, the `sendEmail` method returns an array of `SendEmailResult` objects. These objects can be used to determine the success or failure of each message and include error details in case of failure.

Additional Email Methods

The following list describes useful methods that apply to both `SingleEmailMessage` and `MassEmailMessage` objects:

- **setCcAddresses:** This method accepts a string array of email addresses to carbon copy on the email.

- **setSenderDisplayName:** The sender display name is shown in email reading programs as a label for the sender email address.

- **setReplyTo:** The reply-to address is the email address designated to receive replies to this message. If not specified, it's always the sender's email address.

- **setBccSender:** If this is set to `true`, Force.com blind-carbon-copies the sender's email address. In a mass email, the sender is copied only on the first message. Force.com prevents use of this feature if an administrator has enabled Compliance BCC Email. You can do this in the Administration Setup area by clicking Email Administration → Compliance BCC Email.

- **setUseSignature:** By default, Force.com appends the sending user's signature to the end of outbound emails. You can edit this signature in the Personal Setup area by clicking Email → My Email Settings. To turn off this feature, pass `false` to this method.

- **setFileAttachments:** The argument to this method is an array of `EmailFileAttachment` objects. These objects contain the names and data of attachments to be sent with the message. They provide a method to set the attachment body (`setBody`) and filename (`setFileName`). The total size of the attachments for a single message cannot exceed 10MB.

- **setDocumentAttachments:** Force.com has a native object type for storing content called Document. You can find it in the native user interface by clicking the Documents tab. Here you can create, edit, and delete Documents and group them into folders. Each Document record has a unique identifier, and this method accepts an array of them. Each Document specified is sent as an attachment to the message. All attachments in a single message, including file attachments, cannot exceed 10MB.

- **setOrgWideEmailAddressId:** Use this method to specify the unique identifier of an organization-wide email address. This email address is used as the "from" address rather than the address of the current user. To define organization-wide email addresses and obtain their unique identifiers, go to the Administration Setup area and click Email Administration → Organization-Wide Addresses.

- **setSaveAsActivity:** Force.com's outbound email can be configured to track the behavior of email recipients who are Leads or Contacts in the system. This is accomplished with an invisible image embedded in messages sent using templates. When receivers who haven't blocked multimedia content in their email readers open the message, the Force.com service is contacted and tracks this information. By visiting the receiver's Lead or Contact record, you can see the date the email was first opened, the number of times it was opened, and the date it was most recently opened. By default, this setting is enabled. To disable or enable it for the organization, go to the App Setup area and click Customize → Activities → Activity Settings and select Enable Email Tracking. To disable it for a specific message, pass `false` to this method.

Receiving Email

The two steps for configuring Force.com to process inbound emails are:

1. Write an Apex class that implements a specific interface (`Messaging.InboundEmailHandler`) and method (`handleInboundEmail`). This provides your code access to the envelope (`Messaging.InboundEnvelope`) and content

(`Messaging.InboundEmail`) of inbound emails, including mail headers and attach-ments. It is otherwise standard Apex code with no special restrictions. The return value of this method is a `Messaging.InboundEmailResult`. To indicate processing failure, set the `success` field of this object to `false`. Any explanatory message set in the `message` field is returned to the sender as an email response.

2. Create an Email Service using the native user interface. An Email Service is associ-ated with one or more Force.com-issued email addresses that serve as the gateways to your Apex class. When email arrives at the email address, your Apex class is invoked to process it.

If your Apex code fails with an uncaught exception while processing an incoming email, Force.com treats the email as undeliverable. This is much like a mail gateway behaves when presented with an unknown recipient email address. An email is returned to the sender with diagnostic information about the problem, including the error message from your Apex code.

To personalize email processing based on the identity of the sender, use one of these strategies:

- Have all users share a single inbound email address. Your Apex code reads the sender's "from" address and customizes behavior based on that, perhaps by querying Contact or Lead for more information about them.

- Issue each user or group of users a unique email address. Your Apex code can adjust its behavior based on the "to" address of the incoming message.

> **Caution**
>
> There are governor limits on inbound email. The maximum size of each inbound message, attachments included, is 10MB. The maximum size of each message body, text and HTML combined, is 100KB. The maximum size of each binary attachment is 5MB and 100KB for text attachments. The maximum heap size for Apex email handlers is 18MB. If any of these limits are reached, your Apex code will not be invoked, and the offending message will be returned to its sender.

Getting Started with Inbound Email Processing

Follow these next steps to create a new Apex class to process inbound email in the Force.com IDE. This is a simple example that sends a reply to the inbound message with the original message quoted in the body.

1. Make sure your Force.com project is selected and click New → Apex Class in the File menu.

2. Enter MyEmailService for the name and select the Inbound Email Service template.

3. Click the Finish button. Enter the code given in Listing 6-27, skipping the class and method declarations because they are provided by the template.

Listing 6-27   **Receiving Email**

```
global class MyEmailService implements
  Messaging.InboundEmailHandler {
  global Messaging.InboundEmailResult
    handleInboundEmail(Messaging.InboundEmail email,
      Messaging.InboundEnvelope envelope) {
    Messaging.InboundEmailResult result = new
      Messaging.InboundEmailresult();
    Messaging.SingleEmailMessage outbound = new
      Messaging.SingleEmailMessage();
    outbound.toAddresses = new String[] { email.replyTo };
    outbound.setSubject('Re: ' + email.subject);
    outbound.setHtmlBody('<p>This reply was generated by Apex.'
      + 'You wrote:</p><i>' + email.plainTextBody + '</i>');
    Messaging.sendEmail(new Messaging.SingleEmailMessage[]
      { outbound });
    return result;
  }
}
```

4. In the native user interface, go to the App Setup area and click Develop → Email Services.

5. Click the New Email Service button.

6. Enter a service name. Enter **MyEmailService** as the Apex Class. Leave the other options set to their defaults and click the Save button.

7. Click the Activate button. Then click the New Email Address button to create a Force.com-generated email address.

8. This screen allows you to whitelist email addresses and domains that are allowed to use this email service. By default, it's configured to allow emails only from the current user's email address. Accept this setting by clicking the Save button.

9. You should now see an email address listed at the bottom of the page, as shown in Figure 6-13. Copy the address to your Clipboard, open your favorite email application, and send a test message to this address. Within a minute, you should receive an email in response, generated by your Apex class.

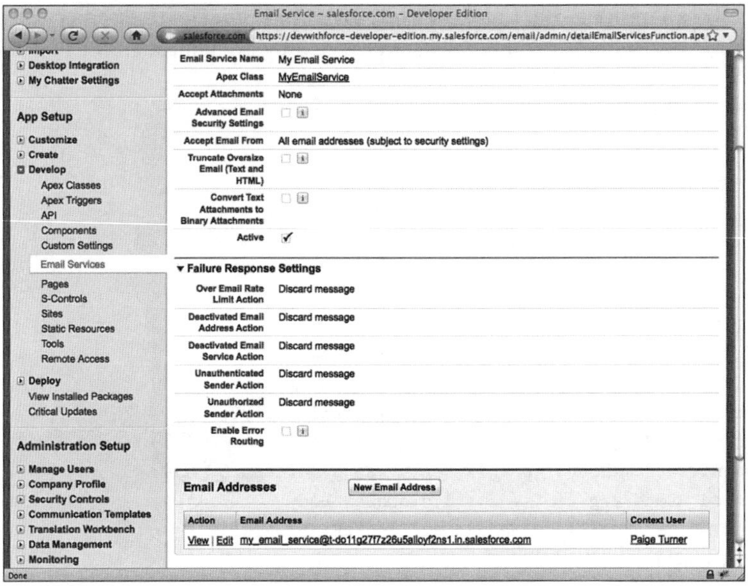

Figure 6-13   Email service configuration

Dynamic Apex

Dynamic Apex describes features of Apex that bypass its typically strongly typed nature. For example, database queries, objects, and fields are part of the language, and references to them are strongly typed, validated at compile time. Dynamic Apex allows you to work with these objects as ordinary strings rather than compiled parts of your program. This has its advantages in that your program can be more dynamic and generic. It also has disadvantages, the primary one being that your code can suffer a greater variety of errors at runtime.

This section describes two dynamic Apex features. Dynamic database queries are SOQL and SOSL queries executed at runtime from strings rather than from compiled code. Schema metadata allows Apex code to introspect the structure of the Force.com database, including its objects, fields, and relationships.

Dynamic Database Queries

In Chapter 5, you learned about bind variables. They are variables whose values are injected into SOQL and SOSL statements in predefined locations, notated with colons. But bind variables are not powerful enough to support an entirely dynamic WHERE clause, one that includes conditional filters added and subtracted based on the behavior of the program. You could write every combination of WHERE clause and use long strings of conditional statements to pick the right one. An alternative is a completely dynamic query, executed using the `Database.query` method.

Listing 6-28 provides an example of two dynamic queries. The first is on the Resource object. The results of the query are returned in list of `Resource__c` objects. Other than the dynamic query itself, this code should be familiar. The second query selects Project records but treats them as a list of SObject objects.

Listing 6-28   **Dynamic SOQL Queries**

```
List<Resource__c> resources = Database.query(
  'SELECT Id, Name FROM Resource__c');
for (Resource__c resource : resources) {
  System.debug(resource.Id + ' ' + resource.Name);
}
List<SObject> projects = Database.query('SELECT Id, Name FROM Proj__c');
for (SObject project : projects) {
  System.debug(project.get('Id') + ' ' + project.get('Name'));
}
```

The SObject is a typeless database object. It allows you to interact with database records without declaring them as a specific type. The get method of the SObject allows the retrieval of a field value by name. The getSObject method returns the value of a related object. These values also have setter methods: set and setSObject. Used in conjunction with DML statements or database DML methods, you can write generic code that operates on a series of database objects. This is particularly useful when you have several objects with the same field names because it can reduce the amount of code.

> **Tip**
>
> Use the escapeSingleQuotes of the String object to prevent SOQL injection attacks. This method adds escape characters (\) to all single quotation marks in a string.

SOSL queries can also be constructed and executed dynamically. The Search.query method returns a list of lists containing SObjects. Listing 6-29 provides an example of its use.

Listing 6-29   **Dynamic SOSL Query**

```
List<List<SObject>> result = Search.query(
  'FIND \'Chicago\' '
  + 'RETURNING Resource__c(Name), Proj__c(Name)');
for (List<SObject> records : result) {
  for (SObject record : records) {
    System.debug(record.get('Name'));
  }
}
```

The SOSL query returns the names of Project and Resource records containing the word *Chicago*. The outer loop is executed for each type of object specified in the

RETURNING clause. The inner loop runs over the matching records of that object type. For example, the first iteration of the loop assigns records to a list of Resource records that matched the search term. The second iteration assigns it to the matching Project records.

> **Note**
> Dynamic queries have all the same governor limits as their static counterparts.

Schema Metadata

Schema metadata is information about the Force.com database, available to your Apex code dynamically, at runtime. It has many potential uses, such as customizing the behavior of Apex code installed in multiple organizations, driving the construction of dynamic queries, or verifying that the database is configured in a certain way. This section describes the five types of schema metadata (object, field, child relationship, picklist, and record type) and includes code that can be run in the Execute Anonymous view to demonstrate accessing them.

> **Note**
> You are limited to a maximum of 100 calls to schema metadata methods. All five types of schema metadata methods contribute equally to the limit.

Object Metadata

Object metadata is information about the database objects in the Force.com organization. It includes custom as well as standard objects. Listing 6-30 provides an example of retrieving object metadata. The metadata of all objects in the database is retrieved, and their names and labels are printed to the debug log.

Listing 6-30   **Retrieving Object Metadata**

```
Map<String, Schema.SObjectType> objects = Schema.getGlobalDescribe();
Schema.DescribeSObjectResult objInfo = null;
for (Schema.SObjectType obj : objects.values()) {
  objInfo = obj.getDescribe();
  System.debug(objInfo.getName() + ' [' + objInfo.getLabel() + ']');
}
```

Field Metadata

Field metadata provides access to all the attributes of fields you configure on a database object. Listing 6-31 demonstrates how to access field metadata. The fields of the Proj__c object are retrieved, including standard and custom fields. The getDescribe method is invoked on each to return its metadata, a Schema.DescribeFieldResult object. The name, label, data type, precision, and scale of each field is displayed in the debug log.

Listing 6-31   **Retrieving Field Metadata**

```
Map<String, Schema.SObjectField> fields =
  Schema.SObjectType.Proj__c.fields.getMap();
Schema.DescribeFieldResult fieldInfo = null;
for (Schema.SObjectField field : fields.values()) {
  fieldInfo = field.getDescribe();
  System.debug(fieldInfo.getName()
  + ' [' + fieldInfo.getLabel() + '] '
  + fieldInfo.getType().name()
  + '(' + fieldInfo.getPrecision()
  + ', ' + fieldInfo.getScale() + ')');
}
```

Child Relationship Metadata

Child relationship metadata contains the child's object type, the relationship name, and an object identifying the field in the child object that relates it to the parent. Listing 6-32 demonstrates the retrieval of child relationship metadata from the Resource object. Compare the results to what you see in the Force.com IDE's Schema Explorer for the Resource object.

Listing 6-32   **Retrieving Child Relationship Metadata**

```
Schema.DescribeSObjectResult res = Resource__c.SObjectType.getDescribe();
List<Schema.ChildRelationship> relationships = res.getChildRelationships();
for (Schema.ChildRelationship relationship : relationships) {
  System.debug(relationship.getField() + ', ' + relationship.getChildSObject());
}
```

Picklist Metadata

Picklist metadata provides access to the master list of available picklist values for a picklist or multi-select picklist field. It does not include the assignments of picklist values to record types, nor does it provide any information about the relationship between picklist values in dependent picklists. Listing 6-33 is an example of its use, printing the picklist values of the Skill object's Type field to the debug log.

Listing 6-33   **Retrieving Picklist Metadata**

```
Schema.DescribeFieldResult fieldInfo =
  Schema.SObjectType.Skill__c.fields.Type__c;
List<Schema.PicklistEntry> picklistValues = fieldInfo.getPicklistValues();
for (Schema.PicklistEntry picklistValue : picklistValues) {
  System.debug(picklistValue.getLabel());
}
```

Record Type Metadata

Record type metadata contains the names and unique identifiers of record types defined on an object. It also indicates the availability of the record type to the current user (isAvailable) and whether the record type is the default record type for the object (isDefaultRecordTypeMapping).

Listing 6-34 provides an example of using record type metadata. It retrieves the record types in the Resource object and prints their names to the debug log.

Listing 6-34   **Retrieving Record Type Metadata**

```
Schema.DescribeSObjectResult sobj = Resource__c.SObjectType.getDescribe();
List<Schema.RecordTypeInfo> recordTypes = sobj.getRecordTypeInfos();
for (Schema.RecordTypeInfo recordType : recordTypes) {
  System.debug(recordType.getName());
}
```

Custom Settings in Apex

You are not limited to using the native user interface for managing data in custom settings, as demonstrated in Chapter 4, "Additional Database Features." Custom settings can also be created, updated, and deleted using standard DML methods. This means you can build your own user interfaces for managing them, or use them to store frequently accessed, simple configuration values needed by your programs. Force.com provides increased performance for custom settings access versus ordinary database access, and custom settings are exempt from the governor limits placed on database access. For example, you might use a custom setting named Debug as a global switch to enable verbose logging within your Apex code.

To get started with custom settings in Apex, run the code in Listing 6-35. It inserts a custom setting record, setting its name and its field value. It assumes you already have defined a List type custom setting object named ConfigSetting containing a single Boolean field named Debug.

Listing 6-35   **Creating a Custom Setting Record**

```
insert new ConfigSetting__c(Name = 'Default', Debug__c = false);
```

Now that your custom setting has a value, try retrieving it. Run the code in Listing 6-36 in the Force.com IDE's Execute Anonymous view.

Listing 6-36   **Retrieving a Custom Setting Value**

```
ConfigSetting__c cfg = ConfigSetting__c.getValues('Default');
System.debug(cfg.Debug__c);
```

The first line retrieves the named record, Default, which you created in Listing 6-35. The second line prints the value of the custom field to the debug log. You can also retrieve a Map of all fields and values using the getAll method.

To update a custom setting value, retrieve it by name, and then update it as you would a database record. Listing 6-37 provides an example.

Listing 6-37   **Updating a Custom Setting Record**

```
ConfigSetting__c cfg = ConfigSetting__c.getValues('Default');
cfg.Debug__c = false;
update cfg;
```

You can also delete custom setting records using the delete DML method, as shown in Listing 6-38.

Listing 6-38   **Deleting a Custom Setting Record**

```
ConfigSetting__c cfg = ConfigSetting__c.getValues('Default');
delete cfg;
```

Hierarchy type custom settings allow a user or profile to be related to them. If no user or profile is specified, they become organization-wide defaults. The code in Listing 6-39 assumes you have created a Hierarchy type custom setting named Hierarchy with a single text field named Field. It creates a new record and relates it to the current user by setting the system field SetupOwnerId to the current user's unique identifier. This same field also accepts a profile unique identifier to make the custom setting apply to a profile instead of a user. And if SetupOwnerId is set to null, it becomes an organization-wide default.

Listing 6-39   **Creating a Hierarchy Type Custom Setting Record**

```
insert new HierarchySetting__c(
  SetupOwnerId = UserInfo.getUserId(),
  Field__c = 'My user preference value');
```

To retrieve a Hierarchy type custom setting value, use the getInstance method of the custom setting object. By default, it returns the "lowest" level of setting value, meaning the value most specific to the current user. If a user-level setting is available, it is returned. Otherwise, the return value is the setting associated with the user's profile. If no user or profile-level settings are present, the organization-wide default is returned. This behavior can be overridden by passing a user or profile unique identifier as an argument to the getInstance method.

Sample Application: Adding Email Notifications

This section applies your knowledge of Apex's outbound email features to enhance the Services Manager sample application. Many scenarios in Services Manager could benefit from email notifications. For example, consultants have requested that they get an email when a timecard is approved or rejected by their project managers.

To implement this change, add a trigger on the after update event of the Timecard object. If the new value of the Timecard's Status field is Approved or Rejected, query the Resource record that created the Timecard. Send an email notification of the change to the Resource.

Listing 6-40 is a sample implementation. It begins by checking to make sure that the updated Timecard contains a new value for the Status field and that the new status is either Approved or Rejected. If so, it makes three queries to retrieve data to send the notification email: the email address of the Resource logging the Timecard, the name of the Project, and the name of the user modifying the Timecard record. It constructs the email message and sends it.

Listing 6-40   **Email Notification Trigger on Timecard**

```
trigger handleTimecardNotifications
  on Timecard__c (after update) {
  for (Timecard__c timecard : trigger.new) {
    if (timecard.Status__c !=
      trigger.oldMap.get(timecard.Id).Status__c &&
      (timecard.Status__c == 'Approved' ||
      timecard.Status__c == 'Rejected')) {
      Resource__c resource =
        [ SELECT Contact__r.Email FROM Resource__c
          WHERE Id = :timecard.Resource__c LIMIT 1 ];
      Proj__c project =
        [ SELECT Name FROM Proj__c
          WHERE Id = :timecard.Project__c LIMIT 1 ];
      User user = [ SELECT Name FROM User
          WHERE Id = :timecard.LastModifiedById LIMIT 1 ];
      Messaging.SingleEmailMessage mail = new
        Messaging.SingleEmailMessage();
      mail.toAddresses = new String[]
        { resource.Contact__r.Email };
      mail.setSubject('Timecard for '
        + timecard.Week_Ending__c + ' on '
        + project.Name);
      mail.setHtmlBody('Your timecard was changed to '
        + timecard.Status__c + ' status by '
        + user.Name);
```

```
        Messaging.sendEmail(new Messaging.SingleEmailMessage[]
            { mail });
    }
  }
}
```

This implementation is not batch-safe. It makes four SOQL queries per Timecard. Even if this were addressed, the code could easily reach the limit of ten email invocations.

To fix this problem, you could change the code to use the `MassEmailMessage`, building a list of recipient Contact objects from the batch. Unfortunately, the `MassEmailMessage`'s `whatIds` field cannot be used with custom objects, so you'll have to forgo the customized message detailing the changes to the Timecard.

An alternative is to anticipate the governor limit. If a batch of Timecards requires more than ten email notifications, send the ten and suppress subsequent notifications.

Summary

This chapter has introduced some of the advanced features of Apex, features that you might not need in every application but that contribute to your knowledge of what is possible with Apex. Before moving on to the next chapter, consider these final points:

- Aggregate queries provide a standard, declarative way to perform calculations on groups of records in the database.
- Rules governing record sharing can be controlled in Apex code using Apex managed sharing.
- You can send and receive emails in Apex code. This provides your applications an additional way to interact with users.
- Although Apex features strongly typed database objects and queries, you can also write code that uses database resources dynamically. This carries with it the risk of runtime errors but opens up new possibilities of dynamic behavior to your applications. It is particularly powerful when writing custom user interfaces.
- You can read and write custom settings from Apex like any database object, but without the governor limits.

7

User Interfaces

Force.com's native user interface provides a consistent and simple way to search, create, update, and delete database records. It combines the definition of database objects with user interface metadata such as page layouts to produce user interfaces through configuration rather than code. For developers and administrators, this makes customization straightforward. For users, the uniformity means that learning to use one screen in Force.com provides the experience to learn all screens with minimal incremental effort.

For applications that require a greater level of control over the appearance and behavior of the user interface, Visualforce offers a solution. Visualforce is a technology in the Force.com platform for building custom user interfaces. Visualforce user interfaces can be built to look nothing like Force.com, exactly like Force.com, or your own unique blend of the two.

This chapter covers the basics of Visualforce in the following sections:

- **Introduction to Visualforce:** Learn the concepts and terminology of Visualforce.
- **Visualforce Controllers:** See how controllers contain the business logic that drives the user interface.
- **View Components:** Learn how view components define the appearance of Visualforce pages.
- **Visualforce and the Native User Interface:** Understand where and how Visualforce pages coexist with the native user interface of Force.com.
- **Visualforce in Production:** Look at how security, governor limits, error handling, and testing are handled with Visualforce.
- **Sample Application:** Implement a feature of the Services Manager sample application called the Skills Matrix. It is a Visualforce page for viewing and editing the skill sets of consultants.

Introduction to Visualforce

This section presents an introduction to Visualforce. It covers the following topics:

- **Overview of Visualforce:** Examine the pieces of Visualforce and how they're put together to aid in understanding this chapter and online reference materials.
- **Getting Started with Visualforce:** Take a brief look at how Visualforce development projects work, learn the tools for Visualforce development, and build a "hello world" example.

Overview of Visualforce

Visualforce is a combination of a page containing the presentation and Apex classes containing the business logic. The presentation is usually HTML rendered in the Web browser, but Visualforce also supports content types such as XML and PDF. HTML output is typically interactive, building up state by collecting user input across a series of related pages.

Force.com processes Visualforce pages on its servers. Only the final rendered page and partial page updates are returned to the Web browser—never the raw data or business logic. Contrast this with S-Controls, an older Force.com user interface technology, which consists of JavaScript programs generating HTML by querying Force.com entirely from within your Web browser.

> **Caution**
>
> Although S-Controls are still visible in the Force.com user interface, they should never be used for new development. Visualforce is the replacement technology for S-Controls and provides a superset of their functionality.

Visualforce is driven by metadata. It can use the definition of fields in the database to provide the appropriate user interface, without custom code. For example, a Visualforce page with an input field mapped to a Date field in the database is rendered with a calendar picker component, consistent with the Force.com native user interface.

The architecture of Visualforce follows the Model-View-Controller (MVC) pattern. This pattern dictates the separation of presentation (View), business logic (Controller), and data (Model). In Visualforce, business logic and data are combined in the controller, named after its MVC counterpart. The presentation lives in the page.

Figure 7-1 shows the relationship between the page and the controller in Visualforce, as well as some of Visualforce's internals.

Controller

The controller is Apex code that reads and writes data in the model, typically the Force.com database. The interaction of the controller with the user interface is accomplished through variables and action methods. Variables are exposed to the presentation layer through getter and setter methods. Getter methods allow the page to retrieve the

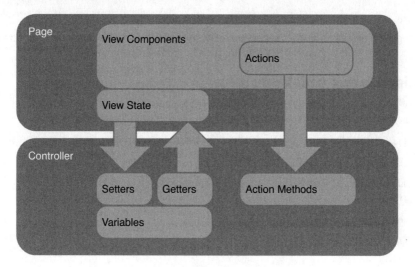

Figure 7-1   Visualforce architecture

value of a variable and display it for the user. Setter methods allow the user to modify the value of a variable through a user interface component such as a text input box.

Action methods perform the processing work on behalf of the user. They are wired up to buttons, links, and even asynchronous events on the user interface.

Force.com provides default controller implementations, called *standard controllers*. Standard controllers replicate the behavior of the native user interface, such as editing and creating records, but allow customization of its user interface without code. Custom behavior can be added to standard controllers using controller extensions, which are classes written in Apex. You can also implement a controller from scratch in Apex. This is called a *custom controller*.

Page

The Visualforce page defines the appearance of your user interface using a mixture of standard HTML and Visualforce-specific XML markup. The XML markup is used to add view components to the page. View components bind the controller to the page, defining how data and user actions are to be rendered in the user interface. Force.com provides a standard set of view components to support common HTML user interface patterns and supports user-defined components.

In Figure 7-1, the arrows between the page and the controller represent expressions. Expressions are embedded in view components to allow the page to reference methods in the controller or in system classes such as UserInfo. Expressions in Visualforce use the same language as formula fields in the database, with a special prefix and suffix added. For example, {!save} is an expression that invokes the save method of the controller.

> **Note**
> Visualforce maintains a strict separation of business logic and presentation. No business logic is allowed in a Visualforce page, not even for trivial formatting tasks.

Getting Started with Visualforce

This subsection offers a path to getting your hands on Visualforce, divided into three parts, as follows:

1. **Development Process:** Begin your development contrasting Visualforce with standard Web application development.

2. **Development Tools:** Take a look at Visualforce development in the Force.com IDE and the native user interface.

3. **"Hello World" Example:** Build your first Visualforce page with a custom controller.

Development Process

Visualforce development projects are much like standard Web application development projects. They have server-side logic to be coded, and user interfaces to be designed, wired up, and tested. User interface developers must collaborate closely with their server-side counterparts to make sure that the necessary data and logic is available to them. The user interfaces themselves are changing rapidly to satisfy the aesthetic and usability demands of project stakeholders.

Unlike with other Web application projects, Force.com eliminates much of the work of choosing and integrating Web frameworks. In terms of simply serving data-driven Web content, Force.com is the only framework you need. The important task then becomes strategizing on how best to use the platform to minimize custom development effort and maintenance cost while maximizing reuse and flexibility.

Walk through the native user interface and think carefully about what features you can reuse, extend, and override. Force.com offers a lot of user interface functionality by default and exposes a variety of hooks into it. Work with the native user interface where possible, rather than circumventing it. The further your project goes toward a fully custom user interface, the more work you spend to implement things that are potentially already provided, maintained, and constantly improved by Force.com.

Development Tools

The two tools for working with Visualforce are the native user interface and the Force.com IDE. The examples in this book can be built in either tool, but all screenshots are shown from the Force.com IDE.

In the native user interface, developers can enable a footer on the bottom of all Visualforce pages that includes syntax highlighting and an integrated help system. Called development mode, it's enabled on a per-user basis; you can enable it by visiting the Personal Setup area and clicking My Personal Information → Personal Information and checking both the Development Mode and Show View State in Development Mode boxes. You must have Customize Application permission enabled on your profile to select these options. With development mode enabled, you can create new Visualforce pages on the fly by visiting them (for example, /apex/myPage) as well as edit existing pages. Figure 7-2 shows an example of editing a Visualforce page in development mode.

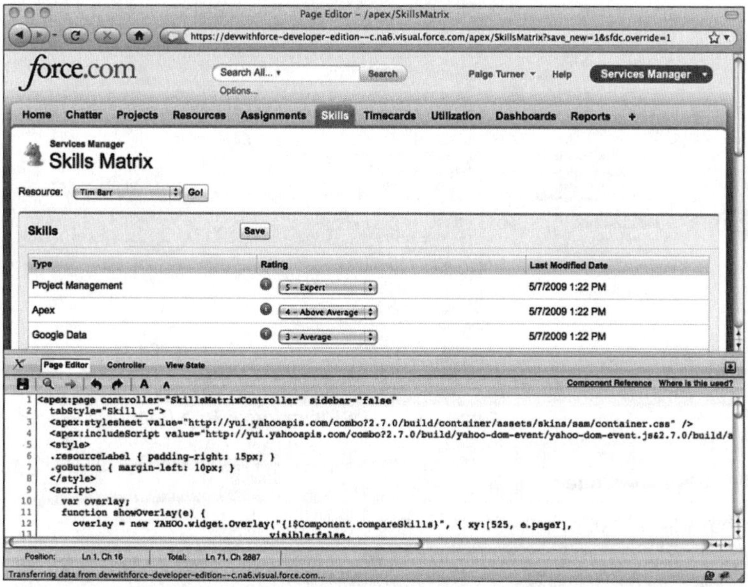

Figure 7-2   Visualforce page in development mode

Force.com IDE integrates Visualforce pages and controllers into the familiar Eclipse user interface. In Figure 7-3, the Visualforce page editor is active. You've already worked with the Force.com IDE to create triggers. Visualforce controllers are displayed in the folder named classes. Visualforce pages are in a separate folder named pages.

"Hello World" Example

To get a sense for Visualforce controllers and pages, follow these steps to create a simple working example.

1. Open Force.com IDE, select a Force.com project, and select File → New → Visualforce Page. Alternatively, you can right-click any object within a Force.com project to reach the New menu.

2. Enter **MyPage** for the label, press Tab, and click the Finish button.

3. In the page editor, enter the code shown in Listing 7-1. Do not save it yet. If you do, it will fail to compile because it references a controller class that doesn't exist.

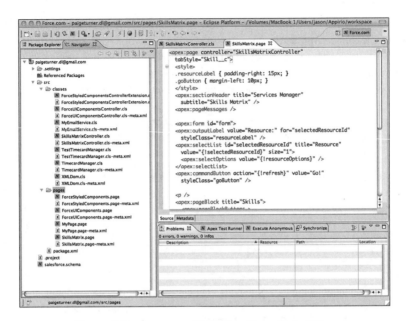

Figure 7-3   Force.com IDE's Visualforce Page Editor

Listing 7-1   **MyPage** **Code**

```
<apex:page controller="MyPageController">
  <apex:form>
    Your name: <apex:inputText value="{!name}" />
    <apex:outputText value="{!message}" />
    <apex:commandButton action="{!hello}" value="Say Hi" />
  </apex:form>
</apex:page>
```

4. Select File → New → Apex Class. Enter **MyPageController** for the name and click the Finish button.

5. In the Apex code editor, enter the code shown in Listing 7-2. Select File → Save All to save both the controller and the page code. Check the Problems view to make sure that there are no compilation errors.

Listing 7-2   **MyPageController** **Code**

```
public class MyPageController {
  public String name { get; set; }
  public String message { get; private set; }
  public PageReference hello() {
    message = 'Hello, ' + name;
```

```
    return null;
  }
}
```

6. In your Web browser, log in to Force.com and edit the URL to remove everything after the hostname, replacing it with /apex/MyPage. Your URL should look something like this: https://na6.salesforce.com/apex/MyPage. You should see your custom Visualforce page. Enter your name and click the Say Hi button to see the hello message.

Visualforce Controllers

Controllers provide the business logic behind Visualforce pages. They supply data to the page, accept input from users through the page, perform actions on behalf of the user, and redirect the browser to new pages. Controllers come in three flavors:

- **Standard Controllers:** Force.com provides default controller implementations called standard controllers. They contain the same functionality as found in the native user interface. No custom Apex code is involved in a standard controller.
- **Custom Controllers:** Custom controllers are the opposite of standard controllers, providing no default functionality and consisting entirely of custom Apex code.
- **Controller Extensions:** Controller extensions are the middle ground between standard and custom controllers. They begin with a standard controller and extend or override its functionality with custom Apex code.

Standard Controllers

Every database object, both standard and custom, has a standard controller. Its name is simply the name of the object. No Apex code exists for a standard controller. The controller implementation is already provided by Force.com.

Working with a Single Record

By default, the standard controller operates on a single record at a time. It receives this record from the id parameter in the URL. Try this for yourself by editing MyPage, the "hello world" example, to look like Listing 7-3.

Listing 7-3   **MyPage with Standard Controller**

```
<apex:page standardController="Proj__c">
  The current project is: {!Proj__c.Name}
  <apex:form >
    <apex:commandButton action="{!edit}" value="Edit {!Proj__c.Name}" />
```

```
    <apex:commandButton action="{!list}" value="Go To List" />
  </apex:form>
<apex:page>
```

If you visit the page in your browser (/apex/mypage) without providing an id, you'll see no current project named in the page. If you append an id value for a Project record (for example, /apex/MyPage?id=a008000000CTwEw), you can get the name of the project and working edit and list buttons.

Listing 7-3 demonstrates a few actions provided by the standard controller, leveraged using expression language in view components. For example, access to the current project record is provided through {!Proj__c}, and access to the navigation actions through {!edit} and {!list}. In general, the following expressions are available in a page that uses a standard controller:

- **Data:** {!id} is the unique identifier of the current record, and {!object} is the current record itself, where object is the lowercase name of your object. All fields of the object are automatically available, including related child objects but not parent objects.

- **Navigation:** {!cancel} navigates to the cancel page, {!edit} to the standard edit page, and {!view} to the standard view page.

- **Action and Navigation:** {!delete} deletes the current record and navigates to the standard delete page, and {!save} saves the current record and refreshes the page.

- **Action Only:** {!quicksave} saves the current record without navigation.

Working with Multiple Records

A variation of the standard controller exists called the standard set controller. It operates on a list of records rather than a single record. The list is produced by executing a view, a user-defined set of column names, filter criteria, and sort criteria for an object. To try it, replace your "hello world" example with the code given in Listing 7-4.

Listing 7-4   **MyPage with Standard Set Controller**

```
<apex:page standardController="Proj__c" recordSetVar="projects">
  <apex:repeat value="{!projects}" var="p">
    {!p.Name}<br />
  </apex:repeat>
</apex:page>
```

Visit /apex/myPage with your browser, and you'll see a list of all projects. Force.com has used the user's most recently executed view to obtain a list of project records, sorted by the first column in the view, even if that column is not displayed in the Visualforce page. The records are available to your page in the variable projects, specified by the page attribute `recordSetVar`. The `recordSetVar` indicates to Force.com that the standard set controller should be used.

The standard set controller allows you to work with up to 10,000 records at once and supports pagination with a variable page size. It also supports multiple selection and actions on a selected set of records.

The following expressions are valid in any page that uses a standard set controller:

- **Data:** The variable name you set in `recordSetVar` is bound to the current list of records, `{!selected}` is an array of SObjects that are selected, `{!resultsSize}` sets or gets the number of records currently displayed, and `{!completeResult}` is a Boolean containing `false` if more than 10,000 records exist.

- **Pagination:** Navigate across multiple pages of data using the `{!first}`, `{!last}`, `{!next}`, and `{!previous}` actions. `{!pageNumber}` sets or gets the current page number, and `{!pageSize}` sets or gets the number of records in a page. `{!hasPrevious}` returns `true` if a previous page exists, `{!hasNext}` returns `true` if a subsequent page exists.

- **Filters:** `{!filterId}` is the unique identifier of the currently selected filter (list view), and `{!listViewOptions}` is an array of SelectOption objects containing the names and identifiers of the available list views.

- **Navigation:** `{!cancel}` navigates to the cancel page, and `{!edit}` to the standard edit page.

- **Action and Navigation:** `{!delete}` deletes the current record and navigates to the standard delete page, and `{!save}` saves the current record and refreshes the page.

- **Action Only:** `{!quicksave}` saves the current record without navigation.

Custom Controllers

Custom controllers provide complete control over the behavior of a page with no default implementation. A custom controller is simply an Apex class designed to be bound to a Visualforce page. There is no new syntax to learn. At a high level, building a custom controller consists of defining the data to make available to the page and the actions that the page can invoke.

Exposing Data

The purpose of exposing data in a controller is to make it available to the page. Within a page, page components can use expressions to bind to it and render HTML or some other representation of the data. This binding is by reference, so data modified in the page can also be modified in the controller.

Simply making a variable public does not provide a Visualforce page access to it. The variable must have a getter method, a setter method, or both, depending on whether you intend to provide read-only or read and write access to the data.

For example, the page component inputText is an input and output component. It renders any existing or default value by invoking the getter and then invokes the setter to update the value after it is changed by the user and the page is submitted.

Expression language allows traversal of an object through dot notation, so providing separate getters and setters for every field in a database record, for example, is not necessary. Expose the object itself and use dot notation to access its fields. For example, the code in Listing 7-5 exposes a Project record for read-only access using the automatic properties feature of the Apex language. The read-only access is accomplished using the private access modifier keyword for the set accessor. Thanks to the Project getter, the page can contain expressions like {!proj.Name} and even {!proj.Account__r.BillingCity} because you've made the parent object's field available through a SOQL statement in the constructor.

Listing 7-5   **Custom Controller, Read-Only Access to Project Record**

```
public class MyPageController {
  public Proj__c proj { get; private set; }
  public MyPageController() {
    proj = [ SELECT Name, Account__r.BillingCity FROM Proj__c
      WHERE Name = 'Tim Barr' LIMIT 1 ];
  }
}
```

> **Caution**
>
> Placing business logic in the getter and setter methods is bad practice and, in many cases, prohibited at runtime. Make a habit of exposing data through Apex automatic properties rather than full getter or setter methods. Automatic properties do not allow a code body to be added.

Expressions are the closest you can get to business logic on the page without resorting to JavaScript. For example, you can combine expressions to form more complex expressions. The expression {!isVisible && isEditable} invokes both the getIsVisible and getIsEditable methods on the controller and evaluates to true if they are both true. Conditionals are also supported. For example, the condition expression {!IF(tabSelected, 'currentTab', 'secondaryPalette')} uses the value of the tabSelected method to determine whether to return one string (currentTab if true) versus another (secondaryPalette if false).

Writing Action Methods

Actions on a page are wired up to action methods in the controller, again by expression language. Action methods are public, nonstatic controller methods that return a PageReference object or null. If null, the current page is refreshed. If not, the PageReference is used to determine the location of the new page.

Actions have three purposes:

1. **Preserve View State:** The view state is maintained by Force.com within your page at runtime and posted back to its servers for the invocation of an action. It consists of the values of all of your controllers' accessible, nontransient variables. It allows you to build stateful interactions consisting of multiple pages without writing boilerplate code to copy values around in hidden fields, in the URL, or by using stateful patterns in the controller such as session objects, which are not supported by Force.com. You can opt out of actions entirely, redirecting the user at a browser level using standard HTML anchors and forms. But by doing so, you're circumventing some of the value provided by Visualforce and giving yourself extra work.

2. **Invoke Custom Logic:** Actions can perform some custom logic, such as using DML methods to upsert a record to the database. Other than the constructor, action methods are the only place you should write new business logic or call existing Apex code in a Visualforce controller.

3. **Trigger Page Navigation:** The `PageReference` object returned by an action determines the page to be refreshed in the browser. Construct a `PageReference` from a page name, such as `new PageReference('MyPage')`. The URL of the browser remains the same, but the body is refreshed with the contents of `MyPage`. This is not always desirable behavior, because a user can click the Reload button in the browser and potentially trigger the same action with the same input data. For example, this would result in duplicate records if the action code performs an insert DML operation. You can tell Force.com to redirect the user to the new page by calling the `setRedirect` method on the `PageReference` and passing `true`. A redirect updates the browser's URL and resets the view state, giving the user a fresh start and preventing any problems with the browser's Reload button.

Listing 7-6 is a sample controller to illustrate a common pattern in Visualforce: wrapping a database object with an Apex class. The wrapper object allows you to enhance a class for participation in user interface tasks, such as formatting data. In Listing 7-6, the wrapper exists to add a `selected` attribute. This attribute is bound to a checkbox view component, shown in Listing 7-7, allowing the user to select multiple items. The action can then perform a mass update based on the selection. In the sample code, it simply outputs the unique identifier of each selected Project record to the debug log.

Listing 7-6   **Controller with Wrapper Pattern**

```
public class MyPageController {
  public List<ResourceWrapper> resources { get; set; }
  public MyPageController() {
    resources = new List<ResourceWrapper>();
    List<Resource__c> records = [ SELECT Name FROM Resource__c ];
    for (Resource__c record : records) {
      resources.add(new ResourceWrapper(record));
```

```
    }
  }
  public PageReference doSomething() {
    for (ResourceWrapper wrapper : resources) {
      if (wrapper.selected) {
        System.debug(wrapper.data.Id);
      }
    }
    return null;
  }
  class ResourceWrapper {
    public Resource__c data { get; private set; }
    public Boolean selected { get; set; }
    public ResourceWrapper(Resource__c data) {
      this.data = data;
      this.selected = false;
    }
  }
}
```

Listing 7-7   **Page with Wrapper Pattern**

```
<apex:page controller="MyPageController">
<apex:form>
  <apex:pageBlock title="Sample Code">
    <apex:pageBlockButtons >
      <apex:commandButton action="{!doSomething}"
        value="Do Something" />
    </apex:pageBlockButtons>
    <apex:pageBlockTable
      value="{!resources}" var="resource">
      <apex:column headerValue="Selected">
        <apex:inputCheckbox value="{!resource.selected}" />
      </apex:column>
      <apex:column headerValue="Resource Name">
        {!resource.data.Name}
      </apex:column>
    </apex:pageBlockTable>
  </apex:pageBlock>
</apex:form>
</apex:page>
```

> **Tip**
>
> To clearly differentiate your controller code from triggers and other Apex code, adopt a naming convention and stick to it. A good one is to suffix your classname with the word *Controller,* so a controller class for `MyPage` becomes `MyPageController`.

Controller Extensions

The final type of controller is the controller extension. A controller extension is a custom controller that extends the behavior of a standard controller. Controller extensions are primarily used to integrate Visualforce more tightly with the native user interface. Many features of Visualforce integration such as overriding standard buttons are not supported for pages that use custom controllers.

Custom controllers can be easily retrofitted to become controller extensions. Multiple extensions can be used in a single page, enabling a large monolithic controller to be divided into smaller controllers by behavior, where some pages might use only a subset of the behaviors.

Listing 7-8 illustrates a trivial controller extension class, and Listing 7-9 shows a page that uses it. The only difference between it and a custom controller is that a constructor is required, allowing the standard controller (`StandardController` for a single record or `StandardSetController` for multiple records) to be passed to the class. In a page that uses the controller extension, all the built-in actions from the standard controller are available implicitly, without any code.

Listing 7-8   Sample Controller Extension with Single Action Method

```
public class MyPageController {
  private ApexPages.StandardController controller;
  public MyPageController(ApexPages.StandardController controller) {
    this.controller = controller;
  }
  public PageReference doSomething() { return null; }
}
```

Listing 7-9   Page Using Sample Controller Extension

```
<apex:page standardController="Resource__c"
  extensions="MyPageController">
  <apex:form>
    <apex:commandButton action="{!doSomething}"
      value="Do Something" />
  </apex:form>
</apex:page>
```

View Components

View components work with the controller to define the appearance and behavior of a Visualforce user interface. They connect variables in the controller to input and output elements such as text boxes and labels, and methods in the controller to action-oriented elements such as buttons and links. Force.com provides a library of standard view components to support common Web user interface design patterns.

This section contains the following subsections:

- **View Component Basics:** Here you'll learn how to add any view component to a page and some of their common characteristics. This material is preparation for the five subsections to follow, which cover specific types of standard view components.

- **Data Components:** Data components enable Visualforce pages to move data in and out of the controller using standard HTML elements.

- **Action Components:** Action components invoke methods on the controller, updating the view state and refreshing the page or navigating to a new page.

- **Primitive Components:** Several components exist with similar syntax to HTML tags, bridging the gap between Visualforce functionality and standard HTML.

- **Force.com-Styled Components:** These components allow Visualforce pages to inherit the appearance of the Force.com native user interface.

- **Force.com User Interface Components:** The Force.com UI components inherit the appearance of the native user interface as well as its behavior. They are large-scale building blocks for incorporating native Force.com user interface functionality wholesale into your custom pages.

View Component Basics

The three important areas to understand about view components are the following:

- **View Component Syntax:** View components are embedded in a Visualforce page using XML markup.

- **Page Definition:** Every user interface page must begin with the `page` component. All Visualforce components must be declared within the `page` component.

- **Component Visibility:** The `rendered` attribute, present on most components, allows conditional rendering of its HTML.

View Component Syntax

Adding view components to a Visualforce page involves constructing XML markup. The markup consists of three parts: the component name, an optional set of attributes, and an optional component body. Listing 7-10 is a sample usage of the view component `dataList`. It demonstrates all three parts of referencing a view component in a Visualforce page.

Listing 7-10   **Sample View Component Usage**

```
<apex:dataList value="{!resources}" var="resource">
  <b>{!resource.Name}</b>
</apex:dataList>
```

Component Name

The component name is specified in the name of the tag. The component is `dataList`, prefaced with the `apex` namespace to instruct Force.com that this is a standard view component. The `dataList` component renders an HTML list, which is a series of `LI` tags within a `UL` tag.

Attributes

Each view component has its own shape. The shape is the set of attributes accepted by the view component and their data types. Attribute values are either static names or expressions.

The `dataList` component iterates over the values in the controller, creating `LI` HTML tags for each. The `value` attribute specifies the source of these values. The value `{!resources}` is expression language syntax that retrieves the reference of the `resources` variable from the controller using its getter method, `getResources`. If this method is not available, its access modifier is not public, or it returns an incompatible data type, then the Visualforce page cannot be compiled. The `var` attribute specifies a variable name that can be referenced in the component body to access each element of the collection.

> ### Note
> Almost every Visualforce component accepts an `id` attribute. This attribute is used to provide a unique identifier to the component. The unique identifier can be used to obtain a reference to the component at runtime, from JavaScript or other Visualforce components. Chapter 8, "Advanced User Interfaces," includes more information on using the `id` attribute.

Component Body

The component body is the text between the start and the end of the XML tag. If no component body is specified, the tag is said to be self-closing. Each component can define its own treatment of the component body.

For example, `dataList` uses the component body to format its list elements. In the sample code, the name of each resource in the list is displayed in bold. The behavior of a self-closing instance of `dataList` depends on the collection type. If you pass a list of primitive types, Force.com can simply return their string representation in the page. But if you pass a list of complex types such as Resource records as in this example, how to dereference the records to produce text for the list items is not clear. If this example had no component body, a list of empty `LI` tags would be produced.

Page Definition

Every Visualforce user interface page must begin with the `page` component. Its main purpose is to connect the page to a controller and optionally override the global appearance of the page.

The `page` component requires either a standard or a custom controller to be specified. The `standardController` attribute is used to reference a standard controller, and its value is the name of a standard or custom object. Optionally, an `extensions` attribute can be provided with a comma-separated list of custom Apex classes that extend the standard controller. To specify a custom controller instead, set the `controller` attribute to the name of a custom controller class.

By default, pages are styled consistently with the Force.com native user interface. They include its stylesheet, sidebar, and header region containing application tabs, banner, and drop-down list of applications. You can override this behavior by setting the `standardStylesheets`, `sidebar`, and `showHeader` Boolean attributes.

Controlling Component Visibility

The `rendered` attribute is available on most standard Visualforce components. It is a Boolean value that indicates whether the component is included in the page. Setting `rendered` to `false` does not hide the component using CSS. It omits it entirely from the rendered page.

For some applications, this server-side approach to visibility is a strong alternative to CSS or JavaScript techniques such as using the `display: none` style directive to hide page elements. The `rendered` attribute is especially powerful when used in conjunction with the partial page refresh feature of Visualforce, discussed in Chapter 8.

Data Components

Data components allow fields and records from the Force.com database to be manipulated within a Visualforce page. They are divided into three categories:

- **Metadata-Aware Components:** The HTML rendered by these smart components varies based on the definition of the field. These components are valid only when bound to database objects.

- **Primitive Data Components:** If your field data is contained in a variable in Apex code rather than a database object, use primitive data components to render input and output HTML elements bound to their values.

- **Repeating Components:** If you have a list of any type of object, you can iterate over it with a repeating component to render its contents.

Metadata-Aware Components

Metadata-aware components use the definition of database objects to determine the appearance of the component on the page. There are two components: one for input (`inputField`) and one for output (`outputField`).

The `inputField` component displays the appropriate input element in HTML for the database field it's bound to. Its `value` attribute defines the binding. For example, an `inputField` bound to a picklist renders HTML including the valid picklist values and selected value. The `inputField` also provides a visual indicator when the database field is required, consistent with the native user interface. The `inputField` component must be contained within a `form` component. Listing 7-11 shows an example of its usage.

Listing 7-11   **Sample Usage of `inputField` Component**

```
<apex:form>
  <apex:inputField value="{!project.Stage__c}" />
</apex:form>
```

The `outputField` formats the value of a field using the correct pattern for that field's data type. For example, an `outputField` bound to a currency field displays the currency type and decimal point. The `value` attribute binds the component to data in the controller. In Listing 7-12, the page expression `{!project.Billable_Hours__c}` provides the source of data for the `outputField`.

Listing 7-12   **Sample Usage of `outputField` Component**

```
<apex:outputField value="{!project.Billable_Hours__c}" />
```

Primitive Data Components

Primitive data components add Visualforce functionality to standard HTML tags. Use these components when you are working with data that is not contained in a database object or when the standard Visualforce rendering or behavior is not desirable.

Table 7-1 describes the primitive data components. With the exception of `outputLabel`, all components listed in the table must be contained in a `form` component or a compilation error results.

Table 7-1   **Primitive Data Components**

Component	Sample Usage	Value Data Type	Sample HTML Output
outputLabel	`<apex:outputLabel value="outputLabel" />`	String	`<label>outputLabel </label>`
inputCheckbox	`<apex:inputCheckbox value= "{!booleanValue}" />`	Boolean	`<input type= "checkbox" checked="checked"/>`

Table 7-1   **Primitive Data Components**

Component	Sample Usage	Value Data Type	Sample HTML Output
`inputFile`	`<apex:inputFile value="{!blobValue}" />`	Blob	`<span>` `<input type="file"/>` `</span>`
`inputHidden`	`<apex:inputHidden value="{!hiddenValue}" />`	String	`<input type="hidden" value= "hiddenValue"/>`
`inputSecret`	`<apex:inputSecret value="{!secretValue}" />`	String	`<input type="pass- word" value=""/>`
`inputText`	`<apex:inputText value="{!textValue}" />`	String	`<input type="text" value= "textValue"/>`
`inputTextArea`	`<apex:inputTextArea value= "{!textAreaValue}" />`	String	`<textarea>textArea Value </textarea>`
`selectList`	`<apex:selectList value= "{!selectedItem}">` `<apex:selectOptions value="{!option Values}" />` `</apex:selectList>`	String or String[] if multiselect (selectList), SelectOption[] (select Options)	`<select size="1">` `<option value="">` `optionValue` `</option>` `</select>`
`selectRadio`	`<apex:selectRadio value= "{!selectedItem}">` `<apex:selectOptions value= "{!optionValues}" />` `</apex:selectRadio>`	String (select Radio), Select Option[] (select Options)	`<input type="radio"/>` `<label>optionValue</ label>`
`selectCheck boxes`	`<apex:selectCheckboxes value= "{!selectedItem}">` `<apex:selectOptions value=" {!optionValues}" />` `</apex:select Checkboxes>`	String or String[] if multiselect (selectCheck boxes), SelectOption[] (select Options) []	`<input type= "checkbox" />` `<label>optionValue </label>`

Repeating Components

Repeating components are bound to a list or set of values. They iterate over them, rendering the component body for each child in the collection.

The three types of repeating components are dataList, dataTable, and repeat. They all require two attributes: value, a binding to the collection, and var, the name of the variable that contains a reference to the current child.

The difference between the three components is in how the HTML is rendered. The dataList component is rendered as an HTML list, with each element of the collection rendered as a list item (LI tag). The dataTable component is rendered as an HTML table, with each element in a table row (TR tag). The repeat component provides no HTML formatting, leaving that entirely up to the Visualforce developer.

Listing 7-13 demonstrates usage of the repeat component to loop over the elements of the collection Skills__r. Each element of the collection is assigned to the variable skill. This variable is valid within the body of the repeat so that you can render its data—in this case, using an outputField component to display each child's Type__c field. A common use of the repeat component is in conjunction with a custom controller method that returns a list of records. You can iterate over the list with repeat, outputting HTML elements as you go.

Listing 7-13   **Sample Usage of repeat Component**

```
<apex:repeat value="{!Skills__r}" var="skill">
  <apex:outputField value="{!skill.Type__c}" />
</apex:repeat>
```

Action Components

Action components allow the page to invoke a method on the controller. The controller method typically performs some operation on the contents of the page, such as updating the database, and then either refreshes the page or navigates to a new page.

Before any refreshing or navigation takes place, the state of the user interface input elements on the page is injected into the variables of the controller using setters. This way, they are accessible from within your action code.

The two basic action components are commandButton and commandLink. The commandButton is rendered as an HTML button, whereas the commandLink is rendered as an anchor. Both are valid only inside a form component. They are typically used with an action attribute that specifies the name of the controller method to invoke or the URL of a new page to navigate to and a value attribute that displays a label to the user. Listing 7-14 is an example of using the commandButton, which invokes the doSomething method of the controller when clicked.

Listing 7-14   **Sample Usage of `commandButton` Component**

```
<apex:form>
  <apex:commandButton action="{!doSomething}"
    value="Do Something" />
</apex:form>
```

The `page` component also has an action, specified in the `init` attribute. This action is called automatically upon page load but should not be used for initialization code. Its purpose is to immediately redirect the user to a new page.

Before invoking a controller method, all action components perform validation on data components, accepting user input that is contained within their parent `form`. For example, if an input component is required but no value is provided, an error results. Errors can be displayed using the `pageMessages` or `messages` component (described in the "Error Handling" subsection of this chapter) and beside any `inputField` components if their database field is defined to do so. You can disable this validation behavior by setting the action component's `immediate` attribute to `true`.

Note

Visualforce includes actions that operate asynchronously, allowing modifications to the page without a full page refresh. These actions are discussed in Chapter 8.

Primitive Components

Many standard components mirror standard HTML tags, summarized in Table 7-2. These primitive components might seem unnecessary, because you can always write the equivalent HTML without using a Visualforce component. But one thing plain HTML cannot do is server-side conditional rendering.

Table 7-2   **Primitive Components**

Component	Sample Usage	Sample HTML Output
outputPanel	`<apex:outputPanel>` `outputPanel` `</apex:outputPanel>`	`<span>outputPanel</span>`
outputText	`<apex:outputText>` `outputText` `</apex:outputText>`	outputText
outputLink	`<apex:outputLink` `value="http://developer.` `force.com">` `Click here` `</apex:outputLink>`	`<a href="http://developer.` `force.com">Click here</a>`
image	`<apex:image` `value="myimage.png" />`	`<img src="myimage.png"/>`

Table 7-2   **Primitive Components**

Component	Sample Usage	Sample HTML Output
iframe	`<apex:iframe src="http://developer.force.com" />`	`<iframe width="100%" scrolling="no" height="600" frameborder="0" title="Content" src="http://developer.force.com"></iframe>`

With regular HTML, your markup always appears in the page, increasing its size and load time, and hiding it requires JavaScript or CSS. Visualforce provides the `rendered` attribute, allowing you to improve the performance of your pages by conditionally rendering markup based on the state of the controller.

There are two additional primitive components, `includeScript` and `stylesheet`. They both accept a `value` attribute to specify the URL of a script or stylesheet resource to load. These components do not have a `rendered` attribute, but using them instead of their HTML counterparts can improve page performance and maintainability. The script and stylesheets are included directly in the HTML HEAD tag for the page, which is not possible to do from a Visualforce page using HTML. Additionally, these components ensure that scripts and stylesheets are not duplicated on the page.

Force.com-Styled Components

Force.com's native user interface makes heavy use of CSS and JavaScript within its Web pages to provide a consistent look-and-feel across the platform. Many Visualforce components deliver this same styling to developers, without requiring any knowledge of Force.com's CSS or other implementation details. The following list groups these components into five categories based on their function:

- **Page Structure:** `sectionHeader`, `pageBlock`, `pageBlockSection`, and `pageBlockSectionItem` are the native structural elements used by Force.com to organize a page into a hierarchy of clearly identifiable sections, subsections, and sets of label/field pairs.
- **Action Containers:** `pageBlockButtons` and `toolbar/toolbarGroup` organize a series of buttons or links for performing actions on the page.
- **Table:** `pageBlockTable` is used like a `dataTable` but renders rows and columns in the Force.com native style.
- **Paging Components:** `panelBar/panelBarItem` and `tab/tabPanel` group components into pages that can be dynamically shown and hidden.
- **Notifications:** `pageMessages` displays errors and information.

Figure 7-4 illustrates all the components in use on a single Visualforce page. Listings 7-15 and 7-16 implement the controller and page shown in Figure 7-4.

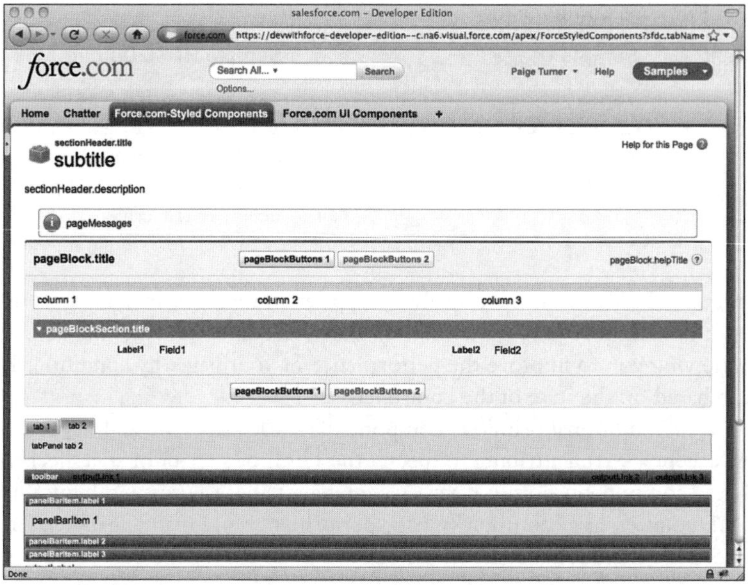

Figure 7-4   Force.com-styled components

Listing 7-15   Sample Controller with Force.com-Styled Components

```
public class ForceStyledComponentsControllerExtension {
  private final List<Resource__c> resources;
  public ForceStyledComponentsControllerExtension(
    ApexPages.StandardSetController stdController) {
    this.resources = (List<Resource__c>)stdController.getRecords();
  }
  public PageReference initPage() {
    ApexPages.addMessage(new ApexPages.Message(
      ApexPages.Severity.INFO, 'pageMessages'));
    return null;
  }
}
```

Listing 7-16   Sample Page with Force.com-Styled Components

```
<apex:page standardController="Resource__c"
  recordSetVar="resources"
  tabStyle="ForceStyledComponents__tab"
  extensions="ForceStyledComponentsControllerExtension"
  action="{!initPage}">
<apex:form>
```

```
<apex:sectionHeader title="sectionHeader.title"
  subtitle="subtitle"
  description="sectionHeader.description"
  help="http://developer.force.com" />
<apex:pageMessages />
<apex:pageBlock title="pageBlock.title"
  helpUrl="http://developer.force.com"
  helpTitle="pageBlock.helpTitle">
  <apex:pageBlockButtons>
    <apex:commandButton action="{!save}"
      value="pageBlockButtons 1"/>
    <apex:commandButton action="{!save}"
      value="pageBlockButtons 2" disabled="true" />
  </apex:pageBlockButtons>
  <apex:pageBlockTable var="r" value="{!resources}"
    title="pageBlockTable.title" rows="1">
    <apex:column>column 1</apex:column>
    <apex:column>column 2</apex:column>
    <apex:column>column 3</apex:column>
  </apex:pageBlockTable>
  <p />
  <apex:pageBlockSection title="pageBlockSection.title"
    columns="2">
    <apex:pageBlockSectionItem>
      <apex:outputPanel>Label1</apex:outputPanel>
      <apex:outputPanel>Field1</apex:outputPanel>
    </apex:pageBlockSectionItem>
    <apex:pageBlockSectionItem>
      <apex:outputPanel>Label2</apex:outputPanel>
      <apex:outputPanel>Field2</apex:outputPanel>
    </apex:pageBlockSectionItem>
  </apex:pageBlockSection>
</apex:pageBlock>
<p />
<apex:tabPanel switchType="client" selectedTab="name2">
  <apex:tab label="tab 1"
    name="name1">tabPanel tab 1</apex:tab>
  <apex:tab label="tab 2"
    name="name2">tabPanel tab 2</apex:tab>
</apex:tabPanel>
<p />
<apex:toolbar>
  <apex:outputText>toolbar</apex:outputText>
  <apex:outputLink value="http://developer.force.com">
    outputLink 1</apex:outputLink>
  <apex:toolbarGroup itemSeparator="line" location="right">
    <apex:outputLink value="http://">outputLink 2</apex:outputLink>
```

```
    <apex:outputLink value="http://">outputLink 3</apex:outputLink>
  </apex:toolbarGroup>
</apex:toolbar>
<p />
<apex:panelBar>
  <apex:panelBarItem label="panelBarItem.label 1">panelBarItem 1
  </apex:panelBarItem>
  <apex:panelBarItem label="panelBarItem.label 2">panelBarItem 3
  </apex:panelBarItem>
  <apex:panelBarItem label="panelBarItem.label 3">panelBarItem 3
  </apex:panelBarItem>
</apex:panelBar>
</apex:form>
</apex:page>
```

Force.com User Interface Components

Four view components are available that each replicate coarse-grained areas of
Force.com's native user interface functionality. These components are a single reference on
your Visualforce page, but they expand to produce many subordinate user interface elements when rendered to users. They are summarized in the following list:

1. **listViews:** The listViews component is rendered by Force.com on the list page
   of an object tab when the Enable Enhanced Lists option is disabled for the organization.

2. **enhancedList:** The enhancedList component consists of a drop-down list of
   view names and a table of records returned by executing the view.

3. **relatedList:** The relatedList component renders the records of any one of an
   object's child objects.

4. **detail:** The detail component provides a subset of the native user interface's
   detail page for an object.

The end of this subsection contains the code for the controller and page used to demonstrate these four components.

listViews Component

The listViews component includes the capability to create and edit list views, as well as
execute them and render their records. The only required attribute of listViews is type,
which binds a database object type to the component. Figure 7-5 shows a listViews
component bound to the Resource custom object.

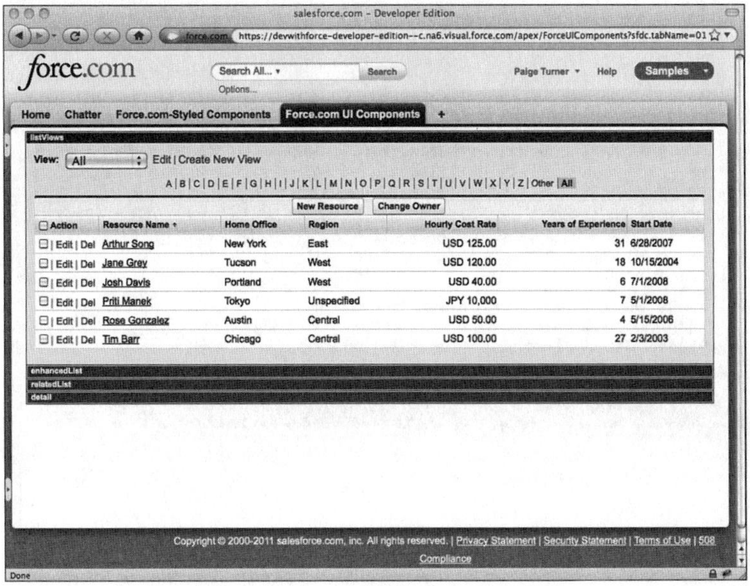

Figure 7-5   `listViews` component

`enhancedList` Component

The `enhancedList` component is a more modern version of the `listViews` component. It has the same functionality but also includes drag-and-drop reorderable columns, sortable columns, and results pagination with dynamic page sizes. It appears in the native user interface only when Enable Enhanced Lists is enabled for the organization.

The required attributes of `enhancedList` are `height` (the height of the component in pixels) and either `type` (the database object type displayed by the component) or `listId` (the unique identifier of the list view). Figure 7-6 demonstrates an `enhancedList` component with its `type` set to the Resource custom object.

`relatedList` Component

The `relatedList` component renders a list of child records. It is the same component that appears in the native interface below the detail for a record. It is paginated and allows related records to be edited, deleted, and created, depending on the object permissions of the current user.

The required attributes of `relatedList` are `list`, the name of the child relationship to be rendered in the list, and `subject`, an expression language reference to the parent record on the controller (defaults to the `id` parameter of the page if not provided). Both Master-Detail and Lookup relationships are supported by `relatedList`.

Figure 7-7 shows the `relatedList` component, with `subject` set to a record in the Resource object, and `list` set to Skills.

Figure 7-6   enhancedList component

Figure 7-7   relatedList component

detail Component

The detail component replicates the functionality of the native user interface on the detail page of a record. It respects the page layout of the record, including page layouts defined per record type. It also supports inline editing for the edit mode of an object.

Like the relatedList component, detail requires a subject or it attempts to read a record identifier from the page's id URL parameter. By default, all related lists are rendered below the detail section unless the relatedList parameter is set to false. In Figure 7-8, detail is bound to a Resource record and configured not to render the related lists.

Figure 7-8   detail component

Demonstration Code

Listings 7-17 and 7-18 implement the controller and page featured in the figures in this subsection.

Listing 7-17   **Sample Controller with Force.com UI Components**

```
public class ForceUIComponentsController {
  public Resource__c subject { get; private set; }
  public ForceUIComponentsController() {
    subject = [ SELECT Id, Name
      FROM Resource__c LIMIT 1 ];
  }
}
```

Listing 7-18   **Sample Page with Force.com UI Components**

```
<apex:page tabStyle="Force_com_UI_Components__tab"
  controller="ForceUIComponentsController">
<style>
.panel {
  background-image: none;
  background-color: #666666;
}
.panelActive {
  background-color: #38197A;
}
</style>
<apex:panelBar headerClass="panel" headerClassActive="panelActive">
  <apex:panelBarItem label="listViews">
    <apex:listViews type="Resource__c" />
  </apex:panelBarItem>
  <apex:panelBarItem label="enhancedList">
    <apex:enhancedList type="Resource__c" height="300" />
  </apex:panelBarItem>
  <apex:panelBarItem label="relatedList">
    <apex:relatedList subject="{!subject}" list="Skills__r" />
  </apex:panelBarItem>
  <apex:panelBarItem label="detail">
    <apex:detail subject="{!subject}" relatedList="false"
      title="false" />
  </apex:panelBarItem>
</apex:panelBar>
</apex:page>
```

Visualforce and the Native User Interface

Force.com provides many places for Visualforce pages to be integrated into its native user interface. You can embed Visualforce pages inside standard user interface pages, override the buttons that navigate between pages, override the standard pages entirely, and add buttons and tabs to navigate to an entirely custom user interface. Areas of the native user interface extensible through Visualforce are summarized here:

- **Standard Pages:** Standard pages provide the default user interface for maintaining records in the Force.com database. These pages can be overridden with your custom Visualforce pages.

- **Standard Buttons:** Standard buttons normally navigate the user to standard pages, such as the New button, which moves the user to the edit page for a new record. But these buttons can be remapped to your custom Visualforce pages, to inject an additional visual step before the standard page or to hide it altogether.

- **Page Layouts:** Page layouts define the position of fields, buttons, and related lists in the native user interface. Visualforce pages can be embedded within page layouts.

- **Custom Button and Links:** Custom buttons appear at the top and bottom of standard pages and links within a detail page. They can navigate the user to a Visualforce page.

- **Custom Tabs:** Custom tabs are added to an application and appear at the top of the Web browser under the application banner. A Visualforce page can be configured as a custom tab.

Standard Pages

The native user interface consists of four standard pages for working with database records. These can all be overridden, as described here:

1. **Tab:** The tab page appears when a custom object tab is clicked. Figure 7-9 provides an example of this page.

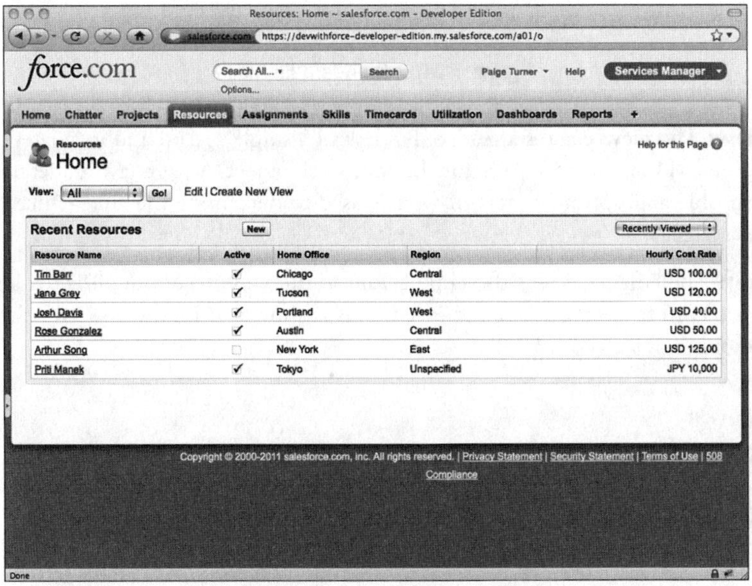

Figure 7-9   Standard tab page

2. **List:** The list page displays a series of records in a tabular view, as shown in Figure 7-10. You reach it by clicking the Go button from the tab page.

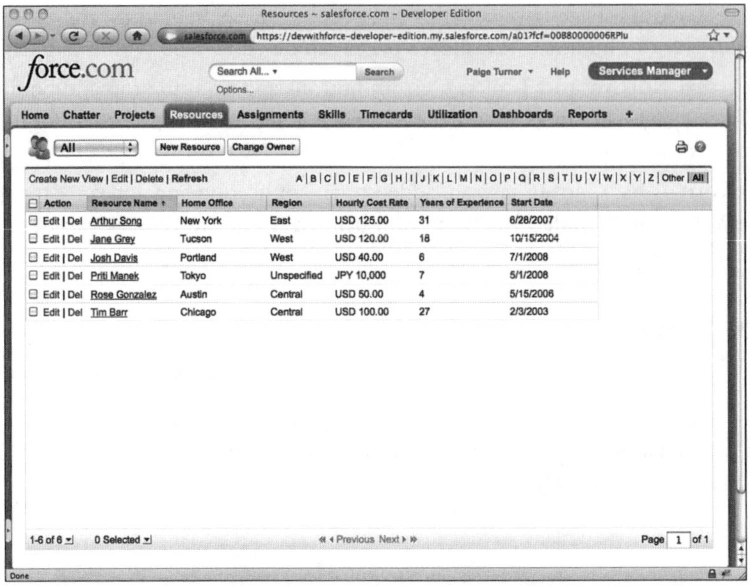

Figure 7-10   Standard list page

3. **View:** The view page is a read-only view of a single record and its related records. Figure 7-11 is the view page for the Resource object. A page layout, determined by profile and optionally record type, is used to determine the appearance of the view page.

4. **Edit:** The edit page uses the same layout as the view page but allows the values of a record to be modified and saved. This is shown in Figure 7-12 for the Resource object.

> **Caution**
>
> Override the standard edit page with caution. The standard edit page provides deep functionality, such as page layouts and record types, that cannot be replicated in a Visualforce page without a significant amount of custom code.

To override a standard page, go to the App Setup area and click Create → Objects and select the object. Scroll to the Standard Buttons and Links section. Tab, view, and edit pages can be overridden only with Visualforce pages that use a standard, single record controller. The list page must use a standard set controller. Controller extensions are supported in all pages.

Figure 7-11   Standard view page

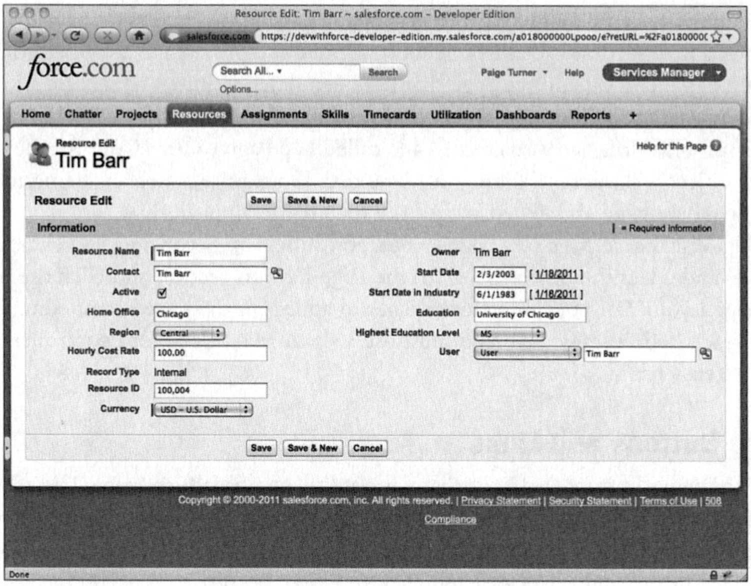

Figure 7-12   Standard edit page

Standard Buttons

Visualforce pages can be shown as the result of clicking a native user interface button, over-riding the button's standard behavior. The following standard buttons can be overridden:

- **New:** The New button normally navigates the user to the edit page on a new record.
- **Delete:** This is the page navigated to after a record is deleted. The default behavior is to navigate to the tab page.
- **Clone:** The Clone button copies the values from the current record into a new record and places the user in edit mode on that record. This behavior can be cus-tomized by overriding the Clone button.
- **Accept:** The Accept button applies to records owned by a queue rather than a sin-gle user. It enables a user to remove a record from the queue, assigning ownership of the record to himself. This button appears on the list page only when it is displaying records owned by a queue.

To override a standard button, go to the App Setup area and click Create → Objects and select the object. Scroll to the Standard Buttons and Links section. Your Visualforce page must use a standard, single record controller, with or without extensions.

Page Layouts

A Visualforce page can be embedded in an object's page layout alongside its fields. Figure 7-13 shows a new section called My Section, defined using the page layout editor. My Page is the name of a Visualforce page that has been dragged into My Section and is now visible whenever a record of that object is viewed or edited.

The result of adding the Visualforce page called My Page to the layout for the Resource object is shown in Figure 7-14. The text "Your page is here" is being rendered by the Visualforce page embedded within the record's detail page.

To add a Visualforce page to a page layout, go to the App Setup area and click Create → Objects and select the object. Scroll to the Page Layouts section and click the Edit link for the page layout. For your Visualforce pages to appear in the page layout editor, they cannot already be in use by a tab and must use a standard single record controller, with or without extensions.

Custom Buttons and Links

You can configure buttons and links that navigate to any Visualforce page. These buttons and links are then added to page layouts. Buttons and links are defined on the database object. In the App Setup area, click Create → Objects, and then click the object. Scroll to the Custom Buttons and Links area and click the New button.

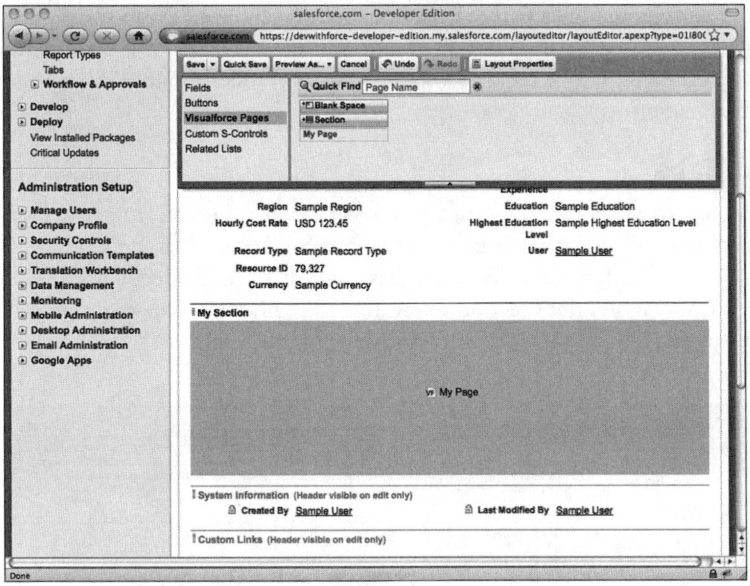

Figure 7-13   Adding a Visualforce page to page layout

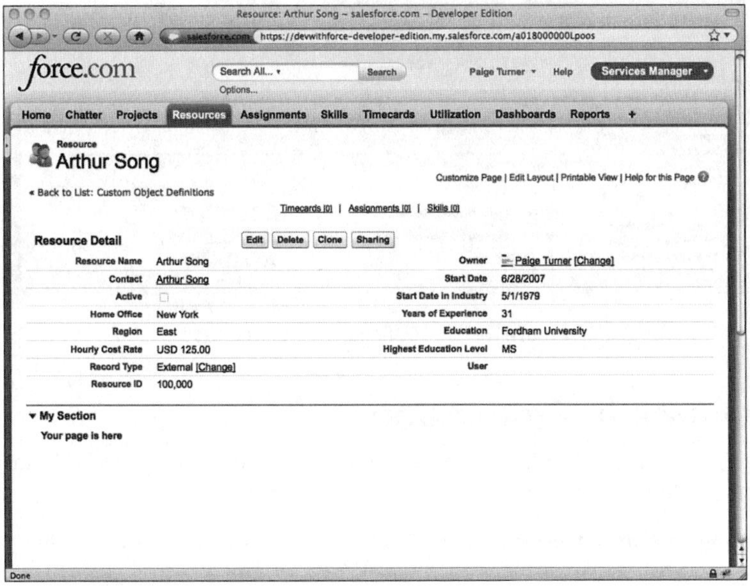

Figure 7-14   Embedded Visualforce page

Custom buttons and links tied to Visualforce pages can be added to the object's detail page layout or a related list page layout. The detail page layout requires a standard controller. The related list layout requires a standard set controller. Controller extensions can be used with either.

Custom Tabs

You can configure any Visualforce page as a new tab in the Force.com native user interface. To add a new Visualforce tab, go to the App Setup area and click Create → Tabs. In Figure 7-15, three custom Visualforce tabs have already been defined. Click the New button in the Visualforce Tabs section to create a tab. Select a Visualforce page, select a tab label and style, set tab visibility on profiles and applications, and click Save.

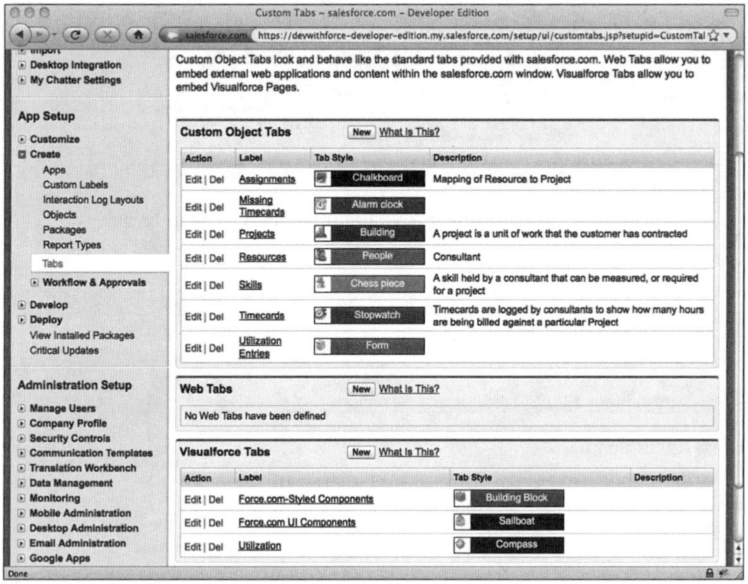

Figure 7-15   Defining Visualforce tabs

Visualforce in Production

This section describes areas of focus for real-world user interfaces written in Visualforce. It includes the following subsections:

- **Debugging and Tuning:** Force.com provides web-based tools for debugging and tuning Visualforce pages.
- **Security:** Securing Visualforce pages is an important task. Visualforce pages can expose users to records they should not see under record sharing rules and cause runtime errors due to lack of object or field visibility.

- **Error Handling:** Error handling in Visualforce is a process of catching all exceptions and handling them thoughtfully, with both the integrity of the database and the user experience in mind.

- **Governor Limits:** The code running in Visualforce controllers is subject to governor limits, applied within the scope of each user-initiated action.

- **Unit Tests:** Force.com requires test coverage on the code in Visualforce controllers and provides system methods to assist.

Debugging and Tuning

The System Log is the first place to look to troubleshoot unexpected behavior from a Visualforce user interface. While the System Log is open, every interaction with Force.com is logged and can be examined in depth. In Figure 7-16, the System Log is active and contains a single log entry, which captured the system activity for the page /apex/SkillsMatrix.

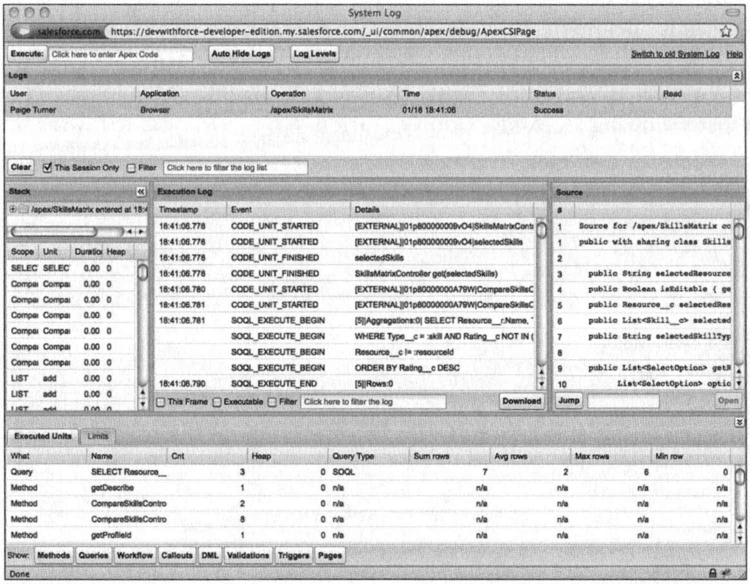

Figure 7-16   System Log

The log entry has been clicked, and the other panels of the System Log are refreshed with detailed information. This information is centered around the Apex code executed in the controller associated with the page, as well as any Apex code executed as a result of controller code. Click the buttons at the bottom of the screen to filter out areas of Apex code such as Workflow that are superfluous to your investigation. If a bug exists in your controller code, it should be obvious in the Stack, Execution Log, and Executed Units panels as you trace the flow of instructions. Remember that like any Apex class, you can sprinkle `System.debug` statements into your controller to help troubleshoot.

Problems in the Visualforce page itself are typically more difficult to debug. If Force.com encounters something invalid in the course of rendering a Visualforce page, such as a null reference in your controller, it might show an unhelpful error message. Trial and error can be helpful in these situations. Comment out portions of your Visualforce page using HTML comment tags (`<!-- sample comment -->`) until the page functions again and you've isolated the troublesome portion. An in-browser development tool such as Firebug is also helpful if the page renders successfully but has a client-side presentation or logic issue. Firebug enables close inspection of the JavaScript, HTML, and CSS in the page.

When you're ready to improve the performance of your Visualforce page, examine the view state. The view state contains the values of local variables in your controller. They are encoded and embedded in the page itself in a hidden field and sent back to Force.com upon every user action. Sending the view state back and forth to the browser and processing it in Force.com can reduce the responsiveness of your user interface. View state is limited to 128K, but performance can be impacted well before the limit is reached.

The Visualforce development mode footer contains a tab called View State, shown in Figure 7-17. With it, you can examine the contents of the view state: the variables saved there, along with their sizes and contents. Double-clicking one of the folders opens a dialog with charts showing the contribution of various types of view state toward the limit.

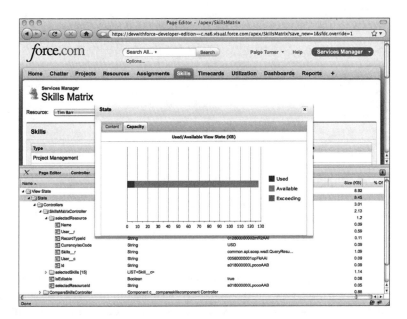

Figure 7-17   View state

Your goal is to minimize the view state. Look for controller variables that do not need to persist across page views, and add the `transient` keyword to them. The `transient` keyword tells Force.com not to save the state of the variable in the web page, removing the round-trip cost of transporting that data to and from the web browser. Avoid querying extraneous information from the database in your SOQL calls. Also, simplify and streamline any nested data structures that are required in the view state.

Security

Securing a Visualforce user interface involves controlling access to the objects, the records, and the page itself. Visualforce obeys the object and field-level security rules configured in profiles. Record security is handled by the controller through special keywords in Apex in conjunction with custom code that can be written to enforce application-specific security rules. Access to the page is granted by the user's profile.

Object-Level Security

Access to database objects and fields is determined by the profile and is consistent with the native user interface. This protects the database and maintains the centralized control of data security, but also exposes the user interface to various runtime errors if improperly configured. For example, if the user's profile denies all access to an object, this object is essentially invisible. When a Visualforce controller attempts to select from it, the page fails with an exception. Other configuration problems are handled more transparently to the user. If the user's profile lacks edit access on an object and a Visualforce page binds an `inputField` to that object, it is automatically rendered as an `outputField`, appropriately blocking user input.

When developing a controller, check that the SOQL, SOSL, and DML operations are fully compatible with the set of profiles expected to use the page. As a developer, you have full visibility to every object and field, but do not assume that your users have the same level of access. Test the Visualforce pages by logging in as a test user or cycling through profiles on a single test user. You can also write unit tests that run under the privileges of a specific user using the `System.runAs` method, covered in more detail in the "Unit Tests" subsection.

Record-Level Security

Standard controllers always honor the record-level security of the current user. But by default, record sharing rules are ignored by code in custom controllers. These controllers run in a system context, like a trigger.

> **Note**
>
> Record sharing rules are still honored by the methods of standard controllers that have extensions defined, but the code in an extension class itself still runs in system mode.

For example, if a user's profile grants the user access to a particular object, your custom controller queries it, and your Visualforce page displays the results, the user can read every record in the object, regardless of the sharing settings.

You can change this behavior in the controller code by specifying a security mode in the class definition. Two security modes are available: `with sharing` and `without sharing`. The controller definition in Listing 7-19 uses `with sharing` to configure the controller to honor record sharing rules.

Listing 7-19   **Custom Controller Using Record Sharing Rules**

```
public with sharing class MyController {
  // the code in this controller honors record sharing rules
}
```

The `without sharing` security mode indicates that a class should not obey record sharing rules, which is the default state. You do not need to change this unless your code accesses objects that have record sharing rules defined that you would like to enforce in your user interface. Subclasses inherit the security mode from their parent class, but inner classes do not. In nested calls, where one class calls another class, the current security mode is applied unless explicitly specified.

After a security mode is chosen, no additional work is required. SOSL and SOQL statements automatically return the correct subset of records based on the sharing rules for each object. But if a record is referenced directly that is not shared with the user, such as through a DML method updating a foreign key, a runtime error is thrown. Use a `try/catch` block around DML methods to make sure that this situation is properly handled.

Page-Level Security

Profiles determine which users are able to use a Visualforce page. Pages must be explicitly enabled for each profile that requires access. If this is not done, users will receive an error page titled Insufficient Privileges when attempting to view the page.

To grant a profile access to a page, go to the Administration Setup and click Manage Users → Profiles. Scroll to the Enabled Visualforce Page Access section, shown in Figure 7-18, and click the Edit button. Select pages from the Available Visualforce Pages list and click the Add button to add them to the Enabled Visualforce Pages list. Click Save when you're done.

> **Note**
>
> Users with the Customize Application permission can access all Visualforce pages in the organization.

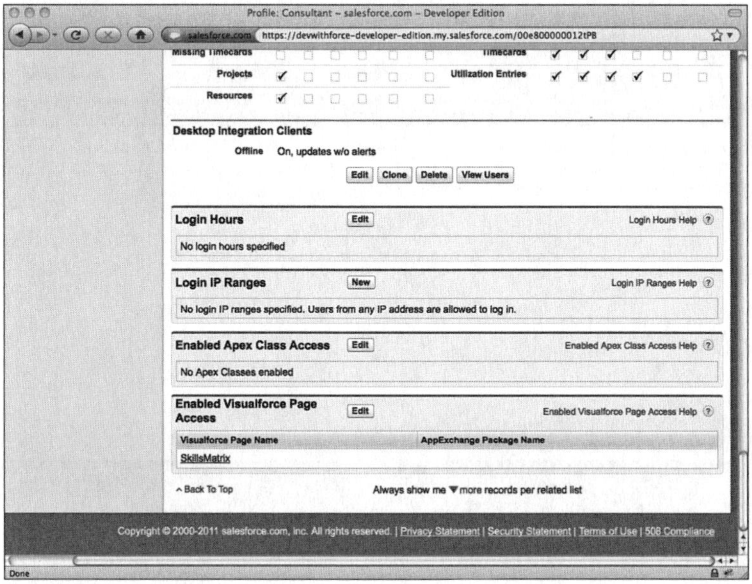

Figure 7-18   Configuring Visualforce page security

Error Handling

The two main concerns when handling errors in Visualforce are how uncaught exceptions impact the user interface and how to communicate caught exceptions to users.

Uncaught Exceptions

Allowing an uncaught exception in a trigger is often an appropriate way to notify the user of a problem because Force.com displays a nicely formatted error message to the user in the native user interface. But in a Visualforce page, uncaught exceptions result in an alarming, generic Force.com error page whose appearance cannot be controlled or customized in any way. Figure 7-19 shows an example of this error page.

As this is typically not consistent with the usability and look-and-feel of a custom user interface, one of the goals of error handling in Visualforce is to avoid these uncaught exceptions. Place a try/catch block around every action method, or at least those that perform SOSL, SOQL, or DML operations.

A benefit of uncaught exceptions in triggers is that they roll back the current transaction. Catching all exceptions in your Visualforce controller forces your code to roll back explicitly if required by your application. For example, if your controller has two DML statements in an action method and fails on the second with a caught exception, the first statement is still committed to the database at the conclusion of the method. If this leaves the database in an undesirable state for your application, set a savepoint at the beginning of the method and roll back to it in the catch block. For an example of using savepoints, refer to Listing 6-19 in Chapter 6, "Advanced Business Logic."

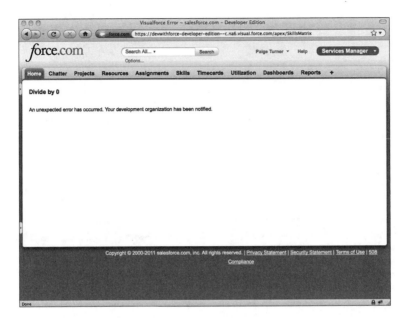

Figure 7-19   Uncaught exception in Visualforce

Error Communication

Visualforce provides page components and corresponding data objects for communicating errors to the user in a consistent way. The page components are messages and pageMessages, which display the page-level errors returned by a controller. These components are placed on pages, typically at the top, and render the ApexPages.Message objects added to the page. Message objects contain a message and optional severity. Severity is used to style the message when displayed in the pageMessages component and can also be filtered on in test methods.

Listing 7-20 is an example of code to add an error-severity message to the page. To be visible, it must be rendered by a messages or pageMessages component.

Listing 7-20   **Sample Usage of Page Messages**

```
ApexPages.addMessage(new ApexPages.Message(
  ApexPages.Severity.ERROR, 'Something went wrong'));
```

Governor Limits

Visualforce controllers have the same set of governor limits as all Apex code. Table 7-3 reviews these limits.

Table 7-3   **Subset of Governor Limits**

Resource Type	Governor Limit
Heap	3MB
Apex code	200,000 lines of code executed
SOQL	100 queries
Records from SOQL	50,000 records cumulatively for all SOQL queries
DML	150 DML statements
Records in DML	10,000 records cumulatively for all DML statements

Governor limits apply during execution of user-initiated actions and are not cumulative. When an action is complete, the governor limits reset. For example, if your controller contains a save method bound to a commandButton, the governor limits apply during the execution of the save method. When the user clicks the button again or takes another action that invokes a method, the governor limits begin counting your resource consumption again from zero.

Unit Tests

Unit tests are mandatory for all Apex code, including Visualforce controllers. Your application code must have at least 75% test coverage before it can be deployed to a production environment.

The mechanics of writing unit tests for controllers is similar to that of triggers, with some additional system methods for test setup. But the strategy for testing controllers is unique, because controller code normally relies on the Web browser to drive it.

Listing 7-21 provides an example of the test setup code. It starts by creating an instance of the controller class and getting a reference to the Visualforce page to test. This is a PageReference instance, created by passing the page name as an argument. The Test.setCurrentPage method sets the context of the test method to the page you want to test.

Listing 7-21   **Sample Controller Test Method**

```
static testMethod void sampleTestMethod() {
  MyPageController controller = new MyPageController();
  PageReference page = new PageReference('MyPage');
  Test.setCurrentPage(page);
}
```

The body of your tests can employ one or more of the following test strategies to exercise code in the controller:

- Directly invoke controller methods and getters/setters.
- Add a test harness to constructor code to read URL arguments to establish controller state or perform actions.
- Verify data in the database using SOQL and SOSL queries.
- Use `System.runAs` blocks to simulate different users; `System.runAs(user)` `{block; }`.

> **Caution**
>
> Even 100% test coverage on the controller class does not guarantee a bug-free user interface. Testing Visualforce pages is like testing any Web application. Test it manually with your Web browser or with an automated Web testing tool.

Sample Application: Skills Matrix

One of the features of the Services Manager sample application is skill set management. The skills of consultants are tracked using the Skill object, a child of the Resource object. Entering skills in the native user interface involves navigating to the Resource's record and clicking the New button in the Skills related list and then selecting a skill type and a rating.

Users of the application have requested a more streamlined way to enter and view skills, called the Skills Matrix. The requirements of Skills Matrix follow:

- **Reduce Navigation Clicks:** Provide a single screen for entering and viewing all skill-related information. The screen shows the skills and ratings of a single resource at a time in tabular format: skill types as rows and a single column to view and edit ratings.
- **Encourage Data Completeness:** All skill types are shown at all times. This is in contrast with the native user interface, which shows only the skills containing ratings. Showing all skill types, including those lacking a rating, encourages users to treat the user interface like a survey and should increase data completeness.
- **Allow All to View, Restrict Editing:** Whether a rating is editable or read-only depends on the current user. If the user is editing her own resource record, all ratings are editable. If the user is a manager, vice president, or system administrator (by profile), the user is allowed to edit the skills of any resource. If the user does not meet any of the previous criteria, the skill ratings are read-only.

This section describes building the feature in three parts. The first part is a basic implementation, to allow the selection of a resource and editing of its skills. The second part adds the finishing touches to implement the full set of requirements. The final section provides a sample, full implementation of the feature, shown in Figure 7-20, and comments on portions of the code.

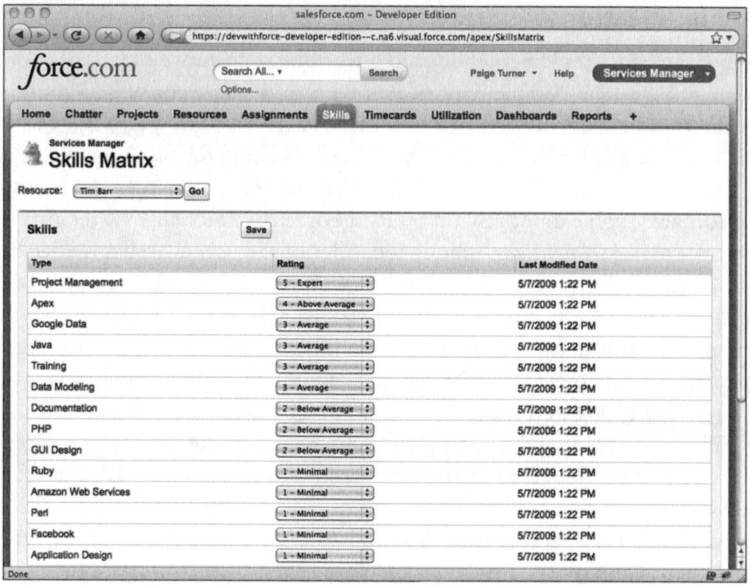

Figure 7-20   Skills Matrix sample implementation

Basic Implementation

In the basic implementation, build a Visualforce page with a drop-down list at the top containing resource names and a table below it with the skills and ratings. The only skills shown are those that already contain ratings for the resource. The ratings can be edited and saved by any user.

Start by creating the page and controller in the Force.com IDE. Add a `selectList` component, and a corresponding getter in the controller to return a list of `SelectOption` objects, constructed from the names and unique identifiers of records of the `Resource__c` object. Add a refresh `commandButton` to fetch the skills for the currently selected resource.

Build and test the drop-down list of resources before moving on to the list of skills. Then flesh out the controller, querying the `Type__c` and `Rating__c` fields of the `Skill__c` records belonging to the selected resource. Iterate over that list in the page, displaying the ratings as drop-down lists. Add an action method to the controller to save changes to the skills list. Use the upsert database method, as later your skills list will contain both new and edited records. Add a `commandButton` on the page to invoke the action method.

Test your user interface frequently during development. Add your page to the native user interface with a Visualforce tab or override the Skills custom object tab. To override the tab, in the App Setup area, click Create → Objects and select Skill. Scroll to the Standard Buttons and Links section. Click the Override link for the tab. For the Content Type, select the Visualforce Page radio button. Select your Skills Matrix page from the Content Names drop-down list and click the Save button.

Full Implementation

After you get the basic implementation into a working state, move on to the more challenging requirements: the complete list of skill types and data security.

To get the complete list of types, use the metadata methods to query the values of the Skill__c.Type__c picklist. Iterate over the values, checking for the presence of corresponding Skill records for the resource. Create Skill records where they are missing.

For data security, you cannot rely on built-in Force.com record-level security alone. It operates on the OwnerId field, the unique identifier of the user who has ownership rights to a record. In the Skills Matrix, ownership of a resource record does not determine who is allowed to edit or view its skills. An administrator might import resource data from a legacy system, or a user in human resources might be the owner of the resource.

The assumption is that every consultant and other user of the Services Manager application has a license to log in to Force.com as an independent user with his own credentials. Each full user license carries with it a unique record in the standard User object. This user identity can be correlated to the resource record to determine at runtime the behavior of the Skills Matrix. To create this correlation, add a lookup field to the Resource object called User, setting its parent to the standard User object. For each resource record, provide a value of the new User field. This lookup of the User from Resource can drive the decision of the controller to make a set of skills editable or not.

When you're done with the implementation, test it against the three user scenarios: privileged user, consultant editing his or her own skills, and consultant viewing the skills of another consultant.

Tip

Only users with the System Administrator profile will have access to your new Skills Matrix page. To open the page to non-administrative users, in the Administration Setup area, click Manage Users → Profiles and select the profile of the users. Scroll to the Enabled Visualforce Page Access section and click the Edit button. Select your page from the Available Visualforce Pages list and click the Add button to move it to the Enabled Visualforce Pages list. Click the Save button when you're done.

Implementation Walkthrough

This subsection provides the code for a sample implementation of the Skills Matrix. It includes the controller, the page, and controller test cases.

Skills Matrix Controller

Listing 7-22 contains a sample implementation of the Skills Matrix controller class. The controller has four variables, each with a getter method for access by the Visualforce page. The selectedResourceId variable contains the unique identifier of the resource selected for editing or viewing. isEditable is a flag used by the page to enable or disable the Save button and to determine whether to render skills as plain-text fields or editable drop-down lists. The selectedResource variable contains several fields from the Resource object needed throughout the controller, queried using the `selectedResourceId`. The `selectedSkills` list contains the skill types and ratings to be displayed and edited in the user interface, and this same list is used to update the database upon a save action.

The controller has two actions: `save` and `refresh`. The save action applies the changes from the drop-down lists of skill ratings by upserting them into the database. The refresh action uses the unique identifier of the currently selected resource (`selectedResourceId`) to query the database for Skill records. It compares them against the complete list of skill types via the database metadata call `getPicklistValues`. Finally, it updates the `isEditable` variable based on whether the current user is privileged or is associated with the currently viewed resource.

Several helper methods are in the controller. `addError` and `addInfo` are shortcuts for adding notifications to the page, displayed using the `pageMessages` component. The `getCurrentUserResource` method queries the Resource record corresponding to the current user. The `isManager` method returns `true` if the user is privileged, enabling the user to edit the skills of any resource.

Listing 7-22   **Skills Matrix Controller**

```
public class SkillsMatrixController {
  public String selectedResourceId { get; set; }
  public Boolean isEditable { get; private set; }
  public Resource__c selectedResource { get; private set; }
  public List<Skill__c> selectedSkills { get; private set; }
  public List<SelectOption> getResourceOptions() {
    List<SelectOption> options = new List<SelectOption>();
      options.add(new SelectOption(
        '', '-- Select Resource --'));
    List<Resource__c> resources = [ SELECT Id, Name
      FROM Resource__c ORDER BY Contact__r.LastName ];
    for (Resource__c resource : resources) {
      options.add(new SelectOption(resource.Id,
        resource.Name));
    }
    return options;
  }
  public PageReference refresh() {
    if (selectedResourceId == null) {
      addError('Select a resource');
      return null;
    }
    selectedResource = [ SELECT Id, Name,
      User__r.UserRoleId,
      User__r.ProfileId,
      (SELECT Type__c, Rating__c, LastModifiedDate
        FROM Skills__r ORDER BY Rating__c DESC)
      FROM Resource__c
```

```
      WHERE Id = :selectedResourceId
      LIMIT 1 ];
    Set<String> skillTypes = new Set<String>();
    selectedSkills = new List<Skill__c>();
    for (Skill__c skill : selectedResource.Skills__r) {
      skillTypes.add(skill.Type__c);
      selectedSkills.add(skill);
    }
    Schema.DescribeFieldResult field = Skill__c.Type__c.getDescribe();
    String picklistValue = null;
    for (Schema.PicklistEntry entry : field.getPicklistValues()) {
      picklistValue = entry.getLabel();
      if (!skillTypes.contains(picklistValue)) {
        selectedSkills.add(
          new Skill__c(Resource__c = selectedResource.Id,
            Type__c = picklistValue));
      }
    }
    if (isManager()) {
      isEditable = true;
    } else {
      Resource__c userResource = getCurrentUserResource();
      isEditable =
        selectedResource != null && userResource != null
        && selectedResource.Id == userResource.Id;
    }
    return null;
  }
  private void addError(String msg) {
    ApexPages.addMessage(new ApexPages.Message(
      ApexPages.Severity.ERROR, msg));
  }
  private void addInfo(String msg) {
    ApexPages.addMessage(new ApexPages.Message(
      ApexPages.Severity.INFO, msg));
  }
  public Resource__c getCurrentUserResource() {
    List<Resource__c> userResource = [ SELECT Id, Name,
      User__r.UserRoleId, User__r.ProfileId
      FROM Resource__c
      WHERE User__c = :UserInfo.getUserId()
      LIMIT 1 ];
    if (userResource.size() == 0) {
      addError('No resource associated with user');
      return null;
    } else {
```

```
        return userResource.get(0);
    }
}
private Boolean isManager() {
    List<Profile> profiles = [ SELECT Id
        FROM Profile WHERE Name IN (
        'Project Manager', 'Vice President', 'System Administrator')
        AND Id = :UserInfo.getProfileId() LIMIT 1 ];
    return profiles.size() == 1;
}
public PageReference save() {
    try {
        upsert selectedSkills;
        addInfo('Changes saved');
    } catch(DmlException e) {
        addError('Could not save changes: ' + e.getMessage());
    }
    return null;
}
}
```

Skills Matrix Visualforce Page

Listing 7-23 contains sample code for the Skills Matrix Visualforce page. It uses
Force.com–styled view components to achieve an appearance that resembles the native
user interface. The pageBlock and pageBlockButtons components visually separate the
selection of the resource from the skills data and Save button, and the sectionHeader
component mimics the appearance of a native object tab.

The pageBlockTable component iterates over the list of skills, displaying them as a
table using standard Force.com styling. Each row of the table includes two columns. The
first column contains the skill type. The second contains two components: one for editing
the skill rating and another strictly for viewing it. Only one of these components is
shown at a time. They are rendered conditionally based on whether the controller has
determined the data to be editable. If the skills data is editable, only the inputField component is rendered. If the current user does not have the rights to edit the ratings, only
the outputField is rendered.

Listing 7-23   **Skills Matrix Visualforce Page**

```
<apex:page controller="SkillsMatrixController"
    tabStyle="Skill__c">
    <style>
    .resourceLabel { padding-right: 15px; }
    .goButton { margin-left: 10px; }
    </style>
```

```
<apex:sectionHeader title="Services Manager"
  subtitle="Skills Matrix" />
<apex:pageMessages />
<apex:form id="form">
<apex:outputLabel value="Resource:" for="selectedResourceId"
  styleClass="resourceLabel" />
<apex:selectList id="selectedResourceId" title="Resource"
  value="{!selectedResourceId}" size="1">
  <apex:selectOptions value="{!resourceOptions}" />
</apex:selectList>
<apex:commandButton action="{!refresh}" value="Go!"
  styleClass="goButton" />
<p />
<apex:pageBlock title="Skills">
  <apex:pageBlockButtons>
    <apex:commandButton action="{!save}" value="Save"
      disabled="{!NOT isEditable}" />
  </apex:pageBlockButtons>
  <apex:pageBlockTable value="{!selectedSkills}" var="skill"
    rendered="{!selectedResourceId != ''}">
    <apex:column value="{!skill.Type__c}" />
    <apex:column headerValue="Rating">
      <apex:outputField value="{!skill.Rating__c}"
        rendered="{!NOT isEditable}" />
      <apex:inputField value="{!skill.Rating__c}"
        rendered="{!isEditable}" />
    </apex:column>
    <apex:column value="{!skill.LastModifiedDate}" />
  </apex:pageBlockTable>
</apex:pageBlock>
</apex:form>
</apex:page>
```

Controller Tests

The test cases in Listing 7-24 achieve 96% coverage of the Skills Matrix controller. They begin with a static initializer and `init` method to prepare the database for the tests. This preparation includes deleting all existing Resource records so that they do not interfere with the tests and adding test data. These actions are not permanent. All database actions during testing are rolled back automatically upon test completion.

The test cases rely on two Resource records: Tim and Barry. To test the behavior of the Skills Matrix on existing data, Tim is given a single Skill record, whereas Barry is left without skills. For testing security, Tim's Resource record is associated with a User record named Tim, whereas Barry's Resource record is not mapped to a User record. Update

the query for the users in the static initializer to match two usernames in your own
organization.

Listing 7-24   **Skills Matrix Unit Test Class**

```
@isTest
private class TestSkillsMatrixController {
  static PageReference page;
  static SkillsMatrixController controller;
  static Resource__c barry, tim;
  static User barryUser, timUser;
  static {
    delete [ SELECT Id FROM Resource__c ];
    timUser = [ SELECT Id FROM User WHERE Name = 'Tim Barr' LIMIT 1 ];
    barryUser = [ SELECT Id FROM User WHERE Name = 'Barry Cade' LIMIT 1 ];
    init();
  }
  private static void init() {
    barry = new Resource__c(Name = 'Barry');
    tim = new Resource__c(Name = 'Tim', User__c = timUser.Id);
    insert new Resource__c[] { barry, tim };
    Skill__c[] skills = new Skill__c[] {
      new Skill__c(Type__c = 'Java', Rating__c = '3',
        Resource__c = tim.Id) };
    insert skills;
    page = new PageReference('SkillsMatrix');
    Test.setCurrentPage(page);
    controller = new SkillsMatrixController();
  }
  static testMethod void testAsUser() {
    System.runAs(timUser) {
      init();
      controller.selectedResourceId = barry.Id;
      controller.refresh();
      System.assert(!controller.isEditable);
      controller.selectedResourceId = tim.Id;
      controller.refresh();
      System.assert(controller.isEditable);
    }
  }
  static testMethod void testNoResourceForUser() {
    System.runAs(barryUser) {
      init();
      controller.selectedResourceId = barry.Id;
      controller.refresh();
      System.assert(ApexPages.hasMessages(ApexPages.Severity.ERROR));
    }
  }
}
```

```
static testMethod void testNoSkills() {
  controller.getResourceOptions();
  controller.selectedResourceId = barry.Id;
  controller.refresh();
  System.assert(controller.selectedSkills.size() > 0);
  System.assert(controller.isEditable);
}
static testMethod void testWithSkills() {
  controller.getResourceOptions();
  controller.selectedResourceId = tim.Id;
  controller.refresh();
  System.assert(controller.selectedSkills.size() > 0);
  System.assert(controller.selectedSkills.get(0).Type__c == 'Java');
}
static testMethod void testNoResourceSelected() {
  controller.selectedResourceId = null;
  PageReference ref = controller.refresh();
  System.assert(ApexPages.hasMessages());
}
static testMethod void testSave() {
  final String skillRating = '5 - Expert';
  controller.getResourceOptions();
  controller.selectedResourceId = barry.Id;
  controller.refresh();
  List<Skill__c> selectedSkills = controller.selectedSkills;
  Skill__c skill = selectedSkills.get(0);
  skill.Rating__c = skillRating;
  String skillType = skill.Type__c;
  controller.save();
  System.assert(ApexPages.hasMessages(ApexPages.Severity.INFO));
  Skill__c savedSkill = [ SELECT Rating__c FROM Skill__c
    WHERE Resource__c = :barry.Id AND
      Type__c = :skillType LIMIT 1 ];
  System.assert(savedSkill != null &&
    savedSkill.Rating__c == skillRating);
  }
}
```

The test methods are described here in the order in which they appear in the code:

- **testAsUser:** This test uses the System.runAs method to assume the identity of Tim. Tim is assigned to a User, so when his corresponding Resource record is selected and the list of skills is refreshed, the isEditable flag should be set to true. If Barry is selected, the flag should be false.

- **testNoResourceForUser:** System.runAs is used again, this time to test for an error condition. Barry's user does not have a child Resource record, so he should receive an error when visiting the Skills Matrix. Without a mapping to the User object, the application cannot determine whether the current user has access to edit skills.

- **testNoSkills:** This test method runs as a System Administrator. It selects Barry from the resource list and refreshes, asserting that there are Skills records. These records are created from the Skill object's Type__c field's picklist values. Another assertion is made that the skill ratings are editable because an administrator can edit the skills of all resources.

- **testWithSkills:** This test retrieves the skills for Tim and asserts that the Java skill is first in the list. This is because Tim already has a Skill record for Java, and existing records should be placed at the top of the user interface.

- **testNoResourceSelected:** The selected resource is set to null to verify that an information message is added to the page. This message instructs the user to select a resource.

- **testSave:** This test uses the controller to rate Barry as an expert in the first skill on the skills list. It then queries the database independently to verify that the controller saved the data correctly.

Summary

This chapter has covered the basics of Visualforce. Visualforce is a challenging but rewarding area of the Force.com platform, enabling the development of custom, data-intensive Web user interfaces using high-level languages for both logic and presentation. Mastering Visualforce requires the application of all of your Force.com skills and knowledge: the database, security model, and Apex code.

Use this chapter as a jumping-off point to the online documentation and Visualforce Developer's Guide. The Visualforce Developer's Guide contains the most current and complete information on the standard Visualforce view components.

Before moving on to the next chapter, consider what you've learned about Visualforce:

- A strong distinction exists between the controller and the page. No business logic is allowed on the page.

- The state of your pages at runtime is maintained automatically by Force.com. This enables you to design stateful interactions across one or many pages without writing custom state transfer code, assuming you always use Visualforce action components rather than raw HTML tags such as anchors.

- Custom controller code runs as the system user by default, meaning record-level security is not honored.

8

Advanced User Interfaces

Now that you are familiar with the basics of Visualforce, this chapter introduces features that enable you to build richer, more interactive user interfaces. The features are divided into the following sections:

- **Asynchronous Actions:** Visualforce has built-in, cross-browser support for Ajax behavior, without requiring you to write JavaScript code or integrate with JavaScript libraries.
- **Modular Visualforce:** Visualforce has a number of features to enable you to write modular pages. You can embed static content, build pages that include other pages, define page templates, and create your own library of custom Visualforce components.
- **Extending Visualforce:** Because Visualforce pages are standard HTML, CSS, and JavaScript when rendered in the Web browser, they can include technology not provided by Force.com, such as JavaScript libraries and Adobe Flex. Pages can also be accessed by users who do not have accounts in your Force.com organization using a feature called Force.com Sites.
- **Sample Application:** The Services Manager sample application's Skills Matrix is enhanced to demonstrate Ajax behavior and the use of JavaScript libraries and custom Visualforce components.

Asynchronous Actions

So far, you've built Visualforce pages that have a simple interaction with their controller. They display data from the controller, potentially allowing the user to change it, and then submit it using an action component such as a `commandButton`. The action component invokes a method on the controller that returns a `PageReference`, navigating the user to a new page or refreshing the current page.

Visualforce actions also support more complex, asynchronous interactions with the page, commonly referred to as Ajax. Visualforce supports Ajax in two ways:

1. It allows actions to run in the background. The user is free to continue working with the page while Force.com processes the result. For example, a duplicate checking algorithm could examine the page while the user is inputting data, flagging duplicate records as they are discovered.

2. Actions can refresh a subset of the Visualforce page, such as a table of data, rather than the entire page. This can create a richer, more interactive experience for users and often better-performing pages.

This section explains how to add Ajax behavior to Visualforce pages. It includes the following subsections:

- **Partial Page Refresh:** Refresh selected elements on the page rather than the whole page.

- **Action as JavaScript Function:** Define a JavaScript function that calls an action method on the controller.

- **Action as Timed Event:** Configure an action method to fire at a predefined time interval.

- **Action as JavaScript Event:** Bind a JavaScript event (such as onclick) to a controller action method.

- **Indicating Action Status:** Reflect the status of an asynchronous action on the page.

Partial Page Refresh

Any action component can refresh part of a page using the reRender attribute. This attribute contains a comma-separated list of identifiers (the id values) of Visualforce view components to be refreshed when the action is completed. The identifiers must be of Visualforce components, not raw HTML elements. If no reRender value is provided or the identifiers are invalid, the entire page is refreshed. This is the default behavior of an action component.

Listings 8-1 and 8-2 are a Visualforce page and controller that demonstrate partial page refresh. A commandButton is defined to increment an integer value in the controller when clicked, via the increment method. The amount to be incremented is passed from the page to controller during the click, using the param component. The increment method returns a null PageReference to remain on the current Visualforce page rather than navigating to a new page. This is a requirement for partial page refreshes.

An outputPanel displays the current value of the integer. The reRender attribute is set on the commandButton to refresh only the outputPanel rather than the entire page.

Listing 8-1   **Visualforce Page Using Partial Page Refresh**

```
<apex:page controller="MyPageController">
  <apex:form>
    <apex:commandButton action="{!increment}" value="Increment"
      reRender="result">
      <apex:param assignTo="{!amount}" value="2" />
    </apex:commandButton>
    <apex:outputPanel id="result">The value is: {!value}
    </apex:outputPanel>
  </apex:form>
</apex:page>
```

Listing 8-2   **Visualforce Controller Using Partial Page Refresh**

```
public class MyPageController {
  public Integer value { get; private set; }
  public Integer amount { get; set; }
  public MyPageController() {
    value = 0;
  }
  public PageReference increment() {
    value += amount;
    return null;
  }
}
```

> **Note**
>
> Not every Visualforce component supports being the target of a `reRender` attribute. If you discover a component that is not refreshing properly, enclose it in an `outputPanel` component, give the `outputPanel` a unique `id` value, and specify that `id` value in the `reRender` attribute.

Action as JavaScript Function

The action component `actionFunction` allows you to call an Apex method in the controller as a JavaScript function. This decouples the user interface representation of the action from the action itself. You've already experienced action components that require a user to click a link or button to trigger a controller action. With `actionFunction`, you can call an action from anywhere in your page, including custom JavaScript code.

To use the `actionFunction` component, minimally specify an action to invoke in the `action` attribute, a JavaScript function name in the `name` attribute, and enclose it in a `form` component. Optionally, you can define arguments on the function by nesting `param` components inside the `actionFunction` tag. You can also define a JavaScript function to be invoked when the action is complete by using the `oncomplete` attribute.

Listings 8-3 and 8-4 contain page and controller code demonstrating the use of
actionFunction and partial page refresh. It multiplies a number by two using a controller
method exposed as a JavaScript function. The resulting value is displayed on the page
using a pageMessages component and also refreshed in the call to the JavaScript function.
This causes a stateful interaction in which the number is multiplied in a series.

Listing 8-3   **Visualforce Page Using `actionFunction`**

```
<apex:page controller="MyPageController">
  <apex:outputPanel id="result">
    <apex:pageMessages />
    <a onclick="timesTwoFunction('{!value}'); return false;">
      Run
    </a>
  </apex:outputPanel>
  <apex:form>
    <apex:actionFunction name="timesTwoFunction"
      action="{!timesTwo}" reRender="result">
      <apex:param name="arg1" value="" assignTo="{!value}" />
    </apex:actionFunction>
  </apex:form>
</apex:page>
```

Listing 8-4   **Visualforce Controller Using `actionFunction`**

```
public class MyPageController {
  public Integer value { get; set; }
  public MyPageController() {
    value = 1;
  }
  public PageReference timesTwo() {
    value *= 2;
    addInfo('The result is: ' + value);
    return null;
  }
  private void addInfo(String msg) {
    ApexPages.addMessage(new ApexPages.Message(
      ApexPages.Severity.INFO, msg));
  }
}
```

Action as Timed Event

The actionPoller component invokes a method on the controller at a constant time
interval. It can be used to perform a long-running operation incrementally, using a series
of smaller steps. Another common usage is to perform a repetitive background task such as

querying the database for some interesting business event. For example, a user interface designed for project staffers might use an `actionPoller` to automatically refresh a list of available resources once per minute.

To use `actionPoller`, provide a value for the `action` attribute, the controller method to invoke, and enclose it in a `form` component. This usage fires the action method every 60 seconds. Optionally, provide a value for the `interval` attribute, the time in seconds to wait between invocations of the action. This value must be 5 or greater. You can also set the `onsubmit` and `oncomplete` attributes, JavaScript functions to call before the action is invoked and after the action is completed.

Listing 8-5 is a sample page that uses the `actionPoller` along with the controller from Listing 8-4. But now instead of clicking a link to multiply the number by two, it happens automatically every five seconds.

Listing 8-5   **Visualforce Page Using `actionPoller`**

```
<apex:page controller="MyPageController">
  <apex:outputPanel id="result">
    <apex:pageMessages />
  </apex:outputPanel>
  <apex:form>
    <apex:actionPoller interval="5" action="{!timesTwo}"
      reRender="result" />
  </apex:form>
</apex:page>
```

Action as JavaScript Event

To invoke an action on the controller as a result of a JavaScript event, use the `actionSupport` component. This component fires an action whenever the event is detected on the enclosing Visualforce component.

The `actionSupport` component is placed within the body of a Visualforce component that fires the JavaScript event of interest. For example, an `inputField` component renders an HTML input element, so it fires standard JavaScript events such as `onfocus`, `onblur`, `onclick`, and so forth. Placing an `actionSupport` component within the `inputField` component allows it to listen for one of these events and invoke a controller method in response.

To use `actionSupport`, specify the name of the controller method to invoke in its `action` attribute, and a single JavaScript event to listen for in the `event` attribute. By default, `actionSupport` overrides the default browser-level handlers for the selected event. To disable this behavior, include a `disableDefault` attribute with the value of `false`. The `onsubmit` and `oncomplete` attributes are also supported to allow pre- or post-processing of the request using your own JavaScript function.

Reusing the controller code from Listing 8-4, the Visualforce page in Listing 8-6 fires the `timesTwo` action when the text field receives focus. Try it by clicking somewhere else on the page, and then into the text field.

Listing 8-6   **Visualforce Page Using `actionSupport`**

```
<apex:page controller="MyPageController">
  <apex:outputPanel id="result">
    <apex:pageMessages />
  </apex:outputPanel>
  <apex:form>
    <apex:inputText>
      <apex:actionSupport action="{!timesTwo}"
        event="onfocus" reRender="result" />
    </apex:inputText>
  </apex:form>
</apex:page>
```

Indicating Action Status

You've learned how to invoke actions asynchronously. To notify users when asynchronous actions are being performed, use the `actionStatus` component in conjunction with any action component.

The `actionStatus` component can notify users of two states: when an asynchronous action is started and when it is stopped. To use it, place it in the location on your page where you want to show the status message. Use the `startText` and `stopText` attributes to specify the messages to be shown to the user. If you need to pass arguments to the action, use a nested `param` component.

Listing 8-7 provides an example of using the `actionStatus` component, building on the page from Listing 8-6 and the controller from Listing 8-4. When the text field receives focus, the action is fired, and the status message changes to Started. When the action is complete, the status message is set to Stopped.

Listing 8-7   **Visualforce Page Using `actionStatus`**

```
<apex:page controller="MyPageController">
  <apex:outputPanel id="result">
    <apex:pageMessages />
  </apex:outputPanel>
  <apex:actionStatus id="status"
    startText="Started" stopText="Stopped" />
  <apex:form>
    <apex:inputText>
      <apex:actionSupport action="{!timesTwo}"
        event="onfocus" reRender="result" status="status" />
    </apex:inputText>
  </apex:form>
</apex:page>
```

To display an image or a stylized message, you can use the start and stop facets. Facets are modifiers accepted by some Visualforce components to specify rich values that cannot be contained in XML attributes, such as nested HTML elements. Listing 8-8 is an example of using the facets to mark up the status message with H2 HTML heading elements.

Listing 8-8   **Code Snippet Using `actionStatus` with Facets**

```
<apex:actionStatus id="status">
  <apex:facet name="stop">
    <h2>Stopped</h2>
  </apex:facet>
  <apex:facet name="start">
    <h2>Started</h2>
  </apex:facet>
</apex:actionStatus>
```

To display a dynamic status message, you can write a JavaScript function to modify HTML elements on the page and call it from the `actionStatus` component. The `actionStatus` component supports the `onStart` and `onStop` attributes, which specify JavaScript functions to be invoked when the associated action is started and stopped. Listing 8-9 provides an example of this usage, using JavaScript to update the HTML content of a `div` tag in response to the `actionStatus` changing state.

Listing 8-9   **Code Snippet Using `actionStatus` with JavaScript**

```
<apex:page controller="MyPageController">
  <script type="text/javascript">
    function start() {
      document.getElementById("myStatus").innerHTML = 'Started';
    }
    function stop() {
      document.getElementById("myStatus").innerHTML = 'Stopped';
    }
  </script>
  <apex:outputPanel id="result">
    <apex:pageMessages />
  </apex:outputPanel>
  <apex:actionStatus id="status"
    onStart="start();" onStop="stop();" />
  <div id="myStatus"></div>
  <apex:form>
    <apex:inputText>
      <apex:actionSupport action="{!timesTwo}"
        event="onfocus" reRender="result" status="status" />
    </apex:inputText>
  </apex:form>
</apex:page>
```

Modular Visualforce

Visualforce pages that are modular, composed of a number of smaller reusable building blocks, improve usability by providing consistent appearance and behavior. They are also easier to develop and maintain. Common functionality is defined once in a single place rather than repeated in multiple pages.

Visualforce provides several features you can use to create modular, highly maintainable pages:

- **Static Resources:** Reusable images, scripts, stylesheets, and other static content can be stored in static resources, available for embedding in all Visualforce pages in the Force.com organization.

- **Inclusion:** The contents of one Visualforce page can be included in another page. A common use for this is page headers and footers.

- **Composition:** Composition allows one Visualforce page to serve as a template for another. The template specifies the static and dynamic portions of a page. Use the template to inject dynamic content while maintaining a consistent page layout and structure.

- **Custom Visualforce Components:** Visualforce provides a library of standard components such as `pageBlock` and `dataTable`, but also allows you to define your own custom components, reusable in any page.

Static Resources

Static resources are containers for content used in Visualforce pages that does not change. Examples of unchanging content include images, stylesheets, and JavaScript files. Although many alternatives to static resources exist, such as Force.com Documents and Amazon S3, static resources have the benefit of being tightly integrated with the Visualforce page. Their names are validated when the page is compiled, preventing the creation of a page that refers to an invalid static resource.

A static resource can be a single file or a zip archive consisting of many files. The maximum size of a single static resource is 5MB, and no more than 250MB of static resources can be defined in any single Force.com organization.

To create a new static resource, follow these steps:

1. In the App Setup area, click Develop → Static Resources.

2. Click the New button to add a new static resource.

3. Enter a name for the static resource. The name cannot contain spaces or other non-alphanumeric characters, must begin with a letter, and must be unique. The name is used to refer to the static resource in Visualforce pages.

4. Specify an optional description to explain the purpose of this static resource to other users.

5. Click the Browse button to find a file in your file system to provide the content for the static resource.

6. Leave the Cache Control setting at its default value, Private. This setting is discussed later in the "Force.com Sites" subsection.

7. Click the Save button to complete the static resource definition.

If your static resource contains a single file, refer to it in your Visualforce page using the syntax `{!$Resource.name}`, where *name* is the name of the static resource to include.

The syntax is different for referring to a single file within a static resource that is a zip archive. Use `{!URLFOR($Resource.name, 'path/tofile')}`, where *name* is the name of the static resource, and *path/tofile* is the full path to the desired file.

Inclusion

A simple way to create modular Visualforce pages is to use the `include` component. It embeds the content of the included page in the current page. The `pageName` attribute specifies the name of the Visualforce page to include. The included page must be a Visualforce page. You cannot include arbitrary URLs.

Listing 8-10 provides an example of using the `include` component. It embeds the page named SkillsMatrix between two horizontal rules.

Listing 8-10   **Visualforce Page Using `include`**

```
<apex:page>
  <hr />
  <apex:include pageName="SkillsMatrix" />
  <hr />
</apex:page>
```

When a single Visualforce page ends up containing multiple controllers due to the `include` component, controllers are isolated from each other and operate independently. The controller of the included page does not have access to the state of the controller on the parent page, and vice versa. But pages are included inline, so JavaScript functions and DOM references can be made across included pages without security restrictions.

Caution

Be careful when using `messages` and `pageMessages` components in pages that are to be included in other pages. If the included page and parent page both supply one of these components, the same page messages will be rendered in multiple locations.

Composition

Composition is a powerful way to create modular Visualforce pages. It allows a Visualforce page to be defined as a template. The template can contain static content and placeholders for content that can be overridden by an implementing page. This enforces a standard structure for the pages without requiring Visualforce developers to remember a sequence of `include` components. It also places more control over the appearance of many pages within the scope of a single page (the template) for easier maintenance.

In the template page, the `insert` component is used to define a named area that can be overridden by a page implementing the template. The implementing page uses the `composition` component to set the name of the page to serve as its template. It then provides content for the named areas of the template using the `define` component.

For example, a template might consist of a header, body, and footer, with horizontal rules between each. Listing 8-11 defines this template page, named `MyPageTemplate`. Note that the header area includes its own default content. This optional content is rendered in the event that content is not provided by an implementing page.

Listing 8-11   **Visualforce Page as Template**

```
<apex:page>
  <apex:insert name="header">
    <h1>Header</h1>
  </apex:insert>
  <hr /><apex:insert name="body" />
  <hr /><apex:insert name="footer">
    Inheriting the footer content
  </apex:insert>
</apex:page>
```

The template is not interesting to render by itself, but in Listing 8-12 it's implemented using the `composition` component. The `template` attribute specifies the template defined in Listing 8-11, which should be named `MyPageTemplate` for this example to work properly. The three dynamic areas are merged into the template to result in the final rendered output. The header area is provided, so it overrides the content defined by the template. The footer is inherited from the template.

Listing 8-12   **Visualforce Page Using Template**

```
<apex:page>
  <apex:composition template="MyPageTemplate">
    <apex:define name="header">
      Overriding the header content
    </apex:define>
    <apex:define name="body">
      This is the body content
    </apex:define>
  </apex:composition>
</apex:page>
```

Composition works with multiple controllers identically to the `include` component. They run independently of each other, but all content is rendered in the same page.

Custom Visualforce Components

Custom components allow you to build a library of reusable user interface elements, encapsulating behavior and appearance while integrating with the data on the page and in the controller using the standard expression language. With custom components, all the functionality of standard components such as `pageBlock` and `inputField` are available to you to define from scratch using Visualforce and Apex code.

Custom components can be used to hide the implementation details of client-side technology like JavaScript. For example, a component can wrap a JavaScript user interface library such as Sencha's Ext JS, freeing Visualforce page developers from the nitty-gritty of integrating Ext JS code into their pages. Custom components can also serve as full-blown pages themselves, reading and writing in the Force.com database through standard or custom controllers.

Defining a Custom Component

To create a new component, select File → New → Apex Component in the Force.com IDE. Or, using the Web browser, navigate to App Setup and click Develop → Components.

Custom components are defined with `component` as the root-level element rather than the familiar `page`. Following the `component` tag is an optional set of `attribute` components specifying the names and types of variables that can be shared between the page and the component. Supported types are primitives, standard and custom database objects, one-dimensional arrays, and custom Apex classes. Attributes can be declared as `required`, meaning that a page using the component must provide a value or it fails to compile. Attributes can also be assigned to member variables in a controller using the `assignTo` attribute.

The remainder of the component definition is identical to a standard Visualforce page, containing a combination of JavaScript, CSS, HTML elements, and standard components, as well as other custom components.

Listing 8-13 provides an example of a component for showing an address on a Google Map. To try the example in Listing 8-13, apply for your own Google Maps API key and replace the "..." in the value of the `includeScript` component. API keys are bound to a domain, so provide the correct URL of your Visualforce pages (for example, https://c.na6.visual.force.com) when you sign up at http://code.google.com/apis/maps/signup.html.

Listing 8-13   **Custom Visualforce Component to Render Google Map**

```
<apex:component>
  <apex:attribute name="address" type="string" required="true"
    description="Address to show on the Google map" />
  <apex:includeScript
    value="http://maps.google.com/maps?file=api&v=2.x&key=..." />
```

```
   <script>
var map = null;
var geocoder = null;
function showAddress(address) {
  initGMap();
  if (geocoder) {
    geocoder.getLatLng(
      address,
      function(point) {
        if (point) {
          map.setCenter(point, 15);
          var marker = new GMarker(point);
          map.addOverlay(marker);
        }
      });
  }
}
function initGMap() {
  if (GBrowserIsCompatible()) {
    map = new GMap2(document.getElementById("map_canvas"));
    if (geocoder == null) {
      geocoder = new GClientGeocoder();
    }
  }
}
function init() {
  showAddress('{!address}');
}
var previousOnload = window.onload;
window.onload = function() {
  if (previousOnload) {
    previousOnload();
  }
  init();
}
</script>
<div id="map_canvas" style="width: 300px; height: 250px"></div>
</apex:component>
```

Using a Custom Component

Using a custom component in a page is much like using a standard component. The difference is that instead of prefacing the component with the apex namespace, you use c. Listing 8-14 shows an example of using the custom component defined in Listing 8-13 to render a Google Map for an address. It references the GoogleMap component, followed by a value for its required `address` attribute containing the street address to render on the map. In this example, the attribute value is hard-coded into the page, but this is not the only way to provide an attribute value. Like standard components, attribute values can include expression language, enabling them to share data with the controller.

Listing 8-14   **Visualforce Page Using Custom Component**

```
<apex:page>
<c:GoogleMap address="1 market st. san francisco, ca" />
</apex:page>
```

Extending Visualforce

You can extend the appearance and behavior of Visualforce pages dramatically using standard JavaScript libraries provided by the open-source community or independent software vendors. Adobe Flex is another path for extending Visualforce, allowing part or all of a page to be covered with a rich, animated canvas that offers developers pixel-level control. You can also extend Visualforce to a new population of users, anonymous users who do not have accounts in your Force.com organization.

This section covers these scenarios in more detail in the following subsections:

- **Using JavaScript Libraries:** For the most part, including open-source and commercial JavaScript libraries in Visualforce is a straightforward process after you learn how to reference Visualforce components dynamically.
- **Adobe Flex and Visualforce:** Achieve rich, pixel-perfect user interfaces across browsers using Adobe Flex, while using Force.com as your data source.
- **Force.com Sites:** Extend Force.com to anonymous users using Sites, opening Visualforce to general-purpose Web development.

Using JavaScript Libraries

You can use a wide variety of open-source and commercial JavaScript libraries in Visualforce pages. These libraries can include user interface widgets, utility functions, and entire frameworks for more productive JavaScript development.

The effort involved in integrating each library with Visualforce varies with the library. In general, the more dynamic your Visualforce page is and the more it deviates from the interaction patterns assumed by the JavaScript library, the more difficult the task becomes.

A common scenario in JavaScript integration is referencing a Visualforce component dynamically in a JavaScript function. Each Visualforce component is assigned a unique identifier, set in its `id` attribute. If you override this `id` attribute and provide your own value, Visualforce does not simply accept your value. It fully qualifies it by affixing the identifiers of any containers included between your component and the root page component.

So, if your JavaScript calls document.getElementById() and provides a plain identifier as an argument, it will fail to retrieve the element. Instead, use {!$Component.id} as the argument, where id is the identifier you set on your Visualforce component. When the page is rendered, Visualforce reads this token and replaces it with the fully qualified value of the identifier. If the identifier cannot be found, the token is replaced with an empty string.

If your component is contained within a form component, you must provide the form with an id value as well and include the form identifier in the component reference. For example, if the form identifier is myForm and the component you want to obtain a reference to is myText, the usage is {!$Component.myForm:myText}.

Listing 8-15 shows an example of a Visualforce page that obtains a component in JavaScript and displays an alert with its value. Click the Run link to try it.

Listing 8-15   **Referencing a Visualforce Component in JavaScript**

```
<apex:page>
  <script type="text/javascript">
    function demo() {
      var component = document.getElementById(
        "{!$Component.myForm:myText}");
      alert('The value is ' + component.value);
    }
  </script>
  <apex:form id="myForm">
    <apex:inputText id="myText" />
    <a onclick="demo();">Run</a>
  </apex:form>
</apex:page>
```

> **Tip**
>
> Use the View Source feature of your Web browser or a plug-in such as Firebug to debug component identifier problems.

Adobe Flex and Visualforce

Adobe Flex is a rich client technology that renders user interfaces using the Adobe Flash player. Flash player is a plug-in installed in most browsers and used by YouTube and other popular Web sites. Flex user interfaces often feature animation and complex data visualizations that might be harder to achieve with standard HTML, CSS, and JavaScript. Flex has the added benefit of being highly consistent in appearance and behavior across different browsers and platforms, without requiring extra effort from developers.

You can add Flex components to Visualforce pages to provide animation and other graphics-intensive user interfaces that are not practical to implement purely using

Visualforce components. These Flex components can interact directly with Force.com using an integration technology called the Force.com Flex framework. They can also integrate with Visualforce components using standard JavaScript.

> **Caution**
>
> Deciding when and when not to use Flex can be a challenge. Although it provides the capability to create exciting user interfaces with little code, it's not a native part of Force.com or the Web browser. Consider the requirements of your user interface carefully to justify its use. Beyond the concerns of load-time performance (the overhead of loading the Flash player and the component itself), performance penalties can occur in moving rendering away from the Force.com service and into the user's Web browser. Additionally, many of the development efficiencies of Visualforce, such as tight, compile-time integration with the database, are lost when you develop in Flex.

Flex is a deep and feature-rich technology unto itself, providing the XML markup language MXML to describe the appearance of the user interface and ActionScript as its JavaScript-like scripting language. This subsection provides a brief introduction to using Adobe Flash Builder for Force.com to integrate with Force.com data. It assumes you are familiar with ActionScript and MXML because these subjects fall well outside the scope of this book.

Introduction to the Adobe Flash Builder for Force.com

Visit http://developer.force.com/flashbuilder to download the latest version of the Adobe Flash Builder for Force.com. It combines the functionality of Adobe Flash Builder and the Force.com IDE into a single development environment. It also provides new functionality to help create Flex applications that interact with Force.com. For example, it includes a new type of project, called a Force.com Flex Project, pre-configured with a library of ActionScript classes to make SOQL calls and perform DML operations. It also provides three new user interface components: FieldContainer, FieldElement, and LabelAndField. They allow quick construction of Visualforce-like, form-based user interfaces that are bound to Force.com data. Figure 8-1 shows Flash Builder for Force.com in action.

Creating a Flex Project

To get started with Flash Builder, follow the steps given next to create a sample project:

1. Create a new Force.com Flex project called `FlexDemo`.

2. In the project's properties, on the Flex Build Path tab, change the Framework linkage menu setting to Merged into code.

3. Enter the MXML code shown in Listing 8-16 and save it. If Project → Build Automatically is checked, `bin-debug/FlexDemo.swf` is generated. If not, select Project → Build Project to explicitly compile the project.

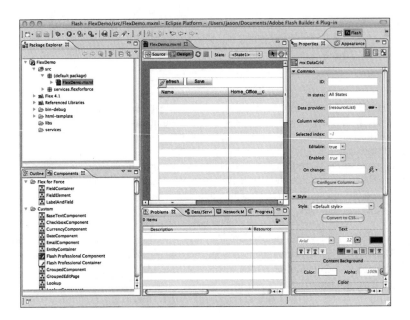

Figure 8-1   Adobe Flash Builder for Force.com

Listing 8-16   **Flex Demo MXML**

```xml
<?xml version="1.0" encoding="utf-8"?>
<mx:Application xmlns:fx="http://ns.adobe.com/mxml/2009"
  xmlns:s="library://ns.adobe.com/flex/spark"
  xmlns:mx="library://ns.adobe.com/flex/mx" width="1000" height="800"
  xmlns:flexforforce="http://flexforforce.salesforce.com"
  creationComplete="login(event)">
  <fx:Declarations>
    <flexforforce:F3WebApplication id="app"
      serverUrl="https://www.salesforce.com/services/Soap/u/17.0"
      loginComplete="loginCompleteHandler(event)"
      loginFailed="loginFailedHandler(event)" />
  </fx:Declarations>
<fx:Script>
<![CDATA[
  import mx.collections.ArrayCollection;
  import com.salesforce.results.QueryResult;
  import mx.utils.ObjectUtil;
  import mx.controls.Alert;
  import mx.rpc.Responder;
  import com.salesforce.events.LoginFaultEvent;
  import com.salesforce.events.LoginResultEvent;
  [Bindable]
```

```
  private var resourceList: ArrayCollection =
    new ArrayCollection();
  private function login(event: Event): void {
    app.serverUrl = parameters.server_url;
    app.loginBySessionId(parameters.session_id);
}
  protected function loginFailedHandler(event: LoginFaultEvent): void {
    Alert.show('Login failed: ' + event);
  }
  protected function loginCompleteHandler(event: LoginResultEvent): void {
    loadData();
  }
  private function handleFault(fault: Object): void {
    Alert.show(ObjectUtil.toString(fault));
  }
  private function loadData(): void {
    app.connection.query("SELECT Id, Name, Home_Office__c, Region__c, " +
      "Hourly_Cost_Rate__c, Start_Date__c FROM Resource__c",
      new mx.rpc.Responder(
        function(qr: QueryResult): void {
          if (qr.size > 0) {
            resourceList = qr.records;
          }
        }, handleFault)
    );
  }
  private function save(): void {
    app.connection.update(resourceList.toArray(),
      new mx.rpc.Responder(handleUpdate, handleFault));
  }
  private function handleUpdate(result: Object): void {
    Alert.show(ObjectUtil.toString(result));
  }
  private function numericSortCompareFunction(
    obj1: Object, obj2: Object): int {
    return ObjectUtil.numericCompare(obj1 as Number,
      obj2 as Number);
  }
]]>
</mx:Script>
<mx:VBox height="100%" width="100%">
  <mx:HBox>
    <mx:Button label="Refresh" click="loadData();" />
    <mx:Button label="Save" click="save();" />
  </mx:HBox>
  <mx:DataGrid dataProvider="{resourceList}"
    editable="true" selectable="false"
```

```
    height="100%" width="100%">
    <mx:columns>
      <mx:DataGridColumn dataField="Name"/>
      <mx:DataGridColumn dataField="Home_Office__c"/>
      <mx:DataGridColumn dataField="Region__c"/>
      <mx:DataGridColumn dataField="Hourly_Cost_Rate__c"
        sortCompareFunction="numericSortCompareFunction" />
      <mx:DataGridColumn dataField="Start_Date__c"/>
    </mx:columns>
  </mx:DataGrid>
</mx:VBox>
</mx:Application>
```

4. Upload `bin-debug/FlexDemo.swf` as a static resource in Force.com called
    FlexDemo. The result is shown in Figure 8-2.

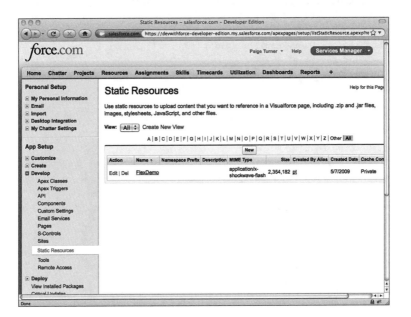

Figure 8-2   FlexDemo SWF as static resource

5. Create a Visualforce page called `FlexDemo` using the code in Listing 8-17.

Listing 8-17   **Visualforce Page for FlexDemo**

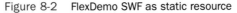

```
<apex:page sidebar="false">
  <apex:flash src="{!$Resource.FlexDemo}"
    height="800" width="100%"
```

```
   flashvars="session_id={!$Api.Session_ID}
   &server_url={!$Api.Partner_Server_URL_200}" />
</apex:page>
```

6. Visit the page /apex/FlexDemo to try it out. It should look as shown in Figure 8-3. Click cells to edit them and then click the Save button to apply all changes to the Force.com database or Refresh to revert them.

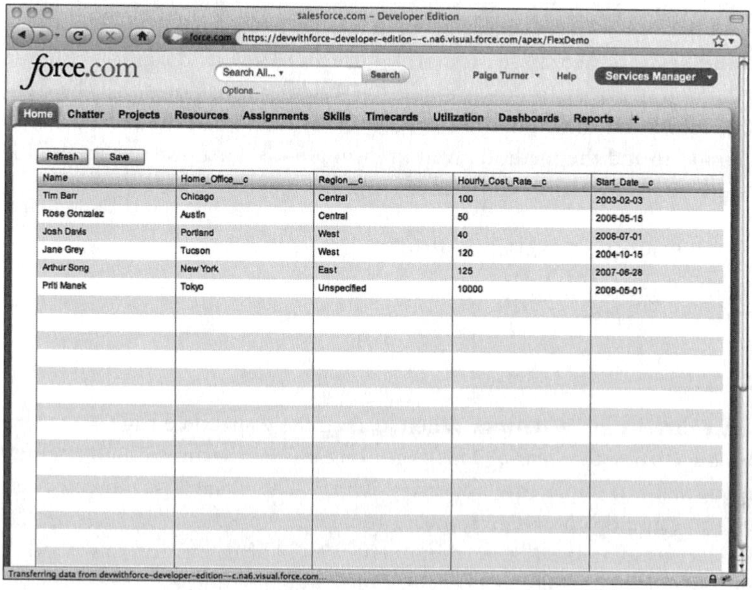

Figure 8-3   Using the FlexDemo page

The following list contains some comments on the code:

- **Sorting of numeric column:** Sorting of the numeric column Hourly_Cost_Rate__c required the definition of a sortCompareFunction. Without this function, the numeric field would be sorted as a string field, resulting in an incorrect order.

- **Brute-force update strategy:** All rows are updated regardless of whether they've been modified. This could be improved by detecting changes in the DataGrid and maintaining state to indicate the list of modified rows, passing only these rows to the update method.

- **No pagination:** The DataGrid displays all records returned by the SOQL query. This is not efficient or usable for large data sets. To improve this example, you could modify the SOQL query to restrict the number of records returned or buffer the results in a data structure in Flex and display subsets of the buffer in the DataGrid.

- **Id column in SOQL:** The Id column is included in the SOQL but not displayed in the DataGrid component. It is required for the `update` method.

Supporting Microsoft Internet Explorer

If you're using the Microsoft Internet Explorer browser, the FlexDemo example might not work properly. Identify the issue from the following list and apply the suggested fix:

- **Invalid session:** Setting the session ID from a merge field can sometimes result in invalid session errors. In this example, the resulting behavior is that the data from Force.com is not shown in the DataGrid. A workaround is to add a controller extension to add the method given in Listing 8-18. Then use this method instead of `{!$Api.Session_ID}` in your `flashvars`.

Listing 8-18   **Controller Extension Method**

```
public String getSessionId() {
  return UserInfo.getSessionId();
}
```

- **Nonsecure items warning:** When loading the Visualforce page, Internet Explorer pops up a dialog that reads, "This page contains both secure and nonsecure items. Do you want to display the nonsecure items?" The `flash` Visualforce component seems to cause this problem. To make your page work better in Internet Explorer, consider replacing the `flash` component with HTML markup to embed the Flex object manually. Listing 8-19 provides an example of this.

Listing 8-19   **HTML for Embedding Flex Object**

```
<object
  width="100%" height="800"
  codebase="https://fpdownload.macromedia.com/get
    /flashplayer/current/swflash.cab">
  <param name="movie" value="{!$Resource.FlexDemo}" />
  <param name="FlashVars"
    value="session_id={!$Api.Session_ID}&
      server_url={!$Api.Partner_Server_URL_200}" />
  <embed src="{!$Resource.FlexDemo}"
    width="100%" height="800"
    FlashVars="session_id={!$Api.Session_ID}&
      server_url={!$Api.Partner_Server_URL_200}"
```

```
        type="application/x-shockwave-flash">
    </embed>
</object>
```

Force.com Sites

Sites is a feature of Force.com that enables public access to your Visualforce pages. A site is a collection of ordinary Visualforce pages and access control settings assigned to a unique base URL. You can define one or many sites within a Force.com organization. Sites can be individually brought up or down by your organization's system administrator.

This subsection divides the discussion of Force.com Sites into four parts, summarized next:

1. **Enabling and Creating a Site:** Turn on the Sites feature and create your first site.

2. **Security Configuration:** Configure the privileges granted to the anonymous user of your site.

3. **Adding Pages to a Site:** Select Visualforce pages that are accessible within a site.

4. **Authenticating Users:** Blend public and private pages by integrating a site with Customer Portal.

Enabling and Creating a Site

To enable Sites for the first time in your organization, go to the App Setup area and click Develop → Sites. You should see the screen shown in Figure 8-4.

> **Note**
>
> If you do not see a link to Sites listed in the Develop options, your organization does not have access to the Sites feature. Visit http://developer.force.com/iwantsites to get access.

You must pick a Force.com domain name to continue. A domain name provides a unique, root address for all of your sites. You can remap this address to your own brand-name address (not Force.com) by configuring a CNAME alias on your domain hosting provider.

Enter your domain name, select the box to indicate that you've read the terms of use, and click the Check Availability button. After your domain name has been accepted, you can define your first site. Adding a site also creates a number of sample components, pages, and controllers in your organization.

After your first site is defined, the main Sites page should look as shown in Figure 8-5.

Security Configuration

When a new site is created, a corresponding profile is also created to manage the privileges of the guest user. The guest user is a special type of Salesforce.com license that represents the anonymous user of your site.

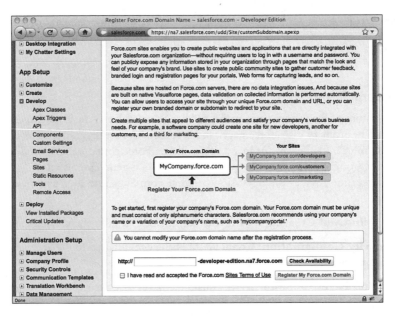

Figure 8-4   Enabling Sites feature

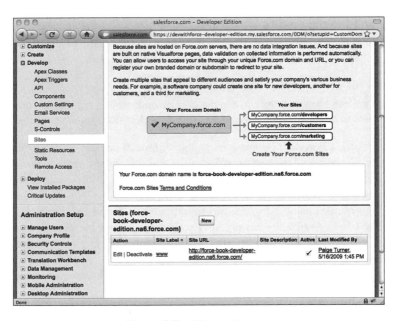

Figure 8-5   Sites main page

The guest profile for each site is configured using the native user interface. To view the profile, navigate to the Site Details page for the site and click the Public Access Settings button. Configure the privileges of the guest profile with extreme caution because mistakes can expose sensitive data in your Force.com organization to the entire world.

> **Note**
>
> The guest profile does not appear with other profiles in the Administration Setup area (Manage Users → Profiles). You must use the Public Access Settings button on the Sites Detail page to reach it.

If a page in a Force.com site uses static resources, make sure that they can be accessed from the guest profile. Go to each static resource and set its Cache Control to Public.

Adding Pages to a Site

A site starts off with a series of system-defined pages such as Exception and FileNotFound. These pages are shown to users in the event of errors in the site. You can redefine them by simply editing them.

You can also add your own custom pages to the site. To add pages, click the Edit button in the Site Visualforce Pages section. Select one or more pages from the list on the left and click the Add button to move them to the list of Enabled Visualforce Pages. Click Save when you're done.

The URL of your pages is the default Web address of the site followed by the name of the page. For example, in Figure 8-6, the default Web address is http://force-book-developer-edition.na6.force.com. If a page named MyPage is added to the site, users can access it at http://force-book-developer-edition.na6.force.com/MyPage.

> **Note**
>
> A site must be activated before any pages in it are accessible. To activate a site, select its Active check box in the Site Detail or click the Activate link on the main Sites page.

Authenticating Users

Anonymous users can be converted to named, authenticated users through the Customer Portal, or portal for short. A portal allows you to extend Force.com to your partners and customers without requiring full user accounts for each of them. It is tightly integrated with Force.com Sites.

Enable portal integration by clicking the Login Settings button on the Site Details page. In the Login Settings section, click the Edit button and select an existing portal from the drop-down list, and then click the Save button. Figure 8-7 shows a site enabled to log in to the portal named Sample Customer Portal.

> **Note**
>
> If no portals are listed, you must configure one that is Login Enabled. Go to the App Setup area and click Customize → Customer Portal → Settings. Setting up a portal is not within the scope of this book, so refer to the online documentation for more information.

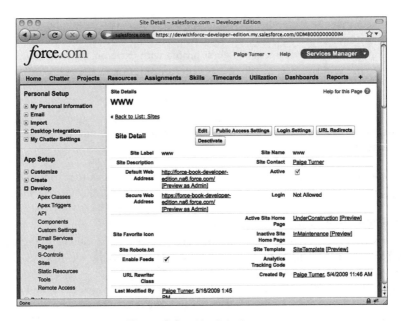

Figure 8-6   Site Details page

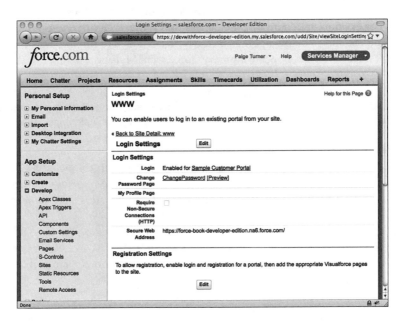

Figure 8-7   Login Settings page

Sample Application: Enhanced Skills Matrix

This section builds on the Services Manager's Skills Matrix feature developed in Chapter 7, "User Interfaces." Users of the Skills Matrix feature have requested the ability to compare a consultant's skills with those of other consultants without navigating to a new page. They would like to see the ratings of other consultants in the same skill visually layered atop the existing Skills Matrix user interface, as shown in Figure 8-8.

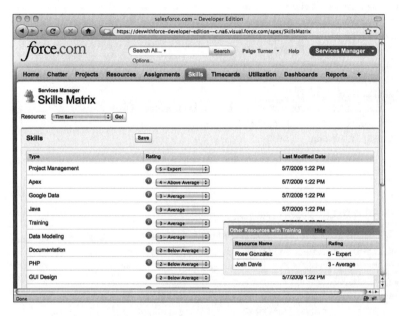

Figure 8-8   Skills Matrix with comparison overlay

The following technologies from this chapter are used in the development of the feature:

- **JavaScript integration:** The Yahoo! User Interface library (YUI) is integrated to provide an easing effect, fading in and out the list of other resources and their skill ratings. YUI is available at http://developer.yahoo.com/yui.

- **Custom Visualforce components:** The overlay containing the other consultants' skills is encapsulated in its own custom Visualforce component and controller.

- **actionSupport component:** This component is used to show and hide the skills comparison overlay when the user hovers over an informational icon.

Begin by developing a custom component for retrieving and rendering a list of skill ratings and consultants. The input to this component is a skill type and a resource identifier of the currently selected consultant. The skill type is the name of a proficiency that consultants are measured on, a picklist value from `Skill__c.Type__c` such as Java or Apex. The resource identifier is used to exclude the current consultant from the list, because their skill ratings are already shown on the Skills Matrix user interface.

Listing 8-20 provides a sample implementation of the controller to support the requirements, and Listing 8-21 shows the custom component that uses it.

Listing 8-20 **CompareSkillsController**

```
public class CompareSkillsController {
  public String resourceId { get; set; }
  public String skill { get; set; }
  public List<Skill__c> getData() {
    return [ SELECT Resource__r.Name, Type__c, Rating__c
      FROM Skill__c
      WHERE Type__c = :skill
        AND Rating__c NOT IN ('', '0 - None') AND
        Resource__c != :resourceId
      ORDER BY Rating__c DESC ];
  }
}
```

Listing 8-21 **CompareSkillsComponent**

```
<apex:component controller="CompareSkillsController">
  <apex:attribute name="skillType" description="Type of skill"
    type="String" required="true" assignTo="{!skill}" />
  <apex:attribute name="resourceId"
    description="Id of resource to compare with"
    type="String" required="true" assignTo="{!resourceId}" />
  <apex:pageBlock>
    <apex:pageBlockSection collapsible="false" columns="1">
      <apex:facet name="header">
        Other Resources with {!skillType}
        <span style="padding-left: 30px;">
          <a onclick="hideOverlay(); return false;"
          href="" style="text-decoration: underline;">Hide</a>
        </span>
      </apex:facet>
      <apex:pageBlockTable value="{!data}" var="item">
        <apex:column value="{!item.Resource__r.Name}" />
        <apex:column value="{!item.Rating__c}" />
      </apex:pageBlockTable>
    </apex:pageBlockSection>
  </apex:pageBlock>
</apex:component>
```

To integrate this component with the Skills Matrix, perform the following steps:

1. Add `sidebar="false"` to the `page` component. This frees up extra horizontal screen real estate that is used to display the skills comparison overlay.

2. Insert the code given in Listing 8-22 to the top of the Skills Matrix page, following the `style` HTML tag.

Listing 8-22   Adding YUI Overlay Support to Skills Matrix Page

```
<apex:stylesheet
  value="http://yui.yahooapis.com/combo?2.7.0/build/
    container/assets/skins/sam/container.css" />
<apex:includeScript
  value="http://yui.yahooapis.com/combo?2.7.0/build/
    yahoo-dom-event/yahoo-dom-event.js&2.7.0/build/animation/
    animation-min.js&2.7.0/build/container/container-min.js" />
<script>
var overlay;
function showOverlay(e) {
  overlay = new YAHOO.widget.Overlay(
    "{!$Component.compareSkills}", {
      xy:[525, e.pageY],
      visible:false, width:"450px", zIndex:1000,
      effect:{effect:YAHOO.widget.ContainerEffect.FADE,duration:0.25}
    }
  );
  overlay.render("{!$Component.form}");
  overlay.show();
}
function hideOverlay() {
  if (overlay != null) {
    overlay.hide();
    overlay = null;
  }
}
</script>
```

3. Add the code shown in Listing 8-23 to the bottom of the `SkillsMatrixController` class. The new method is called to refresh the skills comparison component.

Listing 8-23   **Adding Action Method to Skills Matrix Controller**

```
public PageReference refreshCompareSkills() {
  return null;
}
```

4. Insert the code given in Listing 8-24 to the Skills Matrix page, immediately follow-ing the opening tag of the column component containing the skill rating (headerValue="Rating"). It adds an informational icon beside each skill. Hovering over this icon displays the overlay containing the skills comparison.

Listing 8-24   **Adding actionSupport to Skills Matrix Page**

```
<apex:image value="/img/msg_icons/info16.png"
  style="margin-top: 2px; margin-right: 10px;">
  <apex:actionSupport event="onmouseover"
    action="{!refreshCompareSkills}" rerender="compareSkills"
    oncomplete="showOverlay(event);" onsubmit="hideOverlay();">
    <apex:param name="p1" value="{!skill.Type__c}"
    assignTo="{!selectedSkillType}" />
  </apex:actionSupport>
</apex:image>
```

5. For the last step, insert the code in Listing 8-25 after the closing tag of the form component on the Skills Matrix page. It adds an outputPanel containing the CompareSkillsComponent, which is rendered as an overlay using YUI in the showOverlay JavaScript function.

Listing 8-25   **Adding CompareSkillsComponent to the Skills Matrix Page**

```
<apex:outputPanel id="compareSkills" style="visibility: hidden;">
  <c:CompareSkillsComponent skillType="{!selectedSkillType}"
    resourceId="{!selectedResourceId}" />
</apex:outputPanel>
```

Summary

In this chapter, you've seen some of the ways Visualforce can produce effective user inter-faces, from action components that provide Ajax behavior to the integration of non-Force.com technologies such as Adobe Flex. Before switching gears in the next chapter, take a moment to review these key points:

- Stick with standard and custom Visualforce components wherever possible to keep your user interface running smoothly with the rest of the Force.com today and in future releases.

- Strive to adopt the many features of Visualforce that foster modularity, such as composition and custom components, rather than copying and pasting code from page to page.

- You can use Visualforce to create public-facing Web pages through Force.com Sites. Sites are simply a series of configuration settings that enable a guest profile to access a set of pages, extending your existing investment in Visualforce.

9

Batch Processing

You've learned two ways you can process database records within the Force.com platform: triggers and Visualforce controllers. Each has its own set of platform-imposed limitations, such as how many records can be created at one time. As you accumulate tens of thousands of records or more in your database, you might need to process more of records than permitted by the governor limits applying to triggers and controllers.

Although Salesforce has simplified and incrementally relaxed governor limits in recent Force.com releases, triggers and Visualforce controllers are fundamentally not suited to processing large amounts of data in a multitenant environment. They are driven by user interaction, and must be limited to provide good performance to all users. The Force.com platform carefully controls its resources to maintain high performance for all, so resource-intensive tasks such as processing millions of records must be planned and executed over time, balanced with the demands of other customers.

Batch processing makes this possible, and Batch Apex is the Force.com feature that enables batch processing on the platform. With Batch Apex, data-intensive tasks are taken offline, detached from user interactions, the exact timing of their execution determined by Salesforce itself. In return for relinquishing some control, you the developer receive the ability to process orders of magnitude more records than you can in triggers and controllers.

In this chapter, you learn how to use Batch Apex to create, update, and delete millions of records at a time. It is divided into five sections:

- **Introduction to Batch Apex:** Learn the concepts and terminology of Batch Apex, what it can do, and when you should and should not use it.
- **Getting Started with Batch Apex:** Walk through a simple example of Batch Apex. Develop the code, run it, and monitor its execution.
- **Testing Batch Apex:** Like any other Apex code, proper test coverage is required. Learn how to kick off Batch Apex jobs within test code.

- **Scheduling Batch Apex:** Although Salesforce has the final say on when Batch Apex is run, you can schedule jobs to run using a built-in scheduler. Learn how to use the scheduling user interface and achieve finer-grained control in Apex code.
- **Sample Application:** Enhance the Services Manager application by creating a scheduled batch process to identify missing timecards.

Introduction to Batch Apex

Prior to the availability of Batch Apex, the only options for processing data exceeding the governor limits of triggers and controllers were tricky workarounds to shift work off of the platform. For example, you might have hundreds of thousands of records spanning multiple Lookup relationships to be summarized, de-duplicated, cleansed, or otherwise modified en masse algorithmically. You could use the Web Services API to interact with the Force.com data from outside of Force.com itself, or JavaScript to process batches of data inside the web browser. These approaches are usually slow and brittle, requiring lots of code and exposing you to data quality problems over time due to gaps in error handling and recovery. Batch Apex allows you to keep the large, data-intensive processing tasks within the platform, taking advantage of its close proximity to the data and transactional integrity to create secure, reliable processes without the limits of normal, interactive Apex code. This section introduces you to concepts and guidelines for using Batch Apex to prepare you for hands-on work in the following section.

Batch Apex Concepts

Batch Apex is an execution framework that splits a large dataset into subsets and provides them to ordinary Apex programs that you develop, which continue to operate within their usual governor limits. This means with some minor rework to make your code operate as Batch Apex, you can process data volumes that would otherwise be prohibited within the platform. By helping Salesforce break up your processing task, you are permitted to run it within its platform.

A few key concepts in Batch Apex are used throughout this chapter:

- **Scope:** The scope is the set of records that a Batch Apex process operates on. It can consist of 1 record or up to 50 million records. Scope is usually expressed as a SOQL statement, which is contained in a Query Locator, a system object that is blessedly exempt from the normal governor limits on SOQL. If your scope is too complex to be specified in a single SOQL statement, then writing Apex code to generate the scope programmatically is also possible. Unfortunately, using Apex code dramatically reduces the number of records that can be processed, because it is subject to the standard governor limit on records returned by a SOQL statement.
- **Batch job:** A batch job is a Batch Apex program that has been submitted for execution. It is the runtime manifestation of your code, running asynchronously within

the Force.com platform. Because batch jobs run in the background and can take many hours to complete their work, Salesforce provides a user interface for listing batch jobs and their statuses, and to allow individual jobs to be canceled. This job information is also available as a standard object in the database. Although the batch job is not the atomic unit of work within Batch Apex, it is the only platform-provided level at which you have control over a batch process.

- **Transaction:** Each batch job consists of transactions, which are the governor limit-friendly units of work you're familiar with from triggers and Visualforce controllers. By default, a transaction is up to 200 records, but you can adjust this downward in code. When a batch job starts, the scope is split into a series of transactions. Each transaction is then processed by your Apex code and committed to the database independently. Although the same block of your code is being called upon to process potentially thousands of transactions, the transactions themselves are normally stateless. None of the variables within it are saved between invocations unless you explicitly designate your Batch Apex code as stateful when it is developed. Salesforce doesn't provide information on whether your transactions are run in parallel or serially, nor how they are ordered. Observationally, transactions seem to run serially, in order based on scope.

In the following subsection, these concepts are applied to take you one step closer to writing your own Batch Apex.

Understanding the `Batchable` Interface

To make your Apex code run as a batch you must sign a contract with the platform. This contract takes the form of an interface called `Batchable` that must be implemented by your code. It requires that you structure your processing logic into the following three methods:

- **start:** The start method is concerned with the scope of work, the raw set of records to be processed in the batch. When a batch is submitted to Salesforce for processing, the first thing it does is invoke your start method. Your job here is to return a `QueryLocator` or an `Iterable` that describes the scope of the batch job.
- **execute:** After calling the start method, Force.com has the means to access all the records you've requested that it operate on. It then splits these records into sets of up to 200 records and invokes your execute method repeatedly, once for each set of records. At this point, your code can perform the substance of the batch operation, typically inserting, updating, or deleting records. Each invocation of execute is a separate transaction. If an uncaught exception is in a transaction, no further transactions are processed and the entire batch job is stopped.

> **Caution**
>
> Transactions that complete successfully are never rolled back. So, an error in a transaction stops the batch, but transactions executed up to that point remain in the database. Thinking of an overall Batch Apex job as transactional is dangerous, because this is not its default behavior. Additionally, you cannot use savepoints to achieve a single pseudo-transaction across the entire batch job. If you must achieve job-wide rollback, this can be implemented in the form of a compensating batch job that reverses the actions of the failed job.

- **finish:** The `finish` method is invoked once at the end of a batch job. The job ends when all transactions in the scope have been processed successfully, or if processing has failed. Regardless of success or failure, `finish` is called. There is no requirement to do anything special in the method. You can leave the method body empty if no post-processing is needed. It simply provides an opportunity for you to receive a notification that processing is complete. You could use this information to clean up any working state or notify the user via e-mail that his batch job is complete and its outcome.

With this initial walkthrough of the `Batchable` interface, you can begin to apply it to your own trigger or Visualforce controller code. If you find a process that is a candidate to run as a batch, think about how it can be restructured to conform to this interface and thus take advantage of Batch Apex.

Applications of Batch Apex

Like any feature of Force.com, Batch Apex works best when you apply it to an appropriate use case that meshes well with its unique capabilities. The following list provides some guidelines when evaluating Batch Apex for your project:

- **Single database object:** Batch Apex is optimized to source its data from a single, "tall" (containing many records) database object. It cannot read data from other sources, such as callouts to Web Services. If the records you need to process span many database objects that cannot be reached via parent-child or child-parent relationships from a single database object, you should proceed carefully. You will need to develop separate Batch Apex code for every database object. Although this is doable and you can share code between them, it creates maintenance headaches and quickly exposes you to the limitation of five active batch jobs per organization.
- **Simple scope of work:** Although Batch Apex allows the use of custom code to provide it with the records to process, it is most powerful when the scope of work is expressed in a single SOQL statement. Do some work upfront to ensure that the source of data for your batch can be summed up in that single SOQL statement.
- **Minimal shared state:** The best design for a Batch Apex process is one where every unit of work is independent, meaning it does not require information to be shared with other units of work. Although creating stateful Batch Apex is possible, it is a less mature feature and more difficult to debug than its stateless counterpart. If

you need shared state to be maintained across units of work, try to use the database itself rather than variables in your Apex class.

- **Limited transactionality:** If your batch process is a single, all-or-nothing transaction, Batch Apex is only going to get you halfway there. You will need to write extra code to compensate for failures and roll back the database to its original state.

- **Not time-critical:** Salesforce provides no hard guarantees about when Batch Apex is executed or its performance. If you have an application that has time-based requirements such that users will be prevented from doing their jobs if a batch does not run or complete by a specific time, Batch Apex might not be a good fit. A better fit is a process that must run within a time window on the order of hours rather than minutes.

These guidelines might seem stifling at first glance, but Batch Apex actually enables an impressive breadth of interesting applications to be developed that were previously impossible with other forms of Apex.

Getting Started with Batch Apex

You don't need an elaborate use case or huge data volumes to get started with Batch Apex. This section walks you through the development of a simple Batch Apex class that writes debug log entries as it runs. The class is submitted for execution using the Force.com IDE and monitored in the administrative web user interface. Two more versions of the Batch Apex class are developed: one to demonstrate stateful processing and the other an iterable scope. The section concludes with a description of important Batch Apex limits.

Developing a Batch Apex Class

Although the class in Listing 9-1 performs no useful work, it leaves a trail of its activity in the debug log. This is helpful in understanding how Force.com handles your batch-enabled code. It also illustrates the basic elements of a Batch Apex class, listed next:

- The class must implement the Database.Batchable interface. This is a parameterized interface, so you also need to provide a type name. Use SObject for batches with a QueryLocator scope, or any database object type for an Iterable scope.

- The class must be global. This is a requirement of Batch Apex classes.

Listing 9-1   **Sample Batch Apex Code**

```
global class HelloBatchApex implements Database.Batchable<SObject> {
  global Database.QueryLocator start(Database.BatchableContext context) {
    System.debug('start');
    return Database.getQueryLocator(
      [SELECT Name FROM Proj__c ORDER BY Name]);
```

```
  }
  global void execute(Database.BatchableContext context,
    List<SObject> scope) {
    System.debug('execute');
    for(SObject rec : scope) {
      Proj__c p = (Proj__c)rec;
      System.debug('Project: ' + p.Name);
    }
  }
  global void finish(Database.BatchableContext context) {
    System.debug('finish');
  }
}
```

Before actually running the code in the next subsection, review these implementation details:

- The start method defines the scope by returning a QueryLocator object constructed from an inline SOQL statement. The SOQL statement returns all Proj__c records in ascending order by the Name field. The SOQL statement can use parameters (prefaced with a colon) like any inline SOQL in Apex code. Relationship queries are acceptable, but aggregate queries are not allowed. You can also pass a SOQL string into the getQueryLocator method, allowing dynamic SOQL to define the scope the batch.

- The execute method is called once per transaction with a unique group of up to 200 records from the scope. The records are provided in the scope argument.

- The finish method is called when all transactions have completed processing, or the batch job has been interrupted for any reason.

- The BatchableContext object argument in all three methods contains a method for obtaining the unique identifier of the current batch job, getJobID. This identifier can be used to look up additional information about the batch job in the standard database object AsyncApexJob. You can also pass this identifier to the System.abortJob method to stop processing of the batch job.

Working with Batch Apex Jobs

Batch Apex can be executed from a Visualforce page, scheduled to run automatically at specific times, or kicked off from within a trigger. But the easiest way to experiment with it is in the Execute Anonymous view in the Force.com IDE.

First, enable debug logging for your user in the Administration Setup area; select Monitoring → Debug Logs. This is no different than debugging any Apex class. Using the Execute Anonymous view, enter the code in Listing 9-2 and execute it. The batch is submitted and its unique job identifier displayed in the results box.

Listing 9-2   **Running Sample Batch Apex Code**

```
HelloBatchApex batch = new HelloBatchApex();
Id jobId = Database.executeBatch(batch);
System.debug('Started Batch Apex job: ' + jobId);
```

The `executeBatch` method of the `Database` class does the work here. It queues the batch job for processing when Force.com is ready to do so. This could be in seconds or minutes; it is not specified. The `HelloBatchApex` sample class is very simple, but in many cases you would need to pass arguments, either in the constructor or via setter methods, to adjust the behavior of a batch process. This is no different from any Apex class.

To start a batch in response to a button click or other user interface action, apply the code shown in Listing 9-2 within a Visualforce custom controller or controller extension class. Now that you have submitted your batch job, it's time to monitor its progress. In your web browser, go to the Administration Setup area and select Monitoring → Apex Jobs. This page, shown in Figure 9-1, allows you to manage all the batch jobs in your Force.com organization.

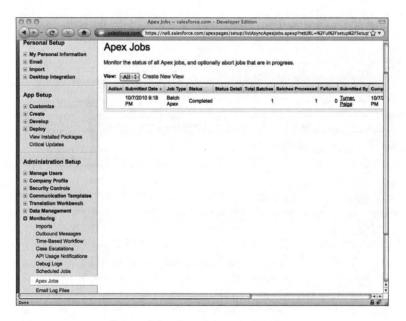

Figure 9-1   Apex Jobs user interface

The single `HelloBatchApex` job you executed should be visible. By this time, it is most likely in the Completed status, having few records to process. If Force.com is very busy, you might see a status of Queued. This means the job has not been started yet. A status value of Processing indicates the job is currently being executed by the platform. If a user interrupts the job by clicking the Abort link on this page, the job status becomes Aborted. A job with a Failed status means an uncaught exception was thrown during its execution. If you scroll to the right, you can also see the Apex Job Id, which should match the one returned by the `Database.executeBatch` method.

Take a closer look at the values in the Total Batches and Batches Processed columns. To avoid confusion, disregard the word "Batches" here. Total Batches is the number of transactions needed to complete the batch job. It is equal to the scope (which defaults to 200) divided into the number of records returned by the `start` method. The Batches Processed column contains the number of times the `execute` method of your Batch Apex class was invoked so far. As the processing proceeds, you should see it increment until it is equal to the Total Batches value. For example, if you have fewer than 200 `Proj__c` records in your database, you should see a 1 in both columns when the batch is complete. If you have between 201 and 400 records, you should see 2 instead. If you have 1,500 records and the system is processing the 300th record, you should see a value of 8 in Total Batches and 1 in Processed Batches. All the information on the page is also accessible programmatically, contained in the standard object named AsyncApexJob.

You have seen the batch job run its course. Proceed back to the debug log page. Here you can review the job's execution in detail, thanks to the `System.debug` statements throughout the code. Figure 9-2 is an example of what you might see there.

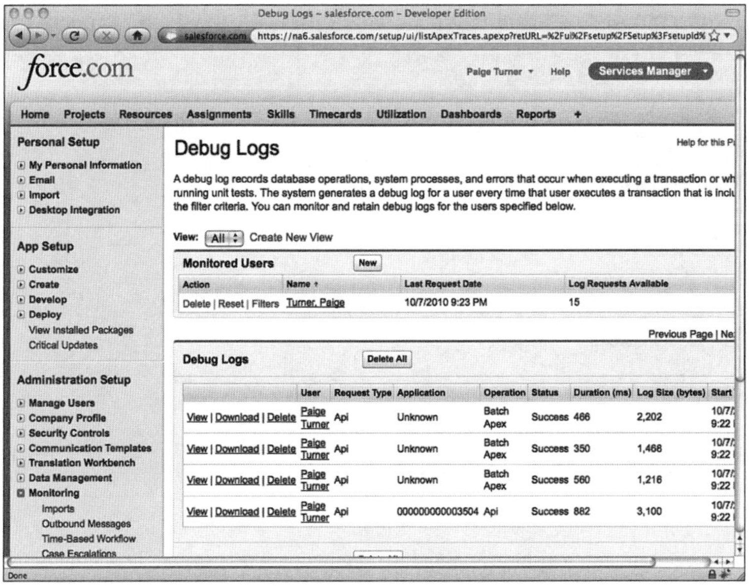

Figure 9-2   Debug logs from Sample Batch Apex Code

Four separate logs each cover a different aspect of the batch execution. Each is described next in the order they are executed, although this might not be the order shown on the Debug Logs page:

1. Results of evaluating the code in the Execute Anonymous view.

2. Invocation of the `start` method to prepare the dataset for the batch.

3. Results of running the `execute` method, where the batch job performs its work on the subsets of the data.

4. All the transactions have been processed, so the `finish` method is called to allow post-processing to occur.

These results are somewhat interesting, but appreciating what the batch is doing is hard without more data. You could add 200 more `Proj__c` records, or you can simply adjust the scope to process fewer records per transaction. Listing 9-3 is an example of doing just that, passing the number 2 in as the scope, the second argument of the `Database.executeBatch` method. This indicates to Force.com that you want a maximum of two records per transaction in the batch job.

Listing 9-3   **Running Sample Batch Apex Code with Scope Argument**

```
HelloBatchApex batch = new HelloBatchApex();
Id jobId = Database.executeBatch(batch, 2);
System.debug('Started Batch Apex job: ' + jobId);
```

After running this code in the Execute Anonymous view, return to the debug logs. You should now see two additional logs in the `execute` phase, for a total of three transactions of two records each. The three transactions are needed to process the six `Proj__c` records.

Using Stateful Batch Apex

Batch Apex is stateless by default. That means for each execution of your `execute` method, you receive a fresh copy of your object. All fields of the class are initialized, static and instance. If your batch process needs information that is shared across transactions, one approach is to make the Batch Apex class itself stateful by implementing the `Stateful` interface. This instructs Force.com to preserve the values of your static and instance variables between transactions.

To try a simple example of stateful Batch Apex, create a new Apex class with the code in Listing 9-4.

Listing 9-4   **Stateful Batch Apex Sample**

```
global class HelloStatefulBatchApex
  implements Database.Batchable<SObject>, Database.Stateful {
  Integer count = 0;
  global Database.QueryLocator start(Database.BatchableContext context) {
```

```
      System.debug('start: ' + count);
      return Database.getQueryLocator(
        [SELECT Name FROM Proj__c ORDER BY Name]);
    }
  global void execute(Database.BatchableContext context,
    List<SObject> scope) {
    System.debug('execute: ' + count);
    for(SObject rec : scope) {
      Proj__c p = (Proj__c)rec;
      System.debug('Project ' + count + ': ' + p.Name);
      count++;
    }
  }
  global void finish(Database.BatchableContext context) {
    System.debug('finish: ' + count);
  }
}
```

Take a moment to examine the differences between this class and the original, stateless version. Implementing the interface `Database.Stateful` is the primary change. The other changes are simply to provide proof in the debug log that the value of the `count` variable is indeed preserved between transactions.

Run the modified class with a scope of two records and examine the debug log. Although the log entries might not be ordered in any discernable way, you can see all the `Proj__c` records have been visited by the batch process. Assuming you have six `Proj__c` records in your database, you should see a total of six new debug log entries: one to begin the batch, one for the `start` method, three entries' worth of transactions (of two records each), and one for the `finish` method.

Notice the value of the `count` variable throughout the debug output. It begins at 0 in the first transaction, increments by two as `Proj__c` records are processed, and begins at 2 in the second transaction. Without implementing `Database.Stateful`, the `count` variable would remain between 0 and 2 for every transaction. The value of the `count` variable is 6 when the `finish` method is reached.

Using an Iterable Batch Scope

All of the sample code so far has used a `QueryLocator` object to define the scope of its batch. This enables up to 50 million records to be processed by the batch job, but requires that the scope be defined entirely using a single SOQL statement. This can be too limiting for some batch processing tasks, so the iterable batch scope is offered as an alternative.

The iterable scope allows custom Apex code to determine which records are processed in the batch. For example, you could use an iterable scope to filter the records using criteria that are too complex to be expressed in SOQL. The downside of the iterable approach is that standard SOQL limits apply. This means you can process a maximum of 50,000

records in your batch job, a dramatic reduction from the 50 million record limit of a
QueryLocator object.

To develop a batch with iterable scope, you must first write code to provide data to the
batch. There are two parts to this task:

- **Implement the Iterator interface:** The Iterator is a class for navigating a collection of elements. It navigates in a single direction, from beginning to end. It
  requires that you implement two methods: hasNext and next. The hasNext method
  returns true if additional elements are left to navigate to, false when the end of
  the collection has been reached. The next method returns the next element in the
  collection. Iterator classes must be global.

- **Implement the Iterable interface:** Think of this class as a wrapper or locator
  object that directs the caller to an Iterator. It requires a single global method to be
  implemented, called Iterator, which returns an Iterable object. Like Iterator,
  classes implementing Iterable must be global.

You could write two separate classes, one to implement each interface. Or you can implement both interfaces in a single class, the approach taken in the code in Listing 9-5.

Listing 9-5   **Project Iterator**

```
global class ProjectIterable implements Iterator<Proj__c>, Iterable<Proj__c> {
  List<Proj__c> projects { get; set; }
  Integer i;
  public ProjectIterable() {
    projects = [SELECT Name FROM Proj__c ORDER BY Name ];
    i = 0;
  }
  global Boolean hasNext() {
    if (i >= projects.size()) {
      return false;
    } else {
      return true;
    }
  }
  global Proj__c next() {
    i++;
    return projects[i-1];
  }
  global Iterator<Proj__c> Iterator() {
    return this;
  }
}
```

With the implementation of the Iterable class ready for use, examine the code in
Listing 9-6. It is very similar to the first Batch Apex example. The only notable differences

are that the parameterized type has been changed from SObject to Proj__c, and the start method now returns the Iterable class developed in Listing 9-5.

Listing 9-6   **Iterable Batch Apex Sample**

```
global class HelloIterableBatchApex implements Database.Batchable<Proj__c> {
  global Iterable<Proj__c> start(Database.BatchableContext context) {
    System.debug('start');
    return new ProjectIterable();
  }
  global void execute(Database.BatchableContext context,
    List<Proj__c> scope) {
    System.debug('execute');
    for(Proj__c rec : scope) {
      System.debug('Project: ' + rec.Name);
    }
  }
  global void finish(Database.BatchableContext context) {
    System.debug('finish');
  }
}
```

Turn on the debug log for your user and run the HelloIterableBatchApex job. Examine the logs and see for yourself that you've accomplished the same work as the HelloBatchApex code using an iterable scope instead of a QueryLocator object.

Limits of Batch Apex

You must keep in mind several important limits of Batch Apex:

- Future methods are not allowed anywhere in Batch Apex.
- Batch jobs are always run as the system user, so they have permission to read and write all data in the organization.
- The maximum heap size in Batch Apex is 6MB.
- Calling out to external systems using the HTTP object or webservice methods are limited to one for each invocation of start, execute, and finish. To enable your batch process to call out, make sure the code implements Database.AllowsCallouts interface in addition to the standard Database.Batchable interface.
- Transactions (the execute method) run under the same governor limits as any Apex code. If you have intensive work to do in your execute method and worry about exceeding the governor limits when presented with the default 200 records per transaction, reduce the number of records using the optional scope parameter of the Database.executeBatch method.

- The maximum number of queued or active batch jobs within an entire Salesforce organization is five. Attempting to run another job beyond the five raises a runtime error. For this reason, you should tightly control the number of batch jobs that are submitted. For example, submitting a batch from a trigger is generally a bad idea if you can avoid it. In a trigger, you can quickly exceed the maximum number of batch jobs.

Testing Batch Apex

Batch Apex can be tested like any Apex code, although you are limited to a single transaction's worth of data (one invocation of the execute method). A batch job started within a test runs synchronously, and does not count against the organization's limit of five batch jobs.

Add the method in Listing 9-7 to the Batch Apex example from Listing 9-1 to achieve 100% test coverage.

Listing 9-7   **Batch Apex Test**

```
public static testmethod void testBatch() {
  Test.startTest();
  HelloBatchApex batch = new HelloBatchApex();
  ID jobId = Database.executeBatch(batch);
  Test.stopTest();
}
```

The new test method simply executes the batch with the same syntax as you have used in the Execute Anonymous view. The batch execution is bookended with the startTest and stopTest methods. This ensures that the batch job is run synchronously and is finished at the stopTest method. This enables you to make assertions (System.assert) to verify that the batch performed the correct operations on your data.

Scheduling Batch Apex

Along with Batch Apex, Salesforce added a scheduler to the Force.com platform. This enables any Apex code, not just Batch Apex, to be scheduled to run asynchronously at regular time intervals. Prior to the introduction of this feature, developers had to resort to off-platform workarounds, such as invoking a Force.com Web service from an external system capable of scheduling jobs.

This section describes how to prepare your code for scheduling, and how to schedule code to run using the administrative user interface and programmatically.

Developing Schedulable Code

An Apex class that can be scheduled by Force.com must implement the Schedulable interface. The interface requires no methods to be implemented; it simply indicates to the platform that your class can be scheduled. Code that is executed by the scheduler runs as the system user, so sharing rules or other access controls are not enforced. At most ten classes can be scheduled at one time.

The class in Listing 9-8 enables the Batch Apex example from Listing 9-1 to be schedulable. It does this by implementing the Schedulable interface, which has a single method: execute. Although you could implement this interface directly on your batch class, the best practice recommended by Salesforce is to create a separate Schedulable class.

Listing 9-8   **Schedulable Batch Apex**

```
global class HelloSchedulable implements Schedulable {
  global void execute(SchedulableContext sc) {
    HelloBatchApex batch = new HelloBatchApex();
    Database.executeBatch(batch);
  }
}
```

Scheduling Batch Apex Jobs

To schedule a job using the user interface, go to the App Setup area and click Develop →
Apex Classes. Click the Schedule Apex button. In Figure 9-3, the HelloSchedulable class has been configured to run Saturday mornings at 11 a.m. between 10/9/2010 and 11/9/2010.

To view and cancel scheduled jobs, go to the Administration Setup area and click Monitoring → Scheduled Jobs. This is shown in Figure 9-4 with the previously scheduled job. At this point, you can click Manage to edit the schedule, or Del to cancel it.

The same management of scheduled jobs available in the user interface can be automated using Apex code, as described next:

- **Create a scheduled job:** Use the System.schedule method to schedule a new job. This method requires three arguments: the name of the job, the schedule expression, and an instance of class to schedule. The schedule expression is a string in crontab-like format. This format is a space-delimited list of the following arguments: seconds, minutes, hours, day of month, month, day of week, and year (optional). Each argument is a value specifying when the job is to run in the relevant units. All arguments except seconds and minutes permit multiple values, ranges, wildcards, and increments. For example, the schedule expression 0 0 8 ? * MON-FRI schedules the job for weekdays at 8 a.m. The 8 indicates the eighth hour, the question mark leaves day of month unspecified, the asterisk indicates all months, and the day of week is Monday through Friday. The time zone of the user scheduling the job is used to calculate the schedule.

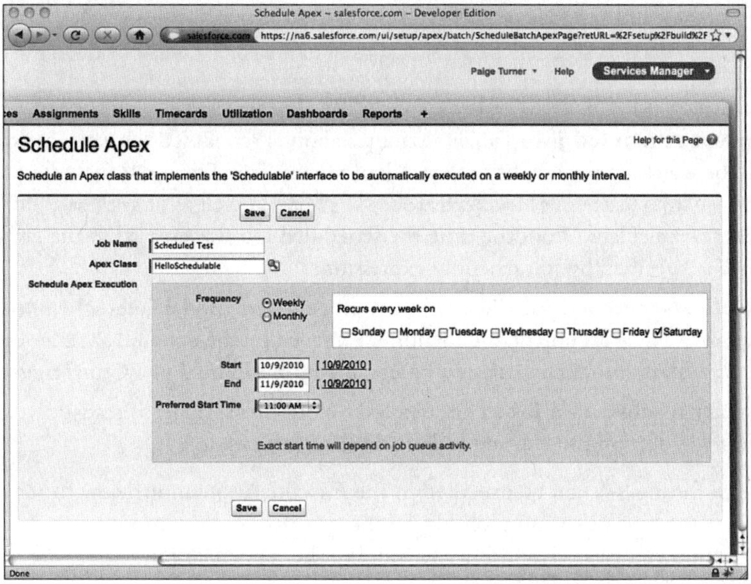

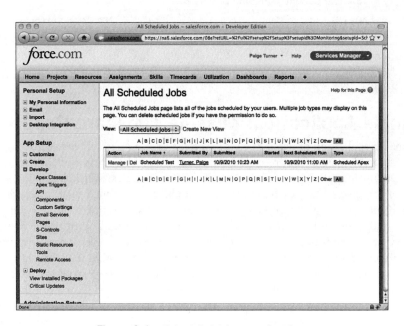

Figure 9-3   Schedule Apex user interface

Figure 9-4   Scheduled Jobs user interface

> **Note**
>
> For a full reference to schedule expressions, refer to the Force.com Apex Code Developer's Guide at www.salesforce.com/us/developer/docs/apexcode/index.htm.

- **View a scheduled job:** To get attributes about a scheduled job, such as when it will be executed next, query the standard object CronTrigger. It includes useful fields such as `NextFireTime`, `PreviousFireTime`, as well as `StartTime` and `EndTime`, calculated from the time the scheduled job was created to the last occurrence as specified by the schedule expression.

- **Delete a scheduled job:** The `System.abortJob` method deletes scheduled jobs. It requires a single argument, the identifier returned by the `SchedulableContext get-TriggerID` method. This can also be obtained from Id field of a CronTrigger record.

- **Modify a scheduled job:** The standard object CronTrigger is read-only, so to modify a job, you must delete it first and then recreate it.

The code in Listing 9-9 can be executed in the Execute Anonymous view to schedule the `HelloSchedulable` class to run monthly on the first day of every month at 1 a.m. in the user's time zone. You can verify this by examining the scheduled job in the user interface, or querying the CronTrigger object.

Listing 9-9   **Sample Code to Schedule Batch Apex**

```
System.schedule('Scheduled Test', '0 0 1 * * ?', new HelloSchedulable());
```

> **Caution**
>
> After an Apex class is scheduled, its code cannot be modified until all of its scheduled jobs are deleted.

Sample Application: Missing Timecard Report

A common application of Batch Apex is to distill a large number of records down to a smaller, more digestible set of records that contain actionable information. In the Service Manager sample application, consultants enter timecards against assignments, specifying their daily hours for a weekly period. When consultants fail to enter their timecards in a timely manner, this can impact the business in many ways: Customers cannot be invoiced, and the budget of billable hours can be overrun without warning. With a large number of timecards, consultants, and projects, manually searching the database to identify missing timecards isn't feasible. This information needs to be extracted from the raw data.

The management users of the Services Manager have requested a tool that enables them to proactively identify missing timecards. They would like to see a list of the time periods and the assignments that have no timecard so that they can work with the consultants to get their time reported. This information could later be used as the basis of custom user interface, report or dashboard component, or automated email notifications to the consultants.

This section walks through the implementation of the missing timecard report. It consists of the following steps:

1. Create a custom object to store the list of missing timecards.

2. Develop a Batch Apex class to calculate the missing timecard information.

3. Run through a simple test case to make sure the code works as expected.

Creating the Custom Object

Your Services Manager users have asked to see missing timecards. Of course, they cannot see the timecards themselves because they're missing, but you can safely assume that they want the dates of missing timecards and the offending consultants and their assigned projects. There are two fields necessary to provide the requested information: the assignment, which automatically includes the resource and project as references, and the week ending date that lacks a timecard for the assignment.

Create a new custom object to store this information, naming it Missing Timecard. Add a lookup field to Assignment and a Date field named Week_Ending__c to mirror the field of the same name in the Timecard object. Create a custom tab for this object as well. When you're done, the Missing Timecard object definition should resemble Figure 9-5.

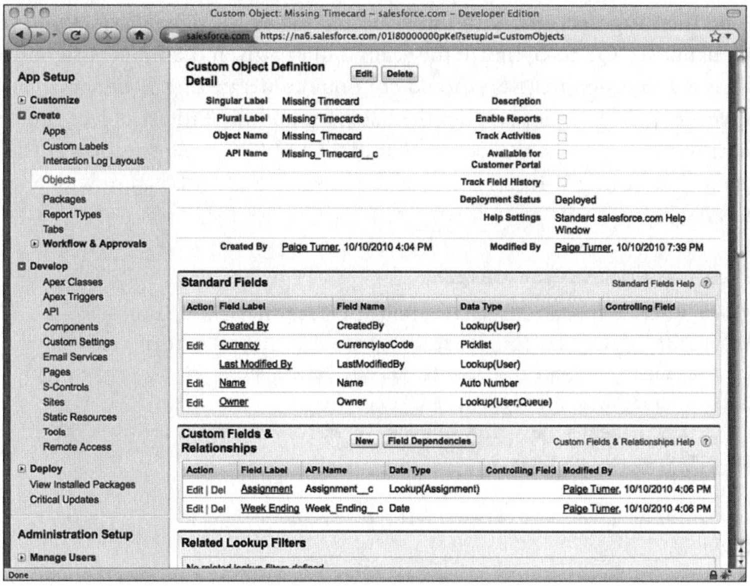

Figure 9-5   Missing Timecard Custom Object Definition

Developing the Batch Apex Class

A good design approach for Batch Apex is to consider the input schema, output schema, and the most direct algorithm to transform input to output. You've already designed the output schema based on what the users want to see: the Missing Timecard object. That leaves the input and the algorithm to be designed.

Consider the algorithm first, which drives the input. The algorithm loops through assignments that are not in Tentative or Closed status. It builds a list of Week Ending dates of valid timecards (in Submitted or Approved status) in the same project as the assignment. It then cycles through the weeks between the start and end dates of the assignment, up to the current day. If a week ending date is not found in the list of timecard Week Ending dates, it is considered missing and its assignment and date is added to the Missing Timecards object.

With the algorithm nailed down, move on to the input. The key to a concise, maintainable Batch Apex class is formulating the right SOQL query to provide the input records. Most of the effort is in finding the optimal SObject to base the query on. If you pick the wrong SObject, you could be forced to augment the input in your `execute` method, resulting in more queries, this time subject to SOQL governor limits.

It is clear from the algorithm that the batch input must include Assignment records and corresponding Timecard records. But Assignment and Timecard are two separate many-to-many relationships with no direct relationship to each other.

Although basing the query on the Assignment or Timecard objects might be tempting, this leads to a weak design. For example, if you query the assignments in the `start` method, and then augment this with Timecard records in the `execute` method, you need to build dynamic SOQL to optimize the second query given the input Assignment records. This is a sure sign that you should continue to iterate on the design.

When you switch tracks and design the batch around the Project object, life becomes easier. From `Proj__c`, you have access to Timecard and Assignment records at the same time. The code in Listing 9-10 implements the missing timecard feature with a query on `Proj__c` as the input.

Listing 9-10   **MissingTimecardBatch**

```
global class MissingTimecardBatch implements Database.Batchable<SObject> {
  global Database.QueryLocator start(Database.BatchableContext context) {
    return Database.getQueryLocator([ SELECT Name, Type__c,
      (SELECT Name, Start_Date__c, End_Date__c
        FROM Assignments__r WHERE Status__c NOT IN ('Tentative', 'Closed')),
      (SELECT Status__c, Week_Ending__c
        FROM Timecards__r
        WHERE Status__c IN ('Submitted', 'Approved'))
      FROM Proj__c
    ]);
```

```
  }
  global void execute(Database.BatchableContext context,
    List<SObject> scope) {
    List<Missing_Timecard__c> missing = new List<Missing_Timecard__c>();
    for (SObject rec : scope) {
      Proj__c proj = (Proj__c)rec;
      Set<Date> timecards = new Set<Date>();
      if (proj.Assignments__r != null) {
        for (Assignment__c assign : proj.Assignments__r) {
          if (proj.Timecards__r != null) {
            for (Timecard__c timecard : proj.Timecards__r) {
              timecards.add(timecard.Week_Ending__c);
            }
          }
        }
/** Timecards are logged weekly, so the Week_Ending__c field is always
 * a Saturday. We need to convert an assignment, which can contain an
 * arbitrary start and end date, into a start and end period expressed
 * only in terms of Saturdays. To do this, we use the toStartOfWeek
 * method on the Date object, and then add 6 days to reach a Saturday.
 */
        Date startWeekEnding =
          assign.Start_Date__c.toStartOfWeek().addDays(6);
        Date endWeekEnding =
          assign.End_Date__c.toStartOfWeek().addDays(6);
        Integer weeks = 0;
        while (startWeekEnding.addDays(weeks * 7) < endWeekEnding) {
          Date d = startWeekEnding.addDays(weeks * 7);
          if (d >= Date.today()) {
            break;
          }
          if (!timecards.contains(d)) {
            missing.add(new Missing_Timecard__c(
              Assignment__c = assign.Id,
              Week_Ending__c = d));
          }
          weeks++;
        }
      }
    }
    insert missing;
  }
  global void finish(Database.BatchableContext context) {
  }
}
```

Testing the Missing Timecard Feature

To achieve adequate test coverage, add unit tests to the Batch Apex class that create assignments and timecards in various combinations, kick off the batch, then query the Missing Timecard object and verify the presence of the correct data.

You can also test informally from the user interface and the Execute Anonymous view in the Force.com IDE. For example, create an Assignment record for the GenePoint project, starting 4/1/2009 and ending 4/30/2009 for Rose Gonzalez. Enter a timecard for her for week ending 4/11/2009 on the GenePoint project, and set its status to Approved. Now run the `MissingTimecardBatch` from Force.com using the code in Listing 9-11.

Listing 9-11   **Running `MissingTimecardBatch`**

```
Database.executeBatch(new MissingTimecardBatch());
```

Check the Apex Jobs to monitor the progress of your batch job. When it's done, visit the Missing Timecard tab. You should see three Missing Timecard records for the Gene-Point assignment, with the dates 4/4/2009, 4/18/2009, and 4/25/2009. The 4/11/2009 date is not included because a valid Timecard record exists for it.

To try some more test scenarios, first clear the Missing Timecard records so you don't have to sift through duplicates. The code in Listing 9-12 is an easy way to do so, and you can run it from the Execute Anonymous view.

Listing 9-12   **Reset Results of `MissingTimecardBatch`**

```
delete [ SELECT Id FROM Missing_Timecard__c ];
```

Summary

Batch processing in Force.com enables you to query and modify data in volumes that would otherwise be prohibited by governor limits. In this chapter, you've learned how to develop, test, and schedule batch jobs, and applied batch processing to the real-world problem of identifying missing database records.

When using Batch Apex in your own applications, consider these key points:

- Batch Apex is optimized for tasks with inputs that can be expressed in a single SOQL statement, and that do not require all-or-nothing transactional behavior.

- With its limit of five active batch jobs per organization, one input dataset per job, and a lack of precise control over actual execution time, Batch Apex is the nuclear option of Force.com data processing: powerful, but challenging to build and subject to proliferation problems. Use it sparingly, when all other options are exhausted. If triggers or Visualforce controllers can do the same job given expected data volumes, consider them first.

- You can use Schedulable Apex to run any Apex code at regular time intervals, not just Batch Apex. Schedules can be managed via the administrative user interface and in Apex code.

10

Integration

The Force.com platform offers various features to integrate its data and processes with those of other applications. These features are leveraged by independent software vendors as part of standalone integration products and also exposed to developers and system administrators of Force.com. This chapter describes the integration features that can bridge Force.com with other applications, with a focus on integration initiated from within Force.com.

Force.com can be configured to send messages to other systems accessible through the Internet. These messages are not email, but messages generated by programs, designed to be consumed by other programs rather than humans. When traveling outside the bounds of the Force.com platform, the messages are sent and received using the standard Web protocols of HTTP and HTTPS.

This chapter is divided into the following sections:

- **Force.com Integration Solutions:** Learn the basics of outbound messaging and Salesforce-to-Salesforce (S2S), Force.com's configuration-based integration features.
- **Developing Custom Integrations:** Use Apex code to communicate with systems outside of Force.com.
- **Sample Application:** Walk through an integration scenario with the Services Manager sample application, extending it to calculate and transmit corporate performance metrics to a fictional industry benchmarking organization.

Force.com Integration Solutions

This section covers integration solutions in Force.com that are configured, not coded. They are outbound messaging and Salesforce-to-Salesforce (S2S). When you have a high degree of control over the design of both sides of an integration, these features provide the most cost-effective options for sending data out from Force.com from a development and operational perspective.

Outbound Messaging

Outbound messaging is a feature of Force.com that sends a Web service request to an endpoint URL that you designate, using HTTP or HTTPS. The outbound message itself is best described as a notification. It is a simple SOAP message that contains one or more fields from a single object.

The configuration of outbound messaging is entirely point-and-click. Workflow rules, another Force.com feature, define the conditions that cause messages to be sent. Messages are sent reliably, queued, and retried upon failure. Retries continue for up to 24 hours until a message is sent.

Although Apex code can also be used to make Web service requests, outbound messaging is the recommended solution. It is reliable, doesn't require code, and is easy to configure and maintain. But it isn't suitable for every integration scenario. The following list describes the two major limitations of outbound messaging:

- **Static Service Definition:** Other than the selection of objects and fields that provide the body of the notification, you have no control over the structure or content of the Web service. There is no field mapping, transformation, or other configurability you might be accustomed to with traditional integration solutions. If the system to receive the Force.com outbound message cannot be modified to adapt to the Force.com outbound message WSDL, you must develop a Web service to mediate between the outbound message and the API of the target system.

- **No Junction Objects:** The object used to define the data in an outbound message can be any type: standard or custom. However, junction objects, the intersection objects in many-to-many relationships, are not supported. A workaround to this is to define an "interface" object, an object that exists only to provide a template for the outbound message. Use a trigger to move data from the junction object to the interface object.

Getting Started with Outbound Messaging

The easiest way to get started with outbound messaging is to build an example. The example described in this subsection uses the Project custom object from the Services Manager sample application.

Suppose your company's financial system requires notification when a consulting project is completed. First, build a workflow rule and outbound message definition to send a message when a project's stage is set to completed. Then implement the Web service for receiving notifications on behalf of the financial system.

Configuring Outbound Messaging

There are two parts to configuring outbound messaging. The first part is to create a workflow rule to specify when to send a message. The second part is to define the outbound message itself, which dictates the contents of the message. Both the workflow rule and the outbound message must be created from the same object. In this example, the custom object Project is used.

To create the workflow rule, follow these steps:

1. Go to the App Setup area and click Create → Workflow & Approvals → Workflow Rules.

2. Click the New Rule button. Select the object to serve as the trigger of this rule. For this exercise, select the Project object. Click the Next button to continue.

3. Enter a rule name and (optionally) a description. Select when the rule should be evaluated and add at least one criteria to determine when the rule is run. Figure 10-1 depicts a rule that runs when the Project Stage field equals Completed. Click the Save & Next button to continue.

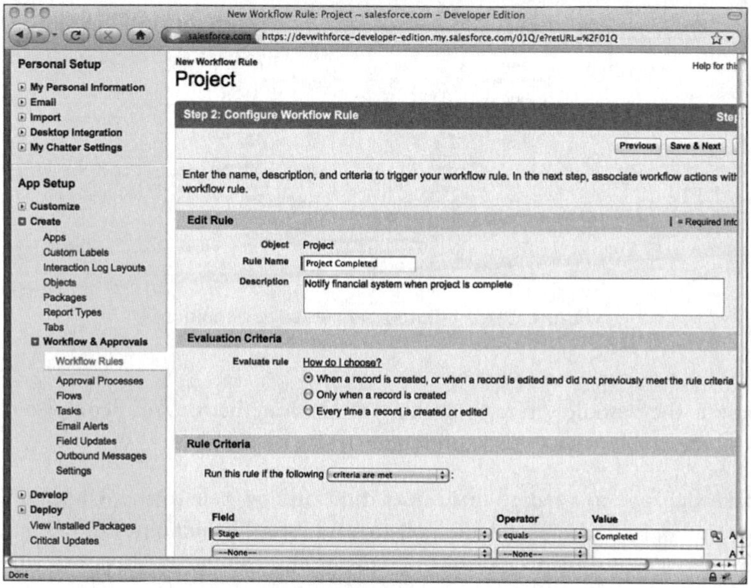

Figure 10-1   Workflow rule definition

4. In the Immediate Workflow Actions section, click Add Workflow Action and select New Outbound Message from the drop-down menu.

5. This is the outbound message definition. Give the message a name and (optionally) a description. Enter the URL of the Web service to receive the outbound message. If you haven't developed one yet, enter `http://localhost` as a placeholder, and

you can update it later. Select fields from the Project object to include in the outbound message. Figure 10-2 shows a sample outbound message definition. Click the Save button to finish the rule and message definition.

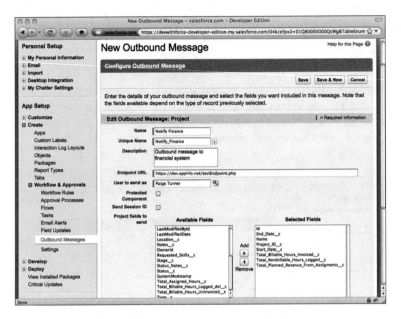

Figure 10-2   Outbound message definition

6. Activate the workflow rule by clicking the Activate button. Your completed rule should resemble what's shown in Figure 10-3.

If you make a change to a record that causes the workflow rule to run, Force.com constructs the outbound message and attempts to send it to the endpoint URL. If you do not have a Web service available to process the message, the sending attempts will fail. To try running the sample rule you just created, modify a Project record and set its stage to Complete.

The progress of outbound messages toward their destinations is visible in an administration page. Go to the Administration Setup area and click Monitoring → Outbound Messages. In Figure 10-4, two messages have been queued for delivery, which has failed due to a 404 error, meaning the endpoint URL is invalid. From this page, you can manually resend a message using the Retry link or remove the message using the Del link. Successfully delivered messages are not shown.

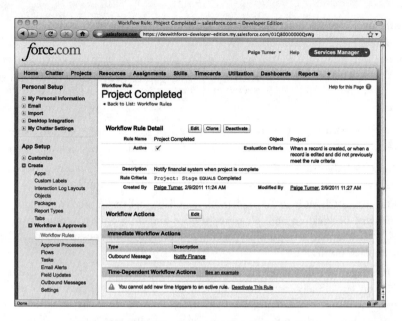

Figure 10-3   Completed workflow rule

Figure 10-4   Outbound messaging delivery status

Creating an External Web Service for Outbound Messaging

Web Services Description Language (WSDL) is a W3C standard XML language for describing Web services. WSDL is used to define the contract between Force.com and the system that is to receive the outbound message. In addition to the methods and types defined in the WSDL, your Web service should take a few additional behaviors into account:

- **Multiple Notifications:** Force.com can send 1 to 100 notifications in a single Web service call. Make sure your Web service can handle single and multiple notifications.

- **Acknowledgements:** Your Web service must synchronously return a Boolean indicating positive or negative acknowledgment for each notification.

- **Duplicate Checking:** To implement its reliable delivery, Force.com might send the same notification multiple times. If once-and-only-once processing is required, your Web service is responsible for implementing it using the unique identifier sent with each notification.

- **Data Age:** The data received in a notification is current as of the time the notification was initially sent. The data might have changed since then in the event of multiple retries and also might have changed from the time the workflow rule was fired. To get the most current data relevant to the notification, enable the Send Session ID option in the Workflow Outbound Message Detail page. This will populate the session ID in the outbound message, enabling your Web service to call back into Force.com using an authenticated session to retrieve the most current information using Apex Web Services. The general scenario of calling into Force.com is covered in Chapter 11, "Advanced Integration."

To continue the example from the preceding subsection, follow these steps to build a test endpoint to receive the outbound message:

1. Download the WSDL for the outbound message endpoint. In the App Setup area, click Create → Workflow & Approvals → Outbound Messages, select the outbound message, and click the Endpoint WSDL link.

2. Save the WSDL on your local machine and copy it to the machine that is to provide the Web service to Force.com.

3. Using the tools and languages of your choice, create a Web service implementation from the WSDL. Listing 10-1 shows a sample implementation in PHP. It simply dumps the fields of the incoming notifications to the error log and returns a positive acknowledgment to Force.com. It assumes you've named the WSDL downloaded from Force.com `workflowOutboundMessage.wsdl`.

> **Note**
>
> You can use Java, C#.NET, or any language that has libraries for working with SOAP and WSDL to build the Web service.

Listing 10-1   **Sample Notification SOAP Service in PHP**

```php
<?php
function dumpNote($note) {
  error_log(print_r($note, 1));
}
function ack($value) {
  return array('Ack' => value);
}
function notifications($data) {
  error_log('Notification from orgId: ' . $data->OrganizationId);
  if (is_array($data->Notification)) {
    $result = array();
    for ($i = 0; $i < count($data->Notification); $i++) {
      dumpNote($data->Notification[$i]->sObject);
      array_push($result, ack(true));
    }
    return $result;
  } else {
    dumpNote($data->Notification->sObject);
    return ack(true);
  }
}
ini_set("soap.wsdl_cache_enabled", "0");
$server = new SoapServer("workflowOutboundMessage.wsdl");
$server->addFunction("notifications");
$server->handle();
```

4. Make sure that the server hosting your Web service is available to the Internet via
    port 80 (HTTP), port 443 (HTTPS), or ports 1024–65535 (HTTP or HTTPS).
    The most secure configuration is to use HTTPS and configure your Web service to
    require an SSL client certificate from Force.com. Go to the App Setup area and
    click Develop → API, and click the Download Client Certificate link.

> **Caution**
>
> If your outbound message endpoint uses HTTPS, the endpoint server's certificate must be
> issued by a Certificate Authority (CA) that is accepted by Force.com. The latest list of accepted
> CAs is available at http://wiki.developerforce.com/index.php/
> Outbound_Messaging_SSL_CA_Certificates.

Salesforce-to-Salesforce (S2S)

S2S allows you to share data between Force.com organizations, the tenants of the multitenant platform. The data exchange takes place entirely within the servers that run the
Force.com platform, eliminating all the overhead associated with traditional integration
over the Internet, such as encryption, message formats, and transport protocols. It can be
valuable for business-to-business scenarios such as partner relationship management and

customer support, providing a point-and-click solution for information sharing that can be set up and managed without additional technology products and their associated costs and complexity.

This subsection walks you through the process of configuring S2S to share records of the Services Manager sample application's Project object between two Force.com organizations. The process is divided into three major steps, listed here:

1. **Establishing a Connection:** Connection is the S2S terminology for an integration point between two Force.com organizations. Connections require manual initiation and acceptance by the administrators of each Force.com organization.

2. **Configured Shared Objects:** To share objects, one organization publishes an object, and the other organization subscribes to it. The subscriber maps the object, fields, and values to counterparts in their organization.

3. **Sharing Records:** After the connection is established and objects are shared, records can begin flowing between the two organizations. Records are forwarded from one organization and accepted by the receiver.

Establishing a Connection

To start, you need at least two separate Force.com organizations. You already have one, so sign up for a second Developer Edition account. Then, enable the S2S feature in both organizations by going to the App Setup area and clicking Customize → Salesforce to Salesforce → Settings. Click the Enable check box and then the Save button, shown in Figure 10-5.

S2S establishes connections between organizations using ordinary email. The process begins with one organization initiating the connection. Initiation requires a Contact record containing the email address of the person who is authorized to accept the connection on behalf of his organization. Users without Modify All Data permission cannot initiate and accept S2S connections unless an administrator has enabled the Manage Connections permission on their profiles.

To prepare to connect, create a new Contact record in your first Force.com organization with the email address of the administrator of your second Force.com organization. Go to the Connections tab and click the New button. Note that the Connections tab is only visible if you have enabled S2S in your organization. Select the Contact and click the Save & Send Invite button to send the invitation email. In Figure 10-6, the user Doug Hole will receive the invitation to connect to this organization.

The invitee receives an automated email from Force.com with a link to log in to his Force.com organization and accept or decline the connection. Clicking the link reveals the screen shown in Figure 10-7. Click the Accept button to complete the connection process.

If the invitation is accepted, the connection moves to an active status as shown in Figure 10-8. Connections can be deactivated by either organization at any time, immediately blocking the exchange of data between the organizations.

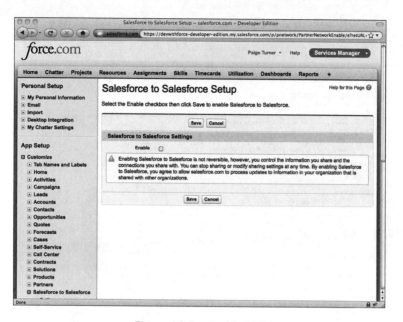

Figure 10-5   Enable S2S

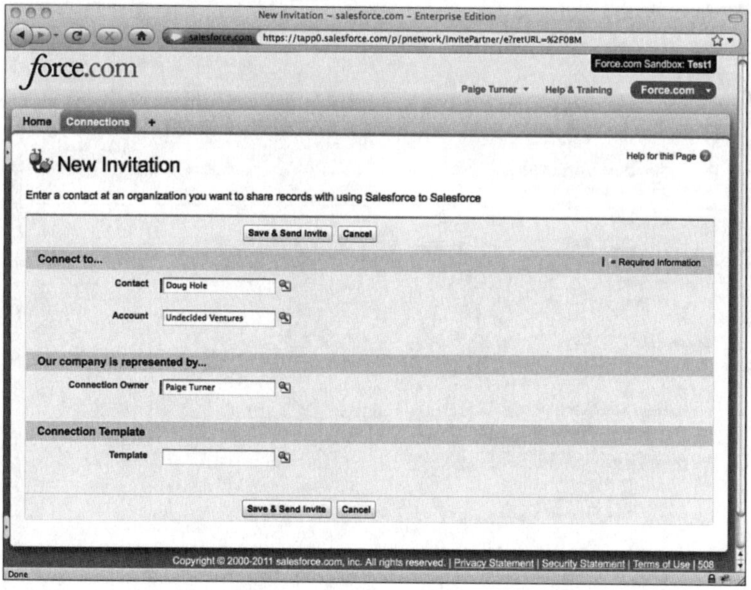

Figure 10-6   Creating new S2S connection

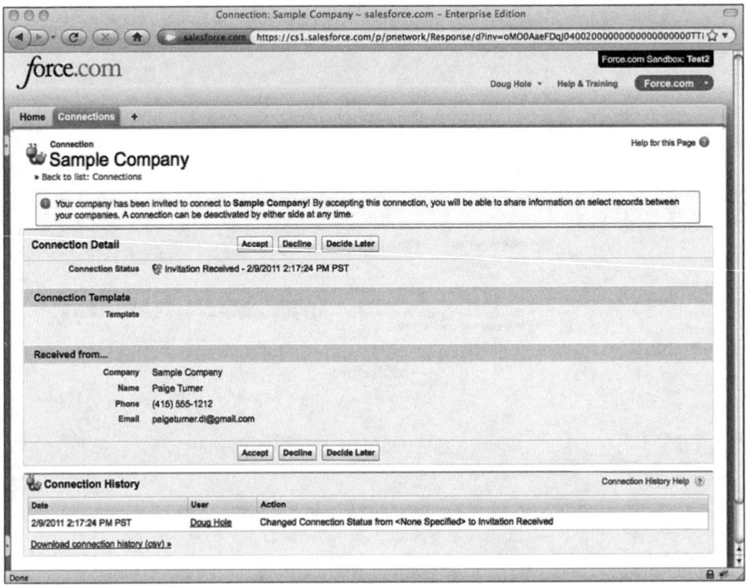

Figure 10-7   Accepting invitation to connect via S2S

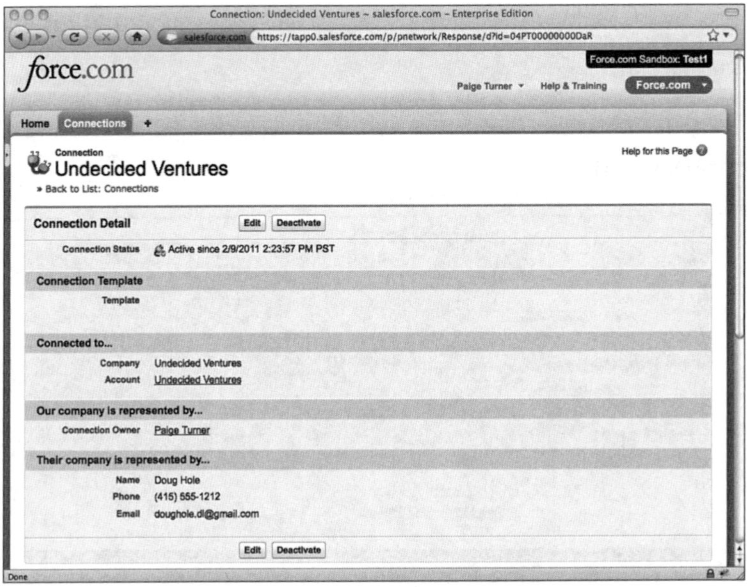

Figure 10-8   Active S2S connection

With an active S2S connection, the next step is publishing objects from one organization and subscribing to them in the other.

Configuring Shared Objects

An object is shared between two organizations when one has published it and another has subscribed to it. Publishing and subscribing are configured per object. All custom objects are supported, but not all standard objects. To get the latest list of standard objects supported by S2S, check the online help by logging into your Force.com organization and clicking the Help & Training link.

On the connection detail page, click the Publish/Unpublish button to edit the list of the objects that are published to the connection. In Figure 10-9, the Project object has been published.

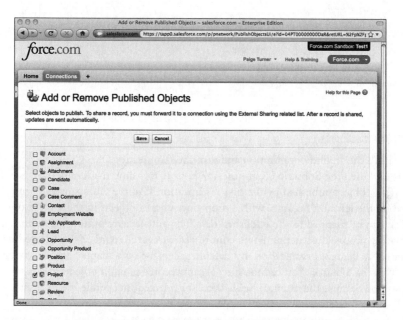

Figure 10-9   Selecting objects to publish via S2S

Publishing is also configured at the field level. Initially only the standard Name field is published. To add more fields, click the Edit link beside the published object. Figure 10-10 shows the publishing of additional fields of the Project object.

You've finished publishing the object and its fields, but records cannot be forwarded until the other organization closes the loop by subscribing to the objects. Subscribing involves mapping the published object, fields, and values so that the published records have a place to call home in the subscribing organization. To keep things simple for this example, use the Force.com IDE to copy and paste the Project custom object and tab from your first organization to the second.

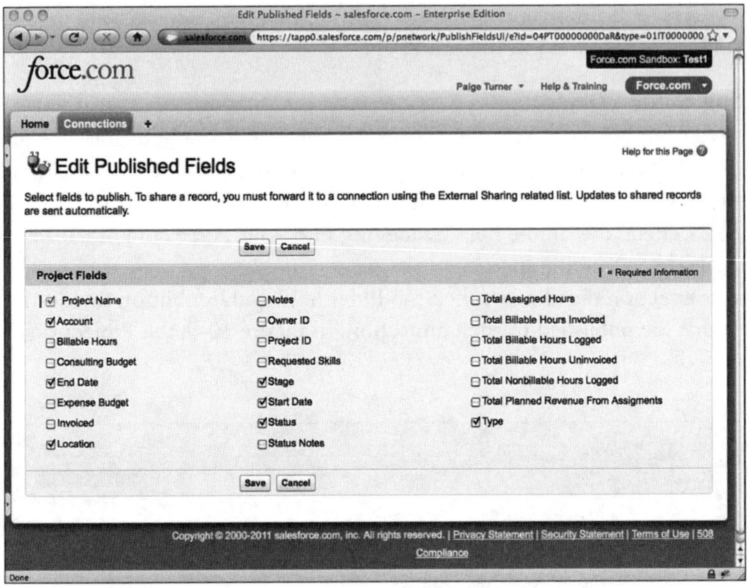

Figure 10-10   Selecting Project fields to publish via S2S

Log in to the second organization and visit the Connections tab. Click the active connection and then the Subscribe/Unsubscribe button, revealing the screen shown in Figure 10-11. Each object published by the first organization (Sample Company in Figure 10-11) is listed on the leftmost column, with a drop-down list of objects in the second organization that can be mapped to the published data. The auto-accept option streamlines the data sharing process, instructing Force.com to accept every record of the selected object forwarded by the first organization. By default, acceptance is a manual process of logging in and clicking a button. You cannot auto-accept records in child objects in Master-Detail relationships, because they cannot be accepted or rejected independently of their parent records.

Like publishing, subscribing takes place at the field level. Click the Edit link beside the subscribed object to edit the field mappings. Figure 10-12 shows an example. The left column contains the fields from the published object; the right, column drop-down lists of fields from the subscribed object. Select a field from the subscribed object to map it or click the Automatically map fields check box to map identical field names from the published object to the subscribed object.

The Account field is a lookup to a parent object, so mapping it means that the destination field receives the name of the parent record. Stage, Status, and Type are picklists, so they have an additional Edit Values link to maintain the mappings of picklist values.

With the connection active and an object shared between the organizations, you're ready to share records.

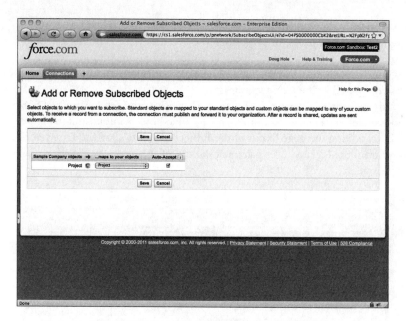

Figure 10-11   Subscribing to objects via S2S

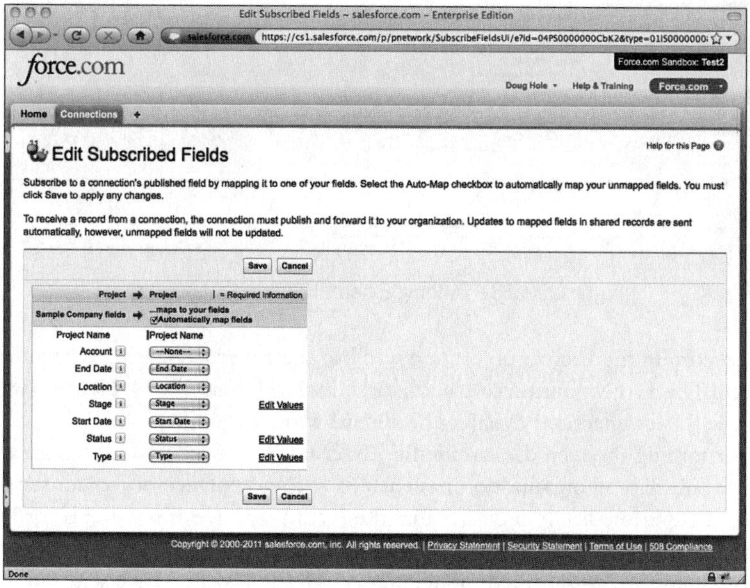

Figure 10-12   Mapping fields in S2S-subscribed object

Sharing Records

To share records between the organizations, the organization publishing the object forwards one or more records of that object. The subscribing organization accepts the records, which creates them in the subscribed object, mapping their fields and picklist values as configured in the Connections tab.

Records are forwarded using the External Sharing related list. This special S2S related list is not visible on page layouts until manually added by an administrator. Figure 10-13 demonstrates editing the page layout of the Project object to drag the External Sharing related list from the Related Lists palette at the top of the screen to the region at the bottom of the screen.

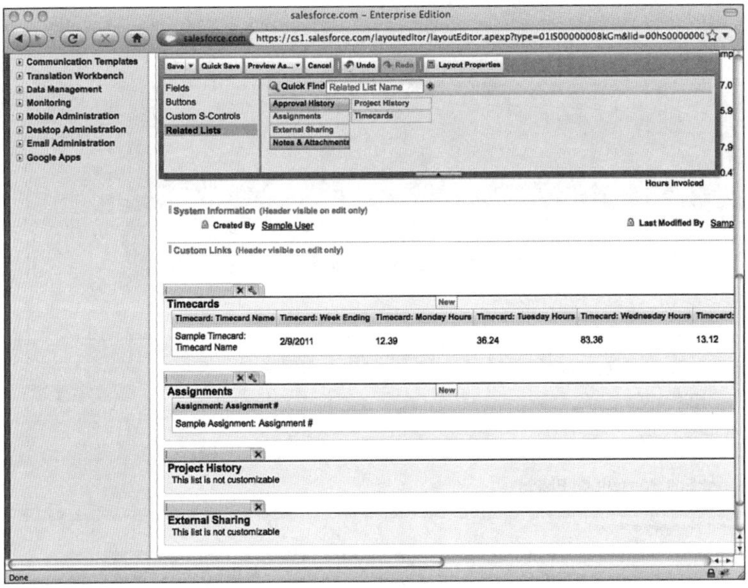

Figure 10-13   Adding External Sharing related list

Visit a record in the Project object and scroll to the External Sharing related list. Click the Forward This Project button to see what's shown in Figure 10-14. Here you can pick one or more S2S connections to share this record with.

After forwarding the record, examine the External Sharing related list for the current status. If the subscribing organization has enabled auto-acceptance of records for this object, the status immediately indicates that the record is active. If not, the record is not active until the subscribing organization manually accepts it. In Figure 10-15, the subscribing organization has accepted the record, as indicated by its Active status in the External Sharing related list.

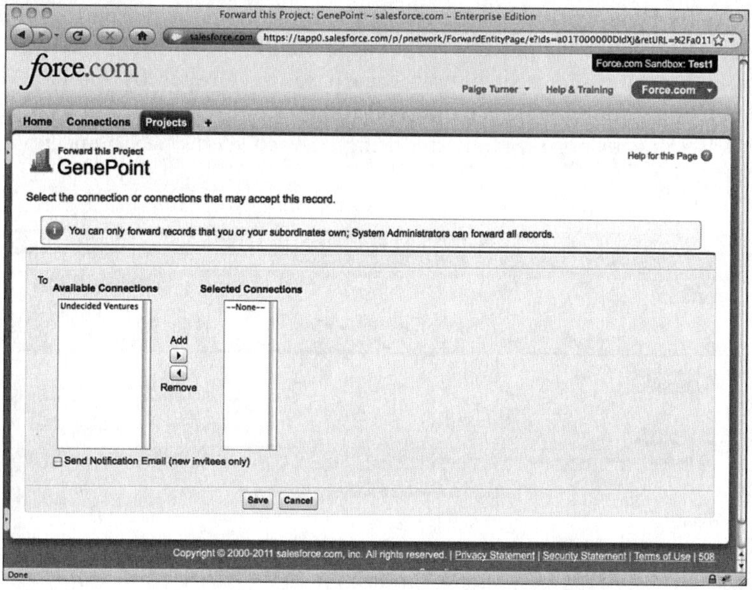

Figure 10-14   Forwarding a record using S2S

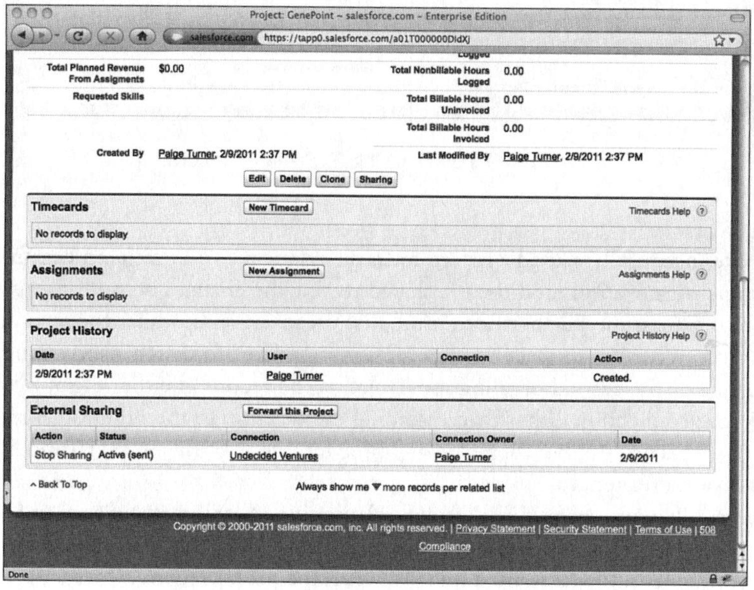

Figure 10-15   Viewing an S2S-forwarded record

Figure 10-16 shows what the shared record looks like from the perspective of the second organization. Notice the message at the top about the record being externally shared from Sample Company, and at the bottom you can see the Created By and Last Modified By value of Connection User. This indicates that the record was created by Force.com itself, not a user in your organization, after being received via the S2S connection.

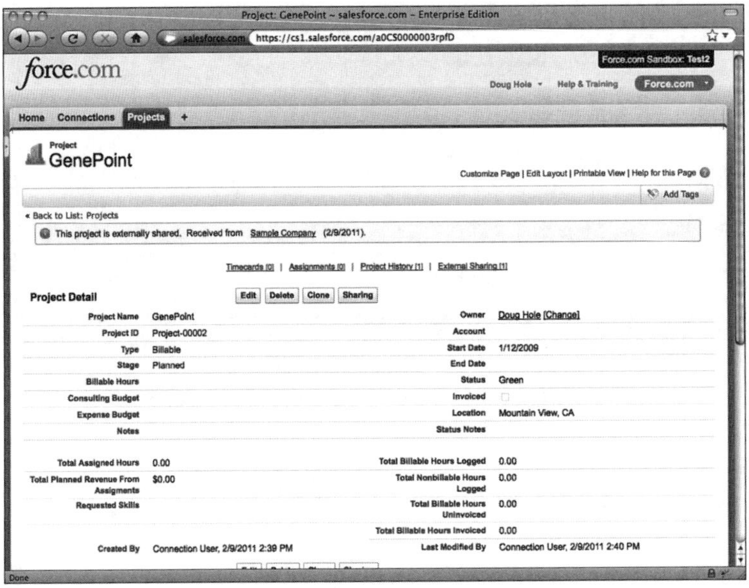

Figure 10-16   Viewing S2S-shared record

You have successfully caused a record to travel between two Force.com organizations. If the second organization modifies the shared record, the changes do not propagate back to the first organization. Furthermore, if the first organization modifies the record, the corresponding record in the second organization is updated to match, overwriting any updates made by the second organization. Deleting the record in either organization simply breaks the connection rather than cascading the deletion to the other organization. Sharing of the record can be stopped at any time by a click of the Stop Sharing link in the External Sharing related list.

Although S2S maps records in a lookup relationship as strings rather than full related objects, it does provide some special functionality for Master-Detail relationships. All child records are automatically forwarded initially, when the parent record is forwarded. Updates of those original child records are also forwarded, but not additions and deletions.

Developing Custom Integrations

With outbound messaging and S2S, Force.com completely handles the low-level details of how data is shared between two systems. These features are not appropriate for every integration scenario because they require a high degree of conformance on the part of the target system. This can be difficult or impossible to achieve with the political and technological barriers commonly present between companies and their applications.

Fortunately, the platform provides two additional features for added control and flexibility over outbound integration:

1. **Calling Web Services from Apex Code:** Apex code can be generated directly from WSDL, producing methods for invoking an external Web service and representing the input and output data in native Apex data structures rather than SOAP.

2. **Using HTTP Integration:** For integration projects that require even more control or that use non-SOAP message formats, Force.com includes classes for issuing HTTP and HTTPS requests, encoding and decoding URLs and Base64 content, and performing cryptographic signing and hashing often needed to comply with the security requirements of external services.

> **Caution**
>
> Force.com tightly controls outbound requests from its platform. Understanding the limits before jumping into development of integrations is important. These limitations apply to both Web service callouts and HTTP requests.
>
> Request and response messages cannot exceed the maximum Apex heap size, normally 3MB. Apex code can make a maximum of ten HTTP requests in a single transaction. By default, a single request cannot run longer than 10 seconds. If a transaction contains more than one request, the total time of all requests cannot exceed 120 seconds.

Calling Web Services from Apex Code

Force.com provides a code generation tool in its native user interface for creating Apex-friendly classes and methods from Web service definitions found in WSDL files. Like most code generation tools, using it is a hit-or-miss experience. When it works on your WSDL, it can save considerable effort over the alternative of manually constructing and parsing SOAP messages. But be prepared for cryptic error messages when code cannot be generated due to the impedance mismatch between WSDL, SOAP, and Apex.

If you're able to use your WSDL wholesale or slim it down to successfully generate Apex code, most of your work is done. Invoking the remote Web service becomes a relatively simple matter of preparing the right input via Apex classes, invoking a method, and using the resulting Apex classes in your program. No interaction with HTTP or XML is necessary because these details are hidden by the generated Apex code.

> **Caution**
>
> For integrations that require a series of Web service calls strung together with cookies to maintain state between them, you cannot use the Apex code generated from WSDL. Additionally, generated code does not support HTTP-level authentication.
>
> In general, no developer-modifiable options exist in the generated code, which uses an internal, undocumented API to perform the actual Web service callout. If your Web service call requires control over the SOAP message content or HTTP headers, you must write code to make the request from scratch using `HTTPRequest`, as described in the next subsection.

Here are the steps needed to generate Apex from WSDL:

1. Save the WSDL file on your local machine.
2. Go to the App Setup area and click Develop → Apex Classes.
3. Click the Generate from WSDL button.
4. Click the Browse button and locate the WSDL in your file system and then click the Parse WSDL button. The WSDL must describe a document-style service because RPC is not supported.
5. Each WSDL namespace can be mapped to an Apex classname to be generated. You can map multiple namespaces to the same class. Force.com suggests an Apex classname based on the WSDL, but you can override this suggestion. When you're done naming the classes, click the Generate Apex code button.
6. If you refresh your Force.com IDE by right-clicking the project and selecting Force.com → Refresh from Server, you should see the new Apex class. If not, make sure that it was generated successfully and that you've subscribed to new Apex classes by right-clicking the Force.com project and selecting Force.com → Add/Remove Metadata Components.

> **Caution**
>
> Due to the complexity of WSDL, mismatches between its naming conventions and Apex, and governor limits on the size of Apex classes, many edge cases exist that you should be aware of when using the WSDL to Apex feature. Investigate these further in the Force.com online help. As a best practice, keep your WSDL as simple as possible. Manually edit it to strip out extraneous services and ports.

Before you can run this code, you must authorize Force.com to make an outbound call to the endpoint of the Web service. Go to the Administration Setup area and click Security Controls → Remote Site Settings and add the host.

Using HTTP Integration

Many integration scenarios require full control over the preparation of requests and processing of responses. Force.com addresses this situation with support in Apex for making direct HTTP requests from the Force.com service to external servers on the Internet. The core Apex classes that allow you to work with HTTP are described here:

- **HttpRequest:** This class contains the parameters for making an HTTP request. It includes methods for working with the request body, HTTP headers, the HTTP method type, client certificates, HTTP compression, and timeouts.

- **HttpResponse:** When an HTTP request is sent, an instance of the HttpResponse class is returned. Methods are available for getting the raw response body, HTTP status code, and HTTP headers.

- **Http:** This class is used to perform the HTTP operation. It contains a single method called send to initiate the operation, which accepts an instance of HttpRequest and returns an HttpResponse.

In addition to these three classes, here are two other useful classes for working with HTTP in Apex:

1. **EncodingUtil:** This class contains methods for URL and Base64 encoding and decoding.

2. **Crypto:** Use the Crypto class to compute cryptographic hashes and signatures commonly required to authenticate to HTTP services. It includes the methods generateDigest to generate a one-way hash digest for a message, generateMac to generate a message authentication code given a private key, and sign to produce a digital signature for a message using a private key.

To get started with HTTP in Apex, try writing a method to invoke a REST service. The REST service used in the following example is provided by Yahoo!. It's a geocoding service, returning latitude and longitude given a street, city, and state. The service is documented at http://developer.yahoo.com/maps/rest/V1/geocode.html. Listing 10-2 is a sample of the result of invoking the service.

Listing 10-2   Sample XML Response from Yahoo! Geocoding REST Service

```
<ResultSet xsi:schemaLocation="urn:yahoo:maps
  http://api.local.yahoo.com/MapsService/V1/
  GeocodeResponse.xsd">
<Result precision="address">
<Latitude>37.555113</Latitude>
<Longitude>-122.300100</Longitude>
<Address>900 Concar Dr</Address>
```

```
<City>San Mateo</City>
<State>CA</State>
<Zip>94402-2600</Zip>
<Country>US</Country>
</Result>
</ResultSet>
```

Inputs to REST services are provided as URL parameters, and the outputs vary but are usually JSON- or XML-encoded. Although you can always manipulate raw strings and JSON in Apex, check the open-source community for existing code to help you construct and parse messages in these and other formats. Check the Force.com Code Share site (http://developer.force.com/codeshare) for the latest list of open-source projects.

In the code sample in Listing 10-3, the geocoding service is called and its response parsed using the XML API provided by Force.com, specifically the DOM.Document and DOM.XmlNode classes. Although the Force.com also includes the XmlStreamReader class for parsing XML, it works at a lower level than DOM.XmlNode and tends to be more difficult to use.

Listing 10-3   Calling the Yahoo! Geocoding REST Service

```
public class YahooGeocode {
  public static List<Result> geocode(
    String street, String city, String state) {
    List<Result> result = new List<Result>();
    HttpRequest req = new HttpRequest();
    String url = 'http://local.yahooapis.com/MapsService/'
      + 'V1/geocode?appid=YD-9G7bey8_JXxQP6rxl.fBFGgCdNjoDMACQA-'
      + '&street=' + EncodingUtil.urlEncode(street, 'UTF-8')
      + '&city=' + EncodingUtil.urlEncode(city, 'UTF-8')
      + '&state=' + EncodingUtil.urlEncode(state, 'UTF-8');
    req.setEndpoint(url);
    req.setMethod('GET');
    Http http = new Http();
    HTTPResponse res = http.send(req);
    DOM.Document doc = res.getBodyDocument();
    List<DOM.XmlNode> nodes = doc.getRootElement().getChildElements();
    if (nodes != null) {
      for (DOM.XmlNode node : nodes) {
        result.add(nodeToResult(node));
      }
    }
    return result;
  }
  public static Result nodeToResult(DOM.XmlNode node) {
    Result r = new Result();
    r.latitude = getText(node, 'Latitude');
```

```
    r.longitude = getText(node, 'Longitude');
    r.address = getText(node, 'Address');
    r.city = getText(node, 'City');
    r.state = getText(node, 'State');
    r.zip = getText(node, 'Zip');
    r.country = getText(node, 'Country');
    return r;
  }
  private static String getText(DOM.XmlNode node, String element) {
    if (node != null) {
      DOM.XmlNode child = node.getChildElement(element, 'urn:yahoo:maps');
      if (child != null) {
        return child.getText();
      }
    }
    return null;
  }
  public class Result {
    public String latitude;
    public String longitude;
    public String address;
    public String city;
    public String state;
    public String zip;
    public String country;
    public String asString() {
      return address + ', ' + city + ', ' + state
        + ', ' + zip + ', ' + country + ' ('
        + latitude + ', ' + longitude + ')';
    }
  }
}
```

Tip

The `YahooGeocode` class will not work without a Remote Site Setting authorizing Force.com to call out to the Yahoo! service. To add this setting, go to the Administration Setup area and click Security Controls → Remote Site Settings. Click the New Remote Site button and enter a name to remember the site (no spaces allowed) and the root of the URL (http://local.yahooapis.com).

To test the code, open the Execute Anonymous view in the Force.com IDE and execute the statements given in Listing 10-4. The result should be a single line containing the latitude and longitude of the input address.

Listing 10-4   **Testing the `YahooGeocode` Class**

```
for (YahooGeocode.Result result : YahooGeocode.geocode(
  '900 Concar Dr', 'San Mateo', 'CA')) {
  System.debug(result.asString());
}
```

Sample Application: Anonymous Benchmarking

In a services organization, utilization is a valuable metric for managing the business. A simple definition of utilization is the number of hours worked, typically hours billable to the client, divided by the total number of hours in a time period, expressed as a percentage.

In this section, the Services Manager sample application is extended with a Visualforce page that performs a basic utilization calculation between two dates. To calculate billable hours worked, it queries the Timecard custom object. For available hours, it uses a built-in Apex function for date arithmetic to compute the number of working hours between the two dates.

Integration comes into the picture with the addition of anonymous benchmarking. Imagine an independent organization that collects and analyzes the performance data of services companies. Companies submit their anonymized metrics and compare their performance to that of other companies in their industry. For the Services Manager sample application, you have access to a fictional benchmarking organization reachable through a Web service call.

The remainder of the section describes the design and implementation of the utilization page, controller, and integration to the anonymous benchmarking Web service. It is divided into the following subsections:

- **Visualforce Page Design:** Build a simple Visualforce page to capture the start and end dates of the utilization calculation, and display the results.

- **Visualforce Controller Design:** Develop a controller to retrieve the billable hours worked and the available hours and perform the utilization calculation.

- **Integrating the Web Service:** Add code to the controller to call out to the anonymous benchmarking Web service to share the results of the utilization calculation.

- **Sample Implementation:** Examine sample code for the utilization page and controller. Try this code in its entirety, copy portions of it, or contrast it with your own implementation.

Visualforce Page Design

The goal of this section is a Visualforce page resembling what's shown in Figure 10-17. A user has entered start and end dates to compute utilization, selected the Share Anonymously check box to indicate that she would like the results sent out over the Web to the benchmarking service, and clicked the Calculate button. This populated the lower three rows with the utilization results. The results include the total hours worked in the time period (from the Timecard object), the total number of consulting resources in the system (from the Resource object), and the utilization as a percentage.

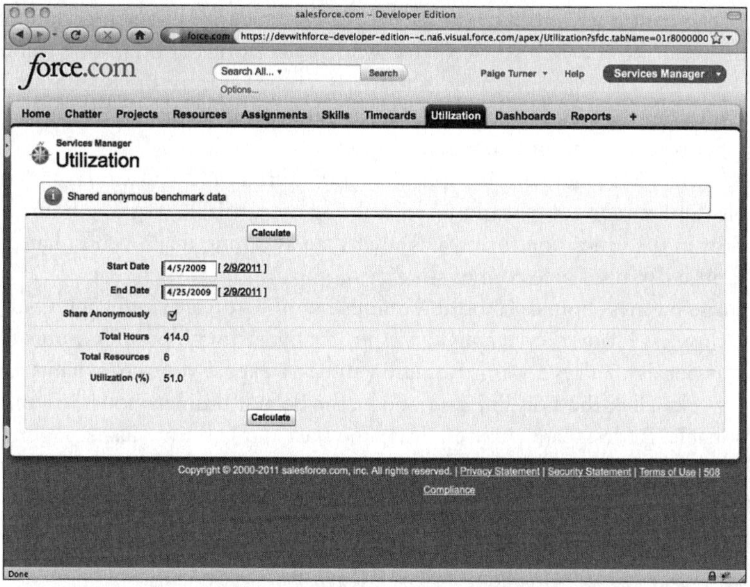

Figure 10-17   Utilization Visualforce page

The page is styled to look like part of the native Force.com native user interface. The sectionHeader component is used to render the heading bar. This is followed by the pageMessages component to show errors and information to the user. The Calculate button is a commandButton, enclosed in a pageBlockButtons component. The Start and End date fields are both inputField components with their value attributes set to SObject Date fields in the controller, providing a calendar picker user interface when focus is received. The styling of each row is accomplished by pageBlockSectionItem components, each with two child components. For example, the pageBlockSectionItem to render the row for Start Date contains an outputLabel and an inputField.

Begin by prototyping this page, focusing on the appearance, layout, and user interaction. Create a custom controller class, adding a placeholder action method to calculate the utilization. Create member variables for the start and end dates, binding them to any Date field in a standard or custom object. This binding means you can use the inputField component to render the start and end date fields, making them calendar input controls rather than plain text fields. Add a Boolean member variable for the Share Anonymously option, bound to an inputCheckbox component.

You're ready to move on to build out the controller to compute utilization and integrate the benchmarking Web service.

Visualforce Controller Design

The job of the controller is to take the user input and calculate utilization, optionally sending the results to the Web service. Real-world calculations of utilization can be complex. For example, some organizations subtract paid time off from the total hours available. Or with a large or diverse pool of resources, utilization might be calculated separately per business unit or geographic region.

In the Services Manager sample application, the utilization calculation is intentionally kept simple. One minor complication is in defining the available working hours, the denominator in the utilization formula. Rather than assuming that all consultants are billable 24 hours a day, use Force.com to store the company's business hours.

To manage business hours, go to the Administration Setup area and click Company Profile → Business Hours. Force.com comes preconfigured with business hours that run for 24 hours per day, 7 days a week. Because you don't expect your consultants to work 168-hour weeks, click the Edit link and update the default business hours to something more reasonable. To designate a day off, leave the start and end time blank. Figure 10-18 shows the business hours configuration for a 45-hour workweek, working 8 a.m. to 5 p.m. weekdays with Saturdays and Sundays off.

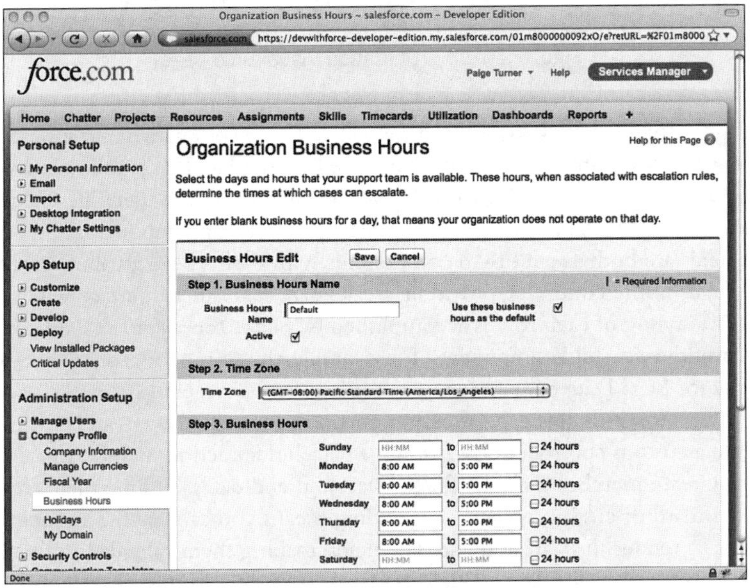

Figure 10-18   Configuring business hours

With business hours configured, you're ready to compute utilization. The following list outlines the steps:

1. Write a SOQL query to select the `Total_Hours__c` field from all timecards that are billable and between the start and end dates entered by the user.

2. Add up all the values of the `Total_Hours__c` field. This is the numerator in the utilization calculation.

3. Assume that the `Week_Ending__c` field of timecards is always a Saturday. If the start or end date entered by the user is not a Saturday, adjust it accordingly. If you do not take this simplifying step, you'll have to compensate for non-Saturday time ranges by subtracting the hours of individual days from the total.

4. The number of hours available must account for the business hours of the organization. The business hours you configured in the Force.com native user interface are stored in a standard object named `BusinessHours`, queryable from SOQL. Write SOQL to obtain the unique identifier of the default `BusinessHours` record. Call the static `diff` method on the `BusinessHours` class, passing the unique identifier and the adjusted start and end dates. This returns a long value with the number of milliseconds elapsed between the two dates during which the organization was open for business.

Integrating the Web Service

The fictional anonymous benchmarking service provides a URL to the WSDL for its Web service. The Web service allows companies to submit their utilization calculations anonymously for contribution in a database. Companies are differentiated by industry only, using a standard industry classification system called the North American Industry Classification System (NAICS), developed by the United States Census Bureau. NAICS codes are six-digit numbers. The list of NAICS codes is available at www.census.gov/eos/www/naics/reference_files_tools/2007/naics07_6.txt. For example, 541511 is the code for companies providing Custom Computer Programming Services.

To integrate the Web service, begin by generating an Apex class from the WSDL. The WSDL is available at http://force-book-developer-edition.na6.force.com/Anonymous-BenchmarkWsdl. Download it to your local machine and then follow these steps:

1. In the App Setup area, click Develop → Apex Classes and click the Generate from WSDL button.

2. Click the Browse button, locate the WSDL file in your file system, and click the Parse WSDL button.

3. You should see the screen shown in Figure 10-19, which is prompting for an Apex classname to receive the generated code. You can name your class anything you want, but this example uses the name BenchmarkWS.

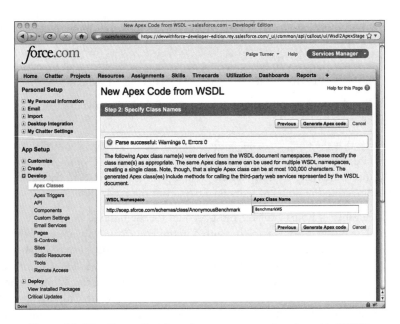

Figure 10-19   Generating Apex from anonymous benchmarking WSDL

You should now have a new Apex class called BenchmarkWS. Before you can test it out, enable the endpoint URL in Remote Site Settings. In the Administration Setup area, click Security Controls → Remote Site Settings. Click the New Remote Site button and enter a name for the site and its URL (https://force-book-developer-edition.na6.force. com). Figure 10-20 shows the result of adding the remote site.

Finally, test the generated Apex class using the code given in Listing 10-5. You can execute this code directly from the Execute Anonymous view.

Listing 10-5   **Testing the Web Service Call from Apex**

```
BenchmarkWS.AnonymousBenchmark service =
  new BenchmarkWS.AnonymousBenchmark();
BenchmarkWS.UtilizationEntry ue =
  new BenchmarkWS.UtilizationEntry();
ue.naicsCode = '541511';
ue.startDate = Date.parse('4/5/2009');
ue.endDate = Date.parse('4/11/2009');
ue.totalHours = 35;
ue.totalResources = 1;
ue.utilization = 88;
BenchmarkWS.SubmissionStatus[] results =
  service.submitUtilizationData(
    new BenchmarkWS.UtilizationEntry[] { ue });
```

```
if (results != null) {
  for (BenchmarkWS.SubmissionStatus result : results) {
    if (!result.success) {
      System.debug(result.errorMessage);
    }
  }
}
```

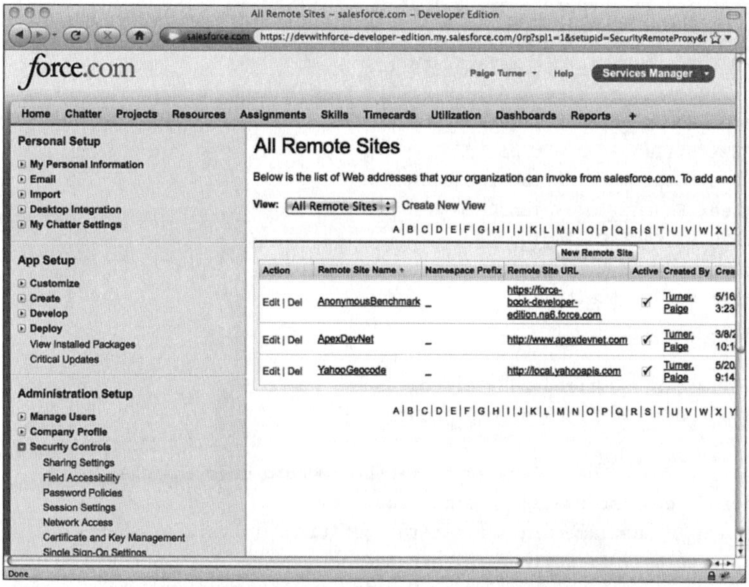

Figure 10-20   Remote site settings

Sample Implementation

Listing 10-6 contains the controller code for the utilization Visualforce page, and Listing 10-7 contains the page itself. This implementation brings together the three elements discussed in this section: the user interface to calculate utilization, the utilization computation itself, and the Web service callout.

Listing 10-6   **Sample Code for Utilization Controller**

```
public class UtilizationController {
  public Timecard__c card1 { get; private set; }
  public Timecard__c card2 { get; private set; }
  public Boolean shared { get; set; }
  public Decimal utilization { get; private set; }
  public Decimal totalHours { get; private set; }
```

```
public Integer totalResources { get; private set; }
public UtilizationController() {
  card1 = new Timecard__c();
  card2 = new Timecard__c();
}
public PageReference calculate() {
  Date startDate = card1.Week_Ending__c;
  Date endDate = card2.Week_Ending__c;
  // assumes all resources are billable
  List<Resource__c> resources = [ SELECT Id FROM Resource__c
    WHERE Start_Date__c < :startDate ];
  List<Timecard__c> timecards = [ SELECT Week_Ending__c,
    Total_Hours__c FROM Timecard__c
    WHERE Billable__c = true AND
      Week_Ending__c >= :startDate AND
      Week_Ending__c <= :endDate
    ORDER BY Week_Ending__c ];
  totalHours = 0;
  if (timecards.size() == 0) {
    return null;
  }
  for (Timecard__c timecard : timecards) {
    totalHours += timecard.Total_Hours__c;
  }
  // adjust start and end dates to match timecard week endings
  Timecard__c firstTimecard = timecards.get(0);
  Timecard__c lastTimecard = timecards.get(timecards.size() - 1);
  if (startDate < firstTimecard.Week_Ending__c) {
    startDate = firstTimecard.Week_Ending__c.addDays(-6);
    card1.Week_Ending__c = startDate;
  }
  if (endDate > lastTimecard.Week_Ending__c) {
    endDate = lastTimecard.Week_Ending__c;
    card2.Week_Ending__c = endDate;
  }
  totalResources = resources.size();
  Long availableHours = totalResources *
    calculateAvailableHours(startDate, endDate);
  utilization = 100 * totalHours.divide(availableHours, 2);
  if (shared) {
    shareUtilization();
  }
  return null;
}
public static Long calculateAvailableHours(
  Date startDate, Date endDate) {
  BusinessHours bh = [ SELECT id FROM BusinessHours
```

```
      WHERE IsDefault = true ];
    DateTime startTime = DateTime.newInstance(
      startDate.year(), startDate.month(), startDate.day(),
      0, 0, 0);
    DateTime endTime = DateTime.newInstance(
      endDate.year(), endDate.month(), endDate.day(),
      0, 0, 0);
    Decimal diff = Decimal.valueOf(
      BusinessHours.diff(bh.id, startTime, endTime));
    return diff.divide(3600000, 0).round();
  }
  private void shareUtilization() {
    BenchmarkWS.AnonymousBenchmark service =
      new BenchmarkWS.AnonymousBenchmark();
    BenchmarkWS.UtilizationEntry ue =
      new BenchmarkWS.UtilizationEntry();
    ue.naicsCode = '541511';
    ue.startDate = card1.Week_Ending__c;
    ue.endDate = card2.Week_Ending__c;
    ue.totalHours = totalHours;
    ue.totalResources = totalResources;
    ue.utilization = utilization;
    BenchmarkWS.SubmissionStatus[] results =
      service.submitUtilizationData(
        new BenchmarkWS.UtilizationEntry[] { ue });
    if (results != null) {
      for (BenchmarkWS.SubmissionStatus result : results) {
        if (!result.success) {
          ApexPages.addMessage(new ApexPages.Message(
            ApexPages.Severity.ERROR, result.errorMessage));
        } else {
          ApexPages.addMessage(new ApexPages.Message(
            ApexPages.Severity.INFO,
            'Shared anonymous benchmark data'));
        }
      }
    }
  }
}
```

Listing 10-7   **Sample Code for Utilization Visualforce Page**

```
<apex:page controller="UtilizationController"
  tabStyle="Utilization__tab">
<apex:sectionHeader title="Services Manager"
  subtitle="Utilization" />
```

```
<apex:form>
<apex:pageMessages id="msgs" />
<apex:pageBlock id="util">
<apex:pageBlockButtons>
  <apex:commandButton action="{!calculate}"
    value="Calculate" rerender="msgs, util" />
</apex:pageBlockButtons>
<apex:pageBlockSection columns="1">
  <apex:pageBlockSectionItem>
    <apex:outputLabel value="Start Date" />
    <apex:inputField value="{!card1.Week_Ending__c}" />
  </apex:pageBlockSectionItem>
<apex:pageBlockSectionItem>
  <apex:outputLabel value="End Date" />
  <apex:inputField value="{!card2.Week_Ending__c}" />
</apex:pageBlockSectionItem>
<apex:pageBlockSectionItem>
  <apex:outputLabel value="Share Anonymously" />
  <apex:inputCheckbox value="{!shared}" />
</apex:pageBlockSectionItem>
<apex:pageBlockSectionItem>
  <apex:outputLabel value="Total Hours" />
  <apex:outputText value="{!totalHours}" />
</apex:pageBlockSectionItem>
<apex:pageBlockSectionItem>
  <apex:outputLabel value="Total Resources" />
  <apex:outputText value="{!totalResources}" />
</apex:pageBlockSectionItem>
<apex:pageBlockSectionItem>
  <apex:outputLabel value="Utilization (%)" />
  <apex:outputText value="{!utilization}" />
</apex:pageBlockSectionItem>
</apex:pageBlockSection>
</apex:pageBlock>
</apex:form>
</apex:page>
```

Summary

With its outbound integration features, the Force.com platform is open for interoperability with other applications and systems running on Force.com, elsewhere on the Internet, and behind your corporate firewall. The capability to call externally from within the platform using Web standards helps to break down the functional silos of Force.com and other applications.

Chapter 11 reverses the integration equation, demonstrating the capability of Force.com to service inbound requests from other systems for its business logic and data. Before jumping in, take a minute to review the following points from this chapter:

- Outbound messaging uses workflow rules to trigger a Web service request to an endpoint, an Internet-accessible HTTP or HTTPS port. The signature of the Web service is dictated entirely by Force.com. If you control the implementation of the endpoint, outbound messaging is the fastest and most robust method of outbound integration.

- Salesforce-to-Salesforce (S2S) enables sharing of records between multiple Force.com organizations. This natural outgrowth of multitenancy provides near-real-time data integration without code.

- WSDL to Apex is a tool in the Force.com native user interface for reading a WSDL and creating Apex code from it. With the generated code, your Apex code has access to the remote methods of the Web service without dealing with the implementation details of XML and HTTP. Apex code also provides access to raw HTTP requests and responses, allowing you to develop your own integration callouts.

11

Advanced Integration

This chapter focuses on integrating with Force.com from outside of the platform, using servers behind your corporate firewall or those of other cloud providers. This approach requires significantly more configuration and development effort than the integrations described in Chapter 10, "Integration," but this extra work is rewarded with increased flexibility.

By integrating from outside of Force.com, you have complete control of the platforms, programming languages, and tools used in building the integration. The only requirement is that the technology supports SOAP or REST (XML or JSON) communication over HTTP. By running the integration code on your own servers rather than Force.com, you are less likely to run into governor limits of Force.com, and those limits you do encounter are readily addressed by following recommended API usage patterns.

This chapter is divided into sections that each address a different aspect of integration with Force.com:

- **Understanding Force.com Web Services:** This section describes high-level concepts common to all the subsequent sections, including how to invoke Web services from Java and C#.NET and the handling of data types and errors.

- **Using the Enterprise API:** The Enterprise API is a set of Web services that allow fine-grained, strongly typed access to the data in your Force.com database, including execution of SOQL and SOSL queries and full read and write capabilities on the records of all objects.

- **Building Custom Web Services in Apex:** Although Force.com provides built-in Web services, you can also define your own using Apex code. Custom Web services are typically written to optimize for application-specific usage patterns; for example, combining what would be many Enterprise API calls into a single, robust method executed entirely on the Force.com platform.

- **Introduction to the Metadata API:** The Metadata API enables you to write code to perform development and configuration management tasks such as database object maintenance and application migration. It is the same API used by the Force.com IDE.

- **Using the Force.com REST API:** The REST API provides much of the same functionality as Force.com Web services, but without the overhead and complexity of SOAP.
- **Sample Application:** In an integration scenario for the Services Manager sample application, a Java program is developed to update Force.com with information from a human resources database.

Understanding Force.com Web Services

Force.com Web services allow data, logic, and metadata to be accessed from outside the Force.com platform by any program that can communicate using SOAP messages over HTTP.

Although the details of the Web services vary, the general procedure for writing a program to invoke them remains constant. With a strongly typed language like Java or C#.NET, stub code is generated from the Force.com WSDL. The program must log in to Force.com to establish a session and can then invoke the Web service methods.

This section describes concepts that can be applied to using any Force.com Web service. It consists of the following parts:

- **Basics of Force.com Web Services:** Learn about the five Web services provided by Force.com, how they are secured, and limits placed on their use.
- **Generating Stub Code:** Walk through the process for generating Java or C#.NET code from Force.com WSDL.
- **Logging In:** The first Web service call typically establishes a session with Force.com by logging in. This session is used to make subsequent Web service calls until it is invalidated explicitly or it expires.
- **Force.com Data Types in SOAP:** Understand how data types in Force.com objects are expressed in Web services.
- **Error Handling:** Force.com Web services signal errors in a few ways, depending on where the errors originate.

Basics of Force.com Web Services

Force.com provides five types of Web service APIs: Enterprise, Partner, Metadata, Apex, and Delegated Authentication. Each has its own WSDL describing the methods and data structures available. The WSDL can be used to generate stub code in strongly typed languages, allowing the Web services to be incorporated in programs without manual construction and parsing of complex SOAP messages.

When accessing data in Force.com using Web services, the choice is between Enterprise and Partner APIs. Both APIs have the same core set of calls, such as query to execute a SOQL query. The difference between the APIs is how database objects are represented in your code.

The Enterprise API provides a strongly typed representation of the objects in your Force.com database. This allows your code to operate naturally with Force.com data, using the field names and data types as you would in Apex code. When you redefine an object or add a new object, the Enterprise WSDL is automatically updated to reflect the changes. You need to manually regenerate the client code from the latest WSDL, but this is a small price to pay for concise, maintainable code.

The Partner API is designed for independent software vendors who write applications that must interoperate with many different Force.com organizations. They cannot rely on a single, static representation of standard and custom objects, because all customers of Force.com are free to create their own database schemas. With the Partner API, you can write generic code to access any object in any Force.com organization. It's more verbose to work with than the Enterprise API, but more flexible as well.

> **Note**
>
> This chapter is intended to familiarize you with the basic Force.com Web service APIs and their usage. It does not cover the Partner API. The full reference for all Force.com Web services is the Force.com Web Services API Developer's Guide, available at www.salesforce.com/us/developer/docs/api/index.htm.

There are also three APIs that do not work with Force.com data. The Metadata API allows manipulation of objects, fields, and other elements of your Force.com configuration. It is described later in this chapter. The Apex API is not covered in this book. It provides access to low-level development-related features such as the generation of Apex from WSDL, test execution, and anonymous Apex execution. The Delegated Authentication API enables a program running outside of Force.com to be invoked whenever a user attempts to log in to Salesforce, allowing it to decide whether the user is valid. It is described in Chapter 12, "Additional Platform Features."

Versions

With each major release of the Force.com platform, new versions of its WSDL are also released. To take advantage of new features, your code must be updated to use the latest WSDL.

If the new features are not needed, no action is required. Your code will continue to work without modification. This is because each WSDL has an endpoint URL in it that includes its version.

> **Note**
>
> In its documentation, Salesforce commits to maintaining Web service versions for a minimum of three years. It also states that one year of notice will be provided for discontinued Web service versions.

Security

Force.com uses Secure Sockets Layer (SSL) v3 and Transport Layer Security (TLS) to protect the communications between your client application and the Force.com platform.

After your client program has logged in, all the API calls respect the full set of data
security features in Force.com at the object, field, and record level. For this reason, configuring a Force.com profile and user account dedicated solely to integration is a good practice. It might have elevated privileges compared with other, Web-based users. You can
configure this profile to accept logins only from the API address of your corporate integration server using the Login IP Ranges on the profile or logins at specific times that
your integration is scheduled to run using the Login Hours section.

API Limits

Salesforce limits the number of API calls that can be executed during a 24-hour period.
Every call into Force.com is counted against this limit, including calls made by the
Force.com IDE. The exact limit depends on the edition of Force.com you have licensed.

To view your API limit and current consumption, go to the Administration Setup area
and click Company Profile → Company Information. For example, the organization in
Figure 11-1 has a maximum of 5,000 API calls and has used 97 of them in the current 24-
hour period.

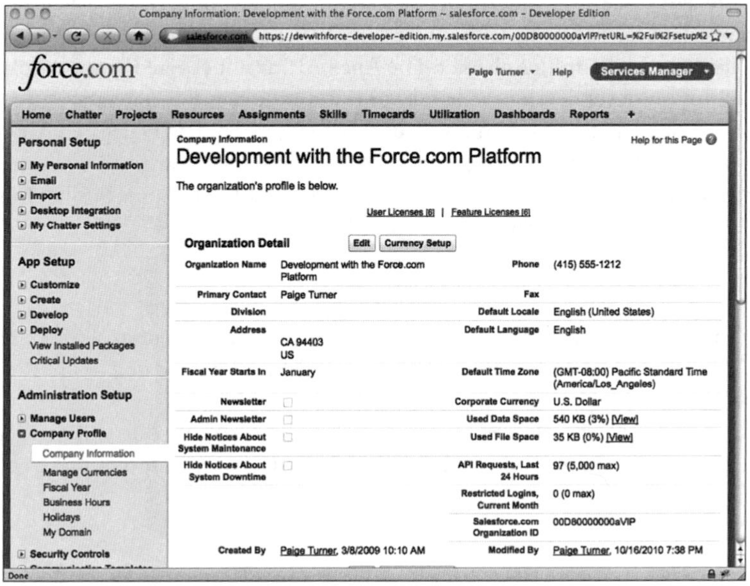

Figure 11-1   Viewing API call usage

You can configure Force.com to email you when your organization is close to its
API call limit. Go to the Administration Setup area and click Monitoring → API Usage

Notifications. Click the New button to define a new notification, specifying the user to receive the notification, the usage threshold that triggers notifications, and how often they are sent. Figure 11-2 shows a configured API usage notification.

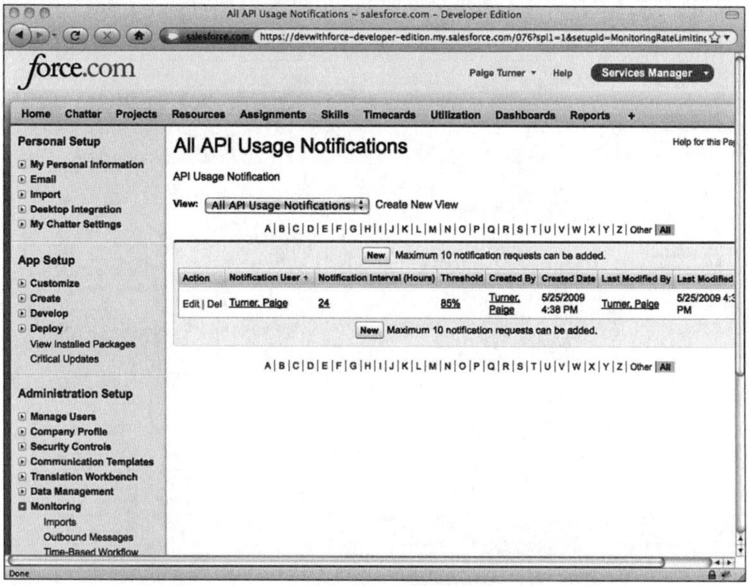

Figure 11-2   Configuring API usage notification

Generating Stub Code

If you're using a strongly typed language like C#.NET or Java to integrate with Force.com, your first step is to generate stub code from a Force.com WSDL. All standard Force.com WSDLs are available in the App Setup area; to access them, click Develop → API. Click each WSDL link and save the resulting document on your local file system.

Each language and development tool typically provides a facility for parsing WSDL and generating stub code that can be incorporated into your program. The steps for generating Java and C#.NET stub code from WSDL are described next.

Java Web Service Client

> **Note**
>
> Salesforce advises that you use the Force.com Web Service Connector (WSC) with its Web services. Download it from http://code.google.com/p/sfdc-wsc.

Follow these steps to create Java stub code using WSC and the Eclipse IDE:

1. Create a new Java project. In this example, the project is named WebServicesDemo.
2. Copy the WSC jar and `enterprise.wsdl` files into the top level of your Java project.

3. Create a new Run Configuration to execute the stub generator. Figure 11-3 shows the Run Configuration.

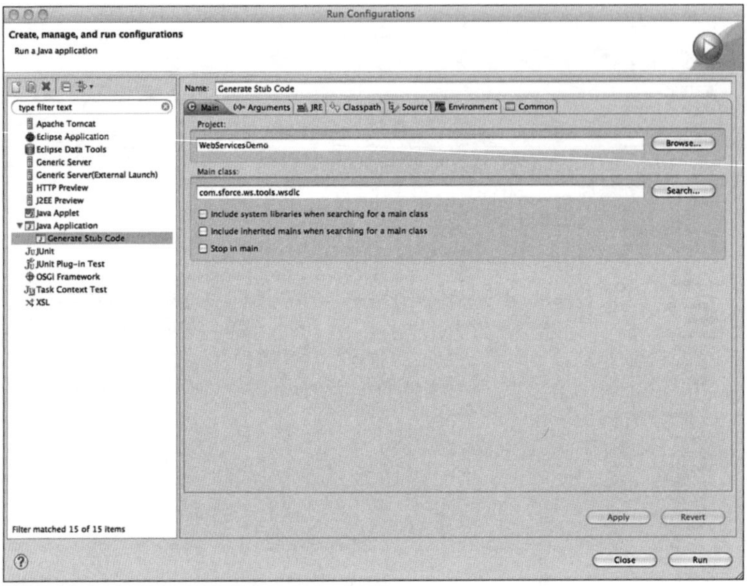

Figure 11-3   Eclipse Run Configuration to generate stub code using WSC

4. Click the Arguments tab and enter `enterprise.wsdl enterprise.jar` in the Program arguments text box. These arguments tell the program to generate the stub code for the `enterprise.wsdl` file into a jar named `enterprise.jar`.

5. Click the Run button on the Run Configuration and refresh your project. It should contain the stub code for the Force.com Enterprise API, as depicted in Figure 11-4.

C#.NET Web Service Client

Note

Salesforce recommends using Visual Studio 2003 or higher with its Web services.

The following steps generate a C#.NET Web service client using Visual Studio 2005:

1. Create a new Visual Studio project. The example here is a C# Windows Console Application.

2. Add a Web Reference and provide the path to the WSDL you saved on your machine and then click the Go button. Visual Studio parses the WSDL and displays the methods.

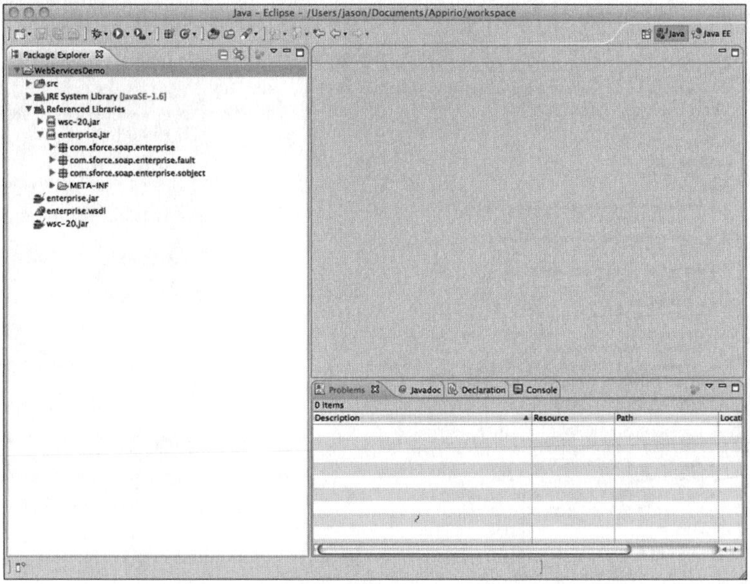

Figure 11-4   Java project with stub code generated

3. Enter a name for the Web reference and click the Add Reference button. This name is the namespace where the generated client classes are placed. Figure 11-5 shows an example with EnterpriseWS as the name.

4. Your project is ready. To use the client in your code, import the namespace generated from the Force.com WSDL. The example in Figure 11-6 shows the project, with sample code importing the namespace WSDemo.EnterpriseWS. WSDemo is the name of the Visual Studio project, and EnterpriseWS is the name of the generated class specified in step 3.

Logging In

Logging in to Force.com from a program begins with the user credentials of username and password, the same as logging in to the native user interface using a Web browser. In addition to a valid username and password, two additional points of configuration are needed to log in, described here:

1. **API Enabled Permission:** The user logging in must have the API Enabled permission on his or her profile.

2. **Security Token or Whitelisted IP Address:** Force.com requires either a security token appended to the password or API calls to be issued from a whitelisted IP address.

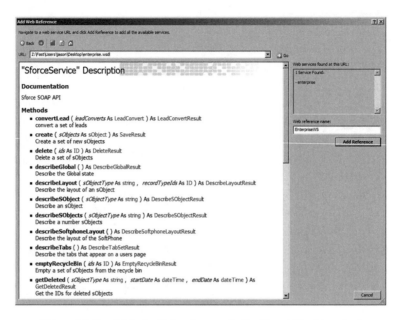

Figure 11-5   Adding a Web reference to the Visual Studio project

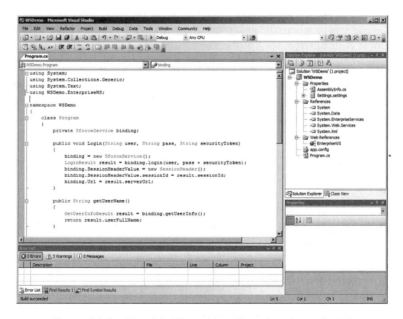

Figure 11-6   Visual Studio project with stub code generated

API Enabled Permission

The user logging in via API must have the API Enabled permission set on his or her profile. This permission is found in the Administrative Permissions section. A profile with API Enabled permission is shown in Figure 11-7.

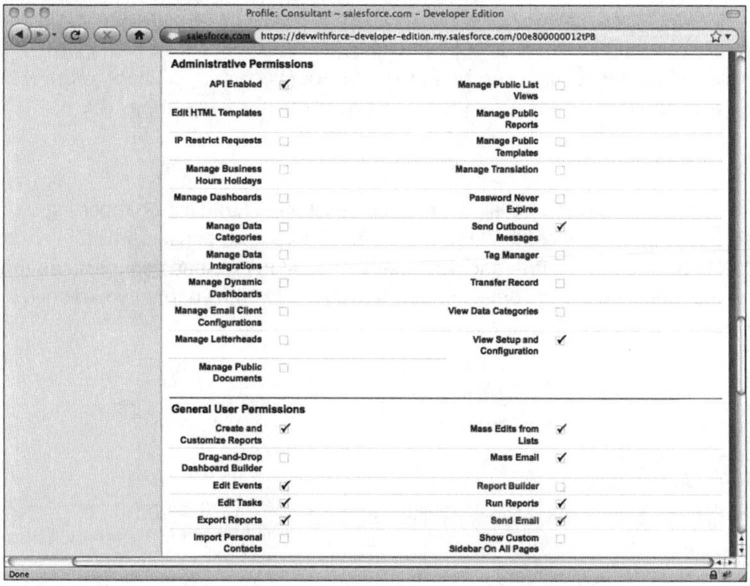

Figure 11-7   Profile with API Enabled permission

Caution

A few editions of Force.com don't allow API access. If you don't see the API Enabled permission on the profile page or cannot enable it, contact Salesforce support.

Security Token or Whitelisted IP Address

The security token is a string of characters appended to the end of a user's password. It allows a user to log in to Force.com from any IP address, assuming that IP address restrictions are not configured on his or her profile. To obtain a security token, visit the Personal Setup area and click My Personal Information → Reset My Security Token. A new security token is generated and emailed to the address associated with the user.

An alternative to security tokens is IP whitelisting. Whitelisting instructs Force.com to accept requests from a specific IP address. To whitelist an IP address, go to the Administration Setup area and click Security Controls → Network Access. Click the New button, enter the IP address in the Start IP Address and End IP Address fields, and then click the Save button.

The Login Web Service

To log in, invoke the `login` Web service with a username and password. If the login is successful, a `LoginResult` object is returned; otherwise, an exception is raised. The `LoginResult` object contains the URL of the server to send Web services requests to and the session identifier that uniquely identifies your authenticated session with Force.com. Both of these attributes must be sent in the HTTP headers of subsequent requests for them to succeed.

Listing 11-1 contains sample Java code to log in. Note that WSC takes care of the details described earlier for logging in, but this is not the case if you use a different Web service stack, such as Apache Axis. Listing 11-2 is the same example in C#.NET.

> **Note**
>
> Code in Listings 11-1 and 11-2 doesn't include exception handling or importing the gener-
> ated stub code. It also doesn't factor in the use of corporate proxies, which might block out-
> bound HTTPS traffic. Both Java and .NET can be configured to pass connections through a
> proxy. If your connections to Force.com are failing, check with your network administrator to
> see whether a proxy could be the cause.

Listing 11-1   **Java Fragment to Log In**

```
ConnectorConfig config = new ConnectorConfig();
config.setUsername(user);
config.setPassword(pass);
EnterpriseConnection connection = Connector.newConnection(config);
```

Listing 11-2   **C#.NET Fragment to Log In**

```
SforceService binding = new SforceService();
LoginResult result = binding.login(user, pass + securityToken);
binding.SessionHeaderValue = new SessionHeader();
binding.SessionHeaderValue.sessionId = result.sessionId;
binding.Url = result.serverUrl;
```

When you're done with a session, you can invoke the logout Web service. It causes the session to become invalid, ensuring that it is not used accidentally elsewhere by your program.

By default, sessions expire after two hours, but you can change this in the Administration Setup area by clicking Security Controls → Session Settings. Web service calls that use an expired or invalid session throw an exception with an `INVALID_SESSION_ID` exception code.

Troubleshooting Login Problems

All logins to Force.com create an entry in the login history, shown in Figure 11-8. To view it, go to the Administration Setup area and click Manage Users → Login History.

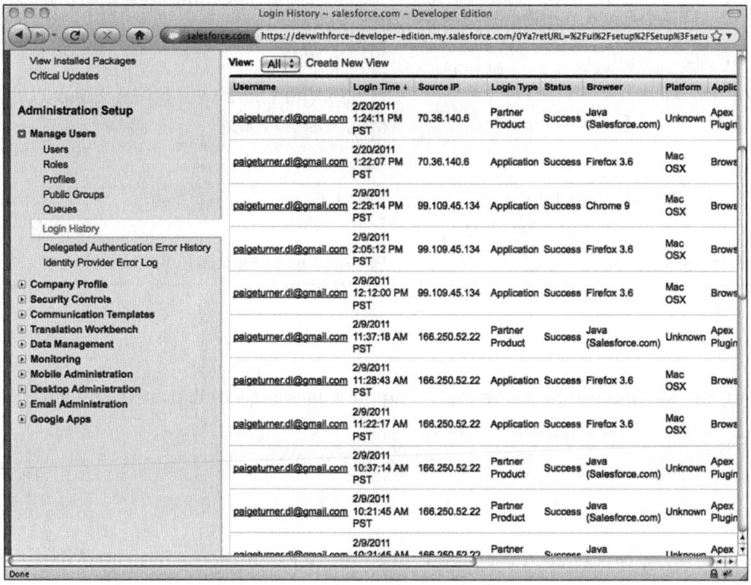

Figure 11-8   Login History Page

The login history can be helpful for troubleshooting login problems. If you see your program's login attempt listed but failed, the login request has successfully reached Force.com's servers but is being rejected. If the request is not listed at all, you need to investigate the connection between your server and Force.com.

Force.com Data Types in SOAP

Table 11-1 lists the Force.com data types and their mapping to SOAP data types.

Table 11-1   **Mapping of Force.com Data Types to SOAP Types**

Force.com Data Type	SOAP Type
Auto Number	String.
Formula	Depends on the data type of the formula. Can be Double, String, Date.
Roll-Up Summary	Double.
Lookup Relationship, Master-Detail Relationship	ID.
Checkbox	Boolean.
Currency	Double.
Date, Datetime	Date. Always UTC, convert to local time zone. If time portion isn't present, midnight is returned.

Table 11-1   **Mapping of Force.com Data Types to SOAP Types**

Force.com Data Type	SOAP Type
Number	Integer (numbers with no fractional component), otherwise Double.
Percent	Double.
Email, Phone, Picklist, Picklist (Multi-Select), Text, Text Area, Text (Long), URL	String.
Binary (Attachment, Document)	Base64-encoded string.

Note

Refer to the documentation for your programming language or Web services library to map SOAP types to language-specific data types.

Error Handling

Three categories of errors are raised by Force.com Web services, described here from lowest to highest level of abstraction:

1. **System Exceptions:** System exceptions are language-specific and indicate lower-level problems occurring in the Web services stack. For example, using Java with the WSC, the ConnectionException contains nested exceptions to indicate specific problems, such as a java.net.SocketException. The C#.NET equivalent is a System.Net.WebException.

2. **API Faults:** API faults are caused by malformed SOAP messages, authentication failures, or query-related problems. They are SOAP-level errors that contain an exception code and a message. For example, in Java, a LoginFault class extends ApiFault and indicates that the login to Force.com failed. A general API fault with an exception code of INSUFFICIENT_ACCESS indicates that the user does not have sufficient access to perform the operation. In C#.NET, these exceptions are instances of System.Web.Services.Protocols.SoapException.

3. **Application Errors:** These are language-neutral, Force.com-specific errors that vary based on the Web services involved. For example, services that modify one or more records return an Error object upon failure. The Error object contains a status code, a message, and an array of fields impacted by the error. As a concrete example, if your record modification violates the referential integrity of the Force.com database, an Error object containing FIELD_INTEGRITY_EXCEPTION as its status code is returned.

Using the Enterprise API

At the highest level, the Enterprise API consists of core services that allow query and modification of Force.com data, plus a set of types reflecting the standard and custom objects defined in your Force.com organization. Using these core services and types is a fairly straightforward exercise after your code has established a session with Force.com.

This section divides the Enterprise API into two functional groups, described here:

1. **Retrieving Records:** Retrieve records using SOQL or SOSL queries, by unique identifier, or based on their modification or deletion timestamp.

2. **Writing Records:** Learn how to create, update, and delete records using the Enterprise API.

Retrieving Records

The most common way to retrieve records is via SOQL. This is accomplished with the query service. A SOQL statement is passed as input, and a `QueryResult` object is returned. This object contains an array of records returned by the query.

The number of records returned by the query service is a function of the batch size. The default batch size in Java using WSC is 2,000 records; 500 for Axis and other Web service clients. If a query result contains more records than the batch size, use the queryMore service to retrieve additional batches of records.

The code in Listing 11-3 demonstrates the query and queryMore services in Java to build a list of Project records. Listing 11-4 is the same code in C#.NET. Note that the connection object in Java and binding object in C#.NET refer to objects created in Listings 11-1 and 11-2, respectively.

Listing 11-3   **Java Fragment to Execute SOQL Query**

```
List<Proj__c> projects = new ArrayList<Proj__c>();
QueryResult qr = connection.query("SELECT Id, Name FROM Proj__c");
boolean done = false;
if (qr.getSize() > 0) {
  while (!done) {
    SObject[] records = qr.getRecords();
    if (records != null) {
      for (SObject record : records) {
        projects.add((Proj__c)record);
      }
      if (qr.isDone()) {
        done = true;
      } else {
```

```
            qr = connection.queryMore(qr.getQueryLocator());
        }
      }
    }
}
```

Listing 11-4   C#.NET Fragment to Execute SOQL Query

```
List<Proj__c> projects = new List<Proj__c>();
QueryResult qr = binding.query("SELECT Id, Name FROM Proj__c");
Boolean done = false;
if (qr.size > 0) {
  while (!done) {
    sObject[] records = qr.records;
    if (records != null) {
      foreach (sObject record in records) {
        projects.Add((Proj__c)record);
      }
      if (qr.done) {
        done = true;
      } else {
        qr = binding.queryMore(qr.queryLocator);
      }
    }
  }
}
```

You can set a custom batch size (up to 2,000 records) by providing a `QueryOptions` header. This is demonstrated in Java in Listing 11-5 and in C#.NET in Listing 11-6.

Listing 11-5   Java Fragment for Setting Query Batch Size

```
connection.setQueryOptions(2000);
```

Listing 11-6   C#.NET Fragment for Setting Query Batch Size

```
binding.QueryOptionsValue = new QueryOptions();
binding.QueryOptionsValue.batchSize = 2000;
binding.QueryOptionsValue.batchSizeSpecified = true;
```

There's no guarantee Force.com will return the requested number of records in a batch. For example, if a SOQL statement selects two or more custom fields of type long text, the batch size will never be more than 200 records. Queries on binary data always return a single record at a time.

Other Ways to Retrieve Records

A few other approaches are available for retrieving records, described next:

- **Using SOSL:** The search service executes a SOSL statement and returns a Search Result object, which contains an array of SearchRecord objects. Each SearchRecord contains an SObject instance representing a matching record. Because SOSL can return many object types, each SearchRecord object can contain a different type of SObject.

- **By Unique Identifier:** If you know the unique identifier of an object you can retrieve it by using the retrieve service. Its inputs are a string containing a comma-separated list of field names to retrieve, the type of object as a string, and an array of up to 2,000 record unique identifiers. It returns an array of SObject instances.

- **By Timestamp:** The getUpdated and getDeleted services return the unique identifiers of records updated or deleted between a range of dates.

Writing Records

The basic services for writing records closely resemble their counterparts in Apex code. Services exist for creating, updating, upserting, deleting, and undeleting records. These services can accept one record at a time or up to 200 records in a single invocation.

Creating Records

To create one or more records, invoke the create service, passing in an array of SObjects. Each SObject must contain at a minimum the values for the required fields defined on the object. The service returns an array of SaveResult objects. Each SaveResult indicates success or failure of an individual record. In the case of failure, the SaveResult also contains an array of Error objects indicating the error reason.

The code in Listing 11-7 demonstrates the create service in Java. It creates a Resource record from the values of firstName and lastName. First, it creates a Contact record, and then it uses its unique identifier as a foreign key when creating the Resource record. Listing 11-8 is the same example written in C#.NET.

Listing 11-7   **Java Fragment to Create Record**

```
String newResourceId = null;
Contact contact = new Contact();
contact.setFirstName(firstName);
contact.setLastName(lastName);
SaveResult[] result = connection.create(
  new SObject[] { contact });
if (result != null && result.length == 1) {
  if (result[0].isSuccess()) {
    Resource__c resource = new Resource__c();
    resource.setActive__c(true);
```

```
      resource.setName(firstName + " " + lastName);
      resource.setContact__c(result[0].getId());
      SaveResult[] result2 = connection.create(
        new SObject[] { resource });
      if (result2 != null && result2.length == 1) {
        if (result2[0].isSuccess()) {
          newResourceId = result2[0].getId();
        } else {
          System.out.println("Failed to create resource: " +
            result2[0].getErrors()[0].getMessage());
        }
      }
    } else {
      System.out.println("Failed to create contact: " +
        result[0].getErrors()[0].getMessage());
    }
  }
}
```

Listing 11-8   C#.NET Fragment to Create Record

```
String newResourceId = null;
Contact contact = new Contact();
contact.FirstName = firstName;
contact.LastName = lastName;
SaveResult[] result = binding.create(
  new sObject[] { contact });
if (result != null && result.Length == 1) {
  if (result[0].success) {
    Resource__c resource = new Resource__c();
    resource.Active__c = true;
    resource.Name = firstName + " " + lastName;
    resource.Contact__c = result[0].id;
    SaveResult[] result2 = binding.create(
      new sObject[] { resource });
    if (result2 != null && result2.Length == 1) {
      if (result2[0].success) {
        newResourceId = result2[0].id;
      } else {
        Console.WriteLine("Failed to create resource: " +
          result2[0].errors[0].message);
      }
    }
  } else {
    Console.WriteLine("Failed to create contact: " +
      result[0].errors[0].message);
  }
}
```

Updating Records

To modify existing records, use the `update` service. Its arguments and return value are identical to those of the `create` method. The major difference is that the SObjects must contain a value for the `Id` field. This value is the unique identifier of the record to be updated.

Use the `upsert` service when you want to create records that don't exist and update them if they do exist. To determine whether a record exists, a match is attempted on a field containing unique identifiers. This field can be the internal `Id` field or a custom field designated as an external identifier. The first argument to the `upsert` service is the name of the unique identifier field, and the second is an array of SObjects. The service returns an array of `UpsertResult` objects. Like the `SaveResult` object, it contains a success or failure indicator and an array of errors upon failure.

> **Note**
>
> When updating or upserting, setting fields to null requires an additional step. Each object instance has a special array field called `fieldsToNull`. To set a field to null, add the name of the field to this list.

Deleting and Undeleting Records

To delete records, call the `delete` service and pass in an array of record unique identifiers to delete. Unlike the other DML operations, `delete` accepts different types of objects in a single call. The service returns an array of `DeleteResult` objects indicating the success or failure of each deletion, as well as any error messages.

The `undelete` service restores deleted records from the Recycle Bin. Like the `delete` service, its input is a list of record unique identifiers. It returns an array of `UndeleteResult` objects for use in tracking the outcome of each undeletion.

Modifications in Bulk

Bulk modifications involve more than one record. You can create, update, upsert, delete, or undelete a maximum of 200 records in a single call. By default Force.com allows partial failure, meaning some records can fail while others succeed. To override this behavior, add the `AllOrNoneHeader` to the call and set it to `true`. This causes Force.com to roll back all modifications made by the call unless all records are successfully processed.

The ability to process multiple object types in a single call is a powerful feature of bulk modifications. This is supported on create, update, delete, and undelete operations, but not upsert. For example, you can create a Resource and Skill in one round-trip to Force.com. This requires that the Skill record references its parent Resource using an external identifier rather than an Id because an Id for the record doesn't exist yet.

There are several important limitations of bulk create and update calls that involve multiple object types:

- Up to ten unique object types are allowed per call.

- You can't reference a new record of the same type in a single call. For example, if two Contact records were related to each other, you would need to create the parent first, then create the child and relate it to the parent in a separate call.

- If there are related records in the call, parent records must be located ahead of child records in the request.

- You cannot modify records of multiple object types if they participate in the Salesforce Setup menu. This limitation includes custom settings objects, GroupMember, Group, and User.

Building Custom Web Services in Apex

In the preceding section, you called into Force.com from your own programs using the Enterprise API. Custom Web services complement the Enterprise API by enabling you to write your own Web services. Like services in the Enterprise API, custom Web services are callable from any program outside of Force.com using SOAP over HTTPS.

This introduction to custom Web services in Apex consists of the following subsections:

- **Understanding Custom Web Services:** Understand how custom Web services can address some of the limitations of the Enterprise API.

- **Service Definition:** Learn how to create a custom Web service in Apex.

- **Calling a Custom Web Service:** Following much of the same procedure as that for the Enterprise API, develop a client program in Java or C#.NET that can invoke a custom Web service in Force.com.

Understanding Custom Web Services

One way to understand the value of custom Web services is to first examine limitations in the Enterprise API. The Enterprise API is a direct representation of the objects in your database as SOAP message types, with methods to query and modify them per record or in batches. This low-level access to the Force.com database through standard protocols and messages opens your Force.com applications to the outside world but isn't perfect for every integration scenario. The following list points out some areas in which the Enterprise API can fall short:

- **Transactions:** There is limited support in the Enterprise API for transactions that span multiple objects. If an external program must modify many objects in an atomic operation, it needs to detect failure for each call and apply a compensating action to reverse prior successes.

- **Integrated Security:** The Enterprise API always applies object, field, and record-level sharing rules of the currently logged-in user. This cannot be disabled by an external program calling into Force.com. If greater rights are needed, an administrator must alter the user's profile or the program must log in with the credentials of a more privileged user. This can complicate integration programs by requiring many logins of varying privileges or put the organization at risk by running integration programs with administrative rights.

- **Performance:** As your integration programs get more complex, they can become chatty, making many calls to Force.com to fetch different types of records and post-process them off-platform. This consumes more of the API calls toward the organization's daily limit and reduces performance by putting more data on the wire.

You can address these limitations by developing custom Web services in Apex. With custom Web services, you can create higher-level APIs of your own directly in the Force.com platform and invoke them from your own programs outside of Force.com using SOAP over HTTP, just like the Enterprise API. Your custom Web services can bundle a series of related queries or updates into a single call, providing an atomic unit of work and reducing network traffic and API call consumption.

> **Caution**
>
> Custom Web services run with administrative rights by default, granting your Apex code access to all data in the organization.

Service Definition

The definition of a custom Web service is slightly different from that of a regular Apex class. The differences are listed here:

- **Global Class Access Modifier:** A class that contains any Web services must use the `global` access modifier. This means the class is visible to all programs running in the Force.com organization.

- **Web Service Methods:** Each method accessible via Web service call must be defined with the `webservice` keyword. These methods must also be static.

- **Security:** Web service methods run as a system administrator, without regard for object, field, or record-level sharing rules. To enforce normal security and sharing rules, define the class with the `with sharing` keyword.

- **Supporting Classes:** User-defined Apex classes, inner or outer, that are arguments or return values for a Web service method must be defined as `global`. Member variables of these classes must be defined using the `webservice` keyword.

- **No Overloading:** Web service methods cannot be overloaded. Overloaded methods result in a compile error.

- **Prohibited Types:** The Map, Set, Pattern, Matcher, Exception, and Enum types are not allowed in the arguments or return types of Apex Web services.

Additionally, Web services written in Apex must abide by its governor limits. A subset of these governor limits is listed in Table 11-2.

Table 11-2 **Subset of Apex Web Service Governor Limits**

Resource Type	Web Service Governor Limit
SOQL	100 queries
Records from SOQL	50,000 records
DML	150 DML statements
Records in DML	10,000 records
Stack Depth	16
Heap	3,000,000 bytes
Apex Code	200,000 lines of code executed

Listing 11-9 defines a simple Web service that creates a record in the Project custom object given a name. Its method body could just as easily create records in three objects, perform some other database operation, or call to an external Web service.

Listing 11-9 **Sample Apex Code for Custom Web Service**

```
global class Custom {
  webservice static ID createProject(String name) {
    Proj__c proj = new Proj__c(Name = name);
    insert proj;
    return proj.Id;
  }
}
```

Calling a Custom Web Service

To call a custom Web service from client code, follow these steps:

1. In the App Setup area, click Develop → Apex Classes.

2. Locate the class containing the Web service and click the WSDL link.

3. Save the WSDL on your local filesystem. You'll need this plus the Enterprise WSDL in order to call the custom Web service.

4. Generate stub code from the custom WSDL and add it to your project.

5. Use the login method of the Enterprise WSDL to get a session identifier. Provide the session identifier when calling the custom Web service.

Listing 11-10 demonstrates the invocation of the custom createProject service in Java using the WSC, with the stub code generated to a .jar file named Custom. Listing 11-11 is the equivalent code in C#.NET, where the WSDL has been generated into a class named CustomWS.

Listing 11-10   **Java Fragment for Invoking Custom Web Service**

```
ConnectorConfig config = new ConnectorConfig();
config.setUsername(user);
config.setPassword(pass);
Connector.newConnection(config);
config.setServiceEndpoint(com.sforce.soap.Custom.Connector.END_POINT);
SoapConnection sconn = new SoapConnection(config);
String projectId = sconn.createProject("Test Project");
```

Listing 11-11   **C#.NET Fragment for Invoking Custom Web Service**

```
public String CreateProject(String sessionId, String name) {
  CustomService service = new CustomService();
  service.SessionHeaderValue = new CustomWS.SessionHeader();
  service.SessionHeaderValue.sessionId = sessionId;
  return service.createProject(name);
}
```

Introduction to the Metadata API

The Metadata API allows the direct manipulation of objects, page layouts, tabs, and most of the other configurable features in Force.com. By using the Metadata API, you can automate many of the click-intensive tasks commonly performed in the Force.com IDE or in the native Web user interface, such as the creation of database objects and fields.

This section provides an introduction to the Metadata API into two parts, described here:

1. **Overview:** The Metadata API is different from the Enterprise API in two major ways. First, it can operate on objects in memory or using zip files containing many objects represented as XML files. Second, its operations are asynchronous, returning immediately with a result identifier to use for follow-up calls to check the status.

2. **Getting Started with the Metadata API:** Walk through a sample of calling the Metadata API to create a new object, using Java and C#.NET.

> **Note**
>
> The details of how the Metadata API operates on each type of metadata in Force.com is outside the scope of this book. Consult the Force.com Metadata API Developer's Guide, found at www.salesforce.com/us/developer/docs/api_meta/index.htm, for the latest information and detailed descriptions of all the available methods of the Metadata API. Salesforce continues to expand the reach of the Metadata API in every release.

Overview

The Metadata API consists of two types of services: file-based and object-based. These service types are summarized next:

1. **File-Based Services:** The file-based services are `deploy` and `retrieve`. The `deploy` service takes a Base64-encoded zip file containing the components to deploy into the Force.com organization. The zip file must contain a manifest file named `package.xml` at its root to describe the contents of the zip. The `retrieve` service downloads metadata from Force.com and returns it as a zip file complete with `package.xml` as manifest. Its input is a `RetrieveRequest` object to specify the types of metadata to download. Both services can operate on up to 1,500 metadata objects per call.

2. **Object-Based Services:** The object-based services are `create`, `update`, and `delete`. To invoke `create` or `delete`, pass an array of `Metadata` objects. The `Metadata` object is the superclass of a wide array of objects that contain metadata for specific features of Force.com. For example, the `CustomObject` class represents a custom database object, and `Layout` represents a page layout. Unlike data records in which a unique identifier (`Id`) field is the key, metadata uniqueness comes from a combination of its type and `fullName` field. The `update` service takes an array of `UpdateMetadata` objects, which each contain a `Metadata` object and the current name of the object to replace.

> **Note**
>
> Force.com's documentation uses the term *declarative* to describe its file-based services, and *CRUD* (for Create, Update, and Delete) to describe its object-based services.

All Metadata API services are asynchronous, returning immediately with an `AsyncResult` object. This object contains a unique identifier for tracking the status of the asynchronous operation. For object-based services, the service to check status is called `checkStatus`. For the file-based service `deploy`, the status service is `checkDeployStatus`, and for `retrieve`, it's `checkRetrieveStatus`.

Getting Started with the Metadata API

To get started with the Metadata API, follow these steps:

1. In the App Setup area, click Develop → API.

2. Right-click the Download Metadata WSDL link and save it on your local filesystem. You'll need this plus the Enterprise WSDL in order to call the Metadata API.

3. Generate stub code from the WSDL and add it to your project.

Listing 11-12 demonstrates usage of the Metadata API in Java by creating a new database object given a name and its plural name. The code assumes the existence of a member variable called `sessionId`, previously populated from the `login` call's `LoginResult`. It prepares the minimum set of metadata required to call the `create` service, which is a custom object name, full name, label, deployment status, sharing model, and name field. After invoking the asynchronous `create` service, it loops to check the status using the `checkStatus` service until the invocation is complete.

Listing 11-12   **Java Fragment for Creating Object**

```java
public void createObject(String name, String pluralName) {
  try {
    ConnectorConfig config = new ConnectorConfig();
    config.setUsername(user);
    config.setPassword(pass);
    com.sforce.soap.enterprise.Connector.newConnection(config);
    config.setServiceEndpoint(Connector.END_POINT);
    MetadataConnection connection = new MetadataConnection(config);
    CustomObject obj = new CustomObject();
    obj.setFullName(name + "__c");
    obj.setLabel(name);
    obj.setPluralLabel(pluralName);
    obj.setDeploymentStatus(DeploymentStatus.Deployed);
    obj.setSharingModel(SharingModel.ReadWrite);
    CustomField nameField = new CustomField();
    nameField.setType(FieldType.AutoNumber);
    nameField.setLabel("Name");
    obj.setNameField(nameField);
    AsyncResult[] result = connection.create(
      new Metadata[] { obj });
    if (result == null) {
      System.out.println("create failed");
      return;
    }
    boolean done = false;
    AsyncResult[] status = null;
    long waitTime = 1000;
    while (!done) {
      status = connection.checkStatus(
        new String[] { result[0].getId() });
      if (status != null) {
        done = status[0].isDone();
        if (status[0].getStatusCode() != null) {
          System.out.println("Error: " +
            status[0].getStatusCode() + ": " +
            status[0].getMessage());
        }
        Thread.sleep(waitTime);
        waitTime *= 2;
```

```
            System.out.println("Current state: " +
               status[0].getState());
         }
      }
      System.out.println("Created object: " +
         status[0].getId());
   } catch (Throwable t) {
      t.printStackTrace();
   }
}
```

Using the Force.com REST API

REST stands for Representational State Transfer, a common form of Web-accessible API. Twitter, Facebook, Yahoo!, Google, and countless others provide REST APIs for their services. REST is designed for lightweight clients, those running inside web browsers or other scripting environments. Rather than generating static language bindings from a metadata description, as found with WSDL in the Web services world, the REST approach is dynamic. Its emphasis is on a concise syntax for URLs that represent resources, and the use of HTTP methods to describe actions on those resources.

The Force.com REST API is a subset of the integration features in the Force.com Web services API. This section provides a brief introduction to the REST API into three parts:

- **Overview of Force.com REST API:** Learn how Force.com functionality is exposed in the REST style.
- **Authentication:** The first step in using the REST API is to authenticate, and the process is significantly different from Web services.
- **API Walkthrough:** Using only your computer's command line, you can take an interactive tour of the Force.com REST API.

Note

This section is not a complete reference to the REST API. Consult the Force.com REST API Developer's Guide, found at www.salesforce.com/us/developer/docs/api_rest/index.htm, for the latest and most detailed information on the REST API, which Salesforce continuously improves in each major release of the platform.

Overview of Force.com REST API

If you're already familiar with the Web services API, you might wonder why another API is available to access identical services. A practical reason is that REST is better aligned with interpreted languages, such as PHP, Ruby, and JavaScript, than SOAP Web services. These languages are standard in the consumer-focused Web world, and are increasingly used by businesses as well. The Force.com platform is simply keeping pace with trends in application development.

The patterns of data access in Force.com translate naturally into the REST style of API. SObjects and rows within them become URLs, and HTTP actions express DML operations: GET for read-only requests for basic information, POST to create records, PATCH to update records, and DELETE to delete them. Because not all HTTP clients support the full range of methods, Force.com also allows a special URL parameter (_HttpMethod) to specify the action. By default, REST API calls return JSON-encoded responses, but you can override this by appending .xml to the end of URLs, or by sending the standard HTTP Accept header with the desired content type.

> **Note**
>
> JSON stands for JavaScript Object Notation, a standard format for representing JavaScript objects as strings. Like XML, it's widely used for communication between programs.

Authentication

Almost every REST API call requires authentication to Force.com. But unlike the Web services API, the REST API does not provide a way to authenticate using a username and password. It requires that you've previously authenticated using OAuth or the Web service API's login method. The token returned by the authentication process is then added to every REST request in the HTTP Authentication header.

OAuth is an industry-standard way of negotiating access to a system without requiring users to share their login credentials. OAuth operates using tokens instead. Tokens have advantages over the typical username/password credentials. They can be audited and revoked by the user. They also typically provide limited access to the system. In the case of Force.com, OAuth access tokens grant bearers the ability to make API calls only. They cannot login to the Salesforce web user interface.

> **Note**
>
> OAuth is a complex subject well beyond the scope of this book. The Force.com REST API Developer's Guide, found at www.salesforce.com/us/developer/docs/api_rest/index.htm, provides some introductory information on using OAuth to authenticate to Force.com.

If you are calling the REST API on behalf of another user, OAuth is the recommended approach for authentication because you do not need to store others' usernames and passwords. But when you're learning and experimenting with simple REST API examples, OAuth can present a significant hurdle. To avoid it, adapt the code in Listing 11-1, which logs into Force.com using the Enterprise Web services API, to output a session identifier. The session identifier is available by calling getSessionHeader().getSessionId() on the EnterpriseConnection object, and can be used in place of the OAuth access token.

API Walkthrough

Because Force.com REST API requests and responses are relatively concise, you can practice using it directly from your computer's command line using standard OS-level tools. The following examples rely on the tool named cURL, available free for every platform at http://curl.haxx.se. Make sure you have already obtained an authentication token (the session identifier) and set it as an environment variable $TOKEN. Also, be sure to replace na6 in the following examples with your own instance of Force.com. To identify your instance, look at the URL in your web browser when you log in. Note that the use of the X-PrettyPrint header throughout the examples is optional and serves only to format responses in a readable way.

Listing 11-13 is an example of one of the simplest REST API calls. It returns the services available via REST in the specified version and instance of the Force.com platform. Here the result indicates four services. In subsequent examples, you'll try all the services, except recent. The recent service returns the same data as you see in the Recent Items box in the web user interface.

Listing 11-13   **Services Available Request and Response**

```
curl https://na6.salesforce.com/services/data/v20.0\
  -H "Authorization: OAuth "$TOKEN -H "X-PrettyPrint:1"
{
  "sobjects" : "/services/data/v20.0/sobjects",
  "search" : "/services/data/v20.0/search",
  "query" : "/services/data/v20.0/query",
  "recent" : "/services/data/v20.0/recent"
}
```

To retrieve basic information on an SObject, use the sobjects service as demonstrated in Listing 11-14. You can also omit the object name (/Proj__c) to get a list of all SObjects, or append /describe to the end of the URL to obtain the full, detailed list of fields on the SObject. If an error occurs in processing this request or any REST request, the response contains message and errorCode keys to communicate the error message and code.

Listing 11-14   **Basic Information Request for an SObject**

```
curl https://na6.salesforce.com/services/data/v20.0/sobjects/Proj__c
  -H "Authorization: OAuth "$TOKEN -H "X-PrettyPrint:1"
```

Another usage of the sobjects service is shown in Listing 11-15. Here an individual record is returned, identified by its unique identifier. The fields parameter specifies a subset of fields to return. You can omit this parameter to retrieve all fields. If your record is a binary object such as a Document, append /body to the URL to retrieve the binary content.

Listing 11-15   **Record Retrieval by Unique Identifier Request and Response**

```
curl https://na6.salesforce.com/services/data/v20.0\
  /sobjects/Proj__c/a008000000CTwEw?fields=Name,Status__c\
  -H "Authorization: OAuth "$TOKEN -H "X-PrettyPrint:1"
```

```
{
  "attributes" : {
    "type" : "Proj__c",
    "url" : "/services/data/v20.0/sobjects/Proj__c/a008000000CTwEwAAL"
  },
  "Name" : "GenePoint",
  "Status__c" : "In Progress",
  "Id" : "a008000000CTwEwAAL"
}
```

Listing 11-16 demonstrates record retrieval by external identifier. The record with a `Resource_ID__c` value of `100000` on the `Resource__c` SObject is returned.

Listing 11-16   Request for Retrieval of Record by External Identifier

```
curl https://na6.salesforce.com/services/data/v20.0\
  /sobjects/Resource__c/Resource_ID__c/100000\
  -H "Authorization: OAuth "$TOKEN -H "X-PrettyPrint:1"
```

A simple SOQL query is shown in Listing 11-17. To run a SOSL query, use `search` instead of `query` in the URL.

Listing 11-17   SOQL Query Request

```
curl https://na6.salesforce.com/services/data/v20.0\
  /query?q=SELECT+Name+FROM+Proj__c\
  -H "Authorization: OAuth "$TOKEN -H "X-PrettyPrint:1"
```

To create a record, make a POST request with the SObject type in the URL and a JSON or XML request body containing the record's field values. Listing 11-18 creates a new `Proj__c` record named Test Project. A successful response provides the new record's unique identifier.

Listing 11-18   Create Record Request and Response

```
echo '{ "Name": "Test Project" }' |\
  curl -X POST -H 'Content-type: application/json'\
  -H "Authorization: OAuth "$TOKEN -H "X-PrettyPrint:1" -d @-\
  https://na6.salesforce.com/services/data/v20.0/sobjects/Proj__c
{
  "id" : "a008000000Fy8oyAAB",
  "errors" : [ ],
  "success" : true
}
```

Updating a record follows a similar process to creating a record. Make a PATCH request with the URL containing the SObject type and unique identifier, and a request body with the field values to update. In Listing 11-19, the record created in Listing 11-18 gets its name updated.

Listing 11-19   **Update Record Request**

```
echo '{ "Name": "Updated Test Project" }' |\
  curl -X PATCH -H 'Content-type: application/json'\
  -H 'Authorization: OAuth '$TOKEN -H "X-PrettyPrint:1" -d @-\
  https://na6.salesforce.com/services/data/v20.0\
  /sobjects/Proj__c/a008000000Fy8oyAAB
```

The only difference between an upsert and update request is that upsert uses an external identifier rather than the unique identifier. If the external identifier value is not found, the request creates the record and its unique identifier is returned. Otherwise, the record is updated, and nothing is returned upon success. Listing 11-20 demonstrates an upsert of a Resource__c record.

Listing 11-20   **Upsert Record Request and Response**

```
echo '{ "Name": "Izzy Impatient" }' |\
  curl -X PATCH -H 'Content-type: application/json'\
  -H "Authorization: OAuth "$TOKEN -H "X-PrettyPrint:1" -d @-\
  https://na6.salesforce.com/services/data/v20.0\
  /sobjects/Resource__c/Resource_ID__c/100050
{
  "id" : "a0180000000jBKLAA3",
  "errors" : [ ],
  "success" : true
}
```

Deleting a record by its unique identifier is shown in Listing 11-21. You can also delete a record by its external identifier. In both cases, nothing is returned by a successful request.

Listing 11-21   **Delete Record Request**

```
curl -X DELETE\
  .-H 'Authorization: OAuth '$TOKEN -H "X-PrettyPrint:1"\
  https://na6.salesforce.com/services/data/v20.0\
  /sobjects/Proj__c/a008000000Fy8oyAAB
```

Sample Application: Database Integration

This section explores a common integration scenario using the Services Manager sample application. It describes the scenario and the implementation strategy and ends with sample code.

Integration Scenario

Force.com applications often require the use of data that is stored in other enterprise systems. This information can initially be pushed to Force.com through Data Loader or another data migration tool. But when Force.com is not the system of record for this information and updates occur, Force.com is left with stale data.

Updated data could be reloaded into Force.com through data migration tools, scheduled to run at regular time intervals, but this approach can quickly become impractical. This is especially true where there are requirements for real-time updates, integration to multiple systems, intricate data mappings, or complex business rules governing the updates.

Imagine that the company using your Services Manager application has a human resources system containing the names, addresses, and other core information about employees. This employee information is duplicated in Force.com in the Resource custom object and the Contact standard object. To prevent the data from being changed directly in Force.com, fields where Force.com is not the system of record can be set to read-only on their page layout. But when the human resources system is updated, Force.com must also be updated. This is the goal of the integration.

Implementation Strategy

To retrieve changes from the human resources system, you could call out from Force.com using HTTP or a Web service call, as described in Chapter 10. But when you would do this is not clear, because Force.com does not receive notifications when the human resource system is updated. Polling the system for changes would be inefficient and quickly hit governor limits on Web service callouts.

Instead, use the Enterprise API to connect to Force.com and upsert the modified records. To simplify the implementation, the target is a single field called `Active__c`, indicating whether the employee is active. After you get this field working, move on to support additional fields such as the address and phone fields of the Resource's associated Contact record.

The first problem is finding a common key to employees in both systems. Assume that the human resources system cannot be changed and focus on adapting Force.com to maintain the mapping between the two systems. Create a new field named Resource ID (API name of `Resource_ID__c`) on the Resource object to store employee identifiers used by the human resources system. For this example, make it a Number type, six digits in length, required, unique, and an external ID. This field configuration is shown in Figure 11-9.

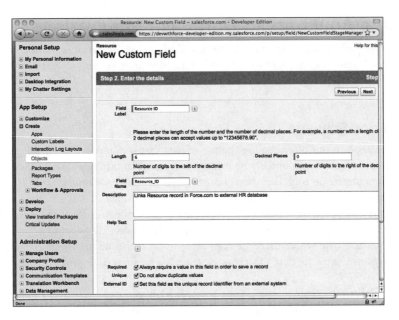

Figure 11-9   Creating the Resource ID field

Caution

Remember that you need to regenerate the client code from Enterprise WSDL after you add this new field; otherwise, it will not be available to your program.

Sample Implementation

The code in Listing 11-22 is a sample Java implementation of the integration. It assumes that you've already generated the Java stub code from Enterprise WSDL using the WSC. It expects a file named import.json to be located in the working directory. This is a JSON-encoded file containing an array of Resource records to update. Listing 11-23 is an example of the file format expected by the program.

Note

The sample implementation uses a JSON library available at www.json.org/java/json.org.

Listing 11-22   **Sample Java Implementation of Integration Scenario**

```
import java.io.BufferedReader;
import java.io.FileReader;
import java.io.IOException;
import java.util.ArrayList;
import java.util.List;
```

```java
import org.json.JSONArray;
import org.json.JSONException;
import org.json.JSONObject;
import com.sforce.soap.enterprise.Connector;
import com.sforce.soap.enterprise.EnterpriseConnection;
import com.sforce.soap.enterprise.UpsertResult;
import com.sforce.soap.enterprise.sobject.Resource__c;
import com.sforce.soap.enterprise.sobject.SObject;
import com.sforce.ws.ConnectionException;
import com.sforce.ws.ConnectorConfig;
public class IntegrationDemo {
  EnterpriseConnection connection;
  public void login(String user, String pass, String securityToken) {
    ConnectorConfig config = new ConnectorConfig();
    config.setUsername(user);
    config.setPassword(pass + securityToken);
    try {
      connection = Connector.newConnection(config);
    } catch (ConnectionException e) {
      e.printStackTrace();
    }
  }
  public void processImportFile(String jsonFile) {
    List<SObject> changes = new ArrayList<SObject>();
    try {
      String json = readFileAsString(jsonFile);
      JSONArray array = new JSONArray(json);
      for (int i=0; i<array.length(); i++) {
        changes.add(importResource(array.getJSONObject(i)));
      }
      if (changes.size() > 0) {
        UpsertResult[] results = connection.upsert("Resource_ID__c",
          changes.toArray(new SObject[changes.size()]));
        int line = 0;
        for (UpsertResult result : results) {
          System.out.print(line + ": ");
          if (!result.isSuccess()) {
            for (com.sforce.soap.enterprise.Error e
              : result.getErrors()) {
              System.out.println(e.getStatusCode() + ": " +
                e.getMessage());
            }
          } else {
            System.out.println("success");
          }
          line++;
```

```
      }
    }
  } catch (Throwable t) {
    t.printStackTrace();
  }
}
private Resource__c importResource(JSONObject rec)
  throws JSONException {
  Resource__c result = new Resource__c();
  result.setResource_ID__c(Double.valueOf(
    rec.getInt("ResourceID")));
  result.setActive__c(rec.getBoolean("Active"));
  return result;
}
private static String readFileAsString(String filePath)
  throws IOException {
  StringBuffer fileData = new StringBuffer(1000);
  BufferedReader reader = new BufferedReader(
    new FileReader(filePath));
  char[] buf = new char[2048];
  int numRead = 0;
  while((numRead = reader.read(buf)) != -1) {
    fileData.append(buf, 0, numRead);
  }
  reader.close();
  return fileData.toString();
}
public static void main(String[] args) {
  IntegrationDemo demo = new IntegrationDemo();
  demo.login("USERNAME", "PASSWORD", "SECURITYTOKEN");
  demo.processImportFile("import.json");
}
}
```

Listing 11-23   **Sample JSON Input File**

```
[
  {
    "ResourceID": 100000,
    "Active": false
  },
  {
    "ResourceID": 100001,
    "Active": false
  }
]
```

Before running the program, change the Resource ID values in the file to match your resources, and the arguments of the login method to your user credentials. Figure 11-10 shows the Resource records after the program has been executed given the sample input file.

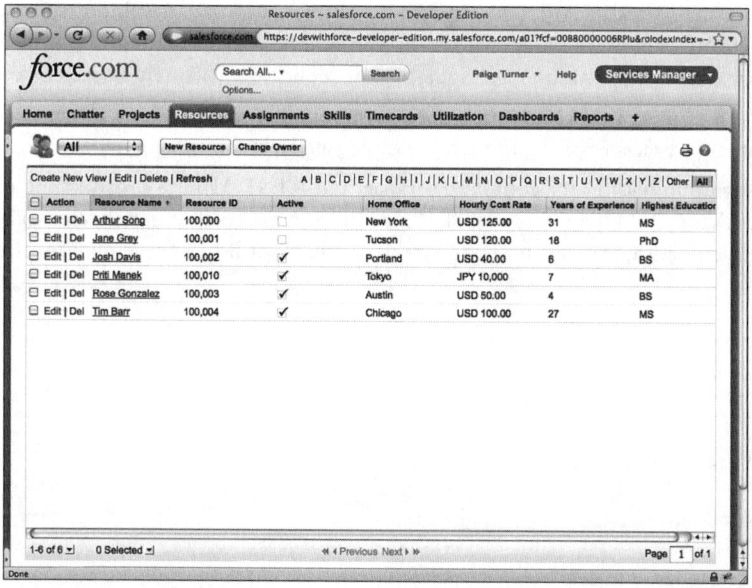

Figure 11-10   Resource records after integration program execution

Note that the only field updated by the sample implementation is `Active__c`. As a challenge, enhance the program to support updates to fields of the Contact object. To do this, you need to first perform a SOQL query on the Resource object to retrieve corresponding Contact Id values from the Resource ID values. Then update contact fields using a separate `upsert` call.

Summary

This chapter has provided the basics of Force.com's Enterprise, Metadata, and REST APIs, with code examples in Java and C#.NET. Consider the following points for review as you move on to the next chapter:

- The core Web services for data integration are found in the Enterprise or Partner APIs. These APIs allow the query, creation, and modification of records in the Force.com database and automatically enforce all Force.com data security features.

- The Enterprise API is intended for corporate use, in which a single Force.com organization is the target. The Partner API is designed for ISVs, in which integration logic must adapt itself to the database schema of any organization.

- Custom Web services can be developed in Apex and called via SOAP and HTTP to wrap a series of calls into a single, atomic unit of functionality for a client program.

- With the Metadata API, you can build tools that automate development tasks, such as creating and modifying database objects and fields. You can also use it to back up your entire organization's configuration or replicate it to a new Force.com account.

- The REST API provides much of the same functionality as the Web services API, but requires less effort to use when developing in scripting languages.

- Integrating with Force.com Web services and REST API is a broad, complex subject that could fill an entire book. To reach the next level of detail, refer to the online documentation and code samples available at http://developer.force.com.

12

Additional Platform Features

Throughout this book, you've been exposed to the nuts and bolts of creating an application on Force.com. This has been discussed in terms of the data model, business logic, user interface, and integrations to other systems. This chapter describes additional features you can leverage when your application runs on the platform. In most cases, the features are inexpensive to use because they are configured with mouse clicks rather than code. They are summarized here:

- **Workflow and Approvals:** Impose business process on the creation and modification of data in your organization using workflow rules and approval processes. These processes can be fully automated or can involve humans in the mix to examine records and take structured actions on them.
- **Introduction to Analytics:** Force.com enables you to create reports that summarize data in several different, highly configurable formats. The reports can also be displayed as dashboards, visual components that can expose users to a wide spectrum of information from across your organization in a single Web page.
- **Force.com for International Organizations:** Using Force.com platform features, your applications can be translated into many languages and support multiple currencies.
- **Using Single Sign-On:** Allow your users to access Force.com applications using your existing corporate identity provider rather than a separate username and password.
- **Sample Application:** A custom dashboard component is developed in Visualforce for the Services Manager sample application to visualize the geographic distribution of consultants on projects.

Workflow and Approvals

Workflow and approvals are extremely configurable features that enable you to describe your own corporate business process in terms that the Force.com platform can understand and act on. Externalizing your business process in this way can reduce the amount of code you write and open the administration and definition of business processes to nonprogrammers. For example, workflow and approvals can help ensure that the right people at your company sign off on a particular document or deal, and that the approval of each person is recorded for auditing purposes.

This section provides an overview of workflow and approvals. It consists of the following subsections:

- **Introduction to Workflow:** Learn how Force.com represents workflows and how to debug them.
- **Getting Started with Approval Processes:** Approval processes are like workflow but incorporate steps that must be performed by humans.

Introduction to Workflow

Workflows are implemented in Force.com by defining workflow rules. A workflow rule consists of five parts:

1. **Object:** Workflow rules are created on objects. A workflow rule can apply to only a single object at a time. For example, a rule that notifies consultants when they have unsubmitted timecards would be created on the Timecard object.

2. **Evaluation Criteria:** The evaluation criteria determines what types of actions on your object cause Force.com to check the rule criteria. An example of this setting is "Every time a record is created or edited."

3. **Rule Criteria:** The rule criteria setting is a list of field expressions or a formula expression that, when true, causes your workflow actions to be triggered. A workflow rule must contain at least one criterion or a formula expression.

4. **Immediate Actions:** When a workflow rule is triggered, its immediate actions are executed. An action can create a task, send an email alert, update a field on the object, or send a SOAP message to a system outside of Force.com. You used the outbound message action to integrate with external systems in Chapter 10, "Integration."

5. **Time-Dependent Actions:** Time-dependent actions are not executed immediately when the workflow is triggered. They are deferred until a user-definable amount of time has passed. After this time, if the rule criteria are still true for the record, the time-dependent actions are executed. A workflow rule is said to be time-based if it includes a time-dependent action.

Additionally, rules exist in one of two states: active and inactive. Active workflow rules are evaluated when data in your organization is created or modified and triggered when the rule criteria are met. Inactive workflow rules are completely dormant. Until they are activated again, they are never evaluated.

To create and manage workflow rules, go to the App Setup area and click Create →
Workflow & Approvals → Workflow Rules. In Figure 12-1, a time-based workflow rule
has been defined that emails a consultant when one of the consultant's timecards is found
to be in an uncommitted state for seven days.

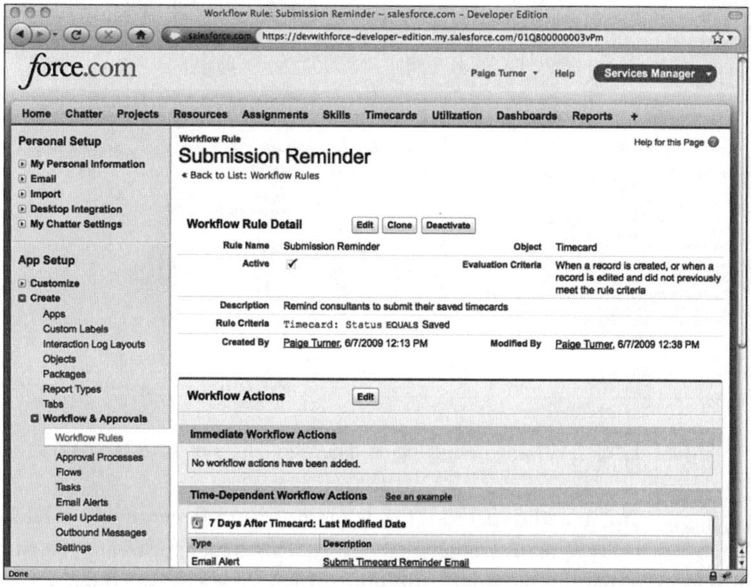

Figure 12-1   Definition of a time-based workflow rule

> **Note**
>
> Workflow rules can become complex quickly, and this book describes only a small subset of
> their capabilities. The context-sensitive online help in Force.com is an excellent resource for
> getting into more depth on the subject.

Because workflow rules run in the background and are largely invisible to users,
debugging them requires some additional work. Force.com offers a tool for capturing logs
of system activity per user, which includes workflow rule evaluation and execution. To
activate the tool, go to the Administration Setup area and click Monitoring → Debug
Logs. Click the New button. Select one or more users to enable debugging on and click
the Save button. As the selected users perform actions in the system, their log entries
become available at the bottom of the page, as shown in Figure 12-2.

The log entries contain information about workflow rules triggered, as well as database
operations, validation rules, resource consumption, and Apex code errors.

Figure 12-2   Viewing debug log configuration, logs of selected users

Force.com provides an additional tool for debugging time–dependent workflow actions. When a workflow rule is triggered, its time-dependent actions are placed in a queue. The actions remain in the queue until they reach their scheduled date.

You can monitor this queue in the Administration Setup area by clicking Monitoring → Time-Based Workflow. In Figure 12-3, the Search button has been clicked, revealing a single record in the queue. The workflow action was triggered on March 1. On March 7, the rule criteria will be evaluated and, if satisfied, the action performed.

Getting Started with Approval Processes

An approval process can be thought of as a specialized workflow template. Like workflow rules, approval processes are defined on a specific object. They define four states that a record can exist in, workflow actions to execute when a record transitions to a new state, and rules used to route the record to users relevant to each state. The four states are described here:

1. **Submitted:** When a record is submitted to an approval process, it is in the submitted state.

2. **Approved:** When a record is approved by a user, it enters an approved state. This state can be further qualified as final if all relevant parties have approved it.

3. **Rejected:** If a record is rejected, it enters the rejected state. Typically, the submitter is notified, fixes the problems with the record, and resubmits the record.

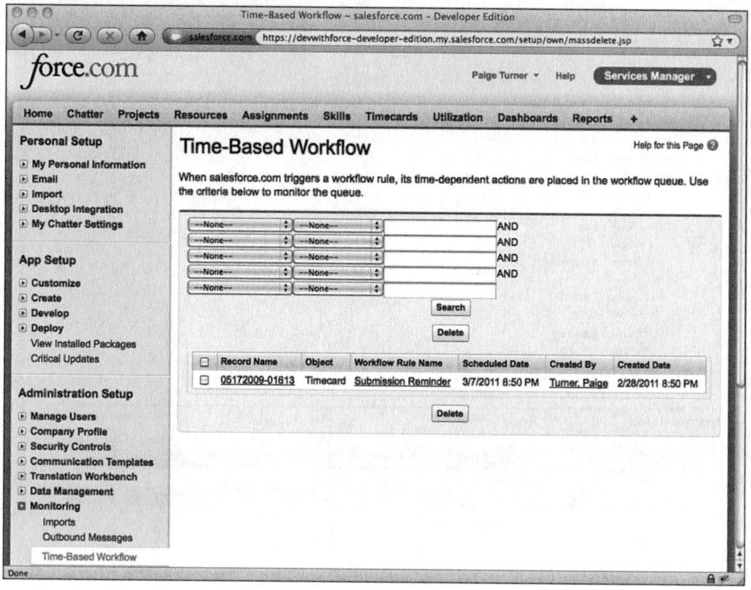

Figure 12-3   Monitoring the time-based workflow queue

4. **Recalled:** If permitted, a submitter can elect to remove a record from an approval process. For example, the submitter might realize that his expense report is missing a receipt and seek to fix it before the report is examined by his manager.

Using Approval Processes

Unlike workflow rules, which are triggered when conditions are met on a record, approval processes are typically driven by explicit user actions. For example, a consultant submits a timecard for approval. The approval process notifies his manager via email. The manager logs in to Force.com, notices the timecard record waiting for her approval, and approves it. In each of these steps, Force.com can also be executing a set of workflow actions in lock step with the user actions. This keeps the business process moving along, synchronized between users and the database.

To get a sense for how an approval process appears to users, examine the three figures that follow. Figure 12-4 is a timecard that has been submitted for approval.

The Approval History related list contains information about the record's progression through the approval process, ordered so that the most recent activities appear first. Tim is the consultant who submitted the timecard record. Paige is his manager who must review the timecard and either accept or reject it. When Tim submits the timecard record, it enters a locked state, as indicated by the lock icon beside the Edit button. This prevents him from changing it while his manager is reviewing it.

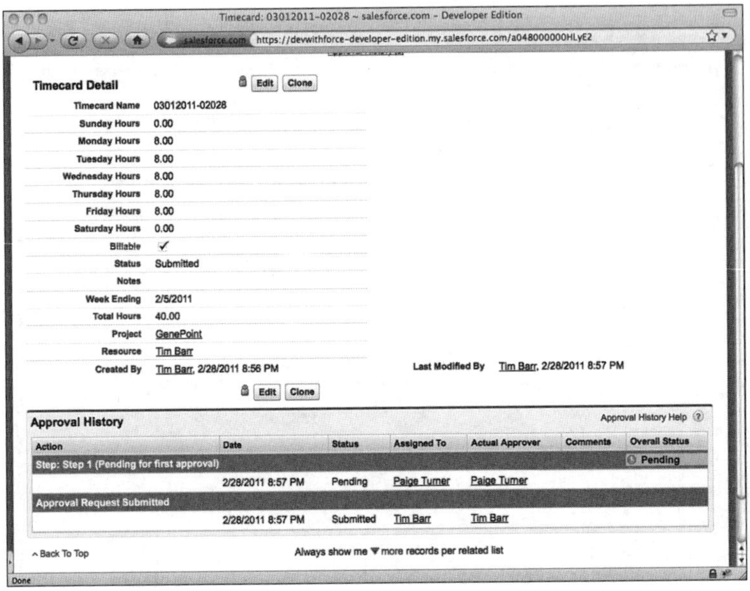

Figure 12-4   Viewing a record submitted for approval

Figure 12-5 shows the reviewer's view of the approval request. Again, the Approval History related list is displayed. The reviewer can supply a comment and then approve or reject the record using the Approve or Reject buttons. These buttons change the state of the record in the approval process.

After approving the record, the reviewer sees the screen shown in Figure 12-6. The Approval History indicates that the record has been approved. It remains locked, but this behavior is configurable in the approval process.

Defining and Managing Approval Processes

Figure 12-7 shows an example of the approval process configuration driving the timecard approval scenario described previously. This is the view a developer or system administrator would have after defining the approval process.

The two wizards for building an approval process are the Standard Setup Wizard and the Jump Start Wizard. If you're just getting started with approval processes, the Jump Start Wizard is the best choice. It makes some simplifying assumptions, enabling you to create a process with very few clicks.

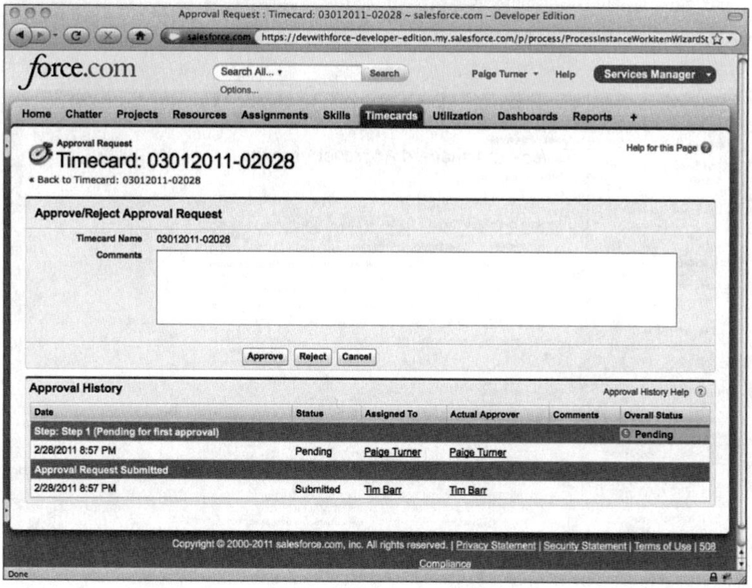

Figure 12-5   Working with an approval request

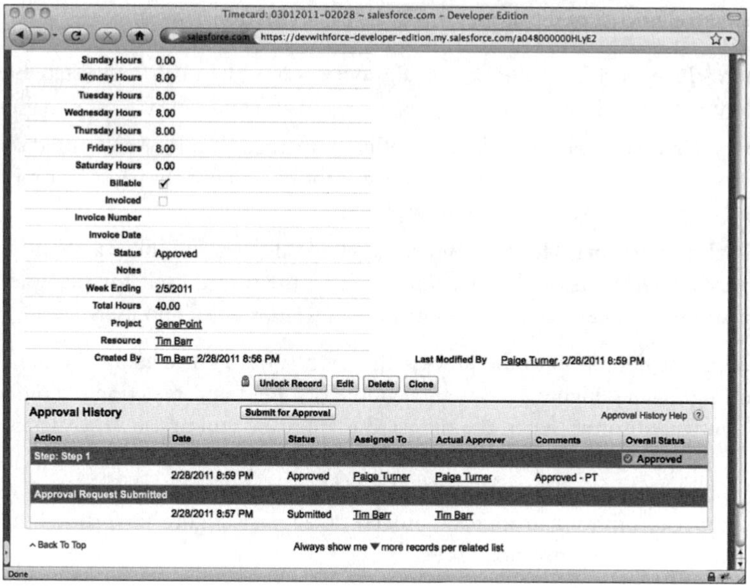

Figure 12-6   Viewing approved record

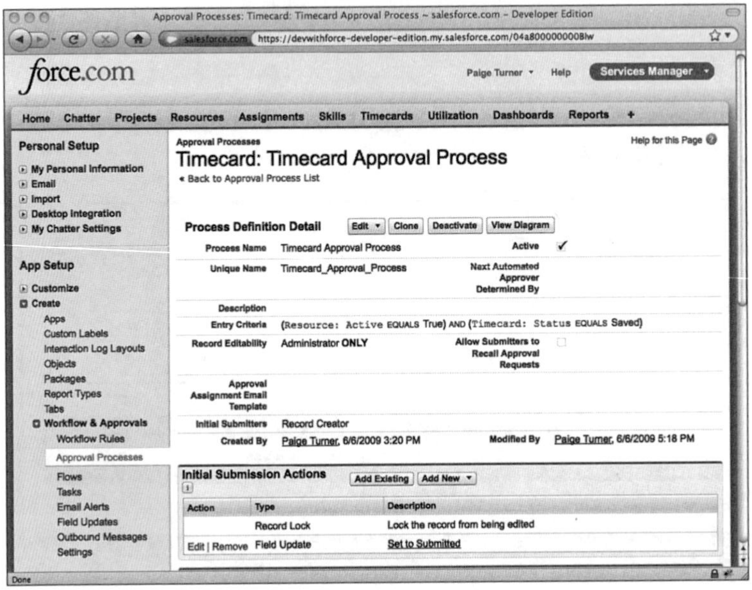

Figure 12-7   Defining an approval process

Like workflow rules, approval processes can become complex very quickly. Here are a few of the key elements of the approval process configuration:

- **Active:** Like workflow rules, approval processes must be in an active state before records can be submitted to them.
- **Entry Criteria:** The entry criteria define what records can be submitted to this approval process. When a user attempts to submit a record that does not meet the entry criteria, an error message is displayed.
- **Initial Submitters:** This field indicates who is allowed to submit a record for approval. Submitters can be dynamic based on the record itself; for example, the creator or owner. They can also be static lists of groups, roles, and users.

In addition to the definition of the process, the process has a set of actions to perform when it changes states. Figure 12-8 is an example of a field update action definition. This action is configured to run when the timecard is approved and updates the picklist field Status__c to Approved.

To get a high-level, read-only view of an entire approval process definition, click the View Diagram button from an approval process detail page. Figure 12-9 shows the diagram for the timecard submission process.

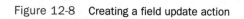

Figure 12-8   Creating a field update action

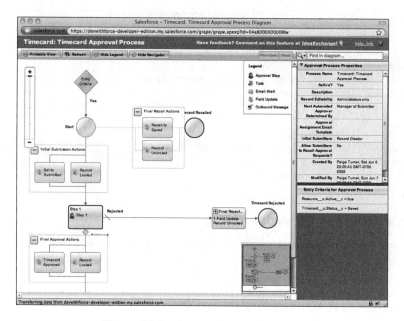

Figure 12-9   Approval process diagram

To incorporate approval processes in the native user interface, add the Approval History related list to your object's page layout. You can also add the Items to Approve component on your Home tab by going to the App Setup area and clicking Customize → Home → Home Page Layouts.

Approval processes leave their mark on your records in two system objects, related as children to your objects. ProcessInstance stores information about approval processes active on your records. ProcessInstanceHistory captures an audit trail of approval activities on your records. These relationships are named ProcessInstances and ProcessSteps, respectively. Listing 12-1 provides a sample query to retrieve approval process–related information for the Timecard object.

Listing 12-1   **Sample SOQL for Retrieving Approval Process Information**

```
SELECT Week_Ending__c, Total_Hours__c,
  (SELECT Status FROM ProcessInstances),
  (SELECT IsPending, StepStatus FROM ProcessSteps)
FROM Timecard__c
```

You can also submit records for approval processing and accept, reject, and recall records from Apex code and the Web Services API. Listing 12-2 provides an example of submitting a record with object ID a048000000BO4W3 from Apex.

Listing 12-2   **Apex Code to Submit Record for Approval**

```
Approval.ProcessSubmitRequest req =
  new Approval.ProcessSubmitRequest();
req.setObjectId('a048000000BO4W3');
Approval.ProcessResult result = Approval.process(req);
System.debug(result.success);
```

> **Note**
>
> Using record identifiers as constants in Apex code is a bad practice, as they can change between environments such as staging and production. This is done in the book only to keep code samples simple and focused.

Introduction to Analytics

So far, you've focused on the transactional aspects of Force.com. You've designed objects, imported records into them, written Apex code to validate and modify records, configured native user interfaces and custom Visualforce pages to enable users to work with data, and exchanged records with systems outside of Force.com using HTTP and Web services.

Force.com also includes built-in reporting and analytic features that you can leverage to get a broader view of your application's data, using a larger number of records than is permitted in Apex code by Force.com governor limits. Getting acquainted with these features can feed valuable insight into the design and development process. Determine as soon as possible which reports your business users need because this can help you design the right object model to support both the transactional and the analytical requirements of the application.

This section is divided into three parts, described next:

1. **Working with Reports:** Reports can provide detail or aggregate-level views on the Force.com database.

2. **Configuring Dashboards:** Dashboards are pages consisting of components that consume data from reports and display it graphically in a uniformly small visual footprint. They can provide a window into various types of data across a business.

3. **Using Analytic Snapshots:** Analytic snapshots copy the output of a report into a custom object on a fixed time schedule. They allow you to leverage the unique, high-volume data aggregation capabilities of the reporting feature in other areas of Force.com.

Working with Reports

This subsection introduces you to the reporting feature of Force.com. It is divided into three parts:

1. **Report Creation:** Force.com provides a drag-and-drop user interface for constructing reports. Reports can query and aggregate data from any object and related objects, displaying results in tabular, summary, or matrix form.

2. **Running Reports:** Reports can be viewed directly by users in the native user interface or scheduled with results emailed to a list of recipients.

3. **Defining Custom Report Types:** Custom report types allow you to group related objects together, reducing the effort required to build complex reports.

Report Creation

Reports are created against a primary object and a set of related objects. Force.com automatically generates combinations of primary and related objects. You can also create these yourself using custom report types.

To create a report, click the Reports tab and click the Create New Custom Report button. The first page of the Report Builder is shown in Figure 12-10 and is used to select the source of the report data. In this case, the selected report data source is a custom report type.

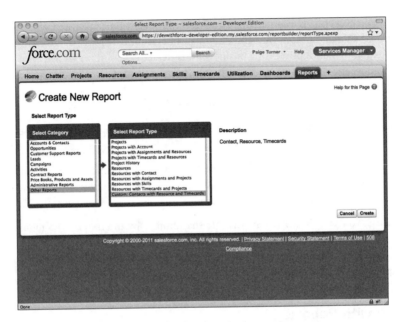

Figure 12-10   Creating a report

After selecting a report type, the Report Builder provides a set of graphical tools for creating the report, including an interactive preview of the report. The tools are described here:

- **Report Format:** Reports can be in one of three formats. The tabular format is the simplest, displaying rows and columns as they appear in the database. The summary report allows you to mix aggregated data and detail data in the same report, with subtotals. Matrix reports contain only aggregated data. To specify the report format, select one of the options from the Report Format drop-down in the preview panel.

- **Fields:** The panel on the left side of the screen displays the fields to be included in the report, divided into folders by their parent object type. Drag and drop fields into the preview panel to add them to the report.

- **Summary Fields:** After you add a field to the report, you can summarize its values to produce an aggregate value. For each column with a compatible data type, you can calculate its sum, average, largest value, and smallest value. To summarize a field, go to the preview panel, click the drop-down menu beside the field name, and select Summarize This Field.

- **Grouping:** You can group records by up to three fields. To group by a field, activate the field's drop-down menu in the preview panel and select Group by this field. This option is valid for summary and matrix report formats only.

- **Order Columns:** Define how columns are ordered visually in the report. You can sort each field in ascending or descending order using the field's drop-down menu in the preview panel.

- **Filters:** Add criteria to limit the amount of data incorporated into the report. You can also set a hard limit on the maximum number of records that are selected. Criteria are specified in the top panel.

- **Chart & Highlights:** You can display your report data graphically by clicking the Add Chart button in the preview panel and selecting a chart type. Valid chart types are bar, column, line, pie, donut, and funnel. You can also configure conditional highlighting of data, defining colors and bounds for low, medium, and high values. The Add Chart button is shown for summary and matrix report formats only.

Running Reports

Reports can be run immediately or scheduled and can be displayed in the native user interface or exported to a comma-delimited (.csv) or Excel (.xls) format.

Scheduled reports run daily, weekly, or monthly, on every day or weekday. The schedule is in effect for a range of dates you select. You can also select a preferred start time from a list of available start times provided by Force.com. When your report is complete, it is emailed to a user or a group of users. Figure 12-11 shows the result of running a custom report named Timecards in the native user interface.

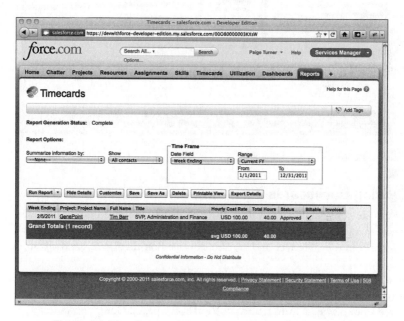

Figure 12-11   Output of a custom report named Timecards

Defining Custom Report Types

Custom report types help simplify object models for reporting by flattening relationships between a primary object and up to two related child objects. To create a custom report type, go to the App Setup area and click Create → Report Types. Click the New Custom Report Type button.

In Figure 12-12, two object relationships have been defined: Resources and Timecards. You can qualify the join relationship using the radio buttons within each related object's colored box. By default, the selected relationship is an inner join, requiring values in the parent object and related object for a record to appear in the report. You can also select a left outer join, in which records from the parent object are displayed even when they do not contain matching records in the child.

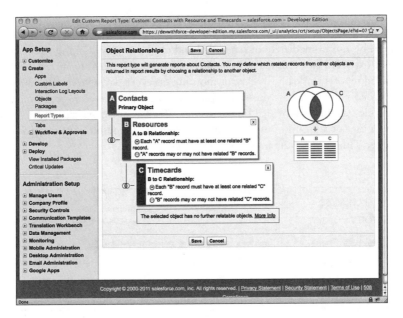

Figure 12-12   Editing object relationships in a custom report type

Configuring Dashboards

Dashboards are configurable pages for displaying many reports at once and rendering report data in a graphical form. Dashboards can be configured to appear on the Home tab of the Force.com user interface and are also displayed on their own standard tab, called Dashboards.

Dashboards are composed of dashboard components. Components are organized into two or three columns on the page and can be individually positioned. Components can be configured to display data from reports or Visualforce pages. Components from reports can be rendered as charts, tables, metrics, or gauges. In Figure 12-13, a dashboard named Company Performance Dashboard is being edited. It organizes components into three columns. Key Metrics, Support, and Pipeline Analysis are the names of dashboard components.

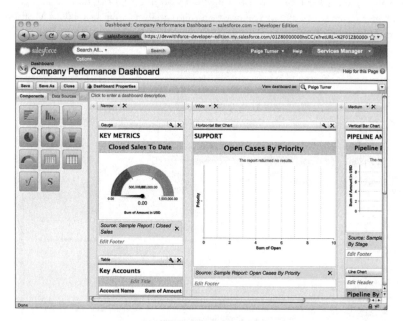

Figure 12-13   Editing a dashboard

To work with dashboards, click the Dashboards tab. To define a new dashboard, click the Go to Dashboards List link at the top of the page and then the New Dashboard button. Force.com comes with many sample dashboards that you can add using the Add Sample Dashboard button. To edit an existing dashboard, locate it in the drop-down list titled View Dashboard and then click the Edit button.

When in edit mode on a dashboard, you can add, edit, or remove components from it. You can move components from one column to another or up and down within a column. You can also change the width of a column using the Narrow, Medium, and Wide links.

Using Analytic Snapshots

Analytic snapshots move data resulting from running a report into a custom object. Ordinarily reports are run interactively by users in the native user interface, scheduled for execution with results emailed to users, or exposed as dashboard components. Force.com does not maintain the report output anywhere within the platform. But when report data is captured in analytic snapshots, it becomes broadly available to the platform, accessible anywhere custom objects are used, without executing the report again.

To manage analytic snapshots, go to the Administration Setup area and click Data Management → Analytic Snapshots. To create a new snapshot, click the New Analytic

Snapshot button. Enter a snapshot name and specify a user whose sharing rules determine which records are included in the snapshot. Then select the report that serves as the information source, select the target custom object to store the report data into and click the Save button. Figure 12-14 shows the creation of an analytic snapshot called Monthly Timecard Summary.

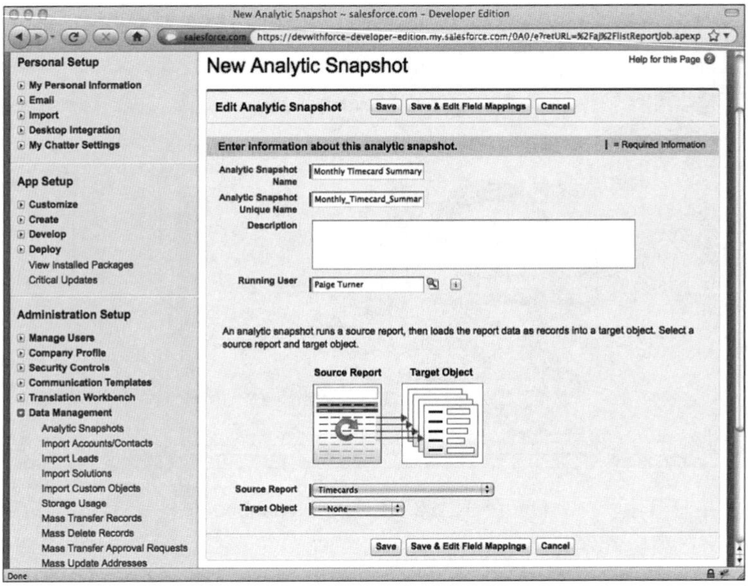

Figure 12-14   Creating a new analytic snapshot

After the snapshot is created, configure its field mappings and schedule it to be executed. To configure field mappings, click the Edit button in the Field Mappings related list. The fields of your custom target object are enumerated on the right side of the screen. On the left are drop-down lists of compatible fields in the source report. To perform the mapping, change the drop-down lists from the default value of Load No Data to the selected field from the source report. When the mapping is complete, click the Save button.

A snapshot can be run only by Force.com itself in accordance with a preset schedule. To set the schedule, click the Edit button in the Schedule Analytic Snapshot related list. The schedule specifies a start and end date, a frequency (daily, weekly, or monthly), and whether the snapshot runs every weekday or every day of the week. Force.com determines the exact time of day to execute the snapshot, but you can get a list of available start times and select one you prefer. Force.com makes no guarantee about executing your snapshot at this precise time. When the snapshot is complete, you or a group of users can be notified via email.

Force.com for International Organizations

One of the advantages of the Force.com platform and other cloud platforms is elasticity. They can scale up and down with less friction than platforms that reside on-premise, in corporate data centers. Additionally, Force.com helps you architect applications that scale geographically and culturally, to operate naturally in multiple countries, languages, and currencies. This is provided by the following platform features, covered in this section:

- **Multilingual Support:** The native Force.com user interface and all of your customizations to it can be translated into any number of 16 supported languages. Custom Apex code and Visualforce pages are also fully supported by the multilingual infrastructure. For details on the supported languages, refer to www.salesforce.com/us/developer/docs/api_meta/Content/meta_translations.htm.

- **Using Multiple Currencies:** Although it defaults to a single global currency per organization, Force.com also supports multiple currencies at the record level.

- **Advanced Currency Management (ACM):** ACM is an optional feature for managing historical currency exchange rates.

Multilingual Support

Force.com provides two major features to support multilingual organizations:

1. **Translation Workbench:** This feature allows the vast majority of the native user interface elements of Force.com to be translated into any number of Force.com's supported languages.

2. **Custom Labels:** Custom labels enable your Apex code and Visualforce pages to be translated into multiple languages by externalizing their strings.

Translation Workbench

Translation workbench is a feature that allows you to translate Force.com's user interface into multiple languages. Tabs, help text, picklist values, field labels, validation rules, and many other elements can be translated. Force.com manages the set of languages supported by your organization, the list of elements to be translated, and users you appoint as translators, and it indicates when translations might be outdated due to configuration changes.

Users of your Force.com organization normally would not use Translation Workbench directly. They simply see the correct user interface based on their preferred language, which they configure in the Personal Setup area by clicking My Personal Information → Personal Information.

By default, Translation Workbench is not enabled in your Force.com organization. To enable it, contact Salesforce support by logging a case. To log a case, log in to your Force.com organization and click the Help link at the top of the page. Click the My Cases tab, and then click the Log a Case link.

When Translation Workbench is enabled, it's visible as an option in the Administration Setup area. Click Translation Workbench → Translation Workbench Setup to get started.

Click the Add button to add supported languages to your organization. Here you can also identify users who are enabled to provide translations in the language. Users who are appointed to translate must also have the View Setup and Configuration permission enabled on their profile.

After you've added languages, click Translation Workbench → Translate Custom Field Labels to get a sense for how translations are performed. Select a language and an object and click the Edit button to begin translating. The Master Field Label is the label set when the field was created. Beside each, you can enter a translation. The Out of Date column indicates that the definition of the field label has changed since it was translated, notifying a translator to double-check that the translation is still valid. When you're done translating the fields, click the Save button. Figure 12-15 shows the result of translating the Resource object to Spanish.

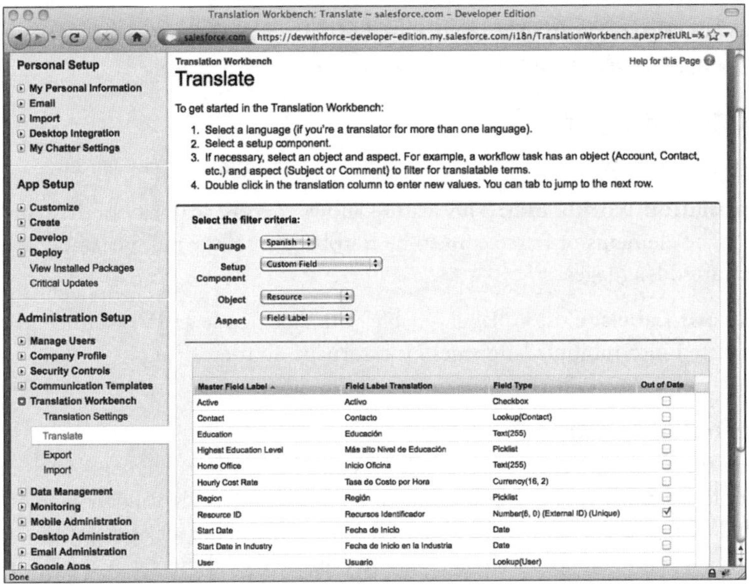

Figure 12-15   Custom field labels in Translation Workbench

Most other features of Force.com that can be translated are shown in the list of Translation Workbench options. One notable exception is custom object tabs. You can have these translated in the App Setup area by clicking Customize → Tab Names and Labels → Rename Tabs and Labels. Select a language from the drop-down list and then click the Edit link for the tab to provide a translation, shown in the Display Label column. The tab is shown as Renamed when a translated value is set.

Custom Labels

Custom labels make your Apex code and Visualforce pages easily localizable. You define custom labels, reference them by name in Apex code and Visualforce pages, and translate the custom labels into all the languages configured for the organization in the Translation Workbench. Users of the Visualforce pages and Apex code automatically receive the translated versions of the custom labels based on their language setting.

Caution

Custom labels can be created and used without enabling Translation Workbench, but labels cannot be translated into different languages.

To get started with custom labels, go to the App Setup area and click Create → Custom Labels. Click the New Custom Label button and provide a unique name for the label. This is the name used by Visualforce pages and Apex code to refer to the custom label. Also provide the text of the label, in the default language, and optionally a comma-separated list of categories, helpful for organizing large numbers of labels.

Figure 12-16 shows a custom label named `Label_Test`. It contains the string `This is a test`, and it has been translated into Spanish and French.

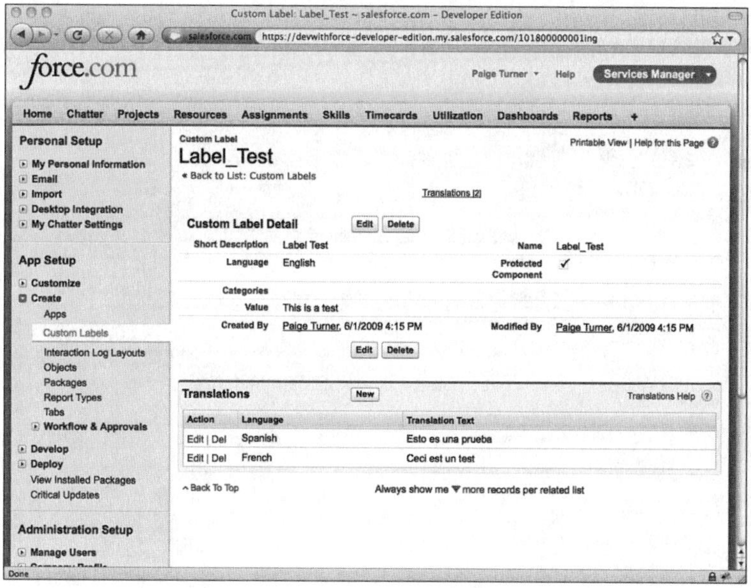

Figure 12-16   Configuring a custom label

A reference to the label in a Visualforce page is `{!$Label.Label_Test}`. The same label included in Apex code is `System.Label.Label_Test`.

Using custom labels during your application development is certainly extra work. The benefit is that your application can support any number of languages with minimal incremental effort and no additional code.

Using Multiple Currencies

By default, Force.com supports a single currency per organization. Every currency field of every object in the system is stored using the same currency. You can set that currency in the Administration Setup area by clicking Company Profile → Company Information. Click Edit and set the Currency Locale of the company. For example, setting the Currency Locale to French (France, Euro) causes all currency fields to be displayed as euros (€).

Alternatively, you can also configure Force.com to use any number of currencies, varying from record to record. You must enable support for multiple currencies by logging a support case with Salesforce. To log a case, log in to your Force.com organization and click the Help link at the top of the page. Click the My Cases tab and then click the Log a Case link.

When you enable multiple currencies, a new configuration option is added in Company Profile called Manage Currencies, shown in Figure 12-17. Here you can set the corporate currency and add the other currencies supported by your organization and their conversion rates to the corporate currency.

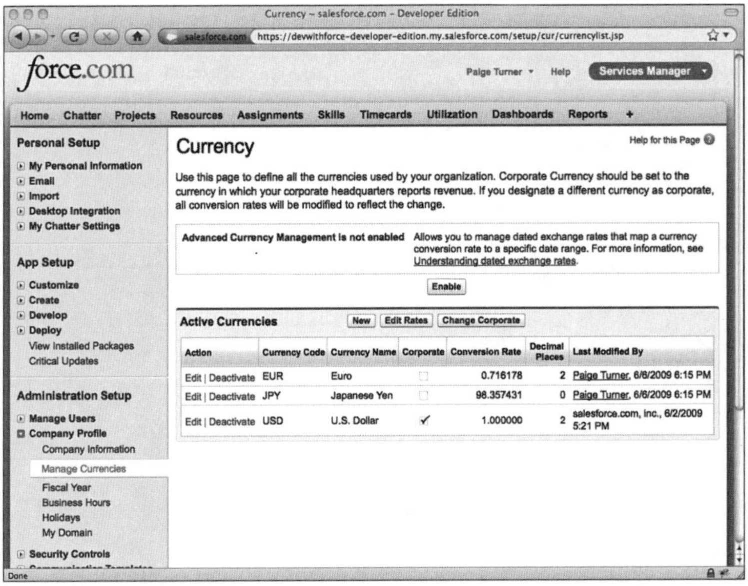

Figure 12-17   Configuring currency exchange rates

With multiple currency support, a new standard field is added to every object called CurrencyIsoCode. This field stores the currency code that applies to every currency field on the record. You can see this field in action when you edit an object that contains currency fields. Figure 12-18 is an example of editing a Resource record. Notice that the Currency is set to Japanese Yen (JPY), making the Hourly Cost Rate field 10,000 JPY.

Figure 12-18   Setting currency on a record

When a user with a different Currency Locale views this record, the user sees the original value and beside it the value converted to the preferred currency. For example, in Figure 12-19, a user with a Currency Locale of United States Dollars (USD) is viewing the record entered in Japanese Yen (JPY).

Leveraging support for multiple currencies in Apex code and Visualforce user interfaces is fairly simple. In Visualforce, the outputField page component formats currency field values correctly. Currency fields retrieved using SOQL or SOSL queries are returned in the currency specified by the record's CurrencyIsoCode value. They are not automatically converted to the current user's preferred currency. To convert them explicitly, use the convertCurrency function. Listing 12-3 provides an example that you can execute in the Execute Anonymous view.

Figure 12-19   Viewing a record with a currency set

Listing 12-3   **Converting Currencies Using SOQL**

```
Resource__c r = [ SELECT Hourly_Cost_Rate__c, CurrencyIsoCode
  FROM Resource__c WHERE Name = 'Priti Manek' LIMIT 1 ];
System.debug(r.Hourly_Cost_Rate__c + ' ' + r.CurrencyIsoCode);
r = [ SELECT convertCurrency(Hourly_Cost_Rate__c)
  FROM Resource__c WHERE Name = 'Priti Manek' LIMIT 1 ];
System.debug(r.Hourly_Cost_Rate__c);
```

The first query selects the value without conversion, and the second uses convertCurrency. For example, running it on the record shown in Figures 11-17 and 11-18 outputs 10,000 JPY and 101.67 USD. This assumes a corporate currency of USD, a current user's currency locale of USD, and an exchange rate from JPY of 98.357431.

Advanced Currency Management (ACM)

ACM is an optional feature of multiple currency support that provides dated exchange rates. With ACM disabled, currency conversion rates are not sensitive to time. The rates are applied uniformly to all records. For currency values that must be converted using rates that vary based on time, enable ACM by going to the Administration Setup area and clicking Company Profile → Manage Currencies.

Note

You must file a support request with Salesforce before you can enable ACM in your organization.

After ACM is enabled, click the Manage Dated Exchange Rates button. Rates are set for ranges of time. Any number of time ranges can be created, with a single day as the lowest level of granularity. In Figure 12-20, the exchange rates for Euro and Japanese Yen that apply beginning on February 28, 2011, are configured.

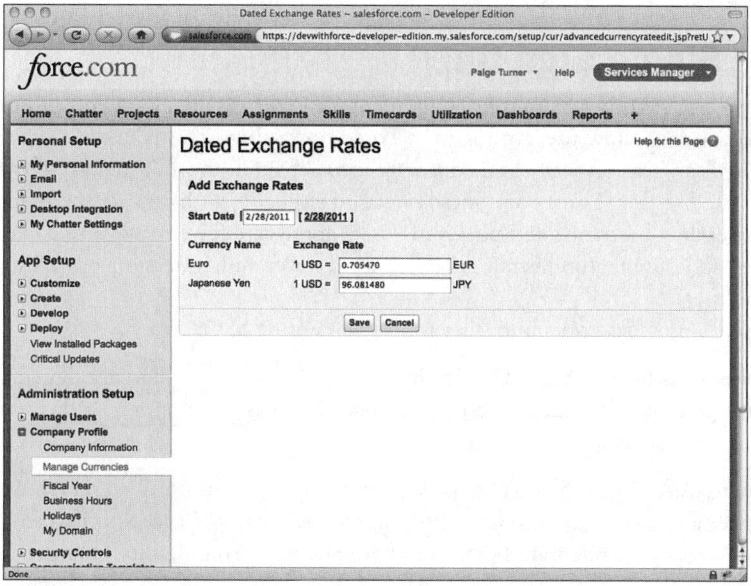

Figure 12-20   Setting dated currency exchange rates

ACM has several limitations. The most notable limitation is that it can be used only for standard fields on the Opportunity object. These fields are automatically converted using the time-based rates you configure. However, fields in other objects continue to use the undated exchange rates.

To use dated currency rates with your own objects, you must develop Apex code and Visualforce pages that perform the conversions manually. The dated conversion rates configured in the native user interface are available to your custom code in the DatedConversionRate standard object. You can query this object using SOQL, and modify it using DML, but you cannot create triggers on it.

Listing 12-4 is an example of using SOQL to retrieve dated currency rates. The dated rates can then be used to manually convert currency values.

Listing 12-4   **Sample SOQL to Retrieve Dated Currency Rates**

```
SELECT StartDate, NextStartDate, IsoCode, ConversionRate
  FROM DatedConversionRate
```

> **Caution**
>
> When updating the present-day currency conversion rates in your organization, always update both the dated and the undated rates. If you do not, you run the risk of showing conflicting data to users. For example, Opportunity records that use dated conversion rates will contain values that disagree with objects tied to the undated rates.

Using Single Sign-On

Single sign-on (SSO) is a common requirement for enterprise deployments of Force.com. The objective is to allow users to log in to Force.com using a trusted session they've established elsewhere, typically in a corporate intranet application or identity provider. With a trusted session, Force.com doesn't need to explicitly authenticate the user with its own independent username and password. Users appreciate fewer passwords to enter and remember, and system administrators benefit from fewer authentication-related support cases from users.

Force.com provides two approaches for implementing SSO:

1. **Federated Single Sign-On:** In the federated approach, a digitally signed assertion message is posted from a Web page into Force.com's login servers. If the assertion is valid, the user is logged in to Force.com.

2. **Delegated Single Sign-On:** Delegated SSO uses a custom Web service you implement to decide whether a user should be permitted access to Force.com, allowing you to integrate Force.com with any back-end identity provider.

Federated Single Sign-On

Federated SSO operates using assertions, which are messages encoded in XML, digitally signed, and posted to Force.com from the Web browser. These messages, when verified, instruct Force.com to create an authenticated session for a user on behalf of your corporate systems. In making the assertion, your corporate system is effectively bypassing Force.com's own authentication mechanism and substituting its own.

Force.com supports Security Assertion Markup Language (SAML) 1.1 and 2.0, which are open standards for implementing federated security models. A system administrator configures Force.com to receive SAML assertions by specifying a digital certificate to verify the signed messages and the location and format of the user's identity in the assertions.

> **Caution**
>
> Federated SSO is not supported for authenticating users to the Web Services API, but it is available for Customer Portal (SAML 2.0 only).

To configure SSO, go to the Administration Setup area and click Security Controls →
Single Sign-On Settings. Click the Edit button and select the SAML Enabled check box.
A sample configuration of federated SSO is shown in Figure 12-21.

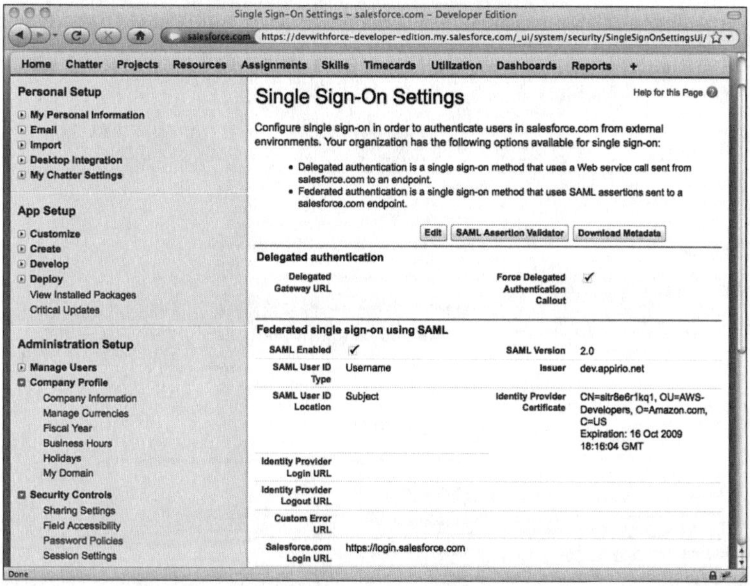

Figure 12-21   Configuring federated single sign-on

The following list describes the fields of the federated SSO configuration:

- **Issuer:** The issuer value must map to the issuer element in the SAML assertion.
- **SAML User ID Type:** This value specifies how Force.com is to interpret the user
  value provided in the assertion. It is either a Force.com username or a federation
  identifier, which is an optional field on the user object.
- **SAML User ID Location:** This setting instructs Force.com on where to find the
  user in the assertion. It is in either a `NameIdentifier` element or an `Attribute`
  element.
- **Salesforce Login URL:** This is a value generated by Force.com. Post your SAML
  assertions to this URL.
- **Identity Provider Certificate:** Your system, the one generating the assertion, is
  the identity provider. The assertion must be digitally signed. This certificate is the
  public half of the credential's key pair, used by Force.com to verify that your system
  indeed signed the assertion. This field displays information about the certificate
  you've uploaded.

After federated SSO is configured, you can generate SAML assertions and test them using the SAML Assertion Validator. On the Single Sign-On Settings page, click the SAML Assertion Validator button. Paste a plain XML or Base64-encoded assertion into the text area labeled SAML Response and click the Validate button. A sample result is shown in Figure 12-22. When your assertion is validated with no errors, you know it can be used to actually log a user in to Force.com when Base64-encoded and posted to the Salesforce Login URL.

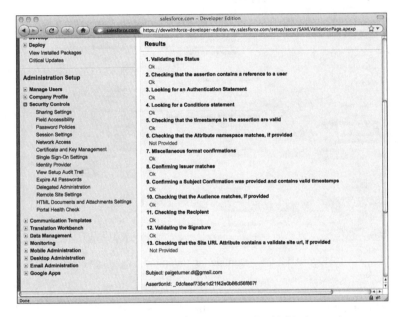

Figure 12-22   Using the SAML Assertion Validation tool

The missing piece in using federated SSO with Force.com is actually generating the signed SAML assertions. This is the most challenging part of the puzzle. Many identity providers support SAML assertions, and configuring them is outside the scope of this book. But you can write your own assertion generator using open-source tools. The following steps describe a SAML 2.0 assertion generator written in Java, using the Open-SAML toolkit:

1. Create a new Java project in Eclipse. Download the OpenSAML 2.0 library from www.opensaml.org. Also download the Simple Logging Facade for Java (www.slf4j.org), Logback (http://logback.qos.ch), and XMLUnit (http://xmlunit.sourceforge.net).

2. Import the endorsed directory from OpenSAML into your Eclipse project. Do the same with the lib directory.

3. Import the `xmlunit` jar, the `slf4j-api` and `slf4j-log4j12` jars, and the `logback-classic` and `logback-core` jars into the `lib` directory of your project.

4. Create a new Java class for your assertion generator. This class must initialize the OpenSAML library, load your private key and certificate, construct the necessary elements of the SAML assertion, sign it, serialize it as XML, and encode it as a Base64 string. Full sample code is provided on the book's Web site (www.informit.com/title/9780321767356) and is far too verbose to include here, but fragments are provided in Listings 12-5, 12-6, and 12-7.

Listing 12-5   Initializing OpenSAML

```
public SAMLDemo() throws ConfigurationException {
  DefaultBootstrap.bootstrap();
  parser = new BasicParserPool();
  parser.setNamespaceAware(true);
  marshallerFactory = Configuration.getMarshallerFactory();
  unmarshallerFactory = Configuration.getUnmarshallerFactory();
  builderFactory = Configuration.getBuilderFactory();
}
```

Listing 12-6   Creating the SAML Assertion and Subject

```
private XMLObject buildXMLObject(QName objectQName)
  throws RuntimeException {
  XMLObjectBuilder builder = Configuration.getBuilderFactory().
    getBuilder(objectQName);
  if (builder == null) {
    throw new RuntimeException("Unable to retrieve builder for
      object QName " + objectQName);
  }
  return builder.buildObject(objectQName.getNamespaceURI(),
    objectQName.getLocalPart(), objectQName.getPrefix());
}
DateTime now = new DateTime();
IdentifierGenerator idGenerator =
  new SecureRandomIdentifierGenerator();
Subject subject = (Subject) buildXMLObject(
  Subject.DEFAULT_ELEMENT_NAME);
NameID nameID = (NameID) buildXMLObject(
  NameID.DEFAULT_ELEMENT_NAME);
nameID.setFormat(NameID.EMAIL);
nameID.setValue("paigeturner.dl@gmail.com");
subject.setNameID(nameID);
SubjectConfirmation conf = (SubjectConfirmation)
  buildXMLObject(SubjectConfirmation.DEFAULT_ELEMENT_NAME);
conf.setMethod("urn:oasis:names:tc:SAML:2.0:cm:bearer");
```

```
SubjectConfirmationData data = (SubjectConfirmationData)
  buildXMLObject(SubjectConfirmationData.DEFAULT_ELEMENT_NAME);
data.setRecipient("https://login.salesforce.com");
data.setNotOnOrAfter(now);
conf.setSubjectConfirmationData(data);
subject.getSubjectConfirmations().add(conf);
Assertion assertion = (Assertion)
  buildXMLObject(Assertion.DEFAULT_ELEMENT_NAME);
assertion.setVersion(SAMLVersion.VERSION_20);
assertion.setID(idGenerator.generateIdentifier());
assertion.setIssueInstant(now);
assertion.setSubject(subject);
```

Listing 12-7   **Signing and Encoding the SAML Assertion**

```
Signature signature = (Signature) buildXMLObject(
  Signature.DEFAULT_ELEMENT_NAME);
signature.setSigningCredential(credential);
signature.setCanonicalizationAlgorithm(
  SignatureConstants.ALGO_ID_C14N_EXCL_OMIT_COMMENTS);
signature.setSignatureAlgorithm(
  SignatureConstants.ALGO_ID_SIGNATURE_RSA);
response.setSignature(signature);
Marshaller marshaller = marshallerFactory.getMarshaller(response);
marshaller.marshall(response);
Signer.signObject(signature);
Response signedResponse = (Response) unmarshallerFactory.getUnmarshaller(
  response.getDOM()).unmarshall(response.getDOM());
Marshaller m = marshallerFactory.getMarshaller(signedResponse);
Element generatedDOM = m.marshall(response, parser.newDocument());
BASE64Encoder be = new BASE64Encoder();
String xml = XMLHelper.nodeToString(generatedDOM);
return be.encode(xml.getBytes());
```

5. Tell the Java Virtual Machine (JVM) about your endorsed jars. Create a Run Configuration for your assertion generator class that includes these JVM arguments: `-Djava.endorsed.dirs=endorsed`.

6. You will need your Identity Provider certificate in X.509 format and your private key in Distinguished Encoding Rules (DER) format. Use OpenSSL to convert your files from other formats. For example, to convert from Privacy Enhanced Mail (PEM), use the commands given in Listing 12-8. In this example, the PEM files are the private key `pk.pem` and certificate `cert.pem`.

Listing 12-8   **Converting from PEM Using OpenSSL**

```
openssl pkcs8 -topk8 -nocrypt -in pk.pem -outform DER -out pk.der
openssl x509 -in cert.pem -inform PEM -out cert.crt -outform DER
```

7. Build a test Web page for submitting the SAML assertion to Force.com. It can be as simple as the page in Listing 12-9. Open the page in your Web browser, paste the generated Base64-encoded SAML assertion into the text area, and click the Submit button. If your assertion is valid, you will be logged in to Force.com immediately, without entering a username or password.

Listing 12-9   **Sample Code for SAML Assertion Test Page**

```
<html>
  <body>
    <form name="form" action="https://login.salesforce.com"
      method="post">
      <textarea name="SAMLResponse" rows="20" cols="80">
      </textarea>
      <input type="submit" value="Submit" />
    </form>
  </body>
</html>
```

8. After testing your SAML assertion with Force.com, you can integrate the assertion generation code with your internal Web applications. This closes the loop, mapping internal application users to the correct Force.com users and extending the trust established with internal applications into Force.com.

Delegated Single Sign-On

With delegated single sign-on, Force.com calls out to a simple Web service you implement for authenticating users. Force.com provides the username, password, and source IP address of the user attempting to log in. Your Web service returns `true` or `false`, indicating whether the user should be authenticated to Force.com.

By default, delegated SSO is not enabled in your Force.com organization. To enable it, contact Salesforce support by logging a case. To log a case, log in to your Force.com organization and click the Help link at the top of the page. Click the My Cases tab and then the Log a Case link.

Caution

Delegated SSO is supported for Customer Portal users, but not for users of the Web Services API.

To get started with delegated SSO, follow these steps:

1. Download the delegated authentication WSDL. Go to the App Setup area and click Develop → API, and click the Download Delegated Authentication WSDL link, shown in Figure 12-23.

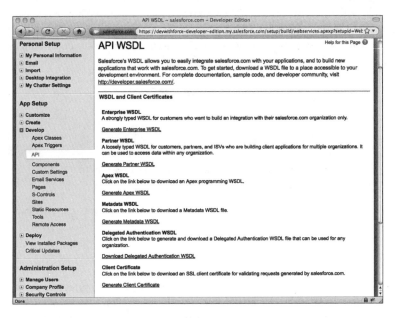

Figure 12-23   Downloading delegated authentication WSDL

2. Using the WSDL, implement a Web service to respond to Force.com delegated authentication requests. Listing 12-10 provides a sample implementation in PHP.

Listing 12-10   **Sample Code for Delegated SSO Authentication Service**

```php
<?php
function authenticated($value) {
  if ($value) {
    return array('Authenticated' => $value);
  } else {
    return null;
  }
}
function Authenticate($data) {
  error_log('Delegated authentication request for username ' .
    $data->username . ' from IP ' . $data->sourceIp);
  return authenticated(false);
```

```
}
ini_set("soap.wsdl_cache_enabled", "0");
$server = new SoapServer("AuthenticationService.wsdl");
$server->addFunction("Authenticate");
$server->handle();
```

3. Make sure the server hosting your Web service is available to the Internet via port 80 (HTTP), port 443 (HTTPS), or ports 1024–65535 (HTTP or HTTPS). The most secure configuration is to use HTTPS and configure your Web service to require an SSL client certificate from Force.com. Go to the App Setup area and click Develop → API and click the Download Client Certificate link.

4. Configure delegated SSO in Force.com to point to your Web service. Go to the Administration Setup area and click Security Controls → Single Sign-On Settings. Enter the URL to your authentication Web service in the Delegated Gateway URL field and click the Save button. Figure 12-24 depicts this configuration page.

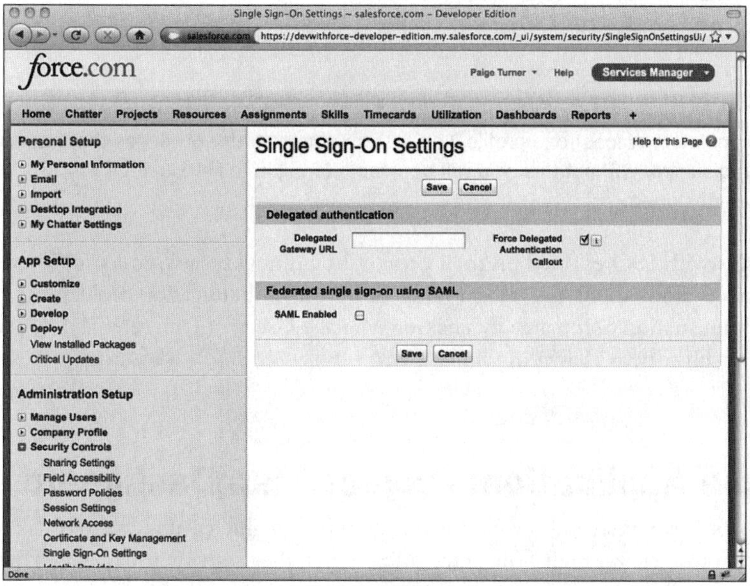

Figure 12-24   Configuring delegated SSO

5. Enable SSO on the profiles of the users. Enable the Is Single Sign-On Enabled check box in the General User Permissions section of the profile, as shown in Figure 12-25.

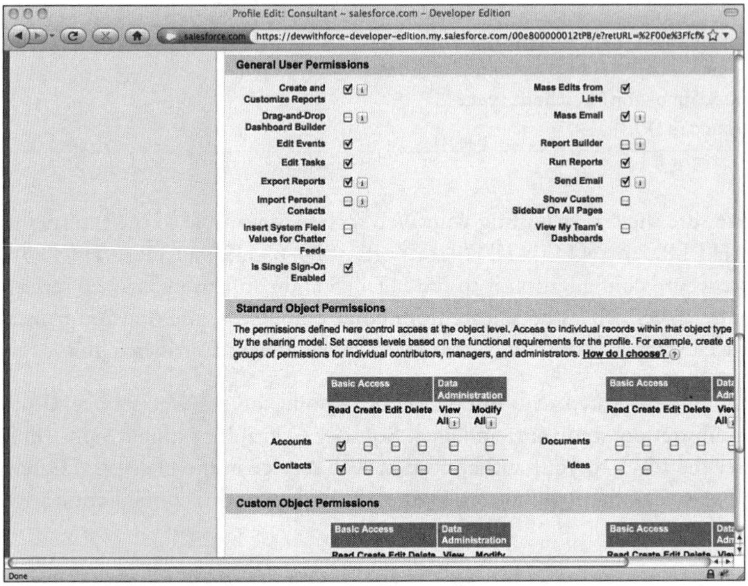

Figure 12-25 Configuring a profile for SSO

> **Caution**
>
> Always maintain at least one profile with system administrator privileges that has single sign-on disabled. Without this, you will be unable to log in to Force.com if your SSO Web service goes down.

6. Users with SSO enabled on their profile should now be able to log in if your Web service allows them. You can monitor delegated authentication problems in the Administration Setup area by clicking Manage Users → Delegated Authentication Error History, as shown in Figure 12-26.

Sample Application: Project Map Dashboard

In this chapter, you've seen how dashboards provide a highly configurable surface for displaying data to users on their home tab, visible when they start their day with Force.com. This section walks through the construction of a custom Visualforce dashboard component for the Services Manager sample application. Called Project Map and shown in Figure 12-27, it renders the locations of the company's active consulting projects on a Google Map.

Project Map demonstrates that what you can show to users on their dashboards is limited only by your imagination in developing with the Force.com platform and freely available JavaScript libraries.

Figure 12-26   Monitoring delegated authentication errors

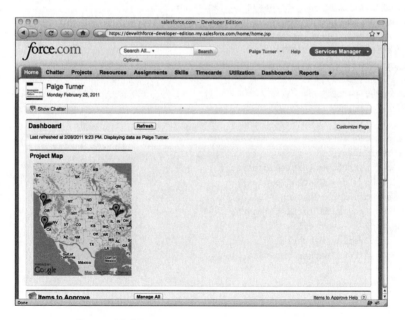

Figure 12-27   Project Map dashboard component

To create the Project Map component, follow these steps:

1. Create a Visualforce component called `GoogleMultiMap` to hide the implementation details of visualizing multiple geographic locations using the Google Maps API. `GoogleMultiMap` has a single input named `mapData`, which is a JSON-encoded string with two keys: `names`, containing an array of project names to plot on the map, and `addresses`, an array of addresses. The component is responsible for taking the addresses and geocoding them to retrieve the latitude and longitude for Google map markers. Each marker is annotated with the project name occurring at that location, displayed when the user hovers over the marker. Listing 12-11 is a sample implementation of the Visualforce component. Be sure to provide your own Google Maps API key in place of the `APIKEY` value.

> **Note**
>
> If you do not have a Google Maps API key, visit http://code.google.com/apis/maps/ signup.html.

Listing 12-11   **`GoogleMultiMap` Component**

```
<apex:component>
<apex:attribute name="mapData" type="String"
  required="true"
  description="JSON-encoded names and addresses
  to show on the Google map" />
<apex:includeScript value="http://maps.google.com/maps?
  file=api&v=2.x&key=APIKEY" />
<script>
var map = null;
var geocoder = null;
var markerList;
var addressList;
var nameList;
var currentIndex;
function finishShowMultipleAddresses() {
  var bounds = new GLatLngBounds();
  map.setCenter(new GLatLng(0,0), 0);
  for (var i=0; i<markerList.length; i++) {
    var marker = markerList[i];
    map.addOverlay(marker);
    bounds.extend(marker.getPoint());
  }
  map.setZoom(map.getBoundsZoomLevel(bounds));
  map.setCenter(bounds.getCenter());
}
```

```javascript
function finishGeocode(point) {
  if (point) {
    var marker = new GMarker(point, {
      'title' : nameList[currentIndex].replace('&', '&')
    });
    markerList.push(marker);
    currentIndex++;
    if (currentIndex == addressList.length) {
      finishShowMultipleAddresses();
    } else {
      geocoder.getLatLng(addressList[currentIndex], finishGeocode);
    }
  }
}
function initGMap() {
  if (GBrowserIsCompatible()) {
    map = new GMap2(document.getElementById("map_canvas"));
    if (geocoder == null) {
      geocoder = new GClientGeocoder();
    }
  }
}
function showMultipleAddresses(names, addresses) {
  initGMap();
  nameList = names;
  addressList = addresses;
  markerList = new Array();
  currentIndex = 0;
  if (geocoder) {
    geocoder.getLatLng(addresses[currentIndex], finishGeocode);
  }
}
function init() {
  var mapData = eval("(" +
    document.getElementById("map_data").innerHTML + ")");
  showMultipleAddresses(mapData.names, mapData.addresses);
}
var previousOnload = window.onload;
window.onload = function() {
  if (previousOnload) {
    previousOnload();
  }
  init();
}
```

```
</script>
<div id="map_data" style="display: none">{!mapData}</div>
<div id="map_canvas" style="width: 300px; height: 300px"></div>
</apex:component>
```

2. Create the ProjectMap Visualforce page. Listing 12-12 is a sample implementation of this page. It simply embeds the GoogleMultiMap component you created in the preceding step and binds its mapData input to an output from your controller. You won't be able to save this page until you've completed step 3 because the controller class does not yet exist.

Listing 12-12 **ProjectMap Visualforce Page**

```
<apex:page controller="ProjectMapController">
  <c:GoogleMultiMap mapData="{!projectLocationsJson}" />
</apex:page>
```

3. Create the controller class for the ProjectMap Visualforce page. The controller is responsible for returning the project names and addresses to be rendered on the Google map. Listing 12-13 provides a sample implementation. It selects the name and address fields from the Account record associated with each Project in progress and then returns them as a JSON-encoded string. This is a simplistic implementation because companies can have multiple locations where a consultant might be working. The on-site location for a project could be stored as a set of address fields added to the project or a separate address object related to both the Account and the Project objects.

Listing 12-13 **ProjectMapController**

```
public class ProjectMapController {
  public String getProjectLocationsJson() {
    List<Proj__c> projects = [ SELECT Name,
      Account__r.BillingStreet, Account__r.BillingCity,
      Account__r.BillingState, Account__r.BillingPostalCode
      FROM Proj__c
      WHERE Stage__c = 'In Progress' ];
    String result = '{ names: [';
    Boolean first = true;
    for (Proj__c project : projects) {
      if (!first) {
        result += ', ';
      } else {
```

```
        first = false;
      }
      result += '\'' + project.Name.replace('\'', '\"') + '\'';
    }
    result += '], addresses: [';
    first = true;
    for (Proj__c project : projects) {
      if (!first) {
        result += ', ';
      } else {
        first = false;
      }
      result += '\'' +
        project.Account__r.BillingStreet + ' ' +
        project.Account__r.BillingCity + ' ' +
        project.Account__r.BillingState + ' ' +
        project.Account__r.BillingPostalCode + '\'';
    }
    result += '] }';
    return result;
  }
}
```

4. Add the ProjectMap Visualforce page as a dashboard component. If the Dashboards tab is not visible on your screen, click the rightmost tab (small arrow pointing to the right) to reach it. Select an existing dashboard or create a new one, and then click the Edit button. In the Components tab panel, select the Visualforce component (vf icon) and drag it into a column of the dashboard. Next, you need to connect the component to a data source. Click the Data Sources tab panel, expand the Visualforce Pages group, and drag the Visualforce page you created in step 2 into the newly created Visualforce dashboard component. When you're done, your dashboard should resemble Figure 12-28.

5. Make sure that users are configured to see the dashboard on their Home tabs. Go to the App Setup area and click Customize → Home → Home Page Layouts. Click the Edit link for the home page layout. In the Select Wide Components to Show list, select the Dashboard Snapshot check box.

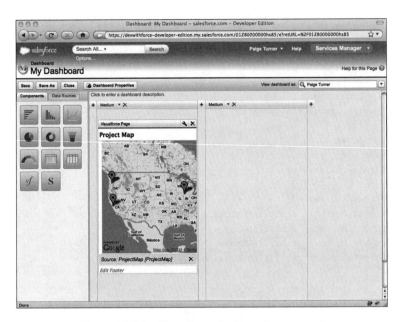

Figure 12-28   Visualforce dashboard component

Summary

In this chapter, you've been exposed to features of the Force.com platform that can enhance the functionality of your applications. Whether or not you've created your first object or line of Apex code, it's worth taking the time to survey the full scope of the Force.com platform's functionality. This investigation will help you assess which applications fit the strengths of the platform and how best to use its features to capture the maximum value from your efforts.

Before finishing the chapter, reflect on a few points:

- Workflow and approval processing impose your own custom business processes on the data in Force.com.

- Although you can always extract Force.com data into on-premise databases and use traditional reporting solutions against them, Force.com provides its own built-in reporting and analytics tools that are worth getting acquainted with.

- Force.com supports single sign-on (SSO) through its federated and delegated authentication options. Federated SSO involves issuing a digitally signed SAML message to Force.com's servers. Delegated authentication is accomplished through a Web service you host that Force.com invokes whenever a user attempts to log in.

13

Social Applications

This chapter introduces Chatter, a layer of functionality that spans all Salesforce applications and the Force.com platform, also referred to collectively as the Collaboration Cloud. Chatter provides the means for users to communicate with each other in the context of the applications and data central to their work, privately and entirely internal to their company. It is delivered securely to their web browsers and most mobile devices. In adopting Chatter, Salesforce customers, partners, and application developers gain the best features of consumer services such as Facebook that form a social glue that makes interacting at work a compelling, relevant, and professional experience.

Chatter includes features for end users and developers alike. Much of the functionality in Chatter is readily accessible to anyone with basic knowledge of the Force.com database, Apex, and Visualforce. Most of the effort as a developer is to first understand the nuances of configuring Chatter as a user and system administrator, discussed in the first section of this chapter. Brief descriptions of all three sections follow:

- **Overview of Chatter:** Chatter brings with it an entire vocabulary necessary for users and developers to understand its features. Learn the new lingo, plus how to configure Chatter as an administrator and user.

- **Understanding the Chatter Data Model:** The heart of Chatter is the data model, standard objects in the Force.com database that allow any application to participate in the conversation and automate Chatter interactions. With a grasp of the data model, incorporating Chatter into your Apex programs is straightforward.

- **Chatter in Visualforce:** Learn how to add Chatter functionality to your custom user interfaces with minimal effort using standard Visualforce components.

In the final section of the chapter, you modify the Services Manager sample application to make staying in touch with resources on a project team using Chatter easy.

Overview of Chatter

Chatter is integrated everywhere into Salesforce, and it wants to be in your custom Force.com applications if you let it. This section covers basic Chatter concepts used throughout the chapter, as well as how to configure Chatter from an administrator and user point of view.

Chatter Concepts

Chatter brings users together socially, inline with the records in the Force.com database relevant to them professionally. You could imagine it as the cloud equivalent of convening a meeting at your desk with an armful of documents to review and annotate with your team. In Chatter, this task is much easier, and less disruptive due to its asynchronous nature.

The following list of Chatter-related terms reflects its focus on marrying social interaction with business data:

- **Posts and comments:** These two terms encompass all communication in Chatter. A post is a public message associated with a record in the database. A comment is also a public message, but related to an individual post rather than a database record, like a footnote to the post. Posts and comments are viewable by anyone in the organization who has access to the parent record. The body of posts and comments can contain text, searchable topics (words prefaced with #), references to users in your organization (using the @ character), and links to web pages. Posts and comments are full-text searchable from the standard Force.com search interface. Posts and comments can also contain any type of file, like attachments in email messages. Individual posts can be "liked" by users, helping to measure and track the popularity of content.

> **Caution**
>
> Unlike other Salesforce data, Chatter posts and comments can be deleted but not undeleted from the Recycle Bin. After a post or comment is deleted, it is gone for good.

- **Follow and unfollow:** The verbs follow and unfollow refer to the social relationship between a user and a database record. A user who seeks to regularly review or participate in the social activity (posts and comments) associated with a record would follow that record. Similarly, when the user is no longer interested in a record's social activity, he would unfollow it. This set of records followed by a user represents his interests, and the Force.com platform summarizes them into a single web page and optionally, periodic email digests.

- **Feed:** The feed is a history of social activity associated with a database record. When users create posts and comments, they are gathered together and displayed as a feed, with the most recent entries appearing first, and subsequent entries in descending order of date posted.

- **Group:** Not to be confused with Public Groups (the grouping of users for authorization purposes), the Chatter Group is a gathering place for users to collaborate on any subject. It's useful when no sensible database object type exists to serve as the locus of Chatter conversation. For example, you could create a group named "Hot Customers" for support employees to work together to fight the fires of unhappy customers.

- **Chatter profile:** The Chatter profile is an additional page associated with each User record. It allows users to share information about themselves, their role in the organization, their interests, and a photo. The profile also contains all Chatter-related information about a user, including group affiliations, records followed, and users following them.

- **Digest:** A digest is a daily or weekly emailed summary of the Chatter feeds followed by a user. The daily digest contains up to 25 of the most recent posts, and the weekly digest has 50. Both include the latest three comments for each post. Digests can be a convenient way to keep current on social activity without logging into Salesforce.

- **Feed-tracked change:** The feed-tracked change is the Chatter version of the standard history tracking feature available on most database fields. After an administrator configures an object and field as feed-tracked, a system-generated Chatter post is created to notify users when the field's value changes. The feed-tracked change Chatter posts serve as a public audit trail, and cannot be deleted. Another unique property of feed-tracked change posts is that they are never included in Chatter search results.

Configuring Chatter

Configuring Chatter involves three main aspects:

- **Administrators:** Users with administrative permissions can enable and disable Chatter for the entire organization. They can also decide which database objects can contain Chatter, and which fields on those objects have feed-tracked changes.

- **Groups:** Data is spread throughout an organization across many standard and custom objects. What objects and records users should follow is not always clear. Groups can provide a meaningful set of Chatter topics for your company.

- **Users:** Individual users can control email digests and notifications of Chatter-related events, such as new posts or new users following them.

Chatter Configuration for Administrators

The first step in adopting Chatter is to enable it for your organization. Unless your organization has explicitly opted out of Chatter, it should be enabled by default. In the App Setup area, click Customize → Chatter → Settings. Figure 13-1 shows this screen with Chatter enabled.

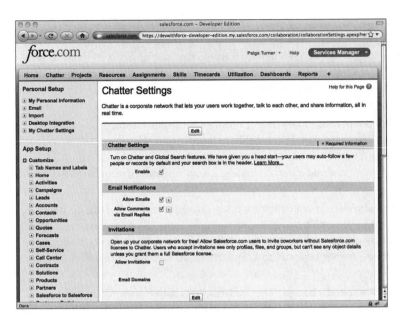

Figure 13-1   Chatter settings for an organization

> **Note**
>
> If you decide to disable Chatter, all of your existing Chatter-related data, such as posts and comments, remains in Salesforce. You can turn it back on again at any time.

After enabling Chatter for the organization, the next step is to Chatter-enable some database objects. Objects that are Chatter-enabled receive a Chatter toolbar at the top of their detail pages. This toolbar is the primary way users interact with Chatter. Figure 13-2 shows it in its expanded state. Clicking the Hide Chatter button collapses it. From the toolbar, users can post, comment, view a list of the followers, and follow or unfollow the record.

To Chatter-enable objects, go the App Setup area and click Customize → Chatter → Feed Tracking. This page also allows configuration of feed-tracked changes, although this is optional. In Figure 13-3, the standard objects Account, Case, Contact, Lead, and Opportunity are Chatter-enabled and have multiple fields with tracked changes. The Chatter Group is a system object that is always enabled. The custom object Project is also Chatter-enabled, but has no fields with feed-tracked changes.

> **Note**
>
> By default, Chatter is enabled on the following standard objects: Account, Case, Contact, Chatter Group, Contact, Lead, Opportunity, and User. Feed-tracked changes are enabled on a few fields of each object: Account (Name, Owner), Case (Owner, Priority, Status), Chatter Group (Description, Group Access, Name, Owner), Contact (Account, Name, Owner), Lead (Name, Owner, Status), Opportunity (Amount, Close Date, Name, Owner, Stage), and User (About Me, Address, E-mail, Manager, Phone, Title).

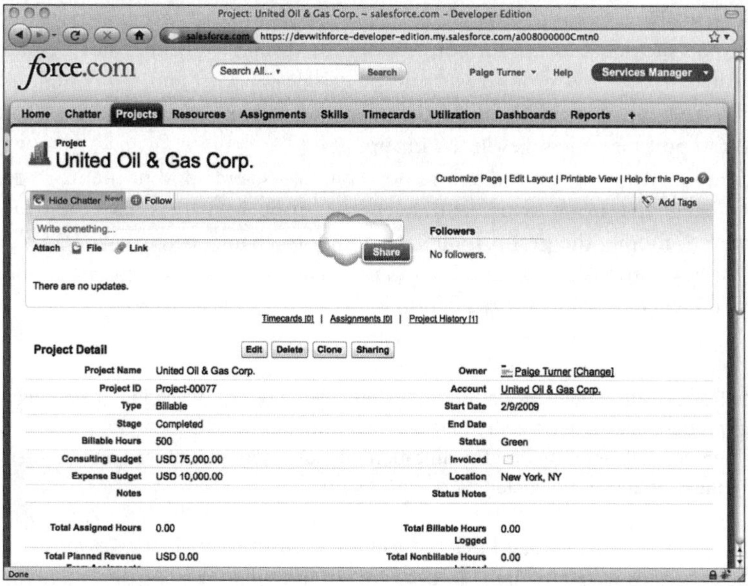

Figure 13-2   Chatter toolbar in the expanded state

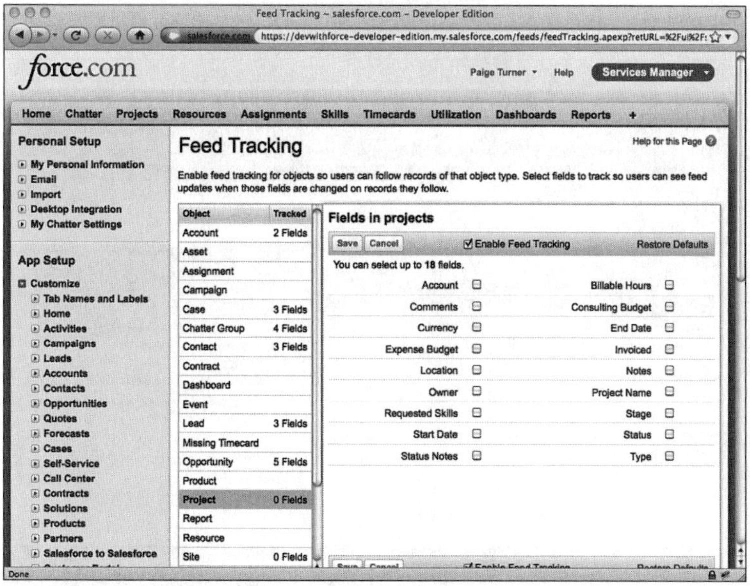

Figure 13-3   Chatter feed tracking settings

Creating Groups

Chatter groups provide a forum for conversation that might not otherwise belong on an ordinary database object. A group has a title, description, photo, and can contain files. Groups also have members who follow the group, see group activity in their Chatter feeds, and can post new messages in the group.

As a group owner, you can add and remove members, and appoint members to serve as managers, change the group owner, and delete the group. Managers have the same rights as the owner to modify the group, minus the ability to change group ownership and delete the group. Groups can be public or private. Anyone can join a public group. But you must be invited to join a private group by its owner or a manager.

> **Note**
>
> Administrators with Modify All Data permissions have special privileges in working with Chatter groups. They can do everything a group owner can do, but cannot post in a group as a non-member. This isn't much of a limitation because administrators can add themselves as a member of any group, including private groups.

Groups are created, edited, and deleted using the Groups tab. If the Groups tab is not visible, click the plus icon (All Tabs) in the toolbar and select it from the list. If you don't see Groups in the list of all tabs, it is hidden in your profile or Chatter is disabled for your organization.

Figure 13-4 shows a sample group called Hot Projects. It has five members, no files, and no photo.

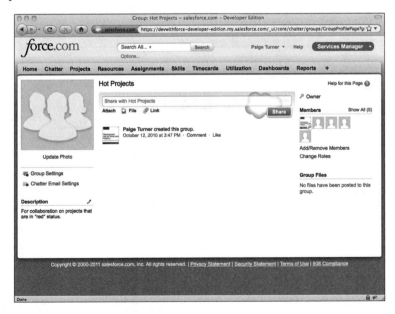

Figure 13-4   Sample group page

Chatter Configuration for Users

When Chatter is enabled for an organization, a new item is added to the Personal Setup area called My Chatter Settings. Within this item are two children, My Feeds and Chatter Email Settings, described here:

- **My Feeds:** By default, Force.com configures your user to follow all Chatter-enabled records that you own. You can disable this behavior on the My Feeds page.

- **Chatter Email Settings:** This page allows the user to control the flow of Chatter-related email. In Figure 13-5, the user is signed up to receive email notification on all Chatter events, daily email digests of Chatter in the Hot Projects group, but no email digests of personal Chatter. To quickly disable all Chatter email, deselect the Receive Chatter emails option.

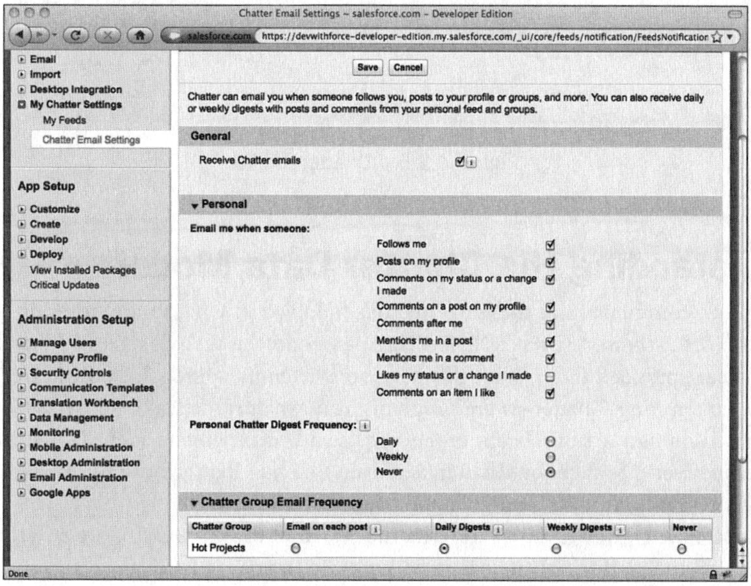

Figure 13-5   Chatter email settings for a user

To get the most out of Chatter, taking a moment to update your Chatter profile with information about yourself is a good idea. This enables other users to find and learn more about you and your role in the organization.

To reach your Chatter profile, click your name on the Home tab, or select your name from the menu bar at the top of the screen and click My Profile. Figure 13-6 shows a sample Chatter profile.

Figure 13-6   Chatter profile

Understanding the Chatter Data Model

Chatter posts, comments, and the list of records followed in Chatter are stored in standard database objects, accessible in SOQL, SOSL, Apex code, the Web Services API, and generally anywhere you need them. With this developer-friendly approach, you can build any number of interesting Chatter-aware programs. You can automatically follow a set of records based on user actions, batch process posts and comments to identify patterns, build an alternative user interface for Chatter, and even extend Chatter outside of your organization by integrating it with external applications.

After you have a good grasp of the data model, all of these scenarios are trivial to implement on the platform. But compared with the standard platform objects such as Contacts and Accounts, Chatter has a slightly more complex data model, including objects with some distinctive qualities, summarized here:

- **Dynamic:** The objects in the Chatter schema can appear and disappear based on the Chatter configuration. For example, when Chatter is disabled in an organization, the Chatter objects are completely hidden, as if they never existed. Also, objects containing Chatter posts are dynamically created when Chatter is enabled for a custom object.

- **Relationship-Rich:** The whole purpose of Chatter is to link social and business data, so Chatter objects consist primarily of foreign keys to other objects.

- **Designed for High Volume:** Chatter objects usually do not allow records to be updated. Some objects can't even be queried directly and must be referenced indirectly from a parent object.

This section introduces you to the Chatter data model by exploring these four areas:

- **Chatter Posts:** Learn how to query, create, and delete the three main types of Chatter posts, based on the parent record's object type.

- **Chatter Comments:** You can query, create, and delete Chatter comments, given a parent post.

- **Feed-Tracked Changes:** Feed-tracked change records are created automatically by Force.com to provide an audit trail of database activity. They can be queried but never directly created, updated, or deleted.

- **Followed Records:** Get a list of followers for a record, and follow and unfollow records by creating and deleting simple Chatter configuration records.

Chatter Posts

Chatter posts are stored using a series of relationships that follow a common pattern, illustrated in Figure 13-7. Starting from the right of the diagram, a Feed object, suffixed with the word Feed, contains Chatter posts. Feed objects exist for each Chatter-enabled parent object type. The parent object is on the left, and the line between them indicates that a single parent record can have zero to many posts.

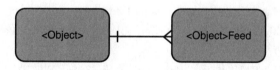

Figure 13-7   Chatter post schema pattern

> **Note**
>
> Feed objects are unusual for Force.com in that they are read-only. To insert or delete Chatter posts, you must use the generic FeedItem object, discussed later in this chapter.

The Feed objects appear and disappear based on the Chatter configuration. For example, if Chatter is enabled on the Proj__c custom object, then an object named Proj__Feed exists, the object used to store posts related to Projects. If Chatter is later disabled for Proj__c, the Proj__Feed object is removed from the Force.com database.

The five types of post content, indicated by the Type field of the Feed objects, are described here:

- **Text (TextPost):** This is the default type of Chatter post. It contains plain text, with no HTML markup or rich formatting allowed. The text is contained in the Body field. The sample code in this chapter focuses on the text post type, because the other post types behave almost identically, differing only on the fields used to store data.

- **URL (`LinkPost`):** The Chatter user interface allows you to attach a single URL to a post, which appears immediately below the post text. The URL value is stored in the `LinkUrl` field, with the URL label in `Title`.

- **File (`ContentPost`):** From the Chatter user interface, you can select a file to attach to a post. The file can be a reference to another Chatter-attached file, or uploaded from your local computer. The file content is base-64 encoded and placed in the `ContentData` field. Several additional file-related metadata fields are also stored with the file: `ContentFileName` and `ContentDescription` (input by the user during upload), `ContentType` (file MIME type), and `ContentSize` (file size in bytes).

- **Field Change (`TrackedChange`):** This post type is relevant only to feed-tracked changes. It is generated by Force.com itself and cannot be created by users or programs.

- **Status Update (`UserStatus`):** Chatter users can change their status from their profile page or any Chatter user interface. This action triggers Force.com to insert a status update Chatter post, with the `Body` field set to the new status.

The remainder of this subsection contains SOQL queries and Apex code snippets to demonstrate how to work with posts and their parent feed objects. They are organized into the following four scenarios:

- **Standard Object Feeds:** When Chatter is enabled for an organization, most standard objects have corresponding Chatter feeds.

- **Custom Object Feeds:** Every custom object that is Chatter-enabled by the administrator has its own feed.

- **User Feeds:** Separate feeds exist for the Chatter user profile as well as the standard User object.

- **Home Tab Feed:** The Home tab has its own feed, called NewsFeed. This contains a collection of all the activity in followed records.

> **Caution**
> Understanding posts and feeds is critical because the rest of the section builds upon this knowledge.

Standard Object Feeds

When Chatter is enabled for an organization, feed objects exist for every standard object that supports Chatter. Listing 13-1 is an example of retrieving the ten most recent Chatter posts on the Contact object using the ContactFeed object.

Listing 13-1   **Chatter Query on Standard Object**

```
SELECT ParentId, Body, Type, CreatedBy.Name, CreatedDate
  FROM ContactFeed
  ORDER BY CreatedDate DESC LIMIT 10
```

To create a post on the Contact object, you need the Id of a Contact record to serve as the parent of the post. This Id becomes the `ParentId` column in `FeedItem`. Force.com takes care of determining which feeds the post belongs to based on the type of object referenced by the `ParentId`. This means you can use the same code to create posts regardless of the type of object you're posting about.

The example code in Listing 13-2 contains a method for creating a Chatter post. Pass it the Id of a Contact record in the `recordId` argument, and the text of the post body in the `text` argument. Make a note of the return value because it is used later to remove the post.

Listing 13-2   **Creating a Chatter Post**

```
public Id post(Id recordId, String text) {
  FeedItem post = new FeedItem(ParentId = recordId, Body = text);
  insert post;
  return post.Id;
}
```

Unlike creating posts, the code to delete posts is object-specific, not generic. It requires the specific feed object containing the post to be known. For example, if you created a post with a Contact record as the `ParentId`, delete the post from the ContactFeed, as shown in Listing 13-3.

Listing 13-3   **Deleting a Chatter Post**

```
public void deleteContactPost(Id postId) {
  ContactFeed post = [ SELECT Id FROM ContactFeed
    WHERE FeedPostId = :postId ];
  delete post;
}
```

Custom Object Feeds

Chatter posts on custom objects behave identically to standard objects, with two exceptions. The naming scheme for the feed objects is slightly different, and a feed object does not exist until Chatter is enabled on the custom object. For example, if you enable Chatter on the `Proj__c` object, the `Proj__Feed` Chatter object becomes available.

Listing 13-4 demonstrates a query for posts on the `Proj__c` object. As you can see, the columns are identical to that of the standard feed, but the FROM clause refers to the `Proj__c`-specific feed object. To get any feed object's name, strip the `__c` from the end of your custom object's API name, and then add the __Feed suffix. You can follow this pattern to access the posts of any custom object.

Listing 13-4   **Chatter Query on Custom Object**

```
SELECT ParentId, Body, Type, CreatedBy.Name, CreatedDate
  FROM Proj__Feed
```

> **Note**
>
> The procedure for creating and deleting Chatter posts in custom objects is identical to that of standard objects.

User Feeds

Two feeds contain user-related Chatter posts:

- **UserFeed:** UserFeed contains feed-tracked changes for fields on your User object, as well as posts by other users on your profile. You cannot query another user's User feed unless you log in to Force.com as that user.
- **UserProfileFeed:** The UserProfileFeed is a superset of the User feed. It includes Chatter from other objects followed by the user, such as groups. It requires the use of the WITH SOQL syntax to query it. This sets the user context, so you can view the UserProfileFeed from the perspective of any user by specifying his UserId.

The SOQL in Listing 13-5 returns the Chatter posts for the current user, the user logged in to Force.com and executing the query.

Listing 13-5   **Chatter Query on UserFeed**

```
SELECT ParentId, FeedPostId, Type, CreatedById, CreatedDate
  FROM UserFeed
```

Listing 13-6 demonstrates the UserProfileFeed. It selects all Chatter posts for the user with the given Id, which is not required to be the same user executing the query.

Listing 13-6   **Chatter Query on UserProfileFeed**

```
SELECT ParentId, FeedPostId, Type, CreatedById, CreatedDate
  FROM UserProfileFeed
  WITH UserId = '00580000001opOPAAY'
```

> **Note**
>
> The procedure for creating and deleting Chatter posts in UserFeed and UserProfileFeed is identical to that of standard objects.

News Feed

If you've experimented with Chatter in the Force.com user interface, you might have noticed that the Home tab aggregates all the posts and comments you follow in one place. The Chatter appearing on the Home tab is also accessible via API using the News-Feed object.

Listing 13-7 is a sample query on the NewsFeed object, returning all the posts in the current user's Home tab. Queries on NewsFeed are limited in scope to the user running the query. You cannot see another user's NewsFeed records unless you log in to Force.com as that user.

Listing 13-7   **Chatter Query on NewsFeed**

```
SELECT ParentId, Body, Type, CreatedBy.Name, CreatedDate
  FROM NewsFeed
```

Chatter Comments

The handling of Chatter comments is slightly different from that of other Chatter data. Comment data is stored in a single, large object called FeedComment that cannot be queried directly. The Feed object becomes a junction object, associating Chatter posts to the subject of the post and zero or more comments. This three-way relationship is shown in Figure 13-8, with the left side the parent of the post and the right side the list of comments.

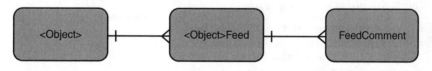

Figure 13-8   Chatter comment schema pattern

The relationship between the Feed junction object and the FeedComment object is called FeedComments. Listing 13-8 provides an example of querying it. The result is all the posts in the Proj__c custom object feed, and for each post all of its comments.

Listing 13-8   **Chatter Query for Comments**

```
SELECT ParentId, Type, CreatedById, CreatedDate, Body,
  (SELECT CommentBody, CreatedById, CreatedDate FROM FeedComments)
  FROM Proj__Feed
```

To create a comment, insert a record into the FeedComment object. Listing 13-9 provides a sample method for doing this. To test it, you need the Id value of a record in a Feed object. For example, if you want to add a comment to an Account post, get the Id of the post to comment on from the AccountFeed object. This Id value is then passed into the method as the first argument, postId. The second argument is the text of the comment to create. Save the postId and the value returned by this method, as these are needed to delete the comment.

Listing 13-9   **Creating a Chatter Comment**

```
public Id comment(Id postId, String text) {
  FeedComment comment = new FeedComment(
    FeedItemId = postId, CommentBody = text);
  insert comment;
  return comment.Id;
}
```

You cannot update a FeedComment record, but you can delete it. Like with deleting posts, deleting comments is tricky because you cannot directly query the FeedComment object to retrieve the record to delete. If your program creates or queries FeedComment records and can keep them around in a cache, that is ideal. If this is not possible, you must query the FeedComment in order to delete it.

Listing 13-10 shows a sample method for deleting a comment by querying it first via its parent post. To use it, you must pass the FeedItemId of the parent post in the Proj__Feed object as the postId, and the Id of the FeedComment record as commentId, returned by the comment sample method. Although this example operates on comments in Proj__Feed only, the same pattern can be applied to comments in all feeds.

Listing 13-10   **Deleting a Chatter Comment**

```
public void deleteComment(Id postId, Id commentId) {
  Proj__Feed post = [ SELECT Id,
    (SELECT Id from FeedComments WHERE Id = :commentId)
    FROM Proj__Feed WHERE FeedPostId = :postId ];
  delete post.FeedComments[0];
}
```

Feed-Tracked Changes

Feed-tracked changes provide an audit trail of modifications to a set of fields. For each record in an object that has feed-tracked changes enabled, there can be many corresponding feed-tracked change records. Each change record captures the original field value, the new field value, the field name, and the new and old currencies if multicurrency is enabled in the organization and the field is a currency type.

The change records for all objects in an organization with feed-tracked changes enabled are stored in a single object called FeedTrackedChange. The schema pattern for this object is illustrated in Figure 13-9.

Figure 13-9   Chatter feed-tracked changes schema pattern

FeedTrackedChange cannot be queried or modified in any way by any user, even an administrator. Like Chatter comments, it must be queried indirectly via its junction object. Listing 13-11 shows an example of querying all posts on Contact records and their corresponding FeedTrackedChanges.

Listing 13-11   **Querying Chatter Feed-Tracked Changes**

```
SELECT ParentId, Type, CreatedById, CreatedDate,
  (SELECT FeedItemId, FieldName, OldValue, NewValue
    FROM FeedTrackedChanges)
  FROM ContactFeed
```

To see the query in action, enable feed-tracked changes on the Contact Phone field; then change the Phone value on a record and run the query. You should see a new record with a Type value of `TrackedChange` containing a nested FeedTrackedChange record. The nested record has the old and new Phone values along with the full field name, `Contact.Phone`. Had you changed two feed-tracked change fields within the same transaction, you would see two nested FeedTrackedChange records instead of one.

Followed Records

Users register interest in the Chatter activity of a record by clicking Follow icons in the Force.com user interface, or by automatically following owned records. Users can follow other users as well as records in standard and custom objects. The information about followers is prominently displayed throughout the standard user interface, and used to email digests and notifications to users if Chatter is configured to do so.

All of this functionality hinges upon a single, simple object, called EntitySubscription. Its two important fields are `ParentId`, the record being followed, and `SubscriberId`, the Id of the user doing the following. For every record-to-user relationship in the organization, a unique record in EntitySubscription exists to express it.

With simple queries on the EntitySubscription object, you can retrieve a list of records followed by a user, or the users following a specific record. Less useful might be a query for the full set of following relationships in the entire organization, as shown in Listing 13-12.

Listing 13-12   **Querying Chatter Following Relationships**

```
SELECT ParentId, SubscriberId, CreatedById, CreatedDate
  FROM EntitySubscription
```

To follow a record programmatically, insert a new `ParentId` and `SubscriberId` pair into the EntitySubscription object. Listing 13-13 provides a sample method to do this. Test it by passing in the Id of a record to follow and the Id of a User record to follow it.

Listing 13-13   **Method for Following a Record**

```
public Id follow(Id recordId, Id userId) {
  EntitySubscription e = new EntitySubscription(
    ParentId = recordId, SubscriberId = userId);
  insert e;
  return e.Id;
}
```

For example, call it with the Id of an Account record and your user's Id value; then refresh the Account's view page to see yourself instantly listed as a follower. Make a note of the Id value returned by the method. This is used later to unfollow the record.

> **Note**
>
> Each EntitySubscription uniquely identifies a relationship between parent record and User record, so a runtime error is thrown if a new record matches an existing record's `ParentId` and `SubscriberId`.

Unfollowing a record involves deleting the appropriate row in EntitySubscription that relates the record to the user. Listing 13-14 provides a sample method for doing just that. To use the method, pass the EntitySubscription record identifier returned by the `follow` sample method in Listing 13-13.

Listing 13-14   **Method for Unfollowing a Record**

```
public void unfollow(Id subscriptionId) {
  delete [ SELECT Id FROM EntitySubscription
    WHERE Id = :subscriptionId ];
}
```

Although this simple example can work, it's unlikely that your program would possess the unique identifier of the EntitySubscription record. You could just as easily delete records on more readily available information, such as the EntitySubscription's `ParentId` or `SubscriberId`.

Chatter in Visualforce

When Chatter is enabled on an object, users viewing a record of that object see a rich user interface to manage posts and comments, followers, and their interest in following the record. This same native user interface functionality is also available to Visualforce developers. Using Chatter components, you can embed the same Chatter toolbar, in its entirety or in pieces, within your custom user interfaces.

Chatter is supported in Visualforce through four dedicated components in the `chatter` namespace, and an additional Chatter-specific attribute on the generic `detail` component, as described here:

- **feed:** This component renders a list of Chatter posts and comments for the selected record. It also provides a text box at the top for creating new posts. The selected record is specified using the `entityId` attribute.
- **feedWithFollowers:** This component embeds the full Chatter toolbar. It includes the functionality of the `feed` component, and adds the list of followers to the right side, the Show/Hide Chatter buttons, and the Follow/Unfollow buttons.
- **follow:** Including this component on a page renders a Follow button if the user is not following the record, and Unfollow button otherwise.
- **followers:** The `followers` component simply displays a list of users following the current record. Users are represented as thumbnail photos, which can be clicked to drill into their profiles.
- **showChatter:** This attribute of the `detail` component, if set to `true`, includes the full Chatter toolbar at the top of the detail page.

To try one of the Chatter components, create a new Visualforce page that uses a standard controller. Pick an object that you know has Chatter enabled. Listing 13-15 shows a custom `Proj__c` page that includes the `feedWithFollowers` component, and Figure 13-10 is the result of visiting the custom page. There are no posts, comments, or followers of the `Proj__c` record, but the `feedWithFollowers` component has made creating and viewing all of these items using the standard Force.com-styled user interface possible.

Listing 13-15   **Visualforce Page with Chatter Component**

```
<apex:page standardController="Proj__c">
  <apex:sectionHeader title="Project"
    subtitle="{!record.Id}" />
  <apex:pageBlock title="Chatter Components">
    <chatter:feedWithFollowers entityId="{!record.Id}" />
  </apex:pageBlock>
</apex:page>
```

You should be aware of a few gotchas with Visualforce Chatter components as you begin using them:

- A Visualforce page cannot contain more than one of the five Chatter components at one time. If you attempt to use more than one, the page cannot be saved.
- Chatter components cannot be added to a Visualforce page unless the API version of the page is at least 20.0. If the API version is set incorrectly, an `Unknown Component` error will prevent the page from being saved.

- You cannot use Chatter components with Visualforce Sites. The Chatter components will be invisible to Sites users.

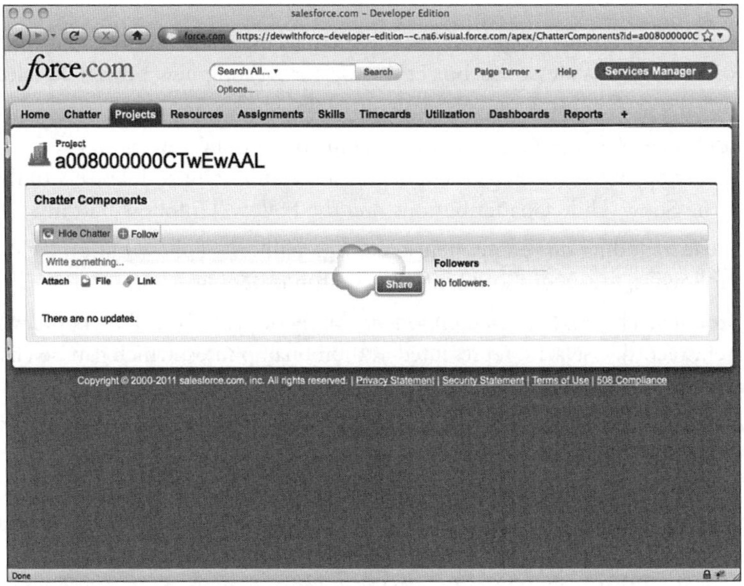

Figure 13-10   Output of Visualforce page with Chatter component

Sample Application: Follow Project Team

One of the initial challenges with using Chatter is building up a relevant set of records to follow. Salesforce's automatic following of owned records is a good start. But users of your Services Manager sample application would like a quick and easy way to follow all the resources assigned to a consulting project.

This section walks through a sample implementation of a custom button called Follow Team, added to the `Project` object's layout. The button launches a Visualforce page that uses the standard `Proj__c` controller and a controller extension. Because the page is shown when the user clicks the button, the `action` attribute of the page invokes the custom controller code to perform the following logic immediately, without additional user action. The results of the following logic are displayed in a page message.

Following records in Chatter using Apex code involves adding records to the Entity-Subscription object. The sample code in Listing 13-16 is the full controller extension implementation.

Listing 13-16   **Controller Extension Code**

```
public with sharing class FollowProjectControllerExtension {
  private ApexPages.StandardController controller;
  public FollowProjectControllerExtension(
    ApexPages.StandardController stdController) {
    this.controller = stdController;
  }
  public PageReference followProject() {
    Id currentUserId = UserInfo.getUserId();
    Set<Id> userIds = new Set<Id>();
    for (List<Assignment__c> assignments :
      [ SELECT Resource__r.User__c FROM Assignment__c WHERE
          Project__c = :controller.getRecord().Id ]) {
      for (Assignment__c assignment : assignments) {
        Id uid = assignment.Resource__r.User__c;
        if (currentUserId != uid && uid != null) {
          userIds.add(uid);
        }
      }
    }
    if (userIds.size() == 0) {
      error('Project has no assignments.');
      return null;
    }
    Set<String> subs = new Set<String>();
    for (List<EntitySubscription> recs :
      [ SELECT ParentId FROM EntitySubscription
        WHERE SubscriberId = :currentUserId
        AND ParentId IN :userIds ]) {
      for (EntitySubscription rec : recs) {
        subs.add(rec.ParentId);
      }
    }
    Integer followCount = 0;
    List<EntitySubscription> adds = new List<EntitySubscription>();
    for (Id userId : userIds) {
      if (!subs.contains(userId)) {
        adds.add(new EntitySubscription(
          ParentId = userId, SubscriberId = currentUserId));
        followCount++;
      }
    }
    insert adds;
    info(followCount + ' users followed');
    return null;
  }
```

```
private static void info(String text) {
  ApexPages.Message msg = new ApexPages.Message(
    ApexPages.Severity.INFO, text);
  ApexPages.addMessage(msg);
}
private static void error(String text) {
  ApexPages.Message msg = new ApexPages.Message(
    ApexPages.Severity.ERROR, text);
  ApexPages.addMessage(msg);
}
}
```

Two tricky areas of the implementation are as follows:

- Duplicate records cannot be added, so existing EntitySubscription records on the assigned users must be checked first. This is done by building a set of record identifiers that are already followed, storing them in the `subs` variable, and consulting them before creating a new EntitySubscription.

- Retrieving the users to follow from a project is somewhat indirect. Start with the list of `Assignment__c` records for the `Proj__c` record. Each `Assignment__c` record contains a `Resource__c` that is assigned to the project. Each `Resource__c` includes a `User__c` field, which optionally contains a reference to a Salesforce User record. The User record identifier becomes the `ParentId`, the record to follow.

The Visualforce page behind the custom Follow Team button is provided in Listing 13-17. Key points in the page are the `action` attribute to invoke the following logic when the page is shown, and the `pageMessages` component to provide feedback to the user about the newly followed records, if any.

Listing 13-17   **Visualforce Page for Custom Button**

```
<apex:page standardController="Proj__c"
  extensions="FollowProjectControllerExtension"
  action="{!followProject}">
  <apex:pageMessages />
</apex:page>
```

Caution

Invoking a controller method upon Visualforce page load is bad practice for security reasons, as it can be exploited in a Cross Site Request Forgery (CSRF) attack. Visualforce pages are normally protected from CSRF using hidden variables that prevent a hijacker from redirecting the browser to a simple URL. To protect a page like the one in Listing 13-17, you could add a token that is checked in the controller before executing the logic. For more information, examine the security-related documents available at wiki.developerforce.com/index.php/Security.

After you have created the controller extension class and the page, add a custom button on the Project object called Follow Team. Figure 13-11 shows the button configuration.

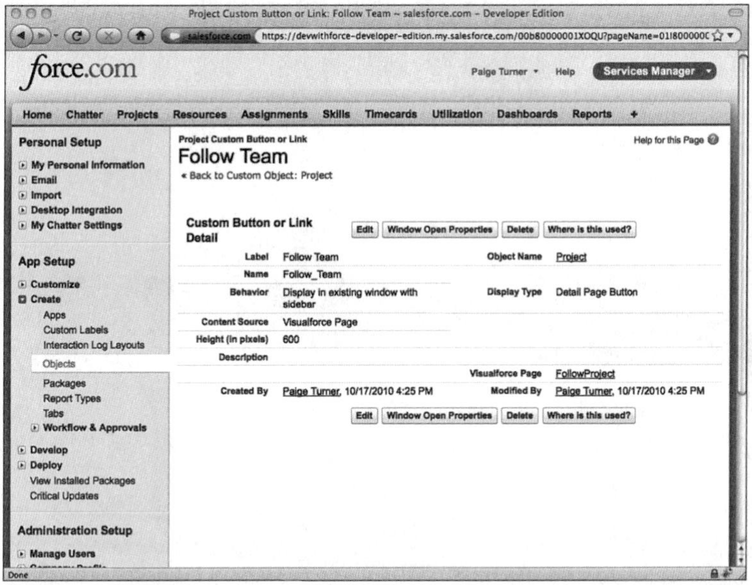

Figure 13-11   Custom button configuration

To manually test the new feature, visit a Project record that has at least one Assignment and where the Assignment has a Resource with a non-null User__c field. Click the Follow Team button. Refresh the current user's profile to verify that the assigned user is followed.

Summary

Chatter offers a unique combination of end-user functionality and building blocks for developers to create socially aware applications. As you review the key features of Chatter, consider the potential it brings to drive new applications and interactions in your organization:

- Chatter provides user profiles, which are customizable pages for every user in your organization. User profiles deliver a stronger sense of user identity than the standard User record.

- As users follow Chatter-enabled records, a corporate-wide social graph of interests in people and data emerges. This graph can be mined in any number of creative applications, inside and outside of the platform.

- Chatter is itself a platform, consisting of a public data model, user interface components, and tight integration with the greater Force.com platform. This provides flexibility for any application to exercise and extend Chatter functionality.

Index

Symbols

A

E

Developer's Library

ESSENTIAL REFERENCES FOR PROGRAMMING PROFESSIONALS

A Developer's Guide to Amazon SimpleDB

Mocky Habeeb

ISBN-13: 9780321623638

Test-Driven JavaScript Development

Christian Johansen

ISBN-13: 9780321683915

Android™ Wireless Application Development

Shane Conder
Lauren Darcey

ISBN-13: 9780321743015

Other Developer's Library Titles

TITLE	AUTHOR	ISBN-13
Drupal's Building Blocks	Earl Miles Lynette Miles	9780321591319
The Python Standard Library by Example	Doug Hellmann	9780321767349
Programming in Objective-C 2.0	Stephen Kochan	9780321711397
Multicore Application Programming	Darryl Gove	9780321711373

Developer's Library books are available at most retail and online bookstores. For more information or to order direct, visit our online bookstore at **informit.com/devlibrary**.

Online editions of all Developer's Library titles are available by subscription from Safari Books Online at **safari.informit.com**.

Addison
Wesley

Developer's Library

informit.com/devlibrary

FREE Online Edition

Your purchase of **Development with the Force.com Platform** includes access to a free online edition for 45 days through the Safari Books Online subscription service. Nearly every Addison-Wesley Professional book is available online through Safari Books Online, along with more than 5,000 other technical books and videos from publishers such as Cisco Press, Exam Cram, IBM Press, O'Reilly, Prentice Hall, Que, and Sams.

SAFARI BOOKS ONLINE allows you to search for a specific answer, cut and paste code, download chapters, and stay current with emerging technologies.

Activate your FREE Online Edition at www.informit.com/safarifree

> **STEP 1:** Enter the coupon code: PUORIWH.

> **STEP 2:** New Safari users, complete the brief registration form.
> Safari subscribers, just log in.

If you have difficulty registering on Safari or accessing the online edition, please e-mail customer-service@safaribooksonline.com